KT-177-832

Contents

Saving the Planet
with Pesticides and Plastic:
The Environmental Triumph
of High-Yield Farming

Saving the Planet
with Pesticides and Plastic:
The Environmental Triumph
of High-Yield Farming

Dennis T. Avery

Hudson Institute
Indianapolis, Indiana

Hudson Institute
Indianapolis, Indiana

ISBN 1-55813-051-9
Copyright © 1995 Hudson Institute, Inc.
Second printing, March 1995

Printed in the United States of America.
This book may be ordered from:
Hudson Institute
Herman Kahn Center
P.O. Box 26-919
Indianapolis, Indiana 46226
(317) 545-1000

Acknowledgments

My thanks go first and foremost to my wife, Anne. She began by cheerfully supporting my efforts to produce this book—and wound up contributing many hours of her own time and her keen editorial eye to its completion. Equally important, she was the only one able to tell me graciously and effectively when I was wrong in my approach to communication with the reader.

My deep appreciation goes also to my longtime friend and colleague, Jo Perrill, who helped organize a diverse set of realities into a coherent book.

I must thank the Hudson Institute for backing a controversial manuscript simply because they thought it would make an important contribution to the public debate. I must also thank my Hudson editor, Sam Karnick, who contributed key ideas that went far beyond the usual editing assistance.

Finally, I must thank my reviewers:

- Dr. Paul Waggoner, distinguished scientist and former director at the Connecticut Experiment Station, and author of the Council for Agricultural Science and Technology's report, *How Much Land Can 10 Billion People Leave for Nature?*
- Dr. John Osmun, former chairman of the Entomology Department at Purdue University and senior official in the Environmental Protection Agency's Office of Pesticides.
- Dr. Douglas Southgate, of the Agricultural Economics faculty at Ohio State, expert on Latin American agriculture and resources, and author of *Economic Progress and the Environment: One Developing Country's Policy Crisis* (Oxford University Press, 1994).

They have done their best to ensure that the book is conceptually and factually correct; if there are errors, they are my fault.

Preface

If one listens to the latest pronouncements from a number of prominent environmentalists, things seem very dire indeed. According to them, the world is running out of food, land, trees, soil, fresh water, and just about any other resource one might think important. They also assert that the planet is becoming overcrowded with people, is being poisoned by chemicals, and is heating up at a dangerous rate. And for all these alleged ills they blame the industrialized nations, particularly the United States.

The media hear the message loud and clear and run a regular parade of terrifying stories warning us of poisonous pesticides in our apples; dangerous genetically engineered additives in our milk; alarming rises in the world's mean temperature; acres of trees being cleared from the world's rain forests, and so on. And they never seem to tire of telling us that organic farming and other ways of going "back to nature" can save the planet.

These assertions, if true, portend a global catastrophe. But, fortunately, there is another side to the story. What the environmentalists and news media usually neglect to tell us is that cancer risks in the industrialized nations are *decreasing;* that the world's temperature rises and falls *naturally;* that *governments,* not agribusinesses, have been encouraging people to cut down rain forests; that the industrial nations pollute *less* than other countries; and that the widespread use of organic farming *threatens* the world's wildlife.

They do not often report that high-tech, high-yield farming saves wildlife by preserving land from the plow; creates new soil through conservation tillage methods; reduces human cancer risks by providing inexpensive, attractive produce year-round; conserves our supplies of fresh water; saves our forests, including the crucial rain forests; and—lest we forget—feeds vastly increasing numbers of people while using fewer resources. And they never mention that, at its current yields, organic farming cannot possibly support the world's population without inducing unprecedented global famine.

This is the story that needs to be heard, and Dennis T. Avery tells it in a thorough and compelling fashion in *Saving the Planet with Pesticides and Plastic: The Environmental Triumph of High-Yield Farming*. According to Avery, most of what we hear about the environment is simply *wrong*, not because of the motivations or research methods of the people who investigate and disseminate it, but because it fails to reflect the big picture. In concentrating on small saplings, the enviro-pessimists do not see the verdant, fertile forest before them—a forest that is standing because of the Green Revolution: the huge advances in mankind's ability to produce food and forest products achieved in the past thirty years.

The accomplishments of the Green Revolution can be used to feed a world of ten or eleven billion people, which Avery predicts is the maximum that will be reached, sometime toward the middle of the next century. And because almost all those people will live in cities, they will not take up much more space than the world's current population. We need not fear either overcrowding or famine.

There are, however, some serpents in the garden. If we fail to support further agricultural research, particularly in the extremely promising field of biotechnology, the Green Revolution will remain the pinnacle of our achievement rather than the foundation of further advances.

Even more detrimental, however, is the possibility that nations will continue to press for food self-sufficiency. Farm trade helps us supply the world's food needs by using the best and most productive acres and technologies to feed the world's people with as little environmental and economic cost as possible. Subsidies, tariffs, and stifling regulations negate these advantages. In this sense, free trade among nations in agricultural goods is *the* environmental issue of the decade. *Saving the Planet with Pesticides and Plastic* provides a crucial and too often overlooked fund of information in the fight to save the planet's people *and* its environment.

This book continues long Hudson Institute traditions of optimism about solving the world's most difficult problems and a healthy skepticism toward the conventional wisdom about them. Many generous contributors to Hudson have helped to make this book possible. Although they bear no responsibility for its conclusions, Hudson Institute gratefully acknowledges their assistance.

Leslie Lenkowsky
President
Hudson Institute

"Then a strange blight crept over the area. . . . Some evil spell had settled on the community: Everywhere there was the shadow of death. There was a strange stillness. The birds, for example—where had they gone? . . . The apple trees were coming into bloom, but no bees droned . . . so there would be no fruit. The roadsides, once so attractive, were now lined with browned and withered vegetation as though swept by fire. . . . Even the streams were now lifeless . . . all the fish had died. . . . A white, granular powder still showed a few patches; some weeks before it had fallen like snow. No witchcraft, no enemy action had silenced the rebirth of new life in this stricken world. The people had done it themselves.

"For the first time in the history of the world, every human being is now subjected to contact with dangerous chemicals, from the moment of conception until death." [Emphasis added.]

Rachel Carson, *Silent Spring*, 1962

FAO photo by G. Tortoli

A PLAGUE OF LOCUSTS—It has been many years since American farms have experienced biblical plagues which destroy everything in their path—thanks to modern-day pesticides.

Introduction

I never meant to write this book.

I had been writing another book, about the critical importance of trade liberalization for American agriculture. Suddenly I realized this one was more important. And due to the vagaries of fate, I knew I was one of the few people who could write it. I had the necessary knowledge of global farming. Nor was I beholden to any of the political or bureaucratic agendas that have so often distorted our understanding of global farming in years past.

My father was a county agricultural agent. His job was to help the local farmers grow more corn from each acre and produce more milk from each cow. Dad's father had been a farmer too, and we lived on a little 80-acre farm. I grew up milking cows and baling hay. When I was a child, high-yield farming was new and glittering, and man's greatest triumph. My father was part of it, spreading word of hybrid corn and artificial insemination across the country. He even volunteered to serve in India with the original "Point Four" program to help raise India's food production (but wasn't selected).

Personally, I wasn't cut out for farming. I could handle cows, but I was hopeless with machinery. I couldn't even adjust the carburetor on our two-cylinder John Deere tractor—about the simplest mechanical task this side of pull-starting a lawn mower. So, instead of farming, I went to college and studied agricultural economics and journalism.

Then I went to work for the Department of Agriculture in Washington. I had wanted to work for one of the land-grant agricultural colleges. But the job at Penn State didn't pan out, and I figured that a year in Washington would be good experience. I stayed 30 years.

In the 1960s, when I was new in Washington, the Green Revolution was being launched. Dr. Norman Borlaug and other seed breeders were creating the miracle wheat and rice varieties that literally saved Asia from massive famine. That seemed to endorse the importance of my father's goal of making two blades of grass grow where only one grew before.

In the 1970s, I didn't pay much attention to the environmental movement. USDA was caught up in the heady era of expanding farm exports. OPEC had spread a lot of money in countries with big populations and poor diets, like Nigeria, Indonesia, and the USSR. Everybody seemed to be importing food from America. The hand-wringers of that day worried that Africa and Latin America would become overdependent on foreign farms.

In the 1980s, the environmental movement was gaining *real* strength—and I began getting drawn into the whirlpool. The guy in the next office mentioned that the State Department was looking for an agriculture specialist. Suddenly, I was the Senior Agricultural Analyst in the State Department. It wasn't a job that my colleagues in USDA took very seriously. State didn't deal in very sophisticated analysis by their USDA/Ph.D. standards. My job was to educate a rather disinterested bunch of Foreign Service officers on what agriculture was and could do. Still, the State Department job had all the breadth any curious farm kid could want: all the countries, commodities, and farm/food problems in the world.

One of my first challenges was to evaluate a memo from a Foreign Service colleague. That fellow had been seriously impressed with Lester Brown's latest scary pronouncement—that soil erosion was rapidly destroying the world's ability to feed itself. Brown even claimed that the Corn Belt would soon erode into a veritable desert. My Foreign Service colleague was recommending that the U.S. drop all of its other foreign policy concerns (Communist expansion, the trade balance, and refugees, to name a few). He wanted us to deal henceforth with the other countries of the world purely on the basis of their soil erosion!

I had known Brown when we were both at USDA. I knew he was a population control activist and not a serious analyst. Still, it took a couple of weeks closeted with the experts to write up the case against the soil erosion scare. Then I got my first lesson in the emotional intensity of environmental concerns. When my State Department colleague's memo was rejected, he tried to sneak it aboard President Reagan's airplane to the Cancun Summit through a friend in the Presidential party!

At State, I found myself being force-fed a diet of 20,000 pages of overseas reports per year. I became a speed reader. I eventually visited 36 countries on four continents. I began to learn how the world fed itself and used its major natural resources. My best information sources turned out to be the USDA agricultural attaches, who were stationed in 150 or so countries. Their post reports were a gold mine of up-to-the-minute facts, trends, and possibilities.

I also got acquainted with the Consultative Group on International Agricultural Research. The group had 13 international farm research centers spread around the Third World. (There are more than 20 now.) They are supported mostly by the Agency for International Development and international banking institutions. Their job was, and is, to take the latest agricultural research methods (mainly developed in the rich countries) and focus them on the farm/food problems of the poorest countries. Norman Borlaug won his Nobel Peace Prize at one of those international research centers, in Mexico. The miracle wheat and rice varieties for the Green Revolution both came from these centers. Later, so did new miracle cassava and hybrid sorghums for Africa.

Through such work, I learned that the Green Revolution was about more than a few seed varieties. It was a research process, building on research discoveries all over the world. The most oft-repeated phrases in my agricultural attache post reports were "record yields" and "record production." From the centers' researchers, I learned *why* we were setting food production records in nearly every country. For the next several years, I put together a steady stream of internal State Department reports designed to help our Foreign Service people understand the real problems and potentials in world food and agriculture. Most of these reports were diametrically opposed to what the environmental activists of the time had to say.

Every year, Lester Brown predicted famine on the front pages of America's newspapers. It became an annual ritual that newspaper reporters would call me for the opposing viewpoint (which they would then duly bury in paragraph 12 on page 9). In 1985, a paper I had written on the global success pattern of farm research fell into the hands of Dr. Philip Abelson, then editor of *Science* magazine. He printed it under the title, "The Global Bad News is Wrong." It was my first successful attempt to present the broader issues of global food production outside the government.

I began getting invitations to speak to farm groups about the patterns and trends in the rest of the world. I began to realize that few Americans, farming or no, have any real understanding of what's happening in the dynamic world beyond our shores.

My federal career ended in 1988 when I jumped through an early retirement window. I wanted to take a more active role in getting a market-oriented agricultural policy for the United States, and in the civil service my hands were tied. Toward that end, I joined the Hudson Institute part-time as their agricultural analyst. (My salary from Hudson nets out at a princely $25,000 per year, but I supplement that by doing long-term international forecasting for farm and agribusiness groups.)

At the time I joined Hudson, I still saw the environmental activists' criticisms of high-yield farming as a secondary problem. What I really wanted to do was tell farmers about their opportunity to help feed an Asia that was getting affluent and that would soon have nine times as many people per acre of arable land as North America. Then about two years ago, I changed my mind about the priorities.

I have never meant to be an "opponent of the environmental movement." Like most rural people, I grew up caring for creatures both domestic and wild. We worried about the health of our dairy cows *and* our pheasant populations. I treasure the deer that wander through my yard, the wild turkeys that call from my mountain, and the bluebirds in our dozen nesting boxes. I even try to care about the 30-pound snapping turtles that lurk in my pond and take a toll of the new mallard ducklings every spring (though I like the ducks a lot better.)

Like many Americans, I am deeply grateful to the environmental movement for raising our level of concern about the environment. But I am also deeply disappointed in many of the environmental activists.

As chapters in this book will show, high-yield agriculture is the *solution*, not the *problem* for wildlife and the environment. It is the only proven way to ensure success for both people and the environment. Yet the environmental leadership refuses to see this.

Similarly, I will argue that there is no upward population spiral in the world, just a one-time surge due to modern medicine lowering death rates —which we can feed. Too many environmentalists seem to reject such realities. They imply that we can starve the people and keep the wildlife. In fact, as I will show, with high-yield crops and forest plantations, we can have *both* people and wildlife. Without high-yield crops, we can have neither.

Consider as a personal example my little retirement farm in Virginia's Shenandoah Valley, which was part of the "nation's bread-basket" in the 1850s. Today, America's grain is being produced on the flat, fertile fields of the Corn Belt and Great Plains, where yields are three times as high and farm machinery doesn't destroy itself on the buried rocks. The Shenandoah, on the other hand, is almost entirely in grass for dairy and beef cattle, and trees for timber and pulpwood. Wildlife is more abundant than in Colonial and even pre-Colonial times, when it was hunted intensely.

Thus, the Shenandoah has lost income, gained beauty, and ended the huge soil erosion losses that cropping inflicted on its steep, rocky slopes. Indiana has gained income and lost woodlands, and its level cropland has comparatively little risk of soil erosion. (It also had historically less biodiversity than the rougher lands.) This is a win-win alteration of the food system. Indiana's grain yields are higher, its economic costs lower, and the environmental balance in both Indiana and the Shenandoah far more sustainable.

More important, we are producing our grain on *fewer acres* by focusing production in Indiana. We can produce the food we need from fewer acres by focusing production on our best and safest cropland. That puts steep and rocky acres back into grass, forest, and wildlife in places like Virginia, West Virginia, Vermont, and Montana. The higher yields achieved by using the best land and high-yield farming methods leave more wildlife habitat than any other approach. The *acres not plowed* will be a continuing focus of this book.

To understand the environmental triumph of high-yield agriculture, we must now extend this sort of analysis beyond the borders of the United States. We must, in fact, look at the global food system as a planetary whole.

We will start that journey now.

1

Saving Lives and Wildlife

MYTHMAKERS SAY:

"Most of our environmental problems are the inevitable result of the sweeping technological changes that transformed the U.S. economic system after World War II . . . (including) the substitution of fertilizers for manure and crop rotation and of toxic synthetic pesticides for ladybugs and birds."

Barry Commoner, "Why We Have Failed," *Greenpeace*,
September/October 1989

"How can we put an end to mass starvation and suffering in this world? There is only one answer."

From a fund-raising letter by Negative Population Growth, Inc.,
Teaneck, New Jersey, Spring 1994

"Just now one of the significant historical roles of the primal people of the world is not simply to sustain their own traditions, but to call the entire civilized world back to a more authentic mode of being."

Thomas Berry, *The Dream of the Earth*, Sierra Club Books, 1988

REALISTS SAY:

"Environmentalists who want to preserve wildlands from the farmer's plow as we feed a burgeoning human population should reconsider an old enemy: chemical-based agriculture."

Ron Bailey, "Once and Future Farming," *Garbage, the Independent Environmental Quarterly*, Fall 1994, pp. 42-48

"This doctrine of accord with Nature has usually marked a transition period. When mythology is dying in its open forms, and when social life is so disturbed that custom and tradition fail to supply their wonted controls . . . natural law is conceived of as the only true divine law. This happened in one form in Stoicism. It happened . . . in the deism of the 18th century with its notion of a benevolent, harmonious, wholly rational order of Nature."

John Dewey, *Human Nature and Conduct*, 1922[1]

"We should like to announce in advance that we have received no support from any industry, government agency or university to write or produce this book. . . . Our conscious intent has been to defend the integrity of the scientific process and to bring to attention the possibility that following the advice of some of the leaders of the environmental movement might be a path to social and economic disasters even more serious than the problems of pollution and poverty . . . "

Dr. George Claus, M.D., Ph.D. (botany) and Ph.D. (microbiology),
and Dr. Karen Bolander, specialist in mass psychology,
in the introduction of their 1977 book, *Ecological Sanity*.[2]

The environmental movement is valid and important. Environmentalists are forcing us to recognize that we are increasingly capable of—and responsible for—saving natural resources. Nevertheless, though they recognize the problems, they do not always see clearly the solution strategies. In the case of agriculture in particular, they have come to exactly the wrong policy solutions.

Mankind is at the most critical moment in environmental history. What we do as people and societies in the next decade will determine whether we have a more crowded but sustainable world to bequeath to future generations—or whether we will bring on the very apocalypse of famine and wildlife destruction that the gloomiest environmentalists have envisioned. Our decisions on agriculture and forestry will be the most crucial of all, because they will govern how we use two-thirds of the earth's surface. They will dictate the habitat—or loss of habitat—for 95 percent of the earth's wildlife species.

So far, we are making the wrong decisions, for the wrong reasons, based on the wrong information. The environmental movement was never more correct than when it coined the slogan, "Think globally and act locally." But today's environmentalists are not thinking about farming and forestry in global terms.

Land, one may argue, is the scarcest resource of all. We need it to produce our food and timber. It is increasingly in demand for human recreation. Now, in addition, we recognize an almost unlimited demand for land as wildlife habitat. Virtually every bit of wildlife habitat is important. Agriculture and forestry are the only sector where we can "create" more land without sacrificing the environment. High yields are the only way to do it.

The environmental movement, however, has been recommending exactly the opposite strategy—low-yield farming. That would almost certainly trigger the plow-down of huge tracts of wildlife habitat as people attempt to avoid famine. As we shall see, the yields from traditional and organic farms are too low to feed people and still protect wildlife.

In the case of forestry, most environmentalists are similarly recommending low-yield forest management and the non-harvesting of trees. That would leave us with fewer trees and less wood—and reliant on more polluting alternatives (like steel) for construction needs. High-yield plantation forestry on a few acres is a key to having lots of forest products and still having lots of wild forests and wildlife.

MODERN COMBINE IN WHEAT—High yields from the best land—this combine is less important than the rust-resistant semi-dwarf wheat that puts more energy into its seed heads and less into stalk. Note the lack of weeds to compete for nutrients.

Much of the green movement has also opposed international trade in general, and farm product trade in particular. They fear that trade will weaken environmental initiatives and threaten small traditional farmers. However, the lack of trade in agriculture and forestry is likely to mean losing big tracts of wildlife habitat in some parts of the world, while safe and renewable farming resources are wasted in other places. The key problem region will be Asia, which will be nine times as densely populated per acre of farmland as North America in the year 2050.

This book will attempt to demonstrate that:

- The world cannot save its wildlife without high-yield agriculture and the careful use of farm chemicals.
- The world cannot afford to do without high-yield plantation forestry *for its environmental benefits* in preserving truly wild forests free from logging pressures.
- Rising crop yields (and thus more food security) haven't encouraged more births; on the contrary, they seem to bring the number of births per woman down more rapidly.
- The methods used to achieve high yields in farming and forestry are already far safer for the environment and for people than the so-called "green" alternatives. There are major risks

USDA

SLIM HARVEST—This 19th-century Russian wheat field helps us understand why Rev. Malthus was pessimistic about feeding more people in the days before farm science launched the Green Revolution.

involved in organic farming. For humans, the organic farming risks include higher cancer rates from unseen natural toxins in untreated grains and oilseeds. They also include higher prices for fruits and vegetables, discouraging the fruit and vegetable consumption that can cut cancer rates in half.

- For wildlife, the low yields of organic farming—and resulting habitat loss—far outweigh the occasional, and unfortunate, losses of wildlife to pesticides. When we factor in these risks, organic farming is the high-risk solution for both people and wildlife.
- For small, traditional farmers, the risk is being condemned to a short, harsh life of toil, disease and ignorance—while raising large, poverty-driven families that destroy forests and erode fragile soils.

Conversely, this book will try to demonstrate that we should be able to feed, house and clothe 10 billion people on less land than we use for farming and forestry today if we:

- Aggressively pursue yield-enhancing agricultural and forestry research. New research is especially important for the Third World, which cannot yet afford to pay for it. Biotechnology is particularly important in both field and tree crops since it represents our biggest reservoir of unexploited new high-yield strategies.
- Use the best and safest land to produce our field and tree crops. The yields on the best land are often twice as high as on the poorer land. That means much more uncropped land can be left to wildlife and recreation. Equally important, there is far less biodiversity on the best and safest lands; biologists theorize that the easy environments allow a few major species to dominate (like the bison, wolf, and prairie dog on our Great Plains). A square mile of rain forest may contain more species than the entire Great Plains.

High-yield farming is not a matter of putting small farmers out of business, anywhere in the world. A planet that must roughly triple the output of its food system has no interest in putting any farmers out of business. The question is where we invest to expand.

High Yields Are the Way to a Better Future

Several Clinton appointees (not in the Department of Agriculture) reacted to my first three draft chapters about high-yield agriculture by saying, "Oh, that high-yield stuff is how we *used* to do farming. Now we have found a better way."

The old way of producing food has been around since before Chief Massasoit taught the Pilgrims how to fertilize their corn with fish. It is called low-yield farming.

The environmental movement has not brought forward any breakthroughs in food production.

Organic farmers, who after all are essentially low-yield, traditional farmers, have not suddenly discovered how to produce lots of extra food. In fact, they are recommending we produce less.

Similarly, biological pest controls are making some progress in controlling a few pests in a few places, but there is little likelihood that they will replace much of our chemical pest control. Biological controls are too narrow and too uncertain.

Integrated pest management (IPM) is also useful, and more producers are using more of it. However, it is not a way to replace pesticides, but rather a way to make them more effective.

Finally, composting and organic fertilizer can only add marginally to our plant nutrient supply. Organic farmers cannot replace the huge quantities of chemical nitrogen and mined phosphate without clearing huge tracts of land for green manure crops—thus sacrificing wildlife habitat.

Nor can the environmental movement bring down the world's population growth trends much more quickly than they are already coming down. The Third World's birth rates have already come more than 60 percent of the way to stability, essentially in one generation. We have a fighting chance at re-stabilizing population at 8 billion people and as early as 2035—mainly because of economic growth and TV. But that won't preclude the need to essentially triple the output of the world's agricultures.

No one is delivering a vegetarian world. Tropical forest is already being cleared to grow low-yielding soybeans for broiler chickens. Big dams are already being built to irrigate more feed grains for hogs. Crop residues are already being stolen to feed more dairy cows to produce more milk, despite the long-term risks to soil productivity.

Obviously, the rising food needs of the world must be met this year, and next year, and the year after that. The key question—and one that the environmental activists and organic buffs refuse to answer—is this: "How many million acres of wildlife habitat are you willing to clear to have chemical-free farming?"

The question of high-yield farming is no arcane or historical debate. Its answer will almost certainly determine the future of the world's wildlife, and probably the futures of billions of people as well.

It Has Been Hard to Hear the High-Yield Message

Unfortunately, it has been tough to get a public hearing for the high-yield viewpoint. It might have been easier if Paul Ehrlich had published his 1968 book, *The Population Bomb*, before Rachel Carson wrote her powerful indictment of pesticides (*Silent Spring*) in 1962. If we had truly become concerned about population before we got frightened of pesticides, we might have been more open to the benefits of high yields. But Rachel Carson got there first. One might say she poisoned the well of public opinion against fertilizers and pesticides.

We know now that manmade chemicals are no more dangerous than natural chemicals. Most chemicals, both natural and manmade, seem to be dangerous to rats in high-dose testing. But high-dose rat tests, as most scientists will admit, overstate the risk to human beings from *all* chemicals.

We also know now that Ms. Carson's fears of widespread human cancer from pesticides have not been borne out. When we adjust for the increasing age of our population, there has been *no* increase in nonsmoking cancer rates as the use of pesticides has spread.

Nor do we have any examples of pesticides threatening wildlife species—or even any major wildlife *populations*. Quite the opposite, in fact. We have pesticides helping to raise crop and tree yields instead of having to plow down wildlife habitat. Every naturalist writing about potential extinction of wild species is worried about three things: habitat, habitat, and habitat. Pesticides help protect the habitat.

Fortunately, the environmental movement no longer needs to indict farm chemicals to justify its existence. The environmental movement has demonstrated its own vital validity. The fact that the movement got its start in the aftermath of *Silent Spring* should not dictate environmental policy recommendations today, when we know so much more about the ecology, and about cancer; and when the pesticides themselves have gotten so much safer.

Such relatively new compounds as the sulfanylureas and the glyphosates are no more toxic than aspirin, need only a few ounces per acre, and can be used around such sensitive species as trout and quail with no harm.

Even given such chemical safety, my claim is not that farm chemicals have zero risk. Rather, I claim that *the major wildlife benefits they offer far outweigh the very small and declining risks they may contain.*

Rising Costs and Tighter Budgets

As budget deficits rise and as the significant costs of environmental policies are becoming clearer, environmental recommendations need to be strongly focused and cost-beneficial. The environmental movement cannot afford to waste its political capital on counterproductive policy thrusts—especially if they mean destruction of the very wildlife which is at the heart of our shared environmental agenda.

Nor can the environmental movement afford to be backed into a set of policies for which continuing popular support and real implementation are almost impossible to generate. The Third World will not accept mud huts and malnutrition as its lot in life. The First World is hardly disillusioned enough to return to them. Virtually the whole world today has a vision of material well-being, and is pursuing it. The environmental movement and the researchers of the First World must offer technologies and policies that support peoples' aspirations *along with* their environmental goals—or the wildlife will lose out.

It's Not a People Problem

Lots of Americans say this country has gotten too crowded. The truth is that America is not a crowded country, nor will it be unless we choose to permit much more immigration. Meanwhile, more and more of our population volunteers to live in the Eastern megalopolis that runs from Boston to Atlanta. There, we make lots of money, have lots of friends nearby—and complain about the traffic.

Hong Kong has a population density of over 14,000 people per square mile. That is far denser than China (288 per square mile) or India (658). The environmental reality is that Hong Kong's impact on the environment is fairly easy to mitigate. Sewage treatment is cheaper in densely populated cities, while energy and land requirements are minimized. (Hong Kong is already beginning to invest in environmental cleanup.) Only if it takes too much land to provide the food and forest products is Hong Kong a long-term threat to the environment. Unfortunately, too many of the environmental activists have turned environmentalism itself into an anti-people crusade— when people are not the problem.

In the environmental context, having 8-10 billion human beings on the planet certainly represents a challenge. But short of poison gas or huge induced famines, the number of humans on earth is not ours to choose. We in the West are not in a position to make the birth decisions for the people of the Third World. Fortunately, the Third World's fertility rate is dropping more rapidly than ever before. We can expect to have a declining world population after about the year 2040.

In the meantime, too many in the environmental movement are still fixated on policy recommendations that pretend we will *not* have 8-10 billion people, and that we will not allow the Third World to become affluent. Such policies cannot possibly generate majority support. Instead, such policy thrusts risk enormous environmental losses.

Slowing World Population Growth with Higher Grain Yields

It's a surprise to many, but high-yield farming seems to help slow down population growth.

The countries that have made the most progress in raising their grain yields have also made the most progress in bringing down their birth rates. Producing more food *has not* aggravated the world's population problems. In fact, the world's population growth rate began to trend down in the very year that the world gave the Nobel Peace Prize to Dr. Borlaug (1970)—in the wake of the Green Revolution.

It is entirely reasonable that higher grain yields should be a leading indicator of lower birth rates. They help produce higher standards of living. They help give parents confidence that their first two or three children will live. More grain makes people more confident that they will be looked after adequately in their old age.

Furthermore, countries generally do not develop cities and urban industries until they have ample food available to feed nonfarm populations. Urban populations almost always have sharply lower birth rates than rural ones, in every culture and on every continent.

We've known for a long time, of course, that higher yields have been associated with low birth rates in the First World:

- America's corn yields have increased 152 percent since 1950, compared with an 89 percent rise in our population. U.S. births per woman are at 2.1, exactly the long-term replacement level.
- French wheat yields have risen 195 percent in the same period, while its population has risen 38 percent. The French fertility rate is now 1.8, below replacement.

The same association seems to hold in the Third World as well:

- India's rice yields have risen 135 percent, and its wheat yields have more than doubled, against a population increase of 149 percent. India's births per woman have fallen from 5.8 to 3.1, with virtually all of the reduction achieved since the beginning of the Green Revolution.
- Indonesia's rice yields are up 160 percent, against population growth of 142 percent. The fertility rate of a *Moslem population* has fallen dramatically, from 5.5 to 2.4 births per woman.

- Emerging Chile has boosted its corn yields by more than fourfold, and easily accommodated a population increase of 130 percent. Births per woman have fallen *in a Catholic country* from 4.0 to 2.1.
- Zimbabwe has long had the best corn-breeding program in Africa. Corn yields among its traditional village farmers have roughly quadrupled, matching the fourfold expansion of its population. Zimbabwe's births per woman started dropping sooner and have come down more sharply than most Sub-Saharan countries, from 7.7 to 3.5.
- China's rice yields have risen 150 percent since 1950, outgaining a population increase of 114 percent. China's births per woman are down to a very low at 1.9, well below re-placement. China has also been famous in recent decades for a harsh policy against large families. However, China's dense population has unquestionably driven both its popula-tion policy and the establishment of one of the Third World's best agricultural research systems.

Unsuccessful Farming Leads to More Births

It may seem counterintuitive, but the countries which have had less success in raising grain yields have also kept the highest birth rates:

- In Ethiopia, grain yields have more than doubled (120 per-cent) but the population has increased 178 percent. The fer-tility rate *increased* from 5.8 in the 1970s to 7.3 in 1993.
- Kenya's corn yields have risen 47 percent, but its population has risen more than 300 percent! The fertility rate was 8 children per woman as recently as in 1970. The population growth rate hovered near 4 percent (one of the highest rates in the world) until the end of the 1980s. A crash family plan-ning effort by the Kenyan government has recently helped start the fertility rate downward more rapidly.
- Ghana's rice yields have risen only 24 percent since 1950, while the population has increased more than 300 percent. The fertility rate is still 5.4 births per women, down from 6.7.

- Rwanda's corn yields have risen only about 25 percent, while its population has increased 250 percent. (Yields for the important potato and bean crops *have* risen significantly.) Births per woman have come down from 7.8 but are still at 4.9.[3]

The lesson is clear. High-yield farming helps bring birth rates down. Cutting off high-yield farming research and discouraging the use of fertilizer in the world will hamper our progress toward restabilizing population.

If the world opts for low-yield farming (or simply fails to support a wholehearted push for higher-yield farming) it will take longer to stabilize the population. Low-yield farming is likely to produce more population growth, not less.

But the First World hasn't learned this yet.

The Senate Hearing

In March 1994, I debated Lester Brown, one of our most prominent environmentalists, at a Senate hearing. For years, Brown and his Worldwatch Institute have been predicting famine and environmental disasters due to population growth. They have also contended that agricultural research and higher yields could not meet the food challenge facing the world. They have argued, instead, for population "management". The occasion for our debate was a hearing of the Senate Agricultural Appropriations Committee on the world food outlook. The chairman was Sen. Dale Bumpers (D-Ark).[4]

Brown predicted that the world was headed for massive famine and chaos. Of course, he has been predicting these calamities virtually every year for 25 years. To date, the big famines have never appeared. Bumpers called Brown a "genius" and noted that he himself didn't think the world could sustain more than 2 to 3 billion people (roughly half of our current world population.)

When my turn came, I testified that there is no need for famine in the world's future. The reasons: First, high-yield agriculture is raising crop yields much faster than population growth. Second, high-yield farming has already tripled the output of land and water in farming since the 1950s, during the very period when Brown has been wrongly predicting famine. Third, plant breeding, biotechnology, and other knowledge advances continue to permit higher and higher crop yields, even in the most advanced countries. Fourth, if we *did* get famine, it would only be after starving people had destroyed virtually all of the world's wildlife in last, desperate efforts to keep their children alive.

The question was not whether we would feed more people. The real question was whether we would feed the world's extra people from a few acres or a lot of acres. Wildlife would be the key beneficiaries of our success—or pay the supreme price for our failure.

I said that there was every reason to believe that if Bumpers' Agricultural Appropriations Committee kept funding high-yield agricultural and forestry research, we would be able to feed the doubled-and-restabilized human population of 2050 and beyond—*and* have at least as much room for wildlife as the planet has today.

I was astonished at the Senator's reaction. "Mr. Avery," he said, "your testimony makes me sorry I convened this hearing." Sen. Bumpers seemed suddenly depressed—by the idea that we wouldn't have famine!

Bumpers had apparently been contemplating a big, mechanistic, guilt-free famine solution to end the world's population growth. Meanwhile, his Senate committee was proposing to cut funds for the international agricultural research which could help produce more food quickly. The funding, instead, was going to provide more condoms and pills for the Third World—though these were unlikely to have any significant impact soon enough to stave off famine or wildlife losses.

The *Washington Post* Story

A few days later, *Washington Post*'s Boyce Rensberger wrote a story on the rapid progress in high-yield farming. "Experts on Farming

Remain Optimistic That Large-Scale Starvation Is Still Unlikely," declared the headline for Rensberger's special feature on agricultural research.[5] The story covered a three-day conference of international farm research experts.

Rensberger quoted Dr. Donald Plucknett, who had recently retired as the senior science advisor to the international research networks. Plucknett said, "I do believe we can continue to raise world food yields if we do the right things." Another top expert, Dr. Piers Pinstrup-Anderson, agreed that the long-term world food picture looked promising because of rising crop yields.

"We're not running out of (farming) resources," he said.[6] However, Rensberger noted that funding was the key problem facing the international farm research centers:

> One dwindling resource, however, is financial support. Last year, 12 countries cut their support—the U.S. by the largest amount, dropping [by] $6.5 million to $41.6 million. Overall, [the research group's] funding for 1993 dropped more than 7 percent. Officials say the promise of further cuts this year could force them to close some research centers.
>
> "Whether food production continues to grow," Pinstrup-Anderson said, "may depend on the willingness of donor countries to maintain their support. It's really up to us whether we want to have a happy future or an unhappy future."

There was no firestorm of front-page media coverage on the funding crisis of the Green Revolution research institutes. There was no groundswell of public opinion demanding more agricultural research, nor any "world conference" to organize support.

Much of the public remained fixed on the idea that there are too many people. The reasons why are perhaps understandable—if prosaic. What proportion of the American population did *not* get caught in a traffic jam last week? How many of us in that week looked at a taller building going up—and felt crowded.

But such phenomena are not population results. They are consequences of an urbanization trend—the fact that most people seem to prefer cities.

Just the week before the hearing, I had a long dinner discussion with Steve, a Nebraska farmer opposed to the use of chemicals. However, it quickly became clear that it wasn't chemicals he opposed so much as more people.

"We have too many people," he finally said, "even if we *can* feed them. We need to cut back our population, not increase it." This man who owned 2,000 acres in western Nebraska was suffering from the "Daniel Boone Syndrome." (Boone supposedly said, "when you can see the smoke from your neighbor's cooking fire, it's time to move on.")

Similarly, I have a good friend who is a fine person and a fine economist. He favors economic growth. But he is also deeply—and, I tell him, irrationally—worried about population growth. He's been reading my reports for years, so he does not subscribe to the famine hypothesis. He is well versed in resource economics, and knows we needn't run out of copper or clean water. His fallback position is to worry out loud about how we can educate all of these people. But all it takes for education, I tell him, is a teacher and some students—and the more people we have, the more potential students and teachers.

Who Will Feed China?

Late in 1994, Lester Brown made global headlines with the rhetorical question, "Who will feed China?"

Brown noted that China's meat demand was already rising by 3 million tons per year, as a result of economic growth and higher per capita incomes. Projections indicated that China might need another 200 to 250 million tons of feed grains by the year 2030 to supply the desire of Chinese consumers for more meat, milk, and eggs.

Brown seemed not to realize that his Chinese question represented the utter failure of his whole population management policy thrust. In 1974, he had written in his book *By Bread Alone* that the world should pursue both population management and higher crop yields—but that was the last time he had anything good to say publicly about higher-yield agriculture.

Since then, Brown and the Worldwatch Institute have been totally fixated on suppressing births.

Now, China confronts them with the bankruptcy of birth suppression as a stand-alone policy.

Condoms cannot raise crop yields. China is already at virtual stability in population, but it is demanding a better diet—and planning to build a big dam on the Yangtse River that will displace 1 million people in order to help get it.

Population management cannot save the wildlife. Only higher-yield agriculture will do that.

The Pattern

The truth about the world's rapidly expanding ability to feed itself with higher yields has been published from time to time in the media, including both the *Washington Post* and the *New York Times*. Yet it hasn't resonated with the public.

In contrast, the misinformation about impending famine has reverberated like a cannon-shot. How else can we explain Lester Brown and Paul Ehrlich? Both have been publicly, radically, and consistently wrong on hunger and population issues for 25 years.

Yet Brown sells hundreds of thousands of his books each year. His Worldwatch Institute is one of the largest outside suppliers of teaching materials to American schools and colleges. Paul Ehrlich's *The Population Bomb* predicted in 1968 that we'd have famine in America in the 1970s, with the corpses of starvation victims piled in our streets. It is the bestselling environmental book in history. In 1990, Ehrlich republished the same failed predictions, under the title *The Population Explosion*—and sold millions more copies!

In reality, of course, we have had surplus grain piled in our streets instead of Ehrlich's anticipated famine victims.

I wrote a good book on food and hunger in 1991. *Global Food Progress* laid out the reasons why the world's food production gains were continuing to outstrip population growth. Despite the upbeat message, it sold 4,000 copies and was reviewed only by the *Chicago Tribune* and the *Journal of the American Agricultural Economics Association*. (Both reviews were favorable, by the way.)

Why the dramatic difference? After all this time, it can't be that the public believes Brown, Ehrlich, and their disciples are correct about famine. It has to be that a sizable part of the American population secretly *wants* them to be right.

Are we a nation of people-phobes? Do we have an instinctive

fear of psychological crowding? There is no real crowding in America, nor is there likely to be. The people who voluntarily choose to subject themselves to life in Manhattan or the commuter traffic of I-95 around Washington are volunteers. They have made choices. If crowding is a key issue, the fact is that most of us can move to less crowded situations.

Yet the fear of crowding persists. In 1992, I wrote a column for the *Wall Street Journal* that was headlined, "Mother Earth Could Feed Billions More."[7] I got reader letters whose main point was, "Yeah, you can feed them, but pretty soon there won't be room to take a Sunday drive."

The fact is, of course, that two billion more people in Asia won't affect our Sunday drives. We will have to resolve our own traffic problems. But surely that can be done without "subtracting" 4 billion people forcibly from the world's population.

Virtually none of the world's population growth will occur in the U.S. Our fertility rate is 0.1 percent. We would require 700 years to double our population without immigration—and we can control our own immigration if we choose.

The Turn Back to "Nature"

Is the environmental movement's turn toward wilderness, wildlife and some sort of "natural" world due to our fear of crowding? Here are a few quotes from some environmental leaders:

> The only hope for Earth (including humanity) is to withdraw huge areas as inviolate natural sanctuaries from the depredations of modern industry and technology. Keep Cleveland, Los Angeles. Contain them. Try to make them habitable. But identify big areas that can be restored to a semblance of natural conditions, reintroduce the Grizzly Bear and wolf and prairie grasses, and declare them off limits to modern civilization.
> Dave Foreman, founder of Earth First! *(Confessions of an Eco-Warrior*, Sierra Club Books, 1988[8]

Yes, wilderness for its own sake, without any need to justify

it for human benefit. Wilderness for wilderness. For bears
and whales and titmice and rattlesnakes and stink bugs. And
. . . wilderness for human beings . . . because it is home.
Dave Foreman, founder of Earth First! *(Confessions of an
Eco-Warrior*, Sierra Club Books, 1988[9]

Restoration is a backward-looking philosophy. But unlike
romanticism, which is a longing for the past, or preservation, which seeks to save what already exists, restoration
implies an active participation in bringing the past back to
life.
Carolyn Merchant, "Restoration and Reunion with Nature,"
Restoration and Management Notes, Winter, 1986

Ironically, few people in the environmental movement have any
significant firsthand experience with nature. By " experience" I do
not mean carefully planned backpack trips into the Rocky Mountains, nor carefully manicured mountain retreats in the Adirondacks.
I am talking about living or working in the wilderness.

Hardly anyone in the modern world has real experience with
wilderness. Mostly, true wilderness residents are people like rubber-
tappers in the Amazon, primitive tribesmen in New Guinea, and Lapps
herding reindeer above the Arctic Circle. The wilderness-yearning in
our society comes mainly from urban people who have never experienced it. Few of them actually plan to, other than an occasional
comfortable visit to a national park. Virtually none of them would
countenance shooting game for food, or cutting trees for cabins and
firewood.

How much of this "call of the wild" is a fantasy?

It's true that urban America today is a currently sobering reality.
William Bennett, my fellow Hudson Fellow, has published a new
Index of Leading Cultural Indicators for America. The Index notes
that, compared with 1960: The rate of violent crime in America has
risen more than fourfold; birth rates among unmarried teenaged girls
are up threefold; scholastic aptitude scores are down 20 points; teen
suicide is up threefold; and violent crime among juveniles is up nearly
threefold. And all of this despite the most prosperous economy the
nation has ever seen. Given the problems in urban America, it should

not be too surprising that many people would like changes in our society.

The surprise to me, however, is that environmental critics do not seem to be suggesting any societal changes—at least not in the way we organize the cities where the vast majority of the people and problems reside. Instead, the critics want to retreat—to running a nice, clean wilderness instead:

> ... [T]he wilderness world (we have) recently rediscovered with heightened emotional sensitivity, is . . . the experience of the entire human community at the moment of reconcilia- tion with the divine after the long period of alienation and human wandering away from the true center.
> Thomas Berry, *The Dream of the Earth*, Sierra Club Books, 1988[10]

> We cannot survive by planning to treat the symptoms such as air pollution, water pollution, soil erosion, etc. . . . First we must reverse the population growth. . . .
> The other thing we must do is to pare down to our Indian equivalents. At one end would be the starving blacks of Mississippi; they would approach unity in In- dian equivalents, and would have the least destructive effect on the land. At the other end of the graph would be the politicians slicing pork for the barrel, the highway contractors, strip-mine operators, real estate developers. . . . Blessed be the starving blacks of the Mississippi with their outdoor privies, for they are ecologically sound and they shall inherit a nation.
> Wayne H. Davis, "Overpopulated America," *The New Re- public*, January 1970[11]

We cannot follow such advice. In the first place, it is physically impossible to yield big stretches of the country back to the grizzly bear, go back to low-yield organic farming—and still feed Cleveland and Los Angeles. Second, there is no point to it. Wilderness as such will not help us deal with our problems.

The critics observe that affluence has not brought us happiness.

Nor will it. It will simply give us long lives (if we choose to live them) and comfortable circumstances in which to work out our personal and social dreams and destinies as best we can.

Few have ever found perfection in the short, mean, dangerous life of the wilderness. The American Indian found no mystic perfection in the life of the hunter-gatherer. (Our current Indians have little more understanding of life in the true wilderness than we do.) When the Indians were running the country, myths about harmony with nature took second place to the desperate need for meat. That meant stalking a wary deer using a homemade bow with a range of 50 yards—or facing hunger. Often, it meant pushing the "old ones" out into the winter snow to die quietly (in their 50s). Even more often, it meant killing people from the neighboring tribes to ensure that one's own tribe would have enough hunting ground to survive.

The white "pioneers" lived longer, more comfortable lives than the Indians—but not by much. Their days in houses made of logs or sod were studded with blizzards, disease, droughts, plagues of insects, hunger, wild animal attacks, and combat with others who coveted the same piece of wilderness. For today's comfortable Americans to say they long for the wilderness is almost an insult to the people who had to contend with the dangers and desperation of the true wilderness.

John Dewey, one of America's most eminent philosophers, notes correctly in the opening quotes of this chapter that humanity has tried before to crawl back into the myth of a "natural" world. It hasn't worked.

The environmental movement derives its power from the millions of solid, responsible people who care about the environment and are trying their best to produce a sustainable, livable world. But there are more than a few highly visible people whom I will call in this book "eco-zealots."

Thanks to high-yield farming, we do not need to lower ourselves to levels of inhumanity never before sanctioned in human society. We do not need to induce mass famine, nor force abortions upon the unwilling.

Even the eco-zealots cannot drive us that far.

Nor do we need to accept the loss of any significant wildlife, wildlife habitat or key environmental resources. We can create the new resources we need from our increasing knowledge of the natural world—and use more intensively the natural resources already supporting humanity.

The loss of high-yield farming, by contrast, would mean famine for billions; and destruction of more wildlife than most of us can imagine.

For nothing.

Notes

[1]John Dewey, "Human Nature and Conduct," reprinted in S. Commins and R. Linscott (eds), *Man and Man: The Social Philosophers*, Washington Square Press, N.Y., p. 427.

[2]Claus and Bolander, *Ecological Sanity*, McKay & Co., New York, 1977.

[3]Yield data from FAO Annual Production Yearbooks; births per woman from "total fertility rates" in World Bank Annual Development Reports, World Bank, Washington, D.C.

[4]Senate Agricultural Appropriations Committee, *Hearing on the World Food Outlook*, February 23, 1994, Dirksen Building, Washington, D.C.

[5]Boyce Rensberger, "Despite Horn of Plenty, Some Feasts of Famine Abound Across the World," *Washington Post*, February 28, 1994, p. A3.

[6]Dr. Piers Pinstrup-Anderson is director of the International Food Policy Research Institute, the policy research unit of the Consultative Group on International Agricultural Research. IFPRI is headquartered in Washington, D.C.

[7]Dennis Avery, "Mother Earth Could Feed Billions More," *Wall Street Journal*, September 19, 1991, p. A14.

[8]Dave Foreman, *Confessions of an Eco-Warrior*, Sierra Club Books, San Francisco, 1988.

[9]Dave Foreman, *Confessions of an Eco-Warrior*, op. cit.

[10]Thomas Berry, *The Dream of the Earth*, Sierra Club Books, San Francisco, 1988.

[11]Wayne H. Davis, "Overpopulated America," *The New Republic*, January 10, 1970, reprinted in *Learning to Listen to the Land*, Island Press, Washington, D.C. 1991, p. 177-182.

2

Wildlife and the Acres
Not Plowed

MYTHMAKERS SAY:

"During 1993, no one knows how many species of plants, animals and other living organisms disappeared forever from the Earth—probably at least 75,000 according to conservative estimates."

"More Pollution, More Loss of Species, More Business As Usual," *The Earth Times*, December 31, 1993, p. 28

"Even if humanity were to depart the earth, recovery of biotic diversity by evolutionary mechanisms would require millions of years. . . ."

Michael E. Soule, "Conservation Tactics for a Constant Crisis," *Science*, Vol. 253, 16 August 1991

REALITY SAYS:

"The difference between wildlife habitat loss and cropland stability in most of the world is rising crop yields. Ecuador's crop yields declined between 1982 and 1987, driving a 2 percent annual expansion in cropland—at the expense of tropical forest. Just down the coast in Chile, cropland remained stable, despite a 17.5 percent annual growth in agricultural exports combined with 1.7 percent annual population growth. In Chile, the yields were rising."

Reported by Dr. Douglas Southgate, Ohio State University, in *Tropical Deforestation and Agricultural Development in Latin America*, London Environmental Economics Centre, 1991

"Much of the recent destruction of biodiversity in the tropics and elsewhere has been the result of government subsidies . . . that allowed the deforestation or plowing of low productivity lands that would not

support agriculture. . . . "
                Michael Huston, "Biological Diversity, Soils and Economics,"
                                              Science, December 10, 1993

"The evolution of cadmium resistance [in the mudworms] could have taken no more than 30 years. . . . This capacity for rapid evolutionary change in the face of a novel environmental challenge was startling. No population of worms in nature could ever have faced conditions like the ones humankind created in Foundry Cove. . . . The rapid evolution of tolerance for high concentrations of toxins seems to be common. Whenever a new pesticide is brought into use, a resistant strain of pest evolves, usually within a few years. The same thing happens to bacteria when new antibiotics are introduced."
                Dr. Jeffrey Levinton, Chairman, Department of Evolution and
                Ecology, State University of New York/Stony Brook, "The Big
                Bang of Evolution," *Scientific American*, November 1992

AND A MYTHMAKER'S REALITY:

"Passing a French Broom plant (a pest plant species) he muttered, 'I wish I had some Roundup.' This from the lips of a dedicated conservationist? Most of those battling exotic plants occasionally use herbicides. With varying degrees of distaste, every single one of the dozens of biologists, land managers and activists with whom I spoke considered judicious herbicide use a lesser evil than the harm caused by exotic plants. . . . 'What the hell do they want,' one asks. 'Do they want a short-term environmental insult or a long-term ecological catastrophe?'"
                "Botanic Barbarians," *Sierra*, Sierra Club,
                                          January/February 1994, p. 57

Saving Wildlife with Pesticides and High Yields

Eco-zealots demand that we either prove that pesticides represent zero risk to wildlife—or ban them.

Unfortunately, pesticides sometimes do inflict localized harm to wildlife, particularly when they are misused or when accidental spills occur. Thus pesticide risk to wildlife is greater than zero. But pesticides are a vital element of the high-yield farming system which is already saving 10 million square miles from being plowed for food production. By 2050, pesticides and fertilizers could be helping to save from plow-down as much as 30 million square miles of forests, prairies and other prime wildlife habitat.

In sum, there has never been an *environmental* triumph to match high-yield farming in the whole of human history.

A study by Texas A&M University indicates that U.S. field crop yields would decline drastically if we substituted the currently available organic pest controls for synthetic pesticides. Soybean yields would drop by 37 percent, wheat by 38 percent, cotton by 62 percent, rice by 63 percent, peanuts by 78 percent, and field corn by 53 percent.[1] Similar cuts in yields would be suffered on farms from France and Finland to Chile and China if they followed this example. Such yield cuts would require plowing down at least that much more acreage to replace the lost production. If the additional land had lower productivity, we would have to plow down even more than the indicated percentages.

(America's government-created farm surplus is beside the point. The world has no "surplus" of farmland, in the U.S., in Western Europe, or anywhere else. The world must virtually triple its farm output in the next 40 years. Inevitably, surplus food stockpiled in America means plowing down more wildlife in some other country.)

If we cut out chemical fertilizers as well, we could expect world crop yields to drop back by two-thirds, to the crop yields harvested in the 1950s before most of the world was using high-yield chemicals.

The world is currently cropping the land area equivalent of South America (5.8 million square miles).[2] We would need the land area of both South and North America (15-16 million square miles) to produce today's food supply without chemistry. If we tried to feed the projected human population for 2050 (8-12 billion) without the help of chemistry, we should expect to plow down another 30 to 40 million square miles of wildlife for food production. That is the equivalent of South America, North America, Europe, and much of Asia.

Compare the 10 million square miles of wildlife habitat saved by high-yield farming with the amount of land saved by the Nature Conservancy (one of the few environmental groups that has actually set land aside for wildlife). The Nature Conservancy says it is administering about 78,000 square miles of land worldwide, about the land area equal to Idaho. High-yield farming is thus protecting 125 times as much wildlife habitat as the Nature Conservancy.[3]

Gain in Crop Yields, 1950-90

	1950s	1960s	*Acres saved*
	(metric tons per hectare)		(millions)
U.S. corn	2.7	6.8	148.0
S. Africa corn	1.0	2.7	15.0
Argentine corn	1.6	2.7	6.8
Chile corn	1.6	8.4	1.1 (irrig)
China rice	2.5	5.7	106 (irrig)
Indonesia rice	1.7	4.4	61 (irrig)
France wheat	2.2	6.7	3.6
Mexico wheat	1.1	4.2	5.8
India wheat	0.7	2.3	138.0
Indonesia cassava	7.8	12.4	1.8
Chile tomatoes	13.4	36.0	0.3 (irrig)
Canada rapeseed	0.9	1.32	3.3
U.S. soybeans	1.4	2.3	33.7
Australia cotton	1.8	3.7	0.4 (irrig)

Source: Computed from FAO Annual Production Yearbook series

Yes! It's the Habitat!

Even the most strident naturalists agree that preventing the loss of wildlife habitat is the key to saving wildlife species.

Insect experts Paul Ehrlich of Stanford and E.O. Wilson of Harvard recently coauthored an article claiming we might lose 25-50 million wild species by the year 2050—through habitat destruction due to population growth and rising affluence.[4] Banning pesticides would leave us with far less wildlife habitat—and thus far fewer wildlife species.

We cannot evaluate the wildlife benefits of high-yield farming by the number of spiders and weeds that survive in an acre of monoculture corn. There is never much wildlife in a monoculture crop field. Nor can we condemn pesticides based on the accidental deaths of 200 birds, or even 2000.

We must give high-yield agriculture the environmental credit for billions of wild organisms thriving in and on the two acres that didn't have to be plowed because we tripled the yield on the best and safest acre.

We Cannot Starve People and Keep Wildlife

Since habitat is the key to saving wildlife, and high-yield farming saves habitat, why aren't environmental organizations leading cheers for the companies that develop effective new pesticides for our crops? Why aren't they praising high-yield farmers? Why aren't they demanding *more* research to get still-higher yields?

The eco-activists would prefer to have fewer people in the world. They would like to have so few that high-yield farming would be unnecessary. But it does no good to say that the world should have fewer people. No one is prepared to murder the people, nor forcibly

USDA

THE ACRES NOT PLOWED—There is a good deal of wildlife habitat, even in intensively farmed areas. But the key to saving wildlife is farming the best land for high yields and leaving the biodiversity on the poorer land undisturbed.

abort the children in the Third World.

Nor can we starve the people and let the animals live; the people would not go quietly. They would not let their children die of starvation while a wildlife preserve sat unplowed next door.

Current evidence suggests that world population will restabilize in the next 40 years. In the meantime, we must take seriously the global requirement to feed the human population as it emerges—while still preserving wildlife habitat.

No Vegetarian World

It will not suffice to mutter about vegetarian diets. *The environmental movement is not delivering a vegetarian world.* On the contrary, most human beings continue to exhibit an urgent and deeply rooted hunger for the high-quality protein found in cooking oil, meat, milk, and eggs.

No country or culture in history has voluntarily accepted a diet based solely on the relatively low-quality protein found in vegetable sources. Meat and milk consumption is rising by millions of tons per year in China and India right now as their incomes rise. Billions of people, in every newly industrializing country in the world, are increasing their demands for the resource-costly protein found in cooking oil, meat, milk, and eggs.

Even in the affluent and environmentally conscious United States, the *New York Times* reported in 1992 that a mere 12 million Americans considered themselves vegetarians.[5] That's a bit under 5 percent of the population (though the *Times* said it was a 20 percent increase over a decade earlier).

Even that 12 million figure has to be seriously questioned. Also in 1992, the *Vegetarian Times* commissioned a profile and attitude survey of self-described vegetarians by Yankelovich, Skelly and White/Clancy, Schulman, a respected polling organization.[6] One of the survey questions was: "In order to satisfy my appetite, a main meal must include meat." *Half* of the vegetarians agreed with the statement. Two-thirds of them said they ate chicken, 40 percent reported daily or weekly consumption of some animal product, and one-third even admitted to eating red meat! Only 4 percent of America's "vegetarians" say they never eat any animal products.

There doesn't seem to be a lot of hope that humanity will voluntarily live on porridge and onions.

Even if the world *became* vegetarian, we probably could not feed the current human population with organic farming. We might have enough arable acres—but the world probably has less than 20 percent of the organic plant nutrients needed to maintain current production. Thus, organic farming would force us to plow far more land for green manure crops—again, radically reducing wildlife habitat.

On the other hand, if we allow ourselves to use our knowledge of chemistry in high-yield farming, we can almost certainly feed everybody the foods they want, including high-quality protein—and still leave more room for wildlife than the wild creatures have today.

REALITY COMMENT:

"It is usually best to avoid saying of any idea—whether socialism, Kenynesianism or Christianity—that it has not been tried. Most of these ideas have been tested to destruction by fallible human beings, and there is no point in invoking perfect versions operated by archangels."

Samuel Brittan, columnist for the *Financial Times*,
August 1, 1994, p. 12

Fragile Land Back in Grass and Trees

We must also give high-yield farming the environmental credit for the steep, erodible, and drought-prone acres of farmland put back into grass and trees in countries like the U.S. and Sweden. This has been possible directly because of high-yield farming on the best and safest acres. In the 19th century, my steep, rocky little farm in the Shenandoah Valley was planted to corn and wheat—with terrible erosion losses. Once Iowa and Indiana learned to grow 100-bushel corn, my Virginia land was put back into grass, where it belonged. In the old days, they also burned my mountainside every spring to kill brush and encourage grass for cattle. With good pasture management and fertilizer, I no longer need to pasture or burn the mountain. It harbors deer and wild turkeys instead, with an occasional black bear and bobcat.

Sweden has increased its forest area by 23 percent since 1970, and is continuing to shift land from farms to forests—because of rising crop yields on its best land. Germany is expanding forest by taking some of its high-risk cropland out of farming. Thus high-yield farming is actually putting millions of acres back into more wildlife-friendly status.

The key is to farm the best and safest acres for all they're worth. Then the remaining acres can be left to nature and recreation.

That doesn't mean misusing pesticides. It doesn't mean using more pesticide than we need to achieve good yields. It doesn't mean using pesticides that are dangerous to wildlife when better alternatives are available. It doesn't mean ignoring integrated pest management. It doesn't mean permitting dangerous pesticide runoff. But it certainly *does* mean using pesticides now—and into the future until we discover still-safer and more powerful productivity alternatives.

Tough, Tenacious Wildlife Species

Our wildlife species, meanwhile, have already proven that they are generally tough and adaptable.

According to Dr. Jeffrey Levinton, chairman of the Ecology and Evolution Department at the State University of New York/Stony

MAKING DO WITHOUT HABITAT—These scissortail chicks are growing up in an oil refinery, but if we keep raising crop yields, most of the world's wildlife can keep its traditional habitat.

Brook, the last big explosion of species in the world occurred 600 million years ago.[7] Virtually all of our major wildlife types (Levinton calls them "body types") have been around for at least that 600 million years. During this period, they have dealt with radical changes in temperature, oxygen and CO_2, new pests, and "wild cards" like concentrations of toxic cadmium in their environments. Levinton concludes that the number of wild species has been gradually increasing throughout this long period. He says there is strong reason to believe that the number of species will continue to expand—if we do not destroy the habitats.

Levinton himself tested mudworms from a cove in the Hudson River near an old battery factory. The mudworms there had successfully adapted to levels of toxic cadmium as high as 25 percent—unprecedented in world history.[8] "Overall . . . the total number of species seems to have been increasing steadily during the past 60 million years. . . . All the evidence from living groups of organisms therefore suggests that contemporary evolution proceeds as fast as ever," says Levinton.

His conclusions underscore the reality that if wildlife species do not lose their habitat, their prospects for survival are bright.

But What About Manmade Poisons?

Even if we grant the importance of saving wildlife habitat, the environmental hard-liners seem to believe that the pesticides will poison the wildlife *in* the habitat. That is a valid concern. The demonstrated answer to it is "no."

Naturalists all over the Western world have focused on possible the loss of species, and none of them have fingered pesticides for any species losses. Their major concern is habitat loss, followed by things like untreated sewage threatening coral reefs, and too much nitrate (from both farming and urban areas) over-fertilizing lakes and streams. Pesticides haven't even eliminated the boll weevil— and we were *trying* to do that.

Recently a devoted birdwatcher named Samuel Florman noted in MIT's *Technology Review* that the birdwatching community was perhaps guilty of crying "wolf" again on bird losses.[9] Since the arrival of the Pilgrims, only four North American bird species have become extinct (the Labrador duck, the great auk, the passenger pigeon, and the Carolina parakeet). All were lost before the introduction of pesticides. Three other extinctions are suspected (ivory-billed woodpecker, Bachman's warbler, and Eskimo curlew) but again, no one is laying these at the door of farm chemicals. "Considering the speed and voracity with which the United States was developed, one looks for reasons why the destruction was not far worse," says Florman.

There is also a lot of habitat managed *for* wildlife. The U.S. Fish and Wildlife Service currently manages 20 million acres, the National Park Service another 80 million, and the national forests an additional 176 million acres. This does not count extensive wildlife management on private lands.

Roger Tory Peterson says there are now one to two *billion* more songbirds in the U.S. than when the Pilgrims landed.[10] Humans—including the suburbs—have created much more "forest edge" which is excellent bird habitat. (Florman notes that old growth forest is not congenial environment for most birds.) Also, a majority of the 254 bird species tracked by the U.S. Fish and Wildlife Service's Breeding Bird Survey *increased* in population between 1966 and 1991.

Safer Handling of Pesticides

Research has shown that a very high proportion of environmental contamination attributed to pesticide spraying has come from careless mixing and rinsing of application equipment, and from accidental spills.[11] Industry research has also shown that 85 percent of all applicator pesticide exposure occurs during the mixing and loading operation. With common liquid products, the exposure is often a result of splashing or spilling while pouring and measuring.[12]

Chemical handling is now being made safer by shifting to dry formulations (to prevent damage from spills) wherever that is practical. Formulations that can't be manufactured and shipped as dry powders are increasingly delivered in pre-measured water-soluble pouches that can be simply dropped into the spray tank. In other cases, the compounds are shipped in large reusable plastic containers which lock onto the farmer's spray equipment, without ever exposing the farmer or permitting spillage.

Cooperative Farmer reported "futuristic" spraying technologies, including sprayers controlled by radar to precisely calculate the tractor's ground speed in relation to spray rates. The magazine noted a direct injection spray system in which the active ingredients and the water are kept separate until they meet in the spray nozzles. This eliminates unused pesticide left in the tank. And since the water tank is never contaminated, it eliminates the problem of rinse water.

A University of Kentucky experimental sprayer uses fiber optic cables to throw a special light beam from the sensor to a receiver lens. Anything that interrupts the wave length of the beam is identified as a weed and activates the spray nozzle. UK designers expect the sprayer to cut the application rates for post-emergence sprays by 30 percent.[13]

What About Biomagnification?

"One of the most remarkable antipesticide allegations used by environmental extremists has been the claim that pesticide levels are 'magnified' at each step of the food chain," says Dr. J. Gordon Edwards.[14] Dr. Edwards is a biology professor at San Jose State who has authored both a respected book on wildlife *(Coleoptera East of the Great Plains)* and a Sierra Club book (*Climbers Guide to Glacier National Park*).

Edwards says the concept of biomagnification as put forth by antipesticide forces is scientifically untenable, and has been refuted by both experimental data and field tests. Today's pesticides are basically metabolized or excreted by fish, birds, and mammals.[15]

The DDT residues that remain in the tissues of many people and creatures have been isolated and rendered harmless; they have never been linked to any health threat.

"Unfortunately," Dr. Edwards writes, "the popular press and some semi-scientific journals have been crammed with 'biomagnification' articles for many years, and antipesticide activists have made profitable use of that myth. Environmental organizations welcomed the radical concept and used it to frighten the public into donating more money to 'help fight pesticides'."[16]

Dr. Edwards says that whenever allegations of biological magnification are brought up, the activists should be challenged to produce the actual data, from analyses of each step in the actual food chain. They should have to specify which methods of analysis were used, which tissues were analyzed, how old the samples were, and whether they were wet or dry weights. They should also have to present valid evidence that the creatures really were in the food chain being studied.

He points out that activists have made such mistakes as saying that herring gulls had to have gotten DDT in their tissues from the fish they ate, even though the subject gulls were also notorious garbage feeders in the dumps of nearby cities. They have also, he argues, taken the highest concentration from the upper element of the food chain and the lowest concentration from the lower element to get the *appearance* of biomagnification. Further, they have put herring gulls in a food chain with marine amphipods (which they don't eat) and old squaw ducks (which they don't eat either).

Pesticides Getting Safer for Wildlife

I recently spoke to a local Chamber of Commerce meeting. When I asserted that pesticides were getting safer for wildlife, one of my neighbors said he used to have more cardinals in his yard than he does now. How could I be sure that the pesticides weren't killing his cardinals?

First of all, we must understand that wildlife numbers ebb and flow due to many factors, including the amount of food for that species, competition for territory, the ratio of predators, weather (both here and in migratory paths), and any number of changes in local habitat.

However, I answered my neighbor by noting that Virginia had recently banned a chemical called Furadan 15G (carbofuran) because of "hundreds" of known bird deaths over a period of years. (The antipesticide movement alleges thousands, and they may well be right.)[17]

The chemical in question was a dry, granular insecticide and nematocide. It was supposed to be incorporated in the soil during seedbed preparation, but some granules were often left lying on the surface. It was a threat to birds if they mistook them for seeds and ate them directly.

Some birds *did* eat the Furadan granules, and died. Some were songbirds. Worse, a number of eagles apparently died from carbofuran poisoning after eating pigeons and other prey birds which had consumed carbofuran. Carbofuran was banned in Virginia as a result of the bird deaths and the compound was withdrawn from the U.S. market.

Several things strike me powerfully about the banning.

First, "hundreds" of bird deaths over a period of years, in a state with 44,000 square miles and literally millions of birds, is a tiny problem. This will probably get me condemned by the Audubon Society, but we can't make huge broad-gauge decisions about the future of the world's food systems, people, and wildlife on the basis of a small number of American bird deaths—as regrettable as they may be. The wildlife in Asia and the people in Africa also deserve at least some consideration.

Second, America is so rich in food productivity today that we banned an otherwise-useful chemical which posed even that small a wildlife problem.

Third, one of the reasons we were able to ban Furadan 15G is that there were other cost-effective pesticides available to attack Furadan's target pests in Virginia. If the state had to ban all pesticides and accept a 50 percent cut in its crop yields, Virginia would have to plow down another 1.5 to 2 million acres to make up the lost production. How many birds (plus other wild creatures) live in 2 million acres of forest and wild meadow?

Finally, pesticides and pesticide regulation are continuing to make the world *safer*, not more dangerous, for both people and wildlife. We are banning any chemicals where significant risks can be proved. (DDT was banned even *without* such proof.)

Pesticides today are tested far more extensively than they used to be—specifically for their safety with wildlife as well as with humans. That's a major element of the 100-plus tests that new chemicals must pass.

However, we don't dare to allay my neighbor's worries about pesticides by banning them all—because the environmental cost would be too high. Too much wildlife habitat would be lost to low-yield farming.

What About Minimizing Pesticide Use?

There are techniques that can reduce pesticide use without much production loss. However, all of them involve trade-offs.

For example, we could be using more integrated pest management to a fuller extent. But lots of farmers already use IPM, and more have tried it. It involves management costs, and sometimes higher risks of pest damage. Similarly, we could be scouting more of our crop fields to see when and whether they *need* spraying, rather than spraying every field just in case. Again, scouting involves management costs and risks.

We could be banding more pesticides right along the rows where the pesticide does the most good, instead of spreading it in the mid-rows too. (This permits lower volumes to do almost as much good). However, the banding has to be done carefully or it risks extra pest damage, and the added time involved in application has to be balanced against the reduced pesticide use.

We could be using more crop rotation to break pest cycles without pesticides (though there is sometimes a trade-off in lowered cropping intensity).

As we develop better baits for insect traps (especially the sophisticated pheromones which mimic insect attractants) we can further reduce field spraying.

It is currently fashionable in some of the agricultural colleges and research stations to advocate "low-input sustainable" (LISA) farming systems. (LISA uses chemicals, but sparingly.) This is certainly a less radical recommendation than demanding chemical-free farming—but moving even partway down the yield ladder may be a step backward for wildlife.

Further, if current pesticides are not dangerous, there is little need to take the decision about pesticide use out of the farmers' hands.

Pesticide Volumes Already Declining

American pesticide use is already declining, as shown in Figure 2.1.

Much of this has been due to the introduction of safer new low-volume pesticides. Some of it has also been due to the spread of

Figure 2.1

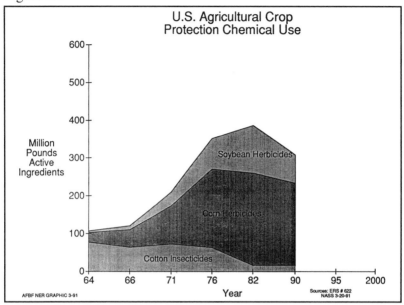

Source: American Farm Bureau Federation

integrated pest management, especially in cotton.

The reduction in pesticides would have been far more dramatic except for the rapid spread of conservation tillage. Herbicides have been the only category of pesticides with any recent increase in usage volume. That's because they're used in the new soil-conserving farming systems, which rely on chemical weed control instead of "bare-earth" farming systems like plowing. But the conservation tillage, now used on more than 100 million U.S. acres, is drastically cutting our soil erosion. The conservation tillage also cuts tractor fuel requirements by millions of gallons compared to plowing. Thus herbicides have increased U.S. pesticide use—but the increased herbicide usage is delivering major environmental benefits.

There *have* been temptations toward prophylactic spraying in the past. One of the awful truths about past weed control has been the "neighbor factor." Farmers didn't want the neighbors to see weeds in their fields. It lowered their prestige. It brought complaints that their weeds were spreading weed seeds onto neighboring fields. It is ironic now, during the low-till revolution, to see these same farmers moving en masse to farming systems like conservation tillage and no-till which feature scruffy-looking fields covered with corn stubble and dead grass.

A far stronger temptation to spray has been offered by the farm subsidy programs of the U.S. and various other rich-country governments. The subsidy programs have given farmers artificial incentives to get high yields—almost literally forcing them into heavier chemical use. Strangely, the environmental movement has been very gentle in approaching these farm subsidies, even though they have clearly played a huge part in boosting farm chemical use in the U.S., Western Europe, and Japan.

In some parts of the world, unfortunately, pesticides *have* been misused and significant damage has been done to wildlife populations. This book is not meant to justify bad management of pesticides. Nor is it intended to justify the over-intensification of farming which has been produced by government farm subsidies in the First World.

However, this book *will* make the argument that any heavy-handed regulatory mandate to drive down pesticide use will provide virtually no safety gain for the public, and may even increase human cancer risks. Nor would it save wildlife.

This book confronts the antipesticide movement with an urgent reality: *Moving now to a chemical-free agriculture on the basis of current knowledge, and thus forcing expansion of cropland to compensate for lower yields, would represent the greatest wildlife loss since the extinction of the dinosaurs.*

Notes

[1]E.G. Smith,, R. D. Knutson, C. R. Taylor, and J. B. Penson, *Impacts of Chemical Use Reduction on Crop Yields and Costs*, Agricultural and Food Policy Center, Department of Agricultural Economics, Texas A&M University, in cooperation with the National Fertilizer and Environmental Research Center of the Tennessee Valley Authority, College Station, TX (undated).

[2]Cultivated land total from John F. Richards, *The Earth As Transformed by Human Action*, Cambridge University Press, 1990.

[3]Land totals from Nature Conservancy, Washington, D.C. (Regina

Perkins), July 12, 1994.

[4]Paul Ehrlich and E. O. Wilson, "Biodiversity Studies: Science and Policy," *Science*, August 1991, pp. 758-761.

[5]Columnist Marian Burros, "Eating Well," *New York Times*, July 8, 1992.

[6]Judy Kizmanic, "Here's Who," *Vegetarian Times*, October 1992, pp. 72-80.

[7]Dr. Jeffrey Levinton, "The Big Bang of Animal Evolution," *Scientific American*, November 1992, pp 84-91.

[8]Op. cit.

[9]Samuel Florman, "Progress for the Birds," *Technology Review*, July 1993, p. 63.

[10]Op. cit.

[11]Richard S. Fawcett, "Pesticides in Ground Water—Solving the Right Problems," *Ground Water Monitoring Review*, Vol. IX, No. 4, Fall 1989.

[12]"Futuristic Spraying Today," *Cooperative Farmer*, February 1993, pp 20-21.

[13]Op. cit.

[14]Dr. J. Gordon Edwards, "The Myth of Food-Chain Biomagnification," *Rational Readings on Environmental Concerns*, op. cit., pp. 125-135.

[15]D. L. Gunn, *Annals of Applied Biology*, 1972, pp. 105-127; G.R. Harvey, "DDT in the Marine Environment," *National Academy of Sciences Committee Report*, August 9, 1973; and J. W. Kanwisher, "DDT in the Marine Environment," *National Academy of Sciences Committee Report*, January 30, 1973.

[16]Dr. J. Gordon Edwards, op. cit.

[17]Diana West, "Taking Aim at a Deadly Chemical," *National Wildlife*, National Wildlife Federation, June/July 1992, pp. 28-41.

3

There Is No Upward Population Spiral

MYTHMAKERS SAY:

"Population, when unchecked, increases in a geometrical ratio. Subsistence increases only in an arithmetical ratio. A slight acquaintance with numbers will show the immensity of the first power in comparison of the second. . . . The power of population is indefinitely greater than the power in the earth to produce subsistence for man."

Thomas Malthus, 1766-1834, *An Essay On the Principle of Population*

"In 1968, *The Population Bomb* warned of impending disaster if the population explosion was not brought under control. Then the fuse was burning; now the population bomb has detonated. . . . In the six seconds it takes you to read this sentence, eighteen more people will be added. Each hour there are 11,000 more mouths to feed; each year, more than 95 million. Yet the world has hundreds of billions fewer tons of topsoil and hundreds of trillions fewer gallons of groundwater with which to grow food crops than it had in 1968."

Paul Ehrlich, *The Population Explosion*, Simon and Schuster, New York, 1990

"Population. I have not spoken about this before. I have been an environmentalist for 20 years, but I have never talked about population. . . . The controversy around contraception and abortion made it politically easier to speak and organize around air pollution, deforestation, toxic waste and biodiversity while ignoring the role our own burgeoning species plays in all this."

Jane Fonda, U.S. Special Goodwill Ambassador to the United Nations Population Fund, 1994

"How long do Americans intend to watch while population growth adds both to poverty and justification for taking more from Nature? . . . With overpopulation, the clash of values grows both more bitter and more illogical. Does Kemp [former Housing and Urban Development Secretary] support open borders *and* housing the poor *and* preserving wetlands? Not possible. These are mutually exclusive goals. . . . Does Vice-President Albert Gore pose as an environmentalist at the same time he plumps for immigration? . . . As an environmentalist, Gore inspires neither confidence nor trust."

Virginia D. Abernethy, *Population Politics*, Plenum Press, New York, 1993, p. 300

REALITY SAYS:

"The new African data mean we will likely get less global population than we imagined. Birth rates in sub-Saharan Africa—the last main redoubt of superhigh fertility—are plunging. . . . This is happening against a backdrop of stunning decreases in fertility over three decades in Latin America (a 50 percent drop), Northern Africa (Egypt down 42 percent) and Asia (Indonesia down 43 percent). The current UN 'medium' projection shows global population growing from 5.4 billion today to 11.1 billion in 2100. But that is based on a 2.1 Total Fertility Rate well above the current levels of modern nations . . . the UN's (more likely) 'low' scenario yields a 6.4 billion population in 2100 (and sinking) and even that is keyed to a 2.0 rate, higher than modern norms."

Ben Wattenberg, American Enterprise Institute, "Unexploding Population?" *Washington Times*, March 17, 1994

"One-quarter of world population has stopped growing. Another quarter of the population is on the verge of arriving at zero-growth fertility. . . . The rate of growth, which had been rising for the past three centuries, dropped to a little above 2 percent around 1970 and has been in decline ever since. The 20-year economic boom after World War II is clearly the reason world population growth dropped to the 1970 level. Another burst of expansion in the world economy could bring the whole population down to zero growth."

Gerard Piel, founder and longtime publisher of *Scientific American*, and author of a forthcoming book on population growth, quoted in *The Earth Times*, June 15, 1994[1]

"Has the world's fear of being overcrowded brought us to a lurking suspicion that additional food production will simply encourage more births? If so, we can set our minds at rest. The evidence shows clearly that higher-yield farming encourages fewer [Third World] births."

Dennis Avery, "Boosting Crop Yields Would Save Habitat,"
Christian Science Monitor, November 1, 1994, p. 19

The most startling thing you can tell the average American is that the world's population is *not* spiraling upward out of control. But that's the reality. What we're seeing is not a population spiral but a onetime surge. In fact, the world is in the final stages of the third—and probably last—human population surge in all history.

The first surge began 10,000 years ago when we invented farming. Farming produced more food per acre, more dependably, than hunting and gathering. With farming, the world's human population rose fairly quickly from perhaps 10 million to about 200 million at the time of Christ.

Population stayed below 700 million until the beginning of the Industrial Revolution in the 18th century.[2] (Agriculture could have supported more people in that period, but epidemic diseases like cholera and bubonic plague kept down the urban numbers.) The second population surge coincided with the Industrial Revolution.

What we're seeing today is what might be called the Public Health Surge in human numbers. Death rates are being brought down by safe drinking water, proper waste treatment, vaccines, and the other public health interventions. Death rates come down quickly.

It takes longer—often several decades—for birth rates to come down to match. In the meantime, we have a surge in populations, country by country.

The Dreaded L-Shaped Curve

The doomsayers claim we can't know that populations will level off again. They imply that human numbers will just go up and up, producing incredible crowding, limitless mountains of waste, and the destruction of virtually every wildlife species. The favorite graphic in book after environmental book shows world population starting at

Figure 3.1

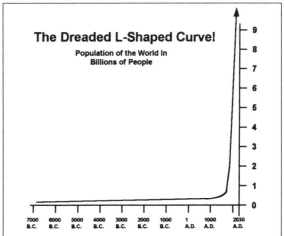

virtually zero in prehistoric times, sloping slowly upward until about 1900, and currently zooming straight up. (See Fig. 3.1.)

The more accurate depiction of human demographics, however, is the S-shaped curve. (See Fig. 3.2.)

The current population surge is expected to be virtually over

Figure 3.2

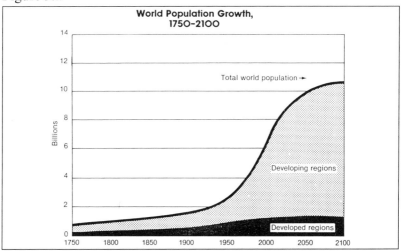

Source: *World Population: Fundamentals of Growth*, copyright Population Reference Bureau, Washington, D.C., 1990

before the year 2050. Total fertility rates in the poorest countries have already come more than 60 percent of the way to stability, essentially in one generation! Births per woman in the whole Third World have dropped from 6.1 in 1965 to a current level of 3.4 in the low-income countries and 3.0 in the middle-income countries.[3] Stability is 2.1 births per woman. The First World is at 1.7 births per woman and seems to have settled at that level.

The Good News on Global Population

One of the reasons that pesticides and fertilizers are *not* politically correct is that many people seem to have that strong psychological fear of overcrowding.

People have not understood that the world's rate of population growth peaked about 1963 and is already headed rapidly toward zero. Even such "responsible" sources such as the UN and the World Bank have continued to predict a world population as high as 12 to 19 billion people in 2100.

What we haven't heard is the *good news* on world population growth: *The most likely projection based on the latest birth data is that the world's population will peak at about 8 billion people in 2030, and then trend downward for the rest of the century.*

We are indebted to Dr. David Seckler of the Winrock Foundation for that good news. He recently used his statistical training to delve into what's behind the UN and World Bank population estimates.[4] (Most of the activists have been telling us the responsible estimates were too *low*.)

Seckler tells us that the UN did *no* research to back up its high, medium and low scenarios. The numbers are not statistical analyses of any sort. Each of the scenarios is *equally probable* in their view.

The World Bank used a slightly more analytic approach—except that the bank assumed long-term fertility rates for every country in the world would stabilize at 2.1, the replacement rate. The bank even assumed that the countries whose fertility rates have dipped far below 2.1 would shortly jump back up.

"There is no statistical reason to believe there is a long-term floor of 2.1," says Dr. Seckler. "On the contrary, over 38 percent of the population of the world is in countries with average fertility rates

Figure 3.3

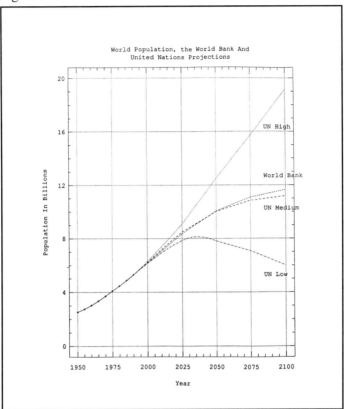

below 2.1. Many countries are at very low levels: Spain, Italy, Germany and Hong Kong are below 1.4. And many countries have been below 2.1 for a long time. We have estimated that if there is a long-term floor, it is in the neighborhood of 1.7 plus or minus 0.2. This independent estimate corresponds to the consensus estimate of a group of demographers interviewed on this subject." [5]

The world's population growth rate apparently peaked at 2.23 percent in the early 1960s. The current rate of population growth is down to 1.5 percent and falling. Population growth in the Third World countries has dropped from a peak of about 2.5 percent to the current 1.6 percent and is falling even faster than the global rates.[6]

The World Bank thinks Ethiopia will be the last major country to reach the ratio of one birth to one death—in 2050. Indonesia, with the fourth-largest population and the largest Moslem population, will get to 1:1 in 2005. India is projected to reach 1:1 in 2010.[7]

How Can We Be Sure Populations Will Level Off?

When I was in Egypt in 1981, women in the upper Nile valleys had just been surveyed on how many children they wanted.

The answer? Sixteen!

That is, in fact, a logical desire—in a primitive country. In a primitive country, children are one of the few assets poor people can have. They are almost immediately useful in the fields and handcrafts. Equally important, kids represent the only social security in poor societies. And if your children keep dying in epidemics, you need a bunch of them to ensure that one or two will be around and solvent when you are in your rocking chair by the fire.

In a wealthy society, by contrast, kids are an expensive ego investment. (I've just gotten my third son through college.) No more child labor. (There are laws.) They need expensive athletic shoes, lots of doctor's checkups, and before you know it they want cars. (Even if they drive yours instead of their own, your car insurance policy will cost you a bundle.)

There has never been a rich country with a continuing high birth rate, and rarely a poor country with a low one.

People have to *want* to limit births, which is why affluence is such a key element in lowering birth rates. Once they decide to limit births, they find ways to do it. A Turkish doctor notes that modern contraception raises the effectiveness of the family's birth decisions from perhaps 80 percent to about 90 percent.

The modern methods are very much preferred; they are used by 80 percent of the Third World women who practice contraception.[8] But the decision to limit births in the first place is the real key.

Recent Income Gains in the Third World

Condoms, pills, and female education all go with declining fertility rates. But none of them work unless people want fewer children.

That comes with higher incomes.

And world economic growth is surging. The world stage is now set to generate more economic growth for more people in poor countries than ever before in history. More important, this is a trend, not an incident.

The General Agreement on Tariffs and Trade (GATT) is now the most successful international institution in world history. It has replaced 200 years of tariff wars with an agreement for all countries to let in the competitive products of their neighbors. This has ushered in decades of economic growth rates higher than we've ever seen before, in countries with no economic growth history. World nonfarm trade has increased more than twelve-fold since 1950, and is still rising fast. The resulting spread of economic growth is headlined by Japan and the other Asian Tigers.

Some observers—I am one—believe that the "GATT miracle" and the Asian Tiger model also triggered the economic liberalization of China, helped bring down the walls of the Kremlin, and are now beginning to rescue Latin America from its traditional, stifling Spanish-style bureaucracy.

The hundred-year ideological struggle between Communism and capitalism is over, and that too is good news for economic growth. The idea that you could make people happier and better-off through government planning and control has been discredited. The idea that six people in Moscow could replace the ideas and energies of millions of on-the-spot Russian decision-makers was unlikely in 1917. It became impossible in the lap-top computer age.

More than 30 poor countries, from India and Poland to Peru and Zimbabwe, are now trying to privatize, attract foreign capital and generate export-oriented manufacturing jobs. Most of them are succeeding, and will continue to succeed, because of the GATT free trade opportunity.

The Cold War has ended. Moreover, the world community of nations stepped in to roll back an invading dictatorship in Kuwait—as it did *not* do with Hitler in the 1930s. That means less money needed for defense and more cash available for civilian needs, all over the world.

Finally, the original Asian Tigers (more properly GATT tigers) are now mature enough to be engines of international economic growth themselves. The imports of Japan, South Korea, and Taiwan—along with their foreign investments—are reinforcing world economic growth.

China, with a billion people, has been boosting its industrial output at more than 12 percent annually for over a decade.

"Between 1977 and 1993," the *Financial Times* said recently, "China's measured gross domestic product rose more than fourfold, the dollar value of its exports increased tenfold, and the annual inflow of direct investment rose from virtually nothing to $26 billion. Above all, hundreds of millions have experienced a transformation in how they live now, and how they hope to live tomorrow." [9]

China's per capita incomes have doubled since 1980, and in the southern part of the country they have quadrupled. Economic growth in *southern* China has been rising 20 percent per year. They are making textiles, shoes, electronics, and a host of other products. Private investors are building superhighways and expanding telecommunications. *The Economist* magazine says half of China's urban households now have refrigerators, and 70 percent have *color* TVs. A 1992 study by McKinsey & Co. estimated that there were 60 million Chinese with incomes above $1,000 (a level at which consumer buying begins to be important.) By the end of the century, McKinsey expects more than 200 million Chinese to top the $1,000 income level.[10]

India's industrial output has been growing three times as fast as its population for a decade. Now India is reducing its socialist red tape and making foreign capital more welcome, so the economic growth rate could increase further. As a result of higher incomes, India's Hindus are increasing their milk consumption 2 million tons per year and are eating more eggs.

Indonesia, with the world's fourth-largest population, is set to become the next Asian tiger with a deregulating economy. In 1970, 60 percent of Indonesians lived in absolute poverty; today less than 15 percent of them do. Indonesia's privatization has been a huge success, pushing economic growth to 8 and 9 percent annually. The poultry industry in Indonesia is expanding at double-digit rates.

This world economic growth pattern is no OPEC boomlet like we saw in the late 1970s. This is permanent, solid growth in the world's economies. And unlike oil money which sticks to the hands of only a few, the income gains from this growth are being spread broadly among workers and active managers.

This is good news for the environment. Forget the guilt being spread by the eco-zealots who claim that the rich countries are the key environmental problem. Rich people stack themselves in cities that don't take much land, treat their sewage, buy cleaner forms of energy, and develop pollution-reducing technologies.

Poor people not only have large families, they also tend to pollute more than affluent families. Most of the Third World's population is already in the most polluting phase of economic growth, extending crops onto fragile farmland, burning trees and soft coal for fuel, and smelting lots of iron.

MYTHMAKER:

"With few exceptions, newborn humans come into a world that can offer them nothing but hunger, disease and squalor. No matter how many relief programs we set up, there is just no way to cope with mass misery that gets worse as numbers increase . . . Our society and all others must adopt deliberate measures that will slow, halt and eventually reverse the appalling multiplication of numbers. There is no other choice . . . NPG advocates a massive increase in funding for U.S. foreign population control programs . . . "

From a fund-raising letter by Negative Population Growth, Inc., Teaneck, N.J., Spring 1994

New Momentum for Lower Birth Rates?

The best recent news is that lower birth rates seem to be gaining a momentum they have never had before. Until now, lower birth rates seemed to require significant gains in affluence. But now population management is becoming a reality even in countries which have not yet achieved high per capita incomes.

Kenya has long been the "fertility Frankenstein" of the developing world. In 1977/78 it had a fertility rate of 8.3 children per woman. By 1989, however, that fertility rate had dropped to 6.7. And in 1993—just four years later—it had fallen to 5.4. "The 20 percent decline in just over four years is one of the swiftest ever recorded," says the Population Reference Bureau of the latest Kenyan fertility drop.

Equally important, the demographers say, there are healthy leading indicators of change elsewhere in southern Africa, even where little economic growth is happening. Women are waiting longer to marry, getting more education, and using more contraceptives. All of this is reported in "The Fertility Decline in Developing Countries," a major article in the December 1993 issue of *Scientific American*.[11]

It is too early to assign a definitive cause for these developments. However, Dr. Seckler of Winrock has broad African and Third World experience. He suggests a "modernization factor."

"This is cultural change," says Seckler. "Changes in the self-image of people—especially people in rural areas and women—due to the rapid spread of modern images and ideas through radio and television in developing countries. This factor plays a major role in lowering the 'demand for children.' We have heard, for example, that family planning messages have been inserted into the television soap-operas in Brazil with great success."[12]

What he's really saying is that with modern electronic communications, even poor women begin to see themselves in a new light. They see Western TV programs on community satellite sets that portray mothers with 2 children who interact with their husbands as equals. They see women doing professional jobs *and* being women. Such exposures may now be driving social change even more rapidly than economics—or more closely in parallel with it.

The new African data mean the world is likely to get quite a lot less population growth than responsible demographers have predicted. The people-phobes will have a harder and harder time justifying their predictions of intolerable global crowding.

Zero Population Growth

I chuckle when I get the mailings touting the need to get zero population growth "right away." These mailings are not being read by the young people begetting Third World children. I laugh out loud when I read about the "rollback" of world population numbers. Are the members of these groups volunteering to subtract themselves? I know we will get zero population growth. We just won't get it fast enough to preclude the need for another tripling in world food production.

Why are we so terrified of this onetime population surge?

We've already accommodated one doubling of population,

between 1950 and 1990.

Certainly, if we *had* a perpetual upward spiral it would eventually defeat our efforts to supply food, forest products, and recreational space. But a onetime surge is a different matter. To repeat: The world has no upward population spiral.

Instead, we will have a population peaking (hopefully at 8-9 billion) about 2035-2040, with the total of humans then gradually declining into the foreseeable future. The Third World will continue to gain affluence and join the 38 percent of the world that is already well below replacement fertility rates.

Obviously, the environmental impacts of a large human population which is also stable and affluent are far different than the zero-population lobby has portrayed.

Food, Crowding, and Violence

Much has been made recently of the idea that crowding produces violence, and that fear of hunger produces wars.

Historically, it is true that tribes and nations have warred over hunting, fishing, and farmland. But we haven't seen much of that lately—or at least not since food production became a matter of technology rather than land.

Japan invaded Manchuria in the 1930s to grow soybeans—but modern Japan has become the world's largest food importer. It is buying wheat, feed grains, and meat on the world market, and exporting cars and other manufactures. Trade has proven a far more secure way for Japan to ensure its food supplies—at far less cost. Aircraft carriers and armies are hugely expensive. Combat with them is even more expensive.

The Serbs and Croatians in Yugoslavia are not warring over farmland. They are warring over ancient, unresolved ethnic frictions, inflamed at least since World War II. Nor is either side gaining a better life.

Look at Ireland, which has been fighting a civil war for decades (or centuries). It was once rooted in land ownership. Now, even the diehard Irish Republican Army is pursuing peace, because it sees the rest of the world outstripping Ireland economically. Food and land are no longer even significant issues; both the Catholics and Protestants assume they'll have food. Both assume the jobs they want are urban ones. But the sons on both sides are going elsewhere to get jobs that won't come to a war-torn land.

In Africa, recent decades have seen a good deal of hunger produced by violence—but not much violence produced by hunger. Civil wars have offered lots of examples of armies trying to keep their opponents from getting food, as in Ethiopia, Angola, Mozambique, Liberia, and Sudan.

In Rwanda, it is said that "crowding" caused the tribal genocide attempted by the Hutus against the Tutsis—with perhaps 1 million murders, systematically carried out according to a plan under development for years.

Why did the people of Rwanda not have faith in "population management"? Why did they not feel secure with the knowledge that contraceptive pills could cut their birth rates to more manageable levels? Any such "solution" must have seemed impossibly far distant. But higher corn and bean yields are immediate and tangible. They provide confidence for the future here and now. Rwanda has not made big gains in corn yields, but it has doubled its potato yields in recent decades, and has recently tripled the yields of its food bean fields. (Since 1985, 500,000 Rwandan farmers have begun growing climbing beans that yield three times as much food per acre; they're the agricultural equivalent of the high-rise office building.)

If food fears *were* to blame in Rwanda, then the Western world bears a more direct responsibility than if it was unresolved ethnic hatred.

We must have failed to communicate our successful experience with high-yield farming to the Rwandans. Maybe we didn't do enough to help them understand that higher-yielding corn, food beans, potatoes and other intensive crops offered food security for their future. We didn't show them the enormous power of a little chemical fertilizer. (High-yield seeds and fertilizer sacks don't try to get revenge in the future.)

Why has there been no internationally funded agricultural research station in Rwanda, prominently displaying the potential food solutions for the future? It couldn't have cost much, if the whole international farm research system has recently gotten only $270 million per year in funding. Why were there not local farm extension agents working intensively with both Hutus and Tutsis to produce more food per acre? As an alternative to murdering people you know by their first names, it should have had a certain basic human appeal.

If we truly are worried about food shortages producing violence, then it is time for the affluent countries to put their money where their mouths have been. It is time to quit complaining about too many births, and trembling about more illegal immigration to the rich countries. If those are our concerns, it is time for us to make real investments in Third World farm research. It is time to double or triple our investments in food production systems for the developing countries. The institutional structure is already in place. The scientific tools already exist. The research thrusts are already under way. It is simply a matter of stepping up the pace and breadth.

One billion dollars per year in Third World farm research . . . as an alternative to genocide . . . ?

The people arguing against high-yield farming research for the Third World may bear a heavy responsibility indeed.

Notes

[1]"Gerard Piel on Population: Assessing the Impact Of Development," *The Earth Times*, June 15, 1994, pp. 28-29.

[2]James Miller, Population Research Institute, Baltimore, MD, personal communication, 1994.

[3]Total Fertility Rate included in the "Demography and Fertility" tables in the *World Development Report 1989* (pp. 216-217) and *World Development Report 1994* (pp. 212-213), World Bank, Washington, D.C.

[4]Seckler and Cox, *Population Projections by the United Nations and the World Bank: Zero Growth in 40 Years*, Winrock International Institute for Agricultural Development, Center for Economic Policy Studies Discussion Paper No. 21, Arlington, VA, 1994.

[5]Seckler and Cox, *Population Projections By The United Nations and The World Bank: Zero Growth in 40 Years*, op. cit, executive summary.

[6]World Bank, Infrastructure for Development, *World Development Report 1994*, Tables 25 & 26, pp. 210-213

[7]*World Development Report* 1994, op. cit.

[8]Robey, Rutstein, and Morris, "The Fertility Decline in Developing Countries," *Scientific American*, December 1993, pp. 60-67.

[9]"Unfinished Revolution," *Financial Times* editorial, August 23, 1994.

[10]"Cracking the China Syndrome," *Financial Times*, December 31, 1992, p. 8.

[11]Bryant Robey, Leo Morris, and Shea Rutstein, op. cit.

[12]Seckler and Cox, op. cit., p. 23.

4

Preventing Cancer
with Pesticides

MYTHMAKERS SAY:

"The problem . . . is whether any of the chemicals we are using in our attempts to control nature play a direct or indirect role as causes of cancer. In terms of evidence gained from animal experiments we shall see that five or possibly six of the pesticides must definitely be rated as carcinogens. . . . Still other pesticides will be added as we include those whose action on living tissues or cells may be considered an indirect cause of malignancy."

Rachel Carson, *Silent Spring*, p. 222

"Farmers have been using these chemicals for decades, and the chemicals have built up in the soil from repeated doses year after year. They get inside the crops and onto their outer coverings. They get into water supplies and into the fish who live in them. And they build up in the bodies of animals whose feed has been grown using these chemicals."

David Steinem, *Diet for a Poisoned Planet*,
Harmony Books, New York, 1990, p. 5

"The most potent cancer-causing agent in our food supply is a substance sprayed on apples to keep them on the trees longer and make them look better."

Opening line of CBS-TV "60 Minutes" segment on
Alar, broadcast February 26, 1989

"The United States . . . will be a desolate tangle of concrete and ticky-tacky, of strip-mined moonscape and silt-choked reservoirs. The land and water will be so contaminated with pesticides, herbicides, mercury, fungicides, lead, boron, nickel, arsenic and hundreds of other toxic substances . . . that it may be unable to sustain human life. . . . Thus, as

the curtain gets ready to fall on man's civilization let it come as no sur-
prise that it shall first fall on the United States."
Wayne H. Davis, "Overpopulated America," *The New Republic,*
January 10, 1970
"The Truth Does Not Kill, Pesticides Do"
Placard at an antipesticide demonstration in Florida,
December 4, 1992

REALITY SAYS:

"The risk of cancer from ingesting minute doses of pesticide residues is so small that it verges on the theoretical."
Harvard Health Letter, January 1994, p. 7-8

"This is nonsense. Every chemical is dangerous if the concentration
is too high. Moreover, 99.9 percent of the chemicals humans ingest are
natural. For example, 99.99 percent of the pesticides humans eat are
natural pesticides produced by plants to kill off predators. About half of
all natural chemicals tested at high doses, including natural pesticides,
cause cancer in rodents. People determined to rid the world of synthetic
chemicals refuse to face these facts."
Dr. Bruce Ames, University of California, Berkeley, who
helped develop the Ames-Gold scale of cancer risk used
around the world, in a statement issued September 13,
1993, in connection with the release of the National
Research Council report, "Pesticides in the Diets
of Infants and Children"

". . . [V]irtually all chemicals are toxic if ingested in sufficiently
high doses. Common table salt can cause stomach cancer. . . . The (high-
dose) rodent test that labels plant chemicals as cancer-causing is
misleading. . . . The standard carcinogen tests that use rodents are an
obsolescent relic of the ignorance of past decades."
Science editorial, Dr. Phillip Abelson, September 21, 1990

"Of the 2,598 (fruit and vegetable) samples taken in this program,
92 percent had no detectable residues . . . we feel these results clearly
confirm what scientists have said for many years: the 'problem' of pesticide residues in fresh produce is more one of perception than reality."
James W. Wells, Director, California Environmental Protection
Agency's Department of Pesticide Regulation, commenting on the

Priority Pesticide Program, in which monitoring
is concentrated on pesticides of
"special health interest"[1]

"All things are poison and none without poison. Only the dose dif-
ferentiates a poison and a remedy."
Paracelsus (1493-1541), German physician and the
father of modern toxicology

In a sense, the public can be forgiven for fearing pesticides. In
the early days, when we knew less about cancer, we adopted (out of
fear and ignorance) the most drastic test we could find. That was the
high-dose rat test.

Then the high-dose rat tests "proved" that the pesticides caused cancer.

There is mounting scientific evidence, however, that high-dose
rat tests tell scientists little about the real risks in our food. The rat
tests in fact mislead the rest of us into fearing the wrong foods and
the wrong dangers.

Rachel Carson was wrong in her belief that five or six pesticides
then in use were causing cancer, and that more would be proven
carcinogenic. In fact, to date we have found one pesticide that caused
cancer—lead arsenate—which was displaced by DDT and the other
modern pesticides. Both lead and arsenic are carcinogenic. But we
no longer use lead arsenate because of its broad, immediate pre-
cancerous toxicity.

The high-dose rat tests find "cancer" in half of the chemicals
tested (natural and manmade). Few consumers realize that there are
no pesticides approved for use in the U.S. today which are known
causes of human cancer. Or that it is unlikely that any human has
ever developed cancer due to pesticide residues.

There are some approved chemicals on the "suspected" carcinogen list. They are mostly there, however, because *the heavy skewing of the diets* in the high-dose tests *itself* apparently causes cell
division and increased cancer risk.

Furthermore, the EPA overstates the dietary risk of pesticide residues to humans by 10,000-fold. For some reason, EPA assumes all
foods carry the maximum pesticide residues, even though only a small
proportion carries any residues at all.

Hunger Before Cancer

Farm chemistry today means life itself for billions of people. All over the world, pesticides and fertilizers mean ample food, free from destruction by locusts, armyworms, witchweed, crabgrass, Johnson-grass, aphids, stem rot, leafrollers, planthoppers, corn borers, dangerous natural toxins, and thousands of other pestilential plagues. Most countries would not be able to sustain life for their populations without farm chemicals.

What is the health trade-off for this abundance, produced with the help of chemicals?

There is no health trade-off. In fact, there are health gains:

- For one, pesticides help prevent the grains and oilseeds we eat from becoming contaminated with bacteria or fungi which produce toxins and mycotoxins which *can* cause cancer. One-fourth of the world's cereals and oilseeds are contaminated with such toxins. Our crops carry much lower risks, because of pesticides.
- Even more important, pesticides permit us to provide an abundance of the low-cost, attractive fruits and vegetables which are humanity's best defense against both cancer and heart disease. Eating five servings of fruits and vegetables per day cuts our cancer risks in half—no matter whether they're organic or not.

Zero Risk from Pesticides?

The eco-zealots demand that we prove zero human risk in pesticides—or ban them. We cannot, in fact, prove zero risk.

But we can prove that the natural chemicals in our foods themselves are 10,000 times more toxic than the pesticide residues. We know the foods are safe; in fact they're beneficial. So we know the pesticide risks are so low they're almost nonexistent.

In high-dose rat tests, pesticide residues have proven *less* dangerous than mustard and pickles!

The rapidly lengthening life spans in countries using farm chemicals are a strong indicator that we thrive on the foods containing both the natural and marmalade "carcinogens" labeled risky in the high-dose rat tests. It makes little sense to suggest that we would be living even longer without the pesticide residues—until after the chemophobes have found ways to deal with the "rat-risky" natural compounds which are ten thousand times more abundant in our diets.

Suppressing Toxins

The UN Food and Agriculture Organization has estimated that up to 25 percent of the world's food crops are contaminated with mycotoxins, many of which have the potential to harm people. A recent report from the Council for Agricultural Science and Technology examined the danger these toxins can represent, and the ways in which Americans avoid them.[2]

Aflatoxin, for example, found most often in moldy corn, peanuts and cottonseed, is a potent carcinogen. In western India, about 100 people died in 1974/75 when 200 villages tried to subsist on heavily molded corn. In England, thousands of turkeys died—of acute liver failure—in the 1960s when fed aflatoxin-contaminated peanut meal from Brazil. When dairy cattle are fed contaminated feed, aflatoxin can be transmitted to milk, and even to such products as cheese and yogurt. In humans it is associated with cancer of the liver and—in severe exposures—with gastrointestinal hemorrhage.

Ergotism, caused by fungal alkaloids, periodically reached epidemic proportions, in the Middle Ages and as recently as the 18th century. Whole populations seemed affected with giddiness. Mass movements with irrational goals appeared suddenly and then faded from sight. (Some historians speculate the Salem witch trials in colonial Massachusetts may have been triggered by ergotism.) In a severe epidemic in Ethiopia in 1978, half of the victims died, while many others developed dry gangrene and lost arms or legs.

Avoiding and minimizing these mycotoxins starts with controlling insect and rodent damage in the field. That's because the insect and rodent damage creates openings for the fungi which produce the mycotoxins. Pesticides are frontline defenses against these toxins. Even after harvest, however, the crops must be protected from storage pests. We have to build safe, dry storage—and sometimes we also have to use low-toxicity antifungal agents such as propionic acid and acetic acid, or even fumigants.[3]

Fighting Cancer and Heart Disease with Produce

Pesticides have been critically important in enabling us to produce ample supplies of attractive and reasonably priced fruits and vegetables for year-round consumption.

Eating more fruits and vegetables, studies show, can cut cancer risks in half and markedly reduce the ratio of heart disease and immune dysfunction.[4,5] Thus, *anything* which boosts fruit and vegetable consumption saves lives.

Dr. Anthony Miller is an epidemiologist at the University of Toronto and a member of the committee which drafted the National Research Council's comprehensive study, *Diet and Health*. He cites examples of findings to date:

- Carotene, found in carrots, broccoli, and many other orange and dark-green leafy vegetables, is converted in our bodies to retinols. The retinols suppress a whole range of cancers— skin, breast, bladder, esophagus, colon, pancreas, lung, and prostate.
- Vitamin C from citrus fruits and vegetables protects against stomach cancer. Stomach cancer was once our most prevalent cancer but the rate of affliction has been cut by three-fourths over the last 40 years. We know that vitamin C inhibits a group of carcinogens called nitrosamines.
- People who eat cabbage once a week have only one-third as much colon cancer as people who eat it less than once a month.
- Nitrate, associated with many vegetables, cuts the risk of lung cancer.
- Oral cancer risks are lower in people who eat lots of citrus fruits and in those who eat lots of dark yellow and cruciferous vegetables.
- Pancreatic cancer is lower in people who eat lots of dietary fiber and vitamin C.[6]

We are only beginning to understand the protective benefits of fruit and vegetable consumption.

For instance, two researchers at Johns Hopkins University in Baltimore recently isolated a single chemical—sulphoraphane—that has "remarkable tumor-fighting ability." It is present in most green and yellow vegetables. Sulphoraphane encourages protective enzymes that work to prevent cancer. There is a strong likelihood that this is only one of several (or many) such compounds.[7]

The Journal of the National Cancer Institute in June, 1990, detailed work done at the Institute for Hormone Research in New York City. "We have identified the compound in cruciferous vegetables which appears to act in a way which should be protective," said doctors Leon Bradlow and Jon Michnovicz. The compound is known as indole-3-carbinol. Their study found that the compound speeded a particular process of estrogen metabolization, thus theoretically reducing the threat of breast cancer. They have since found it reduced cancer risk in laboratory mice. They have begun the 3-5 year process of documenting whether the chemical actually works in humans.

It is this pattern of protection from fruits and vegetable consumption which has led the National Research Council to recommend that Americans double their current average consumption of fruits and vegetables. The National Institutes of Health, dieticians, and most other health professionals support that recommendation. (Incidentally, there is no evidence yet that consuming chemically synthesized vitamins has the same protective impact.)

Only about 9 percent of Americans currently eat the five full servings of fruits and vegetables a day recommended for optimum health. This raises an interesting point. If only 9 percent of the people eat enough fruits and vegetables when they are relatively cheap and attractive, how many of us would eat enough if they were twice as expensive and shabby-looking? What, in sum, is the public health impact of eco-activists frightening consumers about non-organic fruits and vegetables?

REALITY:

"Green and Yellow Veggies Protect Against Blindness

"Two new studies offer tantalizing evidence that chemicals in green and yellow vegetables may protect against heart disease and the most common cause of blindness in the elderly. . . . The compounds, called carotenoids, are the colorful pigments that make squash yellow and spinach green. . . . Nonsmokers with the highest blood levels of carotenoids had 70 percent fewer heart attacks than nonsmokers with the lowest levels. . . .

"People who consumed the most dark green, leafy vegetables were 43 percent less likely to have developed [age-related macular degeneration]. . . . AMD causes vision loss in an estimated 13.1 Americans and accounts for up to a third of the 900,000 U.S. cases of blindness. . . ."

From an Associated Press story published in the
Washington Times, November 9, 1994, p. A4

MORE REALITY:

"In separate studies, scientists in the Netherlands have found that apples are a great source of flavonoids—a naturally occurring chemical in many fruits, vegetables and beverages—which may reduce the risk of death from coronary heart disease and inhibit the development of certain cancers. The October 23 issue of *The Lancet* reports on a five-year study of 805 men, ages 65 to 84. The . . . men who consumed the highest amounts of flavonoids suffered about half as many heart attacks as those who consumed the lowest amounts."

The Packer, January 15, 1994, p. 4A

BOTTOM-LINE REALITY:

Your mother, and grandmother, were right—carrots are good for your eyes and "an apple a day . . . ."

How Much More Costly Without Pesticides?

A group of horticultural researchers associated with Texas A&M University did a recent study of the impact of giving up pesticides for fruits and vegetable production in the U.S. They compared the organic alternative with the costs, yields and practices for commercial producers (most of whom already use various forms of integrated pest management).[8]

They concluded that yields for both fruits and vegetables would drop substantially without pesticides—forcing major increases in cost.

Potato yields would drop "only" 50 percent. The yields of other vegetables were estimated to fall even more sharply, with sweet corn hit the hardest—a 78 percent reduction. Estimated losses in fruit yields ranged from oranges (down 55 percent) to apples (nearly 100 percent losses in commercial orchards). Fresh-market fruits and vegetables would likely suffer even bigger yield losses than processed vegetables.

The experts say a number of famous fruit and vegetable sources would apparently be knocked out completely, including Maine potatoes, Georgia peaches, Washington and Michigan apples, and California grapes. They also believe we would lose the winter production of Florida's tomatoes and sweet corn, making it difficult for the East Coast to keep up its cold-weather fruit and vegetable consumption. (We might have to rely on imports, though there is not as yet any organic fruit and vegetable import trade.)

The Texas A&M group's study is supported by an analysis of the impact of *banning just soil fumigants*, done by the U.S. Department of Agriculture's Economic Research Service (ERS). ERS researchers estimated that the loss of soil fumigants would sharply reduce yields of potatoes and tomatoes, at a cost of perhaps $3 billion to consumers in the short term. (Over time, new organic producers would presumably enter production, somewhat easing the price increases.)[9]

Figure 4.1

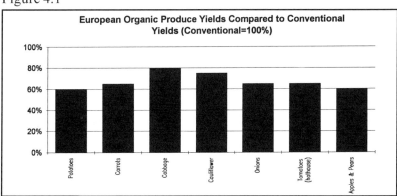

Source: *Organic Farming: Summary of Findings from a Study of Seven European Countries by the Landell Mills Research Group*, copyright European Crop Protection Association, Brussels, 1992

Figure 4.2

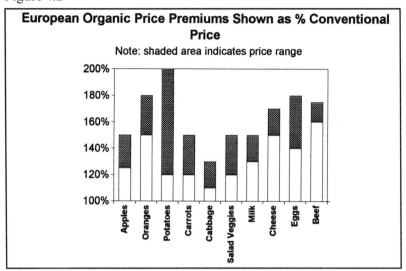

Source: *Organic Farming: Summary of Findings from a Study of Seven European Countries by the Landell Mills Research Group*, copyright European Crop Protection Association, Brussels, 1992

These estimates of commercial yield losses are hypothetical, but they are backed by even stronger real-world evidence. Studies in seven European countries found yields on organic fruits and vegetables averaged far less than commercially grown produce. (See Fig. 4.1)

Equally important, the prices of organic fruits and vegetables are virtually always far higher than the prices of commercially grown fruits and vegetables. (See Fig. 4.2)

Prices for fruits and vegetables are notoriously volatile, but organic produce seems to be priced significantly higher than mainstream produce week in and year out. If it were not more expensive to grow organic produce, the markets would be flooded with organic items with these high price premiums.

Pesticides Aren't Even the Problem

For 30 years, Americans have worried about being poisoned by pesticide residues. Billions of dollars have been spent on studying

**Organic vs. Mainstream Produce Prices
in Washington, D.C., June 1994**

Fruit	Mainstream Price	Organic Price	Premium
oranges	.45 each	.45 each	0%
apples (Red Delicious)	.50/lb	1.35/lb	170%
lemons	3/.99	1.59/lb	60%
pears	.99/lb	.99 each	110%
limes	3/.89	2.89/lb	225%
Vegetables			
carrots	1.49/lb	1.67/bunch	100%
spinach	.59/lb	1.99/bunch	400%
broccoli	.79/lb	1.59/lb	100%
white potatoes	.45/lb	.99/lb	100%
yellow onions	.45/lb	1.29/lb	185%
eggplant	1.29 each	1.95/lb	100%
celery	.99 each	.99 each	0%
mushrooms	1.99/lb	3.75/lb	88%

Source: Price comparisons by the author on the same day in June 1994 at two stores a few blocks apart—in comparable neighbor-hoods—in northwest Washington, D.C.

pesticide risks. Billions more have been spent on costly organic foods and in trying to find better "organic" pest controls. Yet we are still looking for the first human victim of pesticide residues. We have found, instead, that pesticide residues are not a significant health risk.

We have now conducted the high-dose rat tests on some of the natural chemicals in our foods—the same tests used by the eco-zeal-ots to indict pesticides. It turns out that the same proportion of natural chemicals (about half) are "carcinogenic" in the high-dose rat tests as manmade chemicals. They are toxic at about the same range of levels as pesticides. (Nature's own aflatoxin is about as virulent a carcinogen as we've tested.)

The caffeic acid in apples and lettuce, the limonene in orange juice, and the hydrazines in a mushroom have all proven carcinogenic in the rat tests!

The safety of farm chemicals was convincingly demonstrated by Drs. Bruce Ames and Lois Gold at the University of California-Berkeley. They are the scientists who *developed* the cancer risk scale used around the world—appropriately named the Ames-Gold Scale. When they rat-tested both natural and manmade compounds at high dosage levels, they didn't find much difference in the cancer risks.

That means we consume only one ten-thousandth as much cancer risk in the form of pesticide residues as we do in the form of natural carcinogens in our food. Thus, the risk from pesticide resi-

Human Exposure/Rodent Potency Index (HERP)		
Hazard Index	*Daily Human Exposure*	*Risky Compound Involved*
16.0	1 sleeping pill	Phenobarbital
4.7	wine (250 ml)	Ethyl alcohol
0.3	lettuce (1/8 head)	Caffeic acid
0.1	apple	Caffeic acid
0.07	brown mustard	Allyl isothiocyanate
0.04	orange juice	d-Limonene
0.03	peanut butter	Aflatoxin
0.005	coffee (1 cup)	Furfural
0.002	Alar in one glass of apple juice (1988)	UDMH
0.001	tap water	Chlorination
0.0006	mushroom	hydrazines
0.000001	lindane	pesticide
0.000000006	captan	pesticide

Source: Gold et al, "Rodent Carcinogens: Setting Priorities," *Science,* 1992[10]

dues on our foods is truly marginal.[11]

The low risk of pesticide residues is also endorsed by Dr. Robert Scheuplein, the senior cancer expert in the Food and Drug Administration's Food Safety Center. He told the American Association for the Advancement of Science in 1989 that while natural carcinogens may cause an estimated 38,000 of the nation's 500,000 annual cancer deaths, the estimate on cancer deaths from pesticide residues is less than 40.[12] Privately, Dr. Scheuplein says he doubts that anyone has ever developed a fatal cancer from pesticide residues.[13]

More good news: *Less than 3 percent of all our cancer deaths are caused by all the combined forms of environmental contamination and pollution.* That includes not only pesticide residues, but also indoor air pollutants, organic chemicals, hazardous waste, radon, and all of the other "evils" from which the EPA is supposed to protect us.

More than ten years ago, Congress asked two of the world's top cancer experts (Sir Richard Doll and Dr. Robert Peto of Oxford University) to evaluate U.S. environmental cancer risks. They studied American cancer deaths from 1933 to 1978—and concluded that 98-99 percent of our cancer deaths are due to 1) smoking; 2) our own genetics; and 3) bad diet choices, like too much fat and too little fiber.[14]

Who believes the Doll and Peto results? Virtually every regulatory body and medical association. Included are the American Institute of Food Technologists and 14 scientific societies representing over 100,000 microbiologists, toxicologists, veterinarians, and food scientists.[15]

The Environmental Protection Agency, too, confirms the Doll and Peto results. It says so in an EPA publication called *Unfinished Business: A Comparative Assessment of Environmental Problems*, published in 1987.[16]

Doll and Peto wrote, "The occurrence of pesticides as dietary pollutants seems unimportant. There has been no increase in the incidence of liver tumors in developed countries since the long-lasting pesticides were introduced. Yet liver tumors are the most common form of cancer found in animal-based toxicological studies."[17]

If pesticide residues are highly toxic to humans, they should also attack our stomachs as well as our livers. But stomach cancer rates in the countries that use the highest rates of pesticides have been dropping sharply throughout the pesticide era. Stomach cancer rates in the U.S. have dropped 75 percent since the 1930s.[18] Americans currently get about 24,000 stomach cancer cases per year, or one case for each 11,000 residents.[19] A similar declining stomach cancer trend is found in the other developed countries like Europe and Japan—which use farm chemicals even more heavily than the U.S.

Credit for the declining trend in stomach cancer goes both to refrigeration for food storage and to modern chemically assisted farming; both help reduce the molds, toxins, and other pests in the food we consume.

No Rise in Nonsmoking Cancer

None of the nonsmoking cancer statistics have shown any increase in any of the countries where pesticides have become much more heavily used. In fact, there has been no increase in age-adjusted cancer rates—except for tobacco-related cancers.

(Tobacco doesn't just cause lung cancer; cancers of the pancreas, bladder cancer, mouth and uterus/cervix are also associated with tobacco.)

The sole exception is male prostate cancer—but the highest risk for prostate cancer in the world is among black Americans "for reasons not currently known."

The Council on Scientific Affairs reported in the *Journal of the American Medical Association* in 1988, "A large number of pesticidal compounds have shown evidence of genotoxicity or carcinogenicity in animal and in vitro screening tests, *but no pesticides—except arsenic and vinyl chloride (once used as an aerosol propellant)—definitely have been proved to be carcinogenic in man. . . .* Epidemiologic studies offer only conjectural evidence at best that pesticides may be carcinogenic. It may well be as Sharp et al. have stated:

With few exceptions, the delayed effects of pesticides on human health have been difficult to detect. Perhaps the health risks are sufficiently small that they are below the power of

October 22, 1994

Dear Dennis:

One of the principal problems we face continuously is how to get the public to understand that trace amounts of pesticides are seldom, probably never, toxic. Toxicologists explain it this way; it is the dose of a material that determines the poison. We accept this fact every day with medicines and food ingredients. A low dose of a sleeping pill is useful and harmless; an overdose of the same pill is hazardous and sometimes fatal. A sprinkle of table salt is healthy; too much salt has a number of negative effects on the human system.

Toxicity and hazard are *not* the same thing. *Toxicity* is the inherent capacity of a compound to be poisonous at some level. *Hazard* (degree of danger) is linked to *exposure* and toxicity; i.e., it is the chance that the material will or will not elicit a negative response. If someone is not exposed, there is no hazard. If the person is exposed to trace amounts, the chances are that there is still no hazard.

In general, it is a dose/weight relationship. The heavier the animal (or man) the less chance of a negative reaction. Toxicity is expressed as a quantity of the substance as compared to the weight of the animal. There is an amount (a threshold) for toxic response, and any amount below that level is harmless. In general, we are dealing with insignificant quantities that are not capable of being injurious. We are talking about parts per million, or perhaps even parts per billion (ppb), or parts per trillion (ppt). There is a threshold for response and any amount below that level is harmless.

When speaking of pesticides, it is a fallacy to lump them together— or even to do the same when speaking of insecticides, herbicides, or rodenticides. Every chemical is different, and thus the action of each chemical is unique. We would be better off and the public reassured if, like medicine, we would always identify what particular pesticide we are talking about.

Consider this: Pesticides undergo more extensive safety testing than any other product! Some pesticides that in the past caused safety concerns (e.g. ethyl parathion) have been replaced by safer, more readily biodegradable compounds.

It is an insult to the public to talk about banning "pesticides" or fearing to eat vegetables that are not organically grown.

(Letter from Dr. John Osmun, former chairman of the Entomology Department at Purdue University and senior official in the EPA's Office of Pesticides, after reviewing the draft manuscript for this book.)

Here, quoted from *Cancer Facts and Figures 1994*, by the American Cancer Society, is the Society's listing of the major cancer types and their risk factors:[20]

Lung cancer: Cigarette smoking; exposure to certain industrial substances, such as arsenic, certain organic chemicals and asbestos, particularly for persons who smoke.

Colon and Rectum Cancer: Personal or family history. High-fat and/or low-fiber diet may be associated with increased risk.

Breast Cancer: Risk increases with age; personal or family history; late age at menopause; never had children or late age at first live birth; higher education and socioeconomic status. International variability in rates correlates with variations in diet, especially fat intake.

Prostate Cancer: Risk increases with age.

Pancreas Cancer: Incidence is more than twice as high for smokers; suggested associations with diabetes, cirrhosis.

Uterus (Cervix) Cancer: Early age at first intercourse, multiple sex partners, cigarette smoking.

Uterus (Endometrial) Cancer: Early puberty, late menopause, history of infertility, failure to ovulate.

Cancer in Children: Rare. Mortality rates have declined 60 percent since 1950. No risk factors cited.

Leukemia: Cause of most cases unknown. Persons with Down's syndrome and certain other genetic abnormalities have high incidence. Also linked to certain chemicals such as benzene. Certain forms caused by a retrovirus.

Lymphoma: Risk factors largely unknown, but in part involve reduced immune function and exposure to certain infectious agents. HIV virus. Other possible risk factors include exposures to *herbicides*, industrial solvents and vinyl chloride. [emphasis added]

Skin Cancer: Fair complexion. Occupational exposure to coal tar, pitch, creosote, arsenic compounds or radium.

Ovary Cancer: Increases with age. Women who have never had children.

Bladder Cancer: Smokers incur twice the risk of nonsmokers. People living in urban areas and workers exposed to dye, rubber or leather are also at higher risk.

Oral Cancer: Cigarettes, cigars, pipe smoking, chewing tobacco and excess use of alcohol.

epidemiologic studies to detect. Yet it is possible that there are very few effects at all.[21]

INTERESTING REALITY:

"I told my urban caller that we could, indeed, look at pesticides as poisons. But then we must also look at the medicines we take as poisons. We take them because they kill things, like bacteria. As with pesticides, a little medicine can do enormous good. As with pesticides, too much of the medicine can be dangerous. In pesticides, fortunately, the safety factors are several thousand fold, so the dangers are tiny."

Orion Samuelson, syndicated farm broadcaster for
WGN-TV and WGN radio in Chicago, before the
American Crop Protection Association, White
Sulphur Springs, West Virginia, September 26, 1994

MYTHMAKER GOES OVER THE FALLS:

"One of the most famous toxic disasters was Love Canal . . . Hooker Chemical dumped 40,000 metric tons of toxic chemicals, including dioxin, lindane and arsenic trichloride, into Love Canal, which emptied into the Niagara River, adjacent to one of the world's greatest natural wonders—Niagara Falls. The company later filled in the canal and donated the site for the construction of an elementary school."

Helen Caldicott, *If You Love This Planet: A Plan to Heal
the Earth*, W.W. Norton, New York, 1992

Reality Comment: In fact, studies have found *no* health impacts from living on the Love Canal. Nor did Hooker donate the site for a school; it was taken by the school board under condemnation proceedings over Hooker's objections. So far as we know, the chemical disposal had no effect on the view of Niagara Falls.

PROFITABLE MYTH?

". . . Research shows that when people detoxify their bodies, ridding themselves of these industrial pollutants and pesticides, their IQ usually rises." (pp. 313-14).

"For the past five years I have been documenting . . . some of the world's most revolutionary research on detoxifying toxic chemicals that have accumulated in the human body. The program is being carried out at a clinic called HealthMed . . . Thousands of individuals have gone through the HealthMed program with successful reductions in toxic levels and great improvements in overall health and spirit. . . . And it would be wonderful if everybody who needs to be purified could afford the approximately $3,000 the program costs. . . . If you suspect that you're really chemically ill, if you feel sick and disabled, I recommend that you contact HealthMed. . . ." (pp. 295-298).

Excerpts from Diet for A Poisoned Planet, by David Steinman,
Harmony Books, New York, 1990

Reality Comment: There is no scientific or medical basis for Steinman's claims. Environmental "scare" books offer their authors a built-in conflict of interest, since the biggest scares sell the most books. Advertising $3000 treatments for dealing with unspecified toxins offers an even bigger conflict of interest.

Low Pesticide Residues in Food

If you still believe that pesticide residues are a danger to your health, take comfort from the fact that they are present only in tiny amounts.

Food surveys in the First World—where most of the pesticides are used—show consistently low levels of consumer exposure. The latest large-scale monitoring studies in Germany, Ireland, Italy, Sweden, Switzerland, the UK, and the U.S. examined about 50,000 samples.

Most of the samples had no residues at all.[22]

Only about 2 percent of the samples had residues above the maximum residue limit. Most of these "violations" were compounds not approved for that particular food item. These unauthorized residues were found more often in imported produce, but it is also true that pest control is very site-specific. Producers in Honduras may face a different set of pests on snow peas than American growers— and if the American snow pea growers haven't asked for approval on a pesticide, it raises the red flag for the U.S. inspector.

A 1990 Australian survey concluded "The fact that intakes are so much less than the (Acceptable Daily Intake) indicates that there is little health risk from pesticide ingestion in foodstuffs."

A Swiss survey concluded, "Intake of most pesticides is one

hundredth part or less of the ADI. Therefore according to the present toxicological knowledge the residues found do not pose a risk to the health of the consumer." Among the studies, the only one to raise concern was in India, where a 1980-81 survey showed DDT intake was 20 percent of the ADI. (No human health effect has been linked to DDT, however, in India or anywhere else.)

In the U.S., the FDA's quarterly Total Diet studies cover more than 200 food items, table-ready, and analyzed for more than 200 compounds with methods five to ten times more sensitive than the ones used in regulatory monitoring.

- No pesticide residues were found at all on 65 percent of the domestically produced food samples. Less than 1 percent had residues over the EPA tolerances, and less than 1 percent had residues for which there was no established tolerance for that particular commodity.

- On import sampling, FDA found no pesticide residues on 66 percent of the foods, less than 1 percent over tolerance, and 3 percent with residues for which there was no tolerance on that commodity.

- Traces of some 50 compounds have been found each year— but *only in the case of dieldrin did dietary intake exceed 1 percent of the Acceptable Daily Intake.* (Dieldrin residues have ranged as high as 3 percent of the ADI.)

EPA Overstates Pesticide Cancer Risk a Hundred-Fold

The Food and Drug Administration's annual Total Diet Study also shows the EPA's theoretical estimates overstate *everybody's* pesticide exposure by a factor of 100! The EPA, for whatever reason, assumes that all pesticides are used to the legal limit on every crop. They aren't. Not even close.

As we have just noted, the annual Food and Drug Administration food surveys have found that more than 60 percent of our foods have *no* chemical residues when ready for eating. That's because farmers don't spend cash for pesticides except where they're needed. And because many foods are washed, peeled, cooked, or otherwise modified after they leave the field. Without the "table-ready" stipulation, any residues on an orange peel, for example, would be included in "consumption" though we rarely eat the bitter orange peel.

A recent study by Dr. Sandra Archibald of the prestigious Stanford Food Research Institute and Dr. Carl Winter of the University of California-Riverside calculated how much the EPA assumption overstates the real food risk of pesticide residues.[23]

According to the study:

• EPA risk assumptions on tomatoes overstate real risk by 2,600 times.
• The risk on apples is overstated by nearly 21,000 times.
• Lettuce risks are overstated by 300 times.

Overall, the impact of reality on EPA assumptions is to cut our cancer risks from a supposed 1 in 10,000 to as little as 1 in a million.

Dr. Kenneth Olden is director of the National Institute of Environmental Health Sciences, which directs animal toxicology studies for the federal government. Dr. Olden questions the billions of dollars spent each year regulating "carcinogenic" chemicals that may pose little health or environmental risk.

Indeed, other scientists are questioning regulations governing such chemicals as dioxin, DDT, saccharin, and cyclamates, which have produced cancers in some lab animal tests but which experts believe are not harmful to humans at low doses. NIEHS officials estimate that between one-third and two-thirds of substances classed as carcinogenic because of MTD tests in rodents would be benign in humans at normal exposures.[24]

MEAT-AND-PESTICIDE MYTH:

"Cattle spend long hours at the feed troughs. . . . The feed is saturated with herbicides. Today, 80 percent of all the herbicides used in the United States are sprayed on corn and soybeans, which are used primarily as feed for cattle and other livestock. When consumed by the animals, the pesticides accumulate in their bodies. The pesticides are then passed along to the consumer in the finished cuts of beef."

Jeremy Rifkin, *Beyond Beef*, Penguin Books, New York, 1992, pp. 12-13

What About Meat and Pesticides?

What about the safety of our meat supplies in an era of chemical pest controls for feed crops and sophisticated medicines for livestock and poultry?

Jeremy Rifkin demonstrates how far the activists are willing to depart from the truth to frighten the public.

In 1993, a team of Colorado State University researchers presented a study at the American Society of Animal Science national meeting in Spokane, Washington. The team had tested beef tissues from seven packing plants in Colorado, Kansas, Nebraska, and Texas. The beef came from a variety of sources: conventional producers; "natural" beef production (with no medicines used to prevent or treat illness); organic producers (who use neither medicines on their cows nor pesticides on the feed crops); older cull cows; and chronically ill cattle included only for the study.

The samples were tested for 25 different pesticides, including DDT. The researchers found *no* pesticide residues in any of the beef.[25]

"Lead and cadmium were the only residues for which we detected any actual quantities," said Julie Sherbeck, team spokesperson. "These were found in such small amounts as to be nearly undetectable. Thus . . . U.S. beef is unlikely to contain levels of pesticides or any of the compounds or elements considered to be potential hazards to the public health."[26]

Why is Rifkin so wrong? There are a number of reasons.

Herbicides aren't actually sprayed on crops. They are mostly used on the bare ground where the crops *will* be grown (pre-emergence sprays). Or, in the no-till farming system, the herbicides are sprayed on a grass sod before the crop is planted. Even if herbicides are needed once the crops have emerged, they are sprayed or "banded" *between* the rows of crops. (Herbicide that goes onto the crop plant is wasted; the farmer isn't trying to kill the crop plant.)

Second, herbicides are rarely used in a field after the ears of corn or the soybean pods have begun to develop. They are used much earlier, when competition from the weeds would still cut yields.

In fact, neither the ears of corn nor the soybean pods are ever exposed to sprays. The ear of corn is protected by the leafy husks which cover it. The soybeans grow in pods like peas. Both are protected until harvest.

Fourth, herbicides that do get into the crop plants do not concentrate and lurk in the ears or pods. Virtually all are metabolized rapidly by the plants. Nor do cattle "biomagnify" farm chemicals and accumulate them in their meat.

Fifth, no herbicides used on corn or soybeans are a significant danger to humans in the tiny amounts to which consumers are exposed. The biggest of the small dangers is the small amount of atrazine which periodically shows up in stream-fed reservoirs for city water supplies. Few consumers are exposed to atrazine levels above recommended lifetime doses on even a seasonal basis—especially since the EPA in 1993 raised the safety rating of atrazine sevenfold.

Finally, the medicines used on animals must be approved for consumer safety as well as the safety of the animals, and the medicines must be discontinued long enough before slaughter for them to disappear from the tissues of the meat. Obviously, farmers and ranchers are following the recommendations.

The biggest current known risk in beef consumption is E. coli bacteria, which are natural and ubiquitous in our world and our homes. The potential for this bacteria to get into our meat is the reason we should cook hamburger thoroughly instead of eating it rare. (Rare steak is OK.)

Irradiation of our beef would kill this bacteria, and scientists say irradiation is a safe process to use. But irradiation has been opposed by a number of activists—including the same Jeremy Rifkin who claims to be concerned about E. coli in the meat! (Rifkin's solution is for everyone to stop eating hamburger.)

The biggest risk in eating poultry is the danger of salmonella bacteria, not of pesticide or drug residues. Again, irradiation of poultry meat would cost-effectively eliminate even the salmonella threat and again, Rifkin opposes irradiation.

SCARE TACTICS:

Here are samples from the latest round of antipesticide "reports":

"Dr. Daly believes . . . the level of a toxic chemical needed to produce significant behavioral change may be far less than the level needed to produce physical changes."

> *Pesticides and You,* National Coalition Against the Misuse of Pesticides, Winter 1992-93[27]

"... [B]ut more dangerous still is the *fact* that toxic chemicals such as DDT act as neurotoxins, impairing the affected person's mental ability. . . . Even at the very low levels that are now present in the bodies of millions of Americans, chemicals such as DDT have a profound effect on mental clarity and on the ability to think, comprehend and react to outside stimuli." [emphasis added]

> David Steinman, *Diet for a Poisoned Planet*, Harmony Books, New York, 1990, pp. 313-314

"... [T]he [National Research Council] found that virtually no testing had been done on the potential for neurobehavioral damage, birth defects, or toxic effects that might span several generations by passing from parents to offspring."

> Ann Misch, "Assessing Environmental Health Risks," *State of the World 1994*[28]

This latest round of chemical fearmongering is now about non-cancer risks, about sublethal "behavioral modification" and impacts a generation or even two generations removed from the exposure.

These kinds of claims are wonderful for the scare-mongers because they can never be disproved.

I got a very hostile-but-chatty letter from Indianapolis. The lady credited organic foods with saving her life twice, from both ovarian and breast cancers. I had always thought that the organic foods were supposed to *prevent* the cancers, and that once the cancers appeared, the doctors were supposed to get credit if you survived. But this woman's faith in organic food and her fear of manmade chemicals were both unbounded.

Ann Misch, author of "Assessing Environmental Health Risks" in *State of the World 1994*, tries to make us agonize over cancer rates that aren't rising:

> In industrial countries, cancer causes 20 percent of all deaths.
> . . . Explanations for the higher rates of cancer in industrial

countries often invoke the vast differences in diet, smoking habits and methods of preserving food. Compared with these factors, pollution may play a smaller part. Nonetheless, the role of industrial pollutants in cancer is not negligible.[29]

But the big difference between the industrial countries and the developing world is that so many Third World residents don't *live* long enough to die from cancer. They die instead from infectious and parasitic diseases, at earlier ages. (The World Bank's *1993 World Development Report* notes that the residents of the least-developed countries now have a life expectancy of only 55 years at birth, while those in the industrial countries have a life expectancy of 77 years.)
Here is another example of a pesticide myth in action:

Last year, the agency banned pesticide spraying in its more than 40 office buildings. . . . At first, the pesticide ban was widely viewed as a temporary, possibly superfluous precaution were not transmitted to other family members. With a little checking, one woman correlated unexplained sicknesses she and her young daughter periodically experienced with the timing of pesticide applications on her floor of Building 8. . . . Soon, 50 cases of neurological problems had been identified among building occupants. . . . Eventually a number of these sick workers joined our Multiple Chemical Sensitivity Support Group. This group is actively petitioning for "reasonable accommodation" for their disability (chemical sensitivity) under the Americans with Disabilities Act and state human rights laws.

(From "Stopping Pesticide Abuse in Public Facilities," *Pesticides and You: News from the National Coalition Against The Misuse of Pesticides*, Winter 1992-3, pp. 15-17.)

In this instance, the "research" included people remembering, months later, the dates of "stomach viruses" and their timing with office pesticide applications. That is not research. It is legal and environmental activism of the sort most costly to society.

". . . John Graham of the Center for Risk Analysis at the Harvard School of Public Health: 'Less than 5 percent of human cancer can be traced to causes that are within the jurisdiction of the U.S. environmental Protection Agency.' Yet according to a study by the Center for Media and Public Affairs, news stories cite manmade chemicals as a cause of cancer more than any other single cause."

Brent Bozell III, "When the Media Looks at Risk,"
Washington Times, October 17, 1994, p. A17

Finding the Real Causes of Cancer

Despite extensive research, modern pesticides have not been implicated in causing human cancer. Instead, researchers have been finding *genetic* causes for much of our nonsmoking cancer.

Recently, for example, researchers at Johns Hopkins and the University of Helsinki discovered a human gene that—when defective—apparently accounts for a high proportion of our colon cancers. The gene is carried by one in 200 people, and virtually all of them will develop colon cancer. Sporadic mutations of the same gene apparently also cause many other types of cancer including stomach, ovarian, and uterine cancer.

Researchers had previously identified a large number of other genes, called oncogenes, that play a role in initiating cancer when they are defective. The newly discovered gene, called MSH2, goes farther. It effectively creates other dangerous oncogenes by allowing random mutations to accumulate in cells. Eventually, these mutations can produce tumors.[30, 31]

The very process of aging may also play a major role in the onset of cancer, which is fundamentally a disease of old age:

Oxidant by-products of normal (human) metabolism cause extensive damage to DNA, protein and lipid. We argue that this damage (the same as that produced by radiation) is a major contributor to aging and to degenerative diseases of aging such as cancer, cardiovascular disease, immune-system decline, brain dysfunction, and cataracts. Antioxidant defenses against this damage include ascorbate, tocopherol, and carotenoids. Dietary fruits and vegetables are the princi-

Who Is Dr. Bruce Ames?

When it comes to controversy, Dr. Bruce N. Ames, though not physically intimidating at 5 feet 9 inches tall, is no shrinking violet. The man who invented the leading laboratory test to screen chemicals for their ability to damage genes has years of solid science and the accolades of countless colleagues behind him when he makes such provocative and socially unpopular statements as these:

"I think pesticides lower the cancer rate."

"Pollution seems to me to be mostly a red herring as a cause of cancer."

"Environmentalists are forever issuing scare reports based on very shallow science."

"Standard animal cancer tests done with high doses are practically useless for predicting a chemical's risk to humans."

"Nearly all the polluted wells in the U.S. seem less of a hazard than chlorinated tap water."

"Ninety-nine point nine percent of the toxic chemicals we're exposed to are completely natural—you consume about 50 toxic chemicals whenever you eat a plant."

"Elimination of cancer is not in the cards, even if we get rid of every external factor."

"Nearly half of all natural chemicals tested, like half of synthetic chemicals, are carcinogenic in rodents when given at high doses."

"We're shooting ourselves in the foot with environmental regulations that cost over 2 percent of the GNP, much of it to regulate trivia."

Coming as they do from a highly respected scientist who does not do consulting work for industry, such remarks are especially irritating to those who believe that modern industry has touched off an epidemic of cancer and birth defects by contaminating the air, water, soil, and food with toxic chemicals.

Dr. Ames, a biochemist and molecular biologist at the University of California at Berkeley, where he directs the National Institute of Environmental Health Sciences Center, is a member of the National Academy of Sciences, is the recipient of an outstanding investigator grant from the National Cancer Institute and of many highly prestigious awards for excellence in research. His hundreds of technical publications, many in an arena rife with public, political and scientific controversy and punctuated with passionate emotion, have made him one of the two dozen most often cited scientists in the world. "

(Quoted from "Strong Views on Origins of Cancer" by Jane Brod, *New York Times*, July 5, 1994.)

pal source of ascorbate and carotenoids and are one source of tocopherol. Low dietary intake of fruits and vegetables doubles the risk of most types of cancer as compared to high intake and also markedly increases the risk of heart disease and cataracts. Since only 9 percent of Americans eat the recommended five servings of fruits and vegetables per day, the opportunity for improving health by improving diet is great.

(Bruce Ames, Mark Shigenaga, and Tory Hagen, Division of Biochemistry and Molecular Biology, University of California-Berkeley, "Oxidants, Antioxidants and the Degenerative Diseases of Aging," *Proceedings of the National Academy of Science*, Vol. 90, pp. 7915-7922, September 1993.)

If this trio of top cancer experts is correct, cancer is the result of oxidation—part of the process of life. The damage caused by oxidation builds up in our cells, gradually impairing their function. It's almost as though we were exposing ourselves to continual small doses of atomic radiation. Our best defense is to consume anti-oxidents that help protect against the damage. Remember that we know eating more fruits and vegetables lowers cancer risks. We know that some particular compounds in fruits and vegetables inhibit cancer. This would explain why.

It's not glamorous or dramatic. There's no blame to lay. No lawsuits will be filed against big, bad corporations. We know that the public responds much more dramatically when there's blame—as in a plane crash—than when it's their own behavior at fault—as in many car accidents.

On the other hand, it's not all that much fun to spend your life as a chemophobe, terrorized by cabbage, aluminum cookware, pressure-treated lumber and the cotton ticking in your mattress.

Notes
[1]*Issues in Food Safety*, Fresh Produce Council, Los Angeles, May 1992, p. 2
[2]*Mycotoxins: Economic and Health Risks*, Report No. 116, Council

for Agricultural Science and Technology, Ames, Iowa, November, 1989.

[3]*Mycotoxins: Economic and Health Risks*, op. cit.

[4]Ames, Shigenaga, and Hagen, "Oxidants, Antioxidants and the Degenerative Diseases of Aging," *Proceedings of the National Academy of Science*, Vol. 90, pp. 7915-7922, 1993.

[5]Block, Patterson, and Subar, "Fruit, Vegetables and Cancer Prevention," *Nutrition and Cancer* 18, 1992, pp. 1-29.

[6]Miller, Dr. Anthony, "Do Pesticide Scares Raise Cancer Rates?" *Global Food Progress*, Hudson Institute, Indianapolis, 1991, pp. 148-154.

[7]Lisa Hooker, "Molecules for Medicine," *Johns Hopkins Magazine*, June 1992, p. 21.

[8]R.D. Knutson, et al., *Economic Impacts of Reduced Pesticide Use on Fruits and Vegetables*, American Farm Bureau research Foundation, Chicago, IL, September 1993.

[9]J.R. Barse and W. L. Ferguson, "Banning Soil Fumigants: What Cost?" *Agricultural Outlook*, U.S. Department of Agriculture, Washington, D.C., June 1989.

[10]Gold, et al, "Rodent Carcinogens: Setting Priorities," *Science*, Vol. 258, October 9, 1992, pp. 261-265.

[11]Ames, "Science and the Environment: Facts vs. Phantoms," *Priorities*, Winter 1992, American Council on Science and Health, New York.

[12]Warren T. Brookes, "Pesticide Phobia a Dangerous Health Threat," *Detroit News*, April 16, 1990, p. A7.

[13]Personal communication with Dr. Robert Scheuplein, 1990. See Also Dr. Robert Scheuplein, "The Real Cancer Risks in Our Food," *Global Food Progress*, Hudson Institute, Indianapolis, 1991, pp. 155-163.

[14]Doll and Peto, *The Causes of Cancer*, Oxford University Press, 1981.

[15]*Assessing the Optimal System for Ensuring Food Safety: A Scientific Consensus,* Institute of Food Technologists, 1991.

[16]*Unfinished Business: A Comparative Assessment of Environmental Problems*, Environmental Protection Agency, Washington, D.C., 1987.

[17]Doll and Peto, *The Causes of Cancer*, op. cit.

[18]*Cancer of the Stomach*, National Cancer Institute, U.S. Department of Health and Human Services, NIH Publications 88-2978.

[19]Data from U.S. Centers for Disease Control, 1993.

[20]*Cancer Facts & Figures—1994*, American Cancer Society, Atlanta Georgia.

[21]Council on Scientific Affairs, "Cancer Risk of Pesticides in

Agricultural Workers," *Journal of the American Medical Association*, August 19, 1988, Vol. 260 No 7.

[22]Review conducted for the European Crop Protection Association by Dr. Helmut Frehse, former head of the Institute of Residue Analysis, Crop Protection Division, Bayer, AG, copyright ECPA, Brussels.

[23]Warren T. Brookes, "Overstating Pesticide Risks by 2,600 to 21,000 Times?" *Detroit News*, February 26, 1990, p.A9.

[24]*E, The Environmental Magazine*, February 1994, Vol. V, No. 1, p. 14.

[25]Smith, Sofos, Morgan, Aaronson, Clayton, Jones, Tatum, and Schmidt, "Ensuring the Safety of the Meat Supply," paper presented at the Reciprocal Meat Conference of the American Meat Science Association, University Park, PA June 13, 1994.

[26]*Farm Times*, December 1993, p. 6B.

[27]"Toxic Chemicals and Behavior," *Pesticides and You*, Vol. 12, No. 5, Winter, 1992-93, National Coalition Against the Misuse of Pesticides, pp. 6-7.

[28]Ann Misch, "Assessing Environmental Health Risks," *State of the World 1994*, Worldwatch Institute, Washington, D.C., pp. 119-120.

[29]Misch, op. cit. pp. 120-121.

[30]Michael Waldholz, "Cancer Gene is Pinpointed in the Healthy," *Wall Street Journal*, December 30, 1993, p. B1.

[31]*Cell*, December 17, 1993

5

Children, Farmers, and Pesticides

MYTHMAKERS SAY:

"One of the profoundest shocks we have experienced during this chemical age is the realization that the womb is not the secure little niche we had imagined it to be. . . . Doctors for some time now have warned women not to spray their rooms with pesticides during pregnancies."
Frank Graham Jr., Since Silent Spring, Houghton Mifflin,
Boston, 1970, p. 149

"What we don't know are the long-term chronic effects of pesticide exposure on the general population. . . . And in particular—on children."
Bill Moyers, Frontline, PBS-TV, "In Our Children's Food,
March 30, 1993

"Our children are inheriting a dangerous world, dying from pollution and overpopulation, wired up by transnational corporations . . . like a ticking time bomb ready to blow up at any minute from a nuclear war. . . ."
Helen Caldicott, If You Love This Planet, W.W. Norton,
New York, 1992

REALITY SAYS:

"Insufficient fruit and vegetable consumption increases the rate of most types of cancer about two fold. . . . Unfortunately, a high percentage of the American population is eating insufficient fruit and vegetables, particularly the poor and their children. . . . Synthetic pesticides have been a major contributor to health in this century by decreasing the price of fruits and vegetables. . . ."
Dr. Bruce Ames, "Comments on the National Academy Report,

Pesticides In the Diets of Infants and Children," prepared for the
California Department of Pesticide Regulation, September 7, 1993

"The Pacific Northwest's tragic outbreak of hamburger-related food
poisoning (of children) . . . underscores the silliness of a current flap
over agricultural pesticides. . . . EPA Administrator Carol Browner recently requested public comment on the possibility that 35 pesticides
could be banned. . . . The pesticides may be carcinogenic to some animals, but EPA does not consider them carcinogenic to humans. Furthermore . . . the concentrations in which they've been found are so infini-
tesimal that the issue isn't health. . . ."

> Editorial, "Undue Fear of Pesticides Detracts from True Threat,"
> *Spokesman Review*, Spokane, Washington, February 8, 1993

Early in 1993, Bill Moyers hosted a "Frontline" program on PBS-
TV titled "In Our Children's Food." The gist of the program was
that farmers and the regulatory authorities had somehow failed to
realize that *children* will eat the food produced with the help of pesticides. The program implied that pesticide residues are a ticking time
bomb for our kids.

Are children really at greater risk than adults from pesticides?

They may be more at risk because of their smaller body weights.
If they are, the added risk is not more than a factor of three. As we
shall see, the protection factors in our regulatory system add up well
into the thousands.

Let's start our inquiry into children's health by observing that
cancer rates in children have fallen by more than half during the
pesticide era. Childhood cancer was always rare, but it has declined
by 60 percent since 1950. The American Cancer Society estimates
1,600 childhood cancer deaths in 1994. [1]

Even more important, factor in the reality that children born today in the U.S. have a 20-year-longer life expectancy than previous
generations of people—who certainly were NOT exposed to pesticide residues.

Move on to the reality that cancer is basically a degenerative
disease of old age. Only a few rare types of cancers (like leukemia)
attack any significant number of children. Moreover, virtually no
carcinogens can trigger cancer immediately. Virtually none of the

risk estimates would show *any* mortality risk without building on 70 years of lifelong exposure.

Moral: If you want your kids to live long lives, teach them NOT to smoke—and to eat lots more fruits and vegetables, no matter what approved pesticides have been used to grow the produce.

The National Academy Study

In 1993, the National Research Council issued a long-awaited report: *Pesticides in the Diets of Infants and Children.* The report, which had been mandated by the Congress, disappointed some observers because the authoring committee did *not* cite pesticides as a threat to children's health.

In fact, the report stressed that children should eat more fruits and vegetables, even if they were grown with farm chemicals.

The NAS committee *did* attempt to raise a modest scientific point: they felt that we didn't have as much up-to-date information about exactly what American children eat today as researchers would like to have. (They were working with some data which was 10 years old.) Nor did they think we had up-to-date data on exactly how children's pesticide exposure pattern might differ from that of adults.

Whatever the merits of the committee's point about the data base, it never had a chance to be heard.

Activists ambushed the NAS report. *Several days before* the Academy's report was released, activist groups and two government agencies released statements saying that the NAS report "was *expected* to say that children are at particular risk from pesticides." They used this "expectation" as justification to present their own scare reports and press releases *ahead of the NAS report.*

Most of the media swallowed the bait, reporting the scaremongerings of such activist groups as The Environmental Working Group and the Natural Resources Defense Council as if they were the Academy's work. (The Environmental Working Group was a new organization. It got widely quoted—even though it refused to give out the names of its staff or their qualifications!)

Two cabinet officers also abused the NAS report to push the Clinton policy agenda: EPA Administrator Carol Browner and Agriculture Secretary Mike Espy collaborated on an announce-

(Reprinted from the *Wall Street Journal*, April 1, 1993)

"Frontline" Perpetuates Pesticide Myths

by Dennis T. Avery

"Frontline," the Public Broadcasting System's investigative journalism show, is famous for its controversial points of view. But it's now outdone itself. In an episode titled "In Our Children's Food," which aired in most markets earlier this week, a well-meaning Bill Moyers and his PBS colleagues made recommendations that would increase our cancer and heart disease rates, increase the risk of world hunger, and plow down millions of square miles of wildlife habitat. Apparently the "Frontline" staff didn't realize that those calamities would be the result of giving up the farm chemicals it warned us against.

The show was prepared to celebrate the 30th anniversary of Rachel Carson's book, *Silent Spring*. Miss Carson blamed farm chemicals for wildlife losses that we now know were due to lost habitat and to industrial pollutants like mercury and PCBs. In her ignorance, she also feared that pesticides caused human cancer.

We now know that farm pesticide residues contain less food cancer risk than mustard and pickles or even than the environmentalists' beloved mushrooms. We now know that 99.9% of the cancer risk in our food supply come in the foods themselves. So much for the cancer risks in pesticides.

But the indictment against "Frontline" is worse than an omission of these facts. Medical practitioners across the country are telling us today that the best way to reduce both cancer and heart disease is to eat twice as many fruits and vegetables. Fruits and vegetables contain powerful chemicals that inhibit cancer. They are low in fat and high in fiber; their consumption works against heart disease.

But organic farming can't produce low-cost, attractive fruits and vegetables. It produces expensive fruits and vegetables because the insects and diseases eat most of them before they can be harvested from their organically grown gardens. The few that survive

Continued on next page

are shabby-looking, and it's hard to get kids to eat shabby-looking produce. On that basis, organic farming would produce *more* cancer, not less. . . .

Biotechnology may eventually help us engineer the pest protection into plants and creatures so we won't have to spray anything anymore. But most of the ardent environmentalists say they are against biotechnology too. . . .

As evidence of farm chemical dangers, "Frontline" offers one farming town in California that for years has had an unexplained high rate of cancers. But this town is famous in medical circles because its' cancer pattern is unlike any other town's. Medical studies have tried to tie the famous "McFarland Cancer Cluster" to pesticides. All have failed.

Next, Moyers cuts to a guilt-ridden California farmer whose son came down with leukemia ten years ago. He's afraid that his use of pesticides might have caused the leukemia. But farmers and farm kids have lower rates of leukemia and cancer than nonfarm kids. Where is the medical evidence to tie the California farm boy's disease to farm chemicals? The "Frontline" hosts don't tell us anything except how worried they are.

The program also ridicules a Public Health Service toxicology study which reported "There is no evidence that the small doses of pesticides that we do get are causing any harm. The only effect that can be measured . . . is the storage of one of them—DDT—in the tissues of most people. This storage has not caused any injury which we can detect."

Then Mr. Moyers crows: "DDT would be banned ten years later, just as Rachel Carson had predicted." (In the early 1970s.)

But Moyers fails to tell us that DDT was banned against the recommendation of scientists and the Environmental Protection Agency's own hearing examiner. The dozens of experts who testified at the EPA hearing overwhelmingly said DDT should keep its EPA approval because it wasn't dangerous to people or birds. The political appointee who headed EPA feared a public outcry if he concurred with the hearing examiner because so many people had read Miss Carson's book.

Is the rest of PBS' widely noted environmental reporting based on evidence this shaky?"

ment that they would reduce America's future use of farm chemicals. Their statement was also issued *before* the NAS report was released.

When the NAS report failed to indict pesticides as an increased risk to children, Browner and Espy were left with no rationale for their new policy—but regrettably they left the policy goal standing anyway.

MYTHMAKER:

" . . . a 1993 National Research Council report titled 'Pesticides in the Diets of Infants and Children.' The nearly 400-page book advocates more stringent pesticide laws to protect children."

"Ecohealth," *Buzzworm's Earth Journal*, January/February 1994

Reality Comment: The report did *not* advocate more stringent pesticide laws to protect children. It did advocate gathering more data on children's diets and their pesticide exposures. The report also said in its opening statement:

[Pesticide] application has improved crop yields and has increased the quantity of fresh fruits and vegetables in the diet, thereby contributing to the improvements in public health.

Apparently, when the eco-activists don't win, they simply declare victory.

MYTHBELIEVER:

A week after the National Academy study was released, I got an anonymous letter.

"I was shocked when I read your recent article, 'Frontline Perpetuates Pesticide Myths' in the *Wall Street Journal*. Thank God there are people in this world who are not 'paid off' . . . by the corporations promoting the continued use of these 'killers.' It was certainly reassuring to hear this week about the study of the National Academy of Sciences, which concludes exactly the opposite of what your article stated. It's hard to realize how people like you are able to sleep at night. It certainly doesn't take much of a brain to figure out that chemicals are not good for the body. Rachel Carson ignorant? NOT!"

Overstating Pesticide Exposure—For Kids *and* Adults

Dr. Lois S. Gold, one of the country's top experts on cancer and pesticides, said even the NAS committee's call for more data was poorly justified. She said the committee should have used the data from the Food and Drug Administration's annual *Total Diet Study*.

This annual study is the only source of data on the average intake of synthetic pesticide residues from foods as they are consumed. The *Total Diet Study* is thus the most accurate assessment—by far—of real consumer pesticide exposure. It is done each year, and it already includes exactly the information the NAS panel said they needed—estimates broken out for infants, children, and adults.

The *Total Diet Study* indicates that *infants'* exposure to pesticides is roughly three times greater than that of adults. (Of course, infancy doesn't last long, and infants' and children's exposure to pesticides is already factored into the lifetime exposure estimates.)

The risk of pesticide-related cancer in children is trivial. What is *not* trivial is the pesticide scare campaign being mounted *in the name of children* that tells mothers non-organic fruits and vegetables are dangerous. This scare campaign works directly against what should be the number one child dietary health priority—getting kids to eat lots more fruits and vegetables.

Lots of parents can't really afford the high cost of organic produce. Many children object to the appearance of organic fruits and vegetables. Without a second thought, they should be buying the attractive, reasonably priced chemically assisted fruits and vegetables that are in our markets. It's the best thing they can do for their families' health.

Cancer and Farmers

There are no known consumer health impacts from pesticide usage. But what about the most-exposed populations? What about farmers, pesticide plant workers, and pesticide applicators?

We know that the pesticide risks to farmers and farm workers in the First World are low—and declining. We also know that the rates of cancer in farmers, farm workers, and their families are lower than the cancer risks of the general public.

The European Crop Protection Association recently sponsored a review of the medical research in 17 countries, covering 53 mortality studies of the "pesticide-endangered professionals." [2]

They had a lower mortality rate for all causes than the general population, and their cancer mortality was not consistently different from that of the general population. Several studies of farmers showed a lower overall cancer risk.

There are still some questions:

- Swedish studies have firmly concluded a positive association between phenoxyacid herbicides and soft tissue sarcoma, but studies in other countries do not bear this out. Is it a difference in the intensity of exposure? An ethnic difference?
- More reports are beginning to show an increased risk of lymphatic cancers, again associated mainly with phenoxyacid herbicides. A consistently increased risk of multiple myeloma—from low levels—has been observed among farmers. However, no causal agent has been found to link it with pesticides.
- A link has been found between lung cancer and arsenicals, but smoking so strongly confounds the data that assessment is difficult.
- Researchers have also suspected the potential for increased cancers of the urinary tract in pesticide professionals. Farmers have relatively higher (though not high) rates of prostate cancer.

These questions deserve further investigation.

In the U.S., at least one research team has raised questions about a link between non-Hodgkins lymphoma and the use of both 2,4-D and organophosphates. Non-Hodgkins lymphoma is a relatively rare cancer, and farmers have a somewhat higher risk (though not high in absolute terms) than non-farmers.[3]

To demonstrate the level of controversy, however, Dr. John Graham, director of Harvard University's Program on Risk Analysis and Environmental Health, led an independent review of 2,4-D risks in 1990. Here are excerpts from Dr. Graham's conclusions:

The toxicology data by itself provides little reason to expect that 2,4-D causes cancer in people . . . If 2,4-D is ultimately shown to be an animal carcinogen, it is unlikely to be a very potent one. . . . The results of two studies by the same research team suggest an association between the occupational use of 2,4-D and non-Hodgkins lymphoma. However, the workshop participants felt this association needs to be interpreted cautiously, first, because other studies have not shown the same results and second because some factor other than 2,4-D might be involved. . . . None of the panelists felt that the evidence was strong enough to conclude that 2,4-D is either a known or probable cause of cancer. . . . Several members felt that the evidence was barely adequate to support any conclusion.[4]

Another study team is looking at the possibility of a link between leukemia and the use of certain insecticides on farm animals—crotocyphos, dichlorvos, famphur, the chlorinated hydrocarbon methoxychlor, and the natural pesticide pyrethrin.[5]

(Pyrethrin, by the way, is one of the mainstays of *organic* farm production.)

There are some farm chemicals in use that are potentially deadly, such as parathion. These are not the insidious long-term killers the scare books warn about, however; they are dangerous while they are being mixed and applied, and in the hours right after application. Farmers and farm workers must be careful in using them—and must stay out of the field for the specified length of time after spraying.

What are the real risks of pesticides for farmers? The State of Texas in 1986 had only three pesticide-related deaths. One was a suicide who deliberately consumed a potent pesticide. The second was a spray-plane pilot who crashed. The third was a farm worker who went back into a field too soon after spraying.[6] And this was in a huge state with large acreages of fruits, vegetables, and cotton which often need high rates of chemical application per acre.)

RISK REALITY

"From 1982 to 1990, the 48 pesticide-related fatalities in California all involved the mishandling of these chemicals (accidental ingestion, suicides, termite-fumigation accidents) . . . remember the 160,000 Americans who died from tobacco related cancer in (1993 alone)."

Dr. Gordon Gribble, professor of chemistry,
Dartmouth College, Hanover, N.H., letter to the
editor of the *Valley News*, May 18, 1994.)

Fortunately, we continue to develop still-safer pesticides that can be used in ever-smaller amounts. And we deliver them in safer packaging to reduce exposure and the risk of spills.

But even the most dangerous-to-apply pesticides are being used to protect the public health and sustain wildlife habitat, not just to line the pockets of big farmers and chemical companies. They are

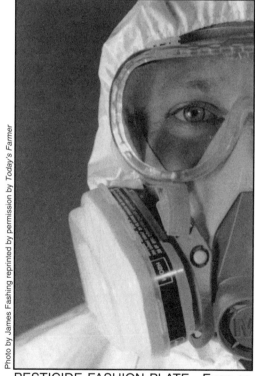

Photo by James Fashing reprinted by permission by *Today's Farmer*

PESTICIDE FASHION PLATE—Even as pesticides have gotten less toxic, modern equipment is expanding the applicators' safety margin.

often needed to attack big pest infestations, and to help control the buildup of resistance to any one pesticide.

I recall as a kid dusting our half-acre of garden with a mixture of lead and arsenic powders, shaken from a burlap bag. Given the toxicity of lead and arsenic, I apparently should have been wearing one of those new EPA "moon suits" when I treated the cabbages and kohlrabi. And talk about needing to wash the produce carefully before it gets to the table!

Today's pesticide risks are not zero, but they are low and declining. The benefits are huge and increasing. When properly used, pesticides promote public health. Most are vital to wildlife conservation.

Protecting Third World Farmers

We know that the risks to farmers in the Third World are not high—but should be a good deal lower than they are. They can be reduced, probably without food production losses, through improved training on which pesticides to use, when and how to apply them more safely, and through better, cheaper, personal protective gear.

Third World farmers have been using more pesticides that are more dangerous to apply and some which are not approved in the First World. The Third World farmers have tended to use pesticides more frequently than First World farmers. Third World farmers have also exposed themselves more openly to the pesticides—because they take fewer safety precautions while mixing, fail to use safety equipment where they should, and because of the backpack sprayers they typically use.

The greatest health hazard to the farm workers is during mixing and transfer of chemical concentrates, not so much the spraying. A First World farmer today typically uses dry mixtures, pre-measured tablets or water-soluble packets. If he's using a liquid, it increasingly comes in a bulk container that locks onto his spray rig in a way that makes spillage nearly impossible. He can read, and the label clearly tells him what he needs to do to protect himself. Some classes of pesticide can only be applied by a certified operator who has been trained and passed an exam on his work.

A Third World farmer, in contrast, usually mixes his pesticides in an old oil drum, and then pours them into his backpack sprayer.

PESTICIDE APPLICATOR SAFETY—This First World spray rig forces the pesticide downward, behind the farmer's enclosed tractor.

He is often illiterate, and he may have bought his chemical from a neighbor with no label or safety warnings on the container

Once the pesticide is mixed, it must then be applied.

Application, too, differs enormously in the two worlds. A First-World farmer is usually sitting on a tractor, with the spray aimed downward in a wide swath *behind him*. He usually encounters little of the spray himself, and is usually wearing protective gear if the pesticide calls for it. A Third World farmer walks through the crop, spraying out in front of his own path. As the crop plants get bigger, the farmer gets more and more pesticide brushed from the plants onto his skin or clothing just from following his own spray pattern. If the backpack sprayer leaks, it leaks onto the farmer's back and legs.

(I know what I'm talking about here; I control the thistles in my 70 acres of pasture by spraying 2,4-D from a backpack sprayer.)

Too few Third World farmers have used protective gear while spraying, especially considering the more dangerous pesticides that are being used in the developing countries. In fact, some Third World farmers often tie cloths over their mouths and noses—which apparently absorb the chemical and *aggravate* the chemical exposure.

Many insecticides that Third World farmers use are rated in the two most dangerous categories, I and II. First World farmers use fewer of these more-dangerous chemicals, and tend to have them

BACKPACK SPRAYER—An Asian farmer must protect his crop, but lack of protective gear and the need to walk behind his spray pattern produce health risks.

custom-applied by high-tech equipment when they do. (Spray planes and special spray rigs with enclosed cabs are two of the high-tech answers to applicator dangers.)

Third World farmers, as a result, have encountered far more health problems from pesticides than First World farmers. These are rarely life-threatening, but they are not trivial either: chronic eye irritation which can cloud vision over long exposure; chronic eczema on exposed skin areas; bronchial asthma; chronic stomach irritation in farmers who smoke or wipe sweat off their faces near their mouths and thus ingest pesticide orally; muscle weakness and lost nerve sensitivity (polyneuropathy), typically in the hands and feet due to absorption of some chemicals by gloves and socks; a somewhat higher rate of abnormal electrocardiogram results.

A recent study by the International Rice Research Institute found that half of the farmers putting on three sprays per year from the I and II danger categories would get chronic eye problems. (The study sample farmers had been using pesticides for 15-25 years, with heavy use of organophosphates.) Fifteen percent of the farmers in one pesticide-using test group had skin problems, and 45 percent in another. Respiratory problems also increased, especially for smokers. Nonsmoking farmers who used pesticides had a 0.3 percent probability of abnormal respiration. Those who smoked and applied two doses of insecticides per year had a 0.45 probability.

Farmers who don't use pesticides have a polyneuropathy probability of only 0.02. Farmers who applied three pesticide sprays per year had a probability of 0.24. If they drank alcohol, their probability was 0.7.

There was also a small increase in heart problems among pesticide-using farmers. Holding age and drinking constant (both produce increased heart problems) the farmers who used pesticides had 7 percent and 11 percent higher rates of functional electrocardiogram impairment.

The study found that health problems were significantly reduced when spinning disc applicators or electrodyn sprayers were used instead of the standard backpack sprayers.[7]

Another study of Ecuadorian potato farmers found 22 percent of the sample farmers had suffered a "pesticide poisoning" incident in their lives, though few of them had gone to a clinic for treatment. ("Poisoning" was defined to include dizziness and nausea.) Chronic dermatitis was almost twice as common among pesticide-using farmers, and neuropsychological tests showed reduced performance on several tests among the farmers who use the pesticides.[8]

There are no validated studies which indicate higher cancer risks for the farmers using pesticides, nor were the chemicals associated with severe neurological problems.

The eco-activists' solution, of course, would be to give up pesticide use altogether. However, this is rarely practical for either the people or the wildlife, due to reduced yields.

In Ecuador, without fungicides, late blight would destroy virtually 100 percent of the potato crop. The Andean weevil can take up to 80 percent of the potatoes in a field. Potatoes are the only crop which can produce enough food for Andean populations, given the high altitudes, limited land and short growing seasons. As a result, Ecuadorian farmers accept the use of pesticides and the health risks involved. Only a few of them use rubber gloves, pants, jackets or other personal protective gear.

Fortunately, there are a variety of specific things that can be done to sharply reduce Third World farmers' risks of pesticide health impairment—far short of banning the chemicals and having to select which people will starve:

- In some cases, safer chemicals are available. As an example, liquid carbofuran in Ecuador's potato fields could be replaced with the granular form which is safer for the farmer (but a greater risk to birds which might mistake the granules for seeds). In some other cases, the safer chemicals are more expensive; farmers would have to choose.
- Better protective gear (gloves, pants, jackets) can be made available, and farmers can be better-educated in the health benefits they will provide.
- Better education of the farmers can help them kill more pests with less chemical. IRRI says that the first three to five sprays that Philippine rice farmers make each season are largely wasted, because they are trying to kill sucking insects with surface sprays. IRRI is trying to help the farmers understand this. Ecuadorian farmers do not understand the life-cycle of the Andean weevil very well, and often spray the wrong pesticide at the wrong time.
- Over time, research will produce safer pesticides. More governments will ban more of the harsh pesticides when they are no longer needed, or will restrict their use. Pesticide research in the First World will lead the way to greater safety—if it is not cut off by inappropriate regulation or prohibition.
- We can expect low-cost spray equipment which does not require the farmer to walk through the newly applied chemicals. Electrostatic and spinning-disc sprayers are already available which carry lower exposure risks.

To summarize, the health problems definitely linked with properly used pesticides on American farms are relatively minor. The linkages with cancer are weak, and the cancers relatively rare. The non-cancer impacts are very minor, such as temporary nausea and skin irritation.

Even in the Third World, where harsher chemicals have been used under more dangerous conditions, the pesticide health risks are rarely severe—and the pesticides are vital to human survival and protection of wildlife habitat.

Notes

[1]*Cancer Facts & Figures*—1994, American Cancer Society, Atlanta.

[2]*Health Effects in Man from Long-Term Exposure to Pesticides: A Review of the 1975-1991 Literature*, International Centre for Pesticide Safety, copyright European Crop Protection Association, Brussels, 1992.

[3]National Cancer Institute, *Occupational Risk of Cancer from Pesticides: Farmer Studies*, National Institute of Health, Washington, D.C., January 1991.

[4]Letter from Dr. John D. Graham, director, Harvard University School of Public Health, program director, Program on Risk Analysis and Environmental Health, to Dr. Richard Stuckey, director, National Association of Wheat Growers' Foundation, February 1, 1990.

[5]*Occupational Risk of Cancer from Pesticides: Farmer Studies*, op. cit.

[6]Curt Lancaster, farm director, USA Radio Network, San Angelo, Texas, personal communication.

[7]Pingali, Marquez, Palis, and Rola, "Impact of Pesticides on Farmer Health: A Medical and Economic Analysis," *Impacts of Pesticides on Human Health and Rice Field Biology in Rice-Growing Areas*, Kluwer, Netherlands (forthcoming in 1995).

[8]C. Crissman and D. Cole, "Pesticide Use and Farm Worker Health in Ecuadorian Potato Production," invited paper for the Allied Social Science Association meetings, Boston, January 3-5, 1994.

6

The Empty Threat of DDT

MYTHMAKERS SAY:

"DDT proved to be toxic not only to insects but to all life. As Worldwatch puts it, DDT 'contaminated the food chain, pushed bald eagles and other predatory birds toward extinction, and accumulated in fish, wildlife and people.' The DDT story is an apt metaphor for all chemical pesticides. Once they seemed ideal; now the evidence is mounting that they are an ecological disaster. They are seeping into groundwater and contaminating drinking water. They are even destroying the soil itself by killing essential organisms, from microbes to earthworms. And they are harmful to humans—especially children."

"Prevent Pests Naturally," *50 Simple Things You Can Do to Save the Earth*, Earthworks, Berkeley, California, 1989

"Banning DDT is the equivalent of the physician's treating syphilis by putting a Band Aid over the first (sore) to appear . . . more serious and widespread trouble will soon appear unless the disease itself is treated."

Wayne H. Davis, "Overpopulated America," *The New Republic*, January 10, 1970

"Dr. Charles Wurster, then chief scientist for the Environmental Defense Fund, responded to a reporter's 1971 question about the world suffering more malaria and malaria deaths if we banned DDT. Dr. Wurster said there were already too many people, and 'this is as good a way to get rid of them as any.' "

Hearings before the House Committee on Agriculture, 92nd Congress on the Federal Pesticide Control Act of 1971, quoted in questions by Mr. Rarick, pp. 266[1]

REALITY SAYS:

"During the less than 30 years of its use (1944-72), DDT prevented more human death and disease than any other manmade chemical in all of recorded history. Without any adverse effects on human health, then or since, DDT prevented thousands of Allied soldiers from contracting typhus (borne by body lice) during World War II and millions of people in the Third World were protected from mosquito-borne malaria in the decades of the 1950s and 1960s."

Dixie Lee Ray, *Environmental Overkill*, 1993, p. 76

Rachel Carson had a deep-seated fear of pesticides. It led her to write an eloquent book. She properly called attention to the fact that DDT was a broad-gauge, persistent insecticide. It did accumulate— and stay—in the tissues of humans, birds, animals, and fish. (DDT was and is nearly unique in that respect.)

The banning of DDT was the first major triumph of the environmental movement. Even today, the movement seems to believe that much of its credibility rests on its successful campaign to ban DDT and related persistent pesticides.

There is no doubt that much of the public concern about pesticides is fundamentally based on the human cancer and wildlife fears aroused during the DDT campaign. DDT has been the trigger for most of the chemophobia in the U.S.

Rachel Carson Didn't Know the Whole Truth

Rachel Carson's fear of manmade chemicals led her to make several major misstatements about the impact of pesticides on wildlife.

For one, she implied that DDT was a serious threat to humans. No danger to humans has yet been identified, more than 30 years after her book was written.

Second, she wrote that pesticides were decimating wild bird populations, which was not true.

The Audubon Society's bird counts *rose* for most species during the 1941-1960 period in which her fear of pesticides developed. The annual Audubon Christmas Bird Counts between 1941 (pre-DDT)

and 1960 (after DDT use had waned) showed that the average numbers of birds seen per observer had increased from 90 to 971! Statistical analyses of the Audubon data confirmed the perceived increases.[2]

Patient research on the bird-destruction claims showed that most
of the bird populations which did decline had begun to decline before DDT was present, or after DDT levels had begun to decline.[3]
The Environmental Defense Fund noted an abundance of game birds
during the DDT years, including pheasants, quail, doves, and turkeys.[4] The Audubon Society added eagles, gulls, ravens, herons,
egrets, swallows, grackles, red-winged blackbirds, cowbirds, *and robins* to the "abundant list."[5]

The U.S. Fish and Wildlife Service's Breeding Bird Survey also
shows that a majority of the 254 bird species tracked between 1966
and 1991 have increased in population.

Third, Ms. Carson wrote in *Silent Spring* that robins were in
danger of extinction.[6] But the Audubon robin counts rose 1,000 percent in the years between 1940 and 1960.[7] DeWitt, in 1955, showed
that robins could resist the fantastically high dose of 10,000 parts
per million of DDT![8] Preeminent bird authority Roger Tory Peterson
stated in 1963 that the robin was the most common bird on the North
American continent.[9]

Fourth, Ms. Carson stated in *Silent Spring* that chickens' eggs
could not hatch after the birds were exposed to DDT. In fact, chickens lay and hatch eggs normally after exposure to DDT.[10]

Fifth, Ms. Carson suggested strongly that DDT would produce
reproductive failure in whole species. "The shadow of sterility lies
over all the bird species, and indeed, lengthens to include all living
things within its potential range."[11] In her view, the threat extended
to all the vertebrate and invertebrate families without exception. She
thought molluscs, crabs, fish, and even small mammals were dying
out. None of this was true.

Sixth, she gave a lengthy description of the method by which she
thought pesticides interfered with cellular respiration:

> We have seen that each step in oxidation is directed and ex-
> pedited by a specific enzyme. When any of these enzymes—
> even a single one of them—is destroyed or weakened, the
> cycle of oxidation within the cell comes to a halt. . . . DDT,

methoxychlor, malathion, phenothiazine and various dinitro compounds are among the numerous pesticides that have been found to inhibit one or more of the enzymes concerned in the cycle of oxidation. . . . This is an injury with the most disastrous consequences. . . . [*Silent Spring*, p. 183.]

Ms. Carson's "explanation" is without scientific merit.

Seventh, Rachel Carson wrote that pesticides were producing a race of "superbugs" that were resistant to more and more pesticides. In fact, the resistant survivors are usually weakened, for they have spent their evolutionary power building resistance to one thing, instead of keeping broad-based tolerance for a range of normal environmental dangers. Even Lamont Cole, a biologist who gave *Silent Spring* a warm review, said, "I do not for a moment believe that the chemicals are producing super insects."[12]

Finally, none of the infamous "robin kills" reported in that period has been duplicated in tests since. (They may have resulted from seeds treated with mercury compounds, which have since been banned.)

(All of this is over and above Ms. Carson's first and most serious error—her erroneous contention that DDT and several other pesticides of the 1960s caused human cancer, as we noted in the cancer chapter.)

The Dangers of DDT

DDT was the first truly effective and widely-used pesticide. It saved hundreds of millions of people from dread diseases like typhus and malaria. It reduced the terrible suffering that continuing bouts of malaria impose on ten times as many malaria victims who *didn't die*. (Most of the world's population lives in the malarial belt.)

DDT was such a powerful force for good that it won its discoverer, Dr. Paul Muller of Switzerland, the Nobel prize in medicine for 1948. In 1971, the Surgeon General of the U.S., Dr. Jesse Steinfeld stated:

DDT has been instrumental in literally changing the course of history for many nations and continues to do so today. Its use in the eradication and control of disease has meant the

difference between hunger, despair and poverty, and good
health, hope and the promise of a better life to billions of
people throughout the world. DDT has been responsible for
returning to man the use of agriculturally rich lands, thereby
making possible improvements in nutrition, providing in turn
the energy and strength for social and economic development. It has had a tremendous impact on the health of the
world, and few drugs can claim to have done so much for
mankind in so brief a period of time as can DDT.[13]

There were other pesticides that killed insects as effectively as
DDT, but most of them were more toxic *and* more expensive.

The power of DDT against malaria was dramatically demonstrated in Ceylon, which had 2.8 million cases of malaria in 1946.
DDT cut the number of cases to a mere *17* in 1963! In 1968, Ceylon
ran out of DDT—and by 1969 was back to 2.5 million malaria cases.[14]

To this day, the Third World has never found anything to equal
the cost-effectiveness of DDT for malarial control. Insect resistance
is a problem with DDT, as it is with other pesticides, but it does
not significantly lower the effectiveness of the DDT malaria control programs.

I have a friend and neighbor whose life was almost certainly
saved by DDT. She was a refugee in Austria after World War II, and
without DDT she would probably have died of typhus. History tells
us the typhus would have spread with deadly speed among the physi-
cally-weakened rescuees—had not the Allies immediately dusted them
with blue DDT powder to kill the fleas that carried the disease.

Ironically, this woman whose life was saved is a chemophobe.
She hated the embarrassing dusting procedure. Due to language problems, she did not understood that millions of people in previous refugee movements had died of typhus.

The Environmental Protection Agency's 1972 hearing on DDT
called more than 100 witnesses. No evidence was presented at the
hearing which demonstrated significant risks to humans. Nor has
any been produced since, though vigorous research efforts continue
to attempt linking DDT with health threats.

The search goes on, however.

In 1993, for example, Dr. Mary S. Wolf of the Mount Sinai School of Medicine announced that her research team had "clearly linked" the risk of breast cancer to DDT exposure. Published in the April 21 issue of the *Journal of the National Cancer Institute*, the report made headlines in the national media as well as in medical circles.[15]

In 1994, however, a larger study covering three times as many cancer cases found no link with breast cancer—in women with 4-5 times as much DDT in their systems! *The Journal of the National Cancer Institute* published an editorial on the disagreement between the studies, titled "Pesticide Residues and Breast Cancer?"

> Hard on the heels of the largest epidemiologic study, until now, showing a positive relationship between breast cancer risk and . . . DDT . . . comes the even larger study reported in this issue, in which no relationship was found. . . . The New York study had only 58 breast cancer cases; the new study has 150. . . . Perhaps most significant, the Kaiser study was focused on women [with] mean levels of [DDT] . . . four to five times those of the New York women . . . Clearly we shall hear more on this topic, but, for the moment, we must conclude that the available epidemiological evidence overall is not supportive of an association between exposure to DDT and increased risk of breast cancer. . . . If science operated in a vacuum, the tendency to over-report suspicious patterns would not necessarily be a bad one . . . we do not operate in a vacuum. . . .[16]

The *removal* of the supposed link between DDT and breast cancer, of course, attracted hardly any media attention at all.

DDT and Wildlife

Evidence of DDT damage to birds and fish was presented at the 1972 hearing to ban the chemical. The anti-DDT evidence was weak and contradictory, however.

For example, the Federal Water Pollution Control Administration had shown in a 1967 report that less than 3 percent of all fish deaths could be attributed to insecticides or other poisons, and almost 80 percent of such deaths were the result of industrial or municipal waste.[17]

Lake Michigan fish production was at a record high in 1967, and fish catch records actually increased nationwide as DDT use increased.

Some of the anti-DDT evidence was found to have been deliberately misleading. It was assembled by two of the three founders of the World Wildlife Fund: by the same Dr. Wurster who thought that malaria was a good way to reduce the world's population, and by Dr. George Woodwell. Woodwell admitted later that he had taken "forest" soil samples near the runway used for a DDT spray program. Woodwell and Wurster measured DDT residues in a marsh along the south shore of Long Island where spray trucks had been rinsed; they reported an average of more than 13 pounds of DDT per acre.[18] Wurster later admitted that more extensive shore sampling showed an overall average closer to 1 pound per acre.[19]

When confronted with the discrepancy in the consolidated DDT hearings, Woodwell said, " . . . this sampling is deliberately biased in order to find the highest residues we could find."

(More recent studies have shown that DDT is photochemically degraded more rapidly than had been thought. As a result, world wide levels of DDT did not build up as much as early warnings had predicted.)[20]

Another opponent of DDT, Dr. Joseph Hickey, implicated DDT in the decline of the peregrine falcon to no more than 140 mating pairs. He was reminded on cross-examination that he had written in a 1942 publication that the number of peregrine falcons had been declining since 1890 and by 1940 (before DDT) there were *no more than 140 mating pairs*.

Some of the *best* studies purporting to show the dangers of DDT to birds—those published in the respected, peer-reviewed scientific journals like *Nature* and *Science*—were so flawed that they should never have passed peer review.[21] There is a strong pattern of evidence that some naturalists apparently shared Rachel Carson's belief that pesticides were an immediate threat to huge groups of wild organisms. They apparently decided to give Ms. Carson some extra help by pushing their "studies" past real science.

DDT Ducks

Nature reported on a study (Heath, et al, 1969)[22] in which ducks were fed DDT and its breakdown products, DDE and DDD.

Then the study scored the birds by the number of fertile eggs laid and live ducklings raised.

The researchers reported that DDT increased embryo mortality by 30 to 50 percent, and cut the number of ducklings raised per hen by up to 75 percent. That sounded bad for DDT.

But the researchers had ignored *huge* differences between their control groups—57 percent in eggs per hen and 63 percent in ducklings. The differences within the controls were bigger than the differences with the DDT groups! That makes it pretty hard to conclude anything at all about DDT.

The researchers apparently also ignored key data that didn't support their thesis. They got 17 percent less fertilization in the *control birds* than in the *experimental* birds (for DDT)—which they didn't mention as significant. But they got only a 21 percent cut in fertilization among the ducks that were fed *high* doses of DDE (40 ppm)—and that was their basis for saying DDT severely cut the ducks' reproductive rate. In fact, it just proved again that there was a lot of variation among the birds.

What's more, *two of the groups fed DDT had 36 and 23 percent more live ducklings than the controls*. The study could have concluded just as validly that moderate doses of DDT *improved* duck reproduction!

The entire study should have been scrapped, not turned into a classic environmentalist citation against DDT. That's the opinion of Dr. George Claus, who holds doctorates in botany, microbiology and medicine, and who went back to reconstruct the DDT controversy for his 1977 book, *Ecological Sanity.*

Another long-term study concluded that DDT thinned birds' eggshells—but the birds' diets were deliberately held down to 0.5 percent calcium when the researchers knew the birds needed at least 3 percent calcium for normal egg formation![23]

Even with this fabricated evidence, however, the EPA hearing examiner ruled that DDT should *keep* its registration.

DDT was banned by the EPA's administrator, Donald Ruckelshaus. He overruled his hearing examiner—because he feared a public backlash from the readers of *Silent Spring.*

What About the Declining Eagles and Other Raptor Birds?

With few exceptions, we save wildlife by saving their habitat.

One of the few exceptions was the decline in some raptor birds, including some eagle and osprey populations, in the 1960s and 1970s. Even here, however, the evidence is mixed. For example, the Hawk Mountain (Pennsylvania) Sanctuary Association's annual reports of hawk counts at that famous migration site show large increases, not decreases, in most kinds of hawks during the DDT years. Even the ospreys increased at Hawk Mountain, from 191 in 1946 to 630 in 1972.

The environmental community said there was a raptor decline, however, and blamed it on DDT. That blame has now become firmly lodged in the public mind.

Tests run during the period, however, show the danger to raptor birds was almost certainly from mercury and PCBs, not DDT.

In 1966, Fish and Wildlife researchers fed elevated levels of DDT to captive eagles for 112 days, and found no ill effects to either birds or eggs.[24]

If DDT was the problem for raptor birds, there has been no adequate explanation of why the 1970s saw the golden eagle population do well in the U.S., but crash in England; or why the osprey populations declined in the Northeast but did well in Alaska despite high DDT residues there; why English herons seemed to be holding their own, whereas in the U.S. they were reported declining. If DDT was the problem, why was there a different response from birds of the same species, with virtually the same food habits?[25]

We almost certainly know the culprits of any raptor decline, and DDT is not among them. Cornell University poultry specialists fed DDT, PCBs, and mercury to chickens and Japanese quail. (Chickens were originally jungle fowl.)

Among the results:

- Chickens given 100 parts per million DDT produced eggs that hatched normally.
- Chickens fed 20 ppm of PCBs had reduced egg production and the hatchability of their eggs was "almost completely eliminated."

• Methyl mercury, at 20 ppm, lowered egg production, hatchability, *and eggshell strength.*[26]

Much of the testing used to indict DDT did not even distinguish between DDT and PCBs! Dr. Scott, who did the comparative tests on DDT, PCBs, and mercury at Cornell, noted in 1975 that "Many reports relating reproductive declines of wild birds to DDT and DDE were based on analytical procedures that did not distinguish between DDT and PCBs"[27]

This was critical because PCBs *do* cause severe effects on fish, birds, and other wildlife. Much of the "DDT and residues" alleged by the anti-DDT literature was later *admitted* to have really been PCBs. In 1969, Anderson, Hickey, and Risebrough reanalyzed the egg samples which they had claimed in 1965 had high levels of DDT. Three of the five sample had no DDT at all, and the other two had only a fraction as much as had been claimed.[28]

The fact that there were lots of eagles and ospreys after the DDT ban seemed proof enough to the public that DDT had been the cause of a "decline." But if there was a decline, it was almost certainly PCBs and mercury, *not DDT*, which caused the reproductive problems and eggshell thinning in our raptor birds.

The birds were probably not saved by the ban on DDT, but by the *concurrent cleanup of industrial effluents* which had been the source of the mercury and PCBs. (The Clean Water Act was passed in 1972.)

FISHY MYTH:

"DDT has been pointed to as a major cause of fish kills. However, the Federal Water Pollution Control Administration showed, in a 1967 report, that less than 3 percent of fish deaths could be attributed to insecticides or other poisons, but that almost 80 percent (8 3/4 million fish) resulted from industrial and municipal wastes, and even manure accounted for 12 percent of these fish kills.

"Many of the dichotomies and inequities of 'data' brought forth can be exemplified by the testimony of Dr. Willion G. Gusey in October 1969, which showed that the extensive publicity given to the Coho salmon's failure to reproduce successfully in Lake Michigan was misleading. The failure was attributed ostensibly to high DDT residues in

Coho eggs. Gusey pointed out that the widely publicized egg hatch figure had occurred actually at only one hatchery in Michigan and that all
other hatcheries in Michigan reported normal reproduction of fish fry.
Since then, in the midst of high levels of DDT 'contamination,' the growth
and abundance of Coho salmon in Michigan attest to their capability to
thrive in the lake. Indeed, figures from the Great Lakes Fishery Commission show that in 1967, the production of all species of fish in Lake
Michigan was greater than ever recorded from that lake since the first
records kept in 1879.

"The extinction of eagles was reported as far back as 1921 in an
article appearing in Ecology entitled, 'Threatened Extinction of the Bald
Eagle,' which blamed the eagle's problems on changes in its habitat
caused by man. In 1964, the Bureau of Sport Fisheries and Wildlife reported that in the Everglades National Park where the eagle's habitat had
not changed, sizeable increases in nests and young occurred between
1959 and 1964 following years of heavy DDT use. Other areas of the
United States also report satisfactory eagle populations."

> From a draft 1974 EPA report, "Review Based on Scientific
> Evidence of the Decision Banning the Use of DDT," by Leonard
> Axelrod, acquired under Freedom of Information appeal, 1975[29]

Looking Realistically at Pesticides

Nearly 1 million people per year are now dying of malaria, and
many millions more suffer fever-wracked lives with low productivity and poverty.[30] Sub-Saharan Africa gets 90 million new malaria
cases per year.[31] Many of these people could be saved and function
as productive citizens if we used more DDT.

DDT is cheap, effective, and persistent against malaria mosqui-
toes. Nothing else is nearly so cost-effective for poor Third World
governments.

The World Health Organization is having to plead with a factory
in Mexico to keep making a small amount of DDT for anti-malaria
programs. The Mexican public is emotionally opposed to DDT. The
plant's owner recently toured malaria countries in South Asia to assure himself that the DDT was truly needed—and came back emotionally stricken by the fever-wracked victims he saw.

I am not crusading for bringing DDT back to the First World.
We have narrower, less-persistent compounds that are cost-effective. And who knows? Someday, the researchers may in fact tag

DDT with honest evidence of sublethal impacts on people or wild-life. The heavy-molecule chlorinated compounds do build up in the tissues of fish, birds, and mammals.

I *am* arguing for a realistic assessment of the currently registered farm chemicals, whose public image has been tainted by the misinformation on DDT. We need these safe and effective chemicals to save ourselves and the environment.

We have let the misreading of the DDT evidence color our whole attitude toward pest control chemicals. Some of the newer pesticides are remarkably safe. One type works on the unique enzymes found in a particular weed family. Another inhibits the shedding of the external skeleton in the insects for which it is applied—and has *no* impact on humans *or* the environment!

Most people today are more afraid of the pesticides used in food production than they are of the pests. That may be because most of us have little recent experience with the pests—thanks to the chemicals we use.

"Sperm counts down? Penises shriveled? Hey Rush, don't blame it on feminists. It may be from chemical pollutants in water and food."
Newsweek, March 21, 1994

FERTILITY ON THE BRINK? THE ESTROGEN DEBATE

Recently, when I made the case for DDT to a wildlife advocate, he replied, "Was cancer ever the issue? Wasn't the original case against DDT that it caused sublethal changes in the endocrine systems of people and wildlife?"

As you have just seen, the eco-zealots charged human cancer and massive reproductive failures in whole species of wildlife. They have failed over 40 years to prove any of it, and their case is getting weaker, not stronger.

Now they have assumed a fall-back position: The claim now is that estrogen-like compounds including DDT (along with such compounds as PCBs and dioxin which are *not* farm chemicals) have caused diverse environmental events such as a worldwide drop in human sperm counts, a decline in the number of alligators born in a Florida lake, and feminized suckerfish in Lake Superior.

Again, they have failed to prove their case.

As with DDT, they simply find events in nature, like Rachel Carson's robin deaths, and speculate that they are "linked" with pesticides.

As with the activists' DDT campaign, the National Wildlife Federation makes no distinction between DDT, which has no proven ill effects on wildlife, and PCBs, which have a long history of major negative wildlife impacts.

MYTHMAKERS:

The following is excerpted from the executive summary of *Fertility on the Brink: The Legacy of the Chemical Age*, published by the National Wildlife Federation, Washington, D.C. 1994:

Toxic Build Up in the Food Chain

An ever-growing body of evidence indicates that certain pollutants that build up through the food chain are capable of entering animals and humans and tampering with vital body systems. The fact that some chemicals persist and bioaccumulate in the food chain has been known for some time now. What is new is the understanding that some of these chemicals interfere with operations of the body's endocrine system.

Representative of this tragic phenomenon are the alligators of Florida's Lake Apopka, which were exposed to DDT and dicofol from a chemical spill. Scientists have found that 75 percent of the alligator eggs at the lake are dead or infertile and almost 60 percent of the juvenile male alligators have severely shrunken penises.

Chemical Hormones and Wildlife

Some of the earliest signs of the ravages of chemical hormones on wildlife showed up in the heavily polluted Great Lakes. Wildlife there exhibit behavior that puts their survival at risk, including gulls that ignore their young and lake trout that swim upside-down. From these behavioral anomalies and clues from reproductive and developmental patterns, scientists theorized that chemical hormones are able to imprint a fetus's endocrine, immune and neurological systems with faulty messages. Scientists speculate that PCBs, DDT and other chemical hormones passing from the mother across the placenta and into the developing fetus. . . .

The Human Connection

People all over the world have in their tissues measurable amounts of DDT and other organochlorine pesticides, PCBs . . . PBBs, dioxins and furans. . . . Scientists have linked human contamination by these chemical hormones to troubling health trends. Breast cancer rates have been increasing at an alarming rate in the U.S., from a 1 in 20 chance of a woman developing breast cancer in the early 1950s to a 1 in 9 chance today. One study showed that women with the highest exposure to DDT had four times the breast cancer risk of women with the lowest exposure. Another major health trend being linked to exposure to dioxin is the 50% drop in sperm counts in men living in industrialized nations. . . .

The Current Regulatory Scheme

Several flaws are inherent in the current approach to regulating toxic substances: 1) pollutants are innocent until proven guilty; . . . loopholes allowing pollution below detectable levels mean that zero discharge is rarely attained. . . .

What Should Be Done

The National Wildlife Federation believes that Congress must give the Environmental Protection Agency an explicit mandate to ban the use, discharge and release of toxic chemicals that poison the environment, build up in humans and wildlife and cause damage to the reproductive system.

Let's look at this astonishing piece of public policy prose.

First of all, look at their level of scientific certainty.

"What is new is the *understanding* that some of these chemicals interfere . . . ."

(They don't say that we *know*, or that *peer-reviewed evidence shows*, nor do they even refer to any *scientific consensus*. What they have is suspicions by a few wildlife researchers about a widely varied set of incidents.)

"Scientists *theorized* . . ."
"Scientists *speculate* . . ."
"Another major health trend being *linked* . . ."

The "evidence" being offered here is just as flimsy as Rachel Carson's evidence on DDT. The document offers three specific pieces of evidence, presumably their strongest:

- Alligators in Lake Apopka, Florida, have reproductive problems. The lake was the site of a major chemical spill in 1980. (In fact, the spill was so bad the lake has been named a Superfund cleanup site.) There is certainly the possibility that the high levels of chemical pollution are causing the reproductive problems. Which chemicals are causing the problem? Through what linkage? At what levels of exposure? What organisms are affected? Which are not? Lake Apopka is certainly not "representative," as the Federation claims.
- A Mt. Sinai Cancer Institute study linked DDT and breast cancer in 1993.[32] But this study has already been trumped by a larger study (Kreiger) of women with even higher levels of DDT *who did not show higher rates* of breast cancer.[33] The rising risk of breast cancer may well be explained completely by the increase in smoking among women and their lengthening life-span.
- There is a study in a British medical journal claiming lower-quality sperm counts among men living in industrialized countries.[34] The National Wildlife Federation suggests it may be dioxin at work. What is the evidence? Moreover, dioxin is also produced in relatively large amounts by *forest fires*, which are almost certainly the major source of exposure to that compound at least for wildlife and possibly for humans. The NWF document itself says, ". . . absolute proof that chemical hormones are causing these and other human health problems may be elusive. . . ."

REINTRODUCING REALITY:

"This natural chemical process occurs in forest fires and volcanos. In fact, it has been estimated that the largest sources of dioxin in the environment is from forest fires, of which 200,000 occur annually. . . . Indeed, dioxins have been identified in 100-year-old preserved soil samples."

Dr. Gordon Gribble, Professor of Chemistry, Dartmouth
University, "Natural Chlorine? You Bet!" *Priorities*, 1994[35]

Real proof of endocrine damage against the chlorinate chemicals may indeed be elusive. As *Fertility on the Brink* admits, "The scientific process of looking for the results of endocrine disruption in animals can be likened to investigating a murder scene in which there is no body, the witnesses are unhelpful, and no motive is known. . . . Investigating chemical hormones . . . forces researchers to examine almost every system, organ and tissue at almost any stage in an animal's development. The possible endpoints are limitless."

The problem for society is that the possible starting points are also limitless. The National Wildlife Federation should still bear the burden of proving the linkages and effects before it demands regulatory action. But NWF wants us to hand down a death sentence on "toxic chemicals"—on suspicion!

Since virtually every natural and manmade chemical ever discovered is toxic at some level, that's a tall order. (Greenpeace, in fact, is demanding that we eliminate our use of chlorine itself, one of nature's most abundant and widely-dispersed chemicals.)

But here's the rub: These are the same organizations that told us acid rain was a desperate problem, destroying trees, lakes, and fish. A $500 million ten-year Federal research project found instead that acid rain was a small and localized problem. It found that of 7,000 Northeastern lakes, only 240 were acidic; and there had historically *never* been fish in those lakes because they were naturally acid (due to a lack of limestone in the soils and rocks of the region). Only after the local forests had been logged and burned (lowering the acidity of the lakes for a few decades) did the Adirondacks' lakes have fish.[36] Asked what would happen to lake and stream acidity in the Northeast if no actions were taken against acid rain, the study director said, "Nothing."[37]

These are the same kinds of activists who demanded that we spend billions of dollars to remove gray asbestos from our public buildings. Now, the evidence is showing that the asbestos is not dangerous except to asbestos miners and plant workers who smoke. Moreover, the "cleansed" buildings are actually a bit *more* dangerous to their occupants because the removal work has left more asbestos fibers floating free inside them.[38]

These are the same folks who told us that Agent Orange was a plague on the earth. Yet another of the most expensive Federal research projects in history has told us that there are no differences from the norm in the health profiles of the men who served in Viet Nam. The birth defects rate in their children (1.5 percent) is the normal rate.[39] Bruce Herbert, Director of the Center for International Security, wrote in a commentary for the *Chicago Tribune* in 1983:

> After nearly five years of almost constant publicity . . . only 16,821 veterans have even filed claims with the VA for suspected Agent Orange damage. Of this number, less than 8,400 present any certifiable medical condition, whether or not these disabilities can ever scientifically be linked to [Agent Orange] exposure. Three thousandths of one percent of the 2.4 million men who could have been exposed to Agent Orange in Vietnam is hardly a compelling statistic. . . .[40]

Dioxin was supposedly the "danger contaminant" in Agent Orange. Here they are bringing it back again. Listen to Dr. Elizabeth Whelan, president of the American Council on Science and Health and recipient of the Walter Alvarez Prize for Distinguished Medical Writing:

> But so far as we know, no human has ever died or become chronically ill from environmental exposure to dioxin in the U.S. The only human illnesses so far proved to occur from exposure to dioxin are chloracne, a severe acnelike skin disorder, and short-term reversible nerve dysfunction. . . . Obviously, there is nothing beneficial about dioxin. And given the chemical's varied toxicity to humans and animals, there is just reason for concern and calm, reasoned and efficient remedial action to clean up

the contaminated areas. . . . But its mere presence in the environment does not translate into a massive public health disaster.[41]

MYTHMAKERS RAIN DIOXIN:

"An ultratoxic herbicide was rained down leaving an endless harvest of genetic defects and cancer; tens of millions of Vietnamese and 2.4 million American soldiers are estimated as having been contaminated. . . . "

Karl Grossman, *The Poison Conspiracy*, The Permanent Press, Sag Harbor, New York, 1983

"The enemy is 2,4,5-T, a powerful phenoxy herbicide contaminated with dioxin, generally considered the deadliest substance ever created by chemists."

Ralph Nader et al., *Who's Poisoning America*, Sierra Club Books, San Francisco, 1981

REALITY:

"Remarkable it is, and indeed a tribute to the power of the media, that a substance of such infamous reputation has never been shown to cause any deaths or serious harm to humans."

Dr. Elizabeth Whelan, *Toxic Terror*, 1983[42]

". . . [D]ioxin is released in very small quantities. Throughout the United States, only 30 pounds of toxic equivalents of dioxins and related compounds called furans are emitted annually, according to the EPA. 'At that level of emission, you clearly have to question how much risk there can be,' a chemical industry spokesman said. But EPA officials acknowledge that new regulations may be in order. . . . Greenpeace advocates a total ban on chlorine. The Sierra club is urging a moratorium on incinerators. . . . Some 95 percent of known U.S. emissions stem from the combustion of waste."

Washington Post, reporting on a 2,000-page, three-year EPA dioxin study, October 14, 1994[43]

The activists also brought us the Love Canal. Remember? That was the toxic dump site in upstate New York on which houses and a school had later been built. The site was evacuated after a series of terrifying health speculations in the *Niagara Gazette* in 1976. The New York State Commissioner of Health issued a report entitled, *Love Canal: Public Health Time Bomb?* It was the beginning of a public fear campaign that resulted in the multi-billion-dollar Superfund legislation. But in 1981, *The New York Times* reported:

> From what is now known, Love Canal, perhaps the nation's most prominent symbol of chemical assaults on the environment, has had no detectable effect on the incidence of cancer. When all the results are in . . . it may well turn out that the public suffered less from the chemicals there than from the hysteria generated by flimsy research, irresponsibly handled.[44]

The world is moving as rapidly away from persistent and broadly-impacting chemicals as rapidly as it can. DDT has been banned in most of the world, and is still used only in foreign tropical anti-malaria programs which directly save hundreds of thousands of human lives per year. PCBs are banned in America, and the existing sources of PCBs are being eliminated as rapidly as possible. The Great Lakes are "rapidly recovering from a range of environmental insults of varying duration and levels."[45]

Certainly, if farm chemicals—or any other chemicals that we use today—are causing significant neural and reproductive damage to humans and wildlife, we want to know about it and stop it.

If the wildlife organizations have the evidence to prove such damage, they should bring it forward. But they admit they do not have the evidence.

Nor are these compounds immediately threatening humans:

> For one thing, they say the basic pharmacology doesn't add up. "Most pesticides and other environmental estrogens are only very weak estrogens," says EPA dioxin researcher Linda Birnbaum. Since background levels of synthetic estrogens are swamped by the body's own [estrogens], says Rutgers' Gallo, there's little chance they would be able to exert an effect. The exception, he suggests, might be cases in which people or wildlife are exposed to massive doses of the estrogens, as . . .

with lab animals [at high doses] or the Lake Apopka alligators. Humans and other primates also have a mechanism for protecting themselves from estrogens that differs from other mammals . . . tack[ing] on a sulfate . . . to disarm circulating estrogens. . . .[46]

REALITY ASSESSES THE MYTHMAKERS:

"When the Clinton Administration unveiled its proposed overhaul of the 1972 Clean Water Act, environmentalists saw a long-cherished dream come true. There in the draft was a provision that called for 'substituting, reducing or prohibiting the use of chlorine or chlorinated compounds' now used in thousands of products, including plastics, medicine and even drinking water . . .

"'We think this is the most meaningful position taken by the Administration in keeping with their campaign rhetoric on pollution prevention since they have taken office,' Rick Hind, legislative director of the Greenpeace Toxics Campaign . . .

". . . [W]hat's missing now in the chlorine controversy is science. The recent stories quote scientists sparingly or not at all. None quotes peer-reviewed articles. None mentions that chlorine fears spring in large part from high-dose animal-to-man extrapolations. Instead, each attempts to cover the scientific issues related to chlorine as though they were merely political."

Kenneth Smith, "The Media's War on Essential Chemicals:
Targeting Chlorine," *Priorities*, Vol. 6, No. 2, 1994[47]

"Concern continues that the U.S. Environmental Protection Agency (EPA) might curtail or ban the production of chlorine and compounds containing it. This perception has been fostered by indications that EPA policy is being predominantly influenced by Greenpeace and its allies. Part of the impetus for banning organochlorine compounds has been an imbalanced media treatment of controversial assertions about hormonal effects of some of them. . . .

"Nature produces many [chlorinated chemicals]. The number identified exceeds 1500. . . . Some are highly toxic. Others are benign and present in edible seaweed. In total the annual global emission rate of [methyl chloride] is 5 million tons. Annual [manmade] emissions total only 26,000 tons.

"The smoke of burning wood contains more than 100 organochlorine compounds. . . . Because most forest fires are caused by lightning, our ancestors were exposed to dioxin long before the first cave dweller. . . .

". . . A serious outbreak of cholera followed when chlorination of water was temporarily stopped in Peru. Waterborne diseases cause the deaths each day of 25,000 children in less developed countries. A costly gamble in the United State to use means of disinfection less effective than chlorine would be irresponsible.

"There is reason to hope that the EPA will not continue to act like a tool of Greenpeace. A plethora of EPA regulations and unfunded mandates coupled with examples of brutality in enforcing them has cost the EPA support in Congress."

Science editorial, "Chlorine and Organochlorine Compounds,"
Philip Abelson, Vol. 265, August 26, 1994, p. 1155

Since there's no immediate threat of further widespread damage, let's let Greenpeace and the National Wildlife Federation complete their scientific research. Let them bring forward the evidence for peer review. Let the regulatory agencies hold hearings.

But please, let's not have another of these media-hype panic campaigns such as we've already seen in DDT and acid rain and Agent Orange and Alar.

They cost us too much. The money, research capacity, and public emotion thrown away on these non-problems should have been invested in resolving demonstrated health problems, not wasted on trivia.

Notes

[1]C. F. Wurster, *Congressional Record* S4599, May 5, 1969.

[2]42nd Annual Christmas Bird Census, *Audubon Magazine*, January/ February, 44, pp. 1-75. Cruickshank, A.D., (ed.) 61st Annual Christmas Bird Census, *Audubon Field Notes* 15(2), pp. 84-300.

[3]J.G. Edwards, Testimony, U.S. Congressional Committee on Agriculture, Washington, D.C., 18 March, 1971, Published in S.N.92-A, pp. 575-594; see also W.E. Hazeltine, Statement to Secretary of State's Advisory Committee: UN Conference on Human Environment, published March 16, 1973.

[4]C.F. Wurster, 1960, *Congressional Record* S4599, May 5, 1969.

[5]42nd Annual Christmas Bird Census, *Audubon Magazine*, 1961, op. cit.

[6]Rachel Carson, *Silent Spring*, p. 108.

[7]Claus and Bolander, *Ecological Sanity*, David McKay, New York, 1977, p. 308.

[8]J. B. DeWitt, "Effects of Chlorinated Hydrocarbon Insecticides Upon Quail and Pheasants," *Journal of Agricultural Food Chemistry*, Vol. 3, 1969, pp. 672-673.

[9]Samuel Florman, "Progress for the Birds," *Technology Review*, (MIT) July, 1993, p. 63.

[10]Scott, et al, "Effects of PCBs, DDT and Mercury Compounds Upon Egg Production, Hatchability and Shell Quality in Chickens and Japanese Quail," *Poultry Science*, Vol. 54, 1975, pp. 350-368.

[11]Rachel Carson, *Silent Spring*, op. cit., p. 101.

[12]L.C. Cole, "Rachel Carson's Indictment of the Wide Use of Pesticides," *Scientific American*, Vol. 207, No. 6, 1962, pp. 173-180.

[13]Dr. Jesse Steinfeld, 1971, quoted in Claus and Bolander, *Ecological Sanity*, op. cit., pp. 293-294.

[14]Claus and Bolander, *Ecological Sanity*, op. cit., pp. 291-292.

[15]Elyse Tanouye, "Breast Cancer, DDT Exposure Linked in Study," Wall *Street Journal*, April 21, 1993, p. B1.

[16]Brian MacMahon, "Pesticide Residues and Breast Cancer?" *Journal of the National Cancer Institute*, Vol. 86, No 8, April 20, 1994, pp. 572-3. Study reported was Kreiger, Wolff, Hiatt, et al., "Breast Cancer and Serum Organochlorines: A prospective study among white, black and Asian women," *Journal of the National Cancer Institute*, vol 86, 1994, pp. 589-599. The study is part of the Kaiser Foundation multiphasic health examination cohort in the San Francisco area.

[17]Axelrod, Leonard, "Review Based on Scientific Evidence of the Decision Banning the Use of DDT," EPA Draft, June 5, 1974. Acquired through Freedom of Information action by Dr. William Hazeltine, Pacific Legal Foundation.

[18]Woodwell, G.M., and Martin. "Persistence of DDT in Soils of Heavily Sprayed Forest Stands," *Science* 145 (1964), p. 481.

[19]Wurster, C.F., "DDT and the Environment," *Agenda for Survival*, (ed. Helfrich), Yale University Press, 1970, p. 234.

[20]Coulston, Frederick, "Reconsideration of the Dilemma of DDT for the Establishment of an Acceptable Daily Intake," *Regulatory Toxicology and Pharmacology*, Vol. 5, 1985, pp. 332-383.

[21]George Claus and Karen Bolander, *Ecological Sanity*, op. cit.

[22]Heath, R.G.; Spann, J.W.; Kreitzer, J.F. 1969. "Marked DDE Impairment of Mallard Reproduction in controlled Studies," *Nature*, 224, pp. 47-48. (DDE is a metabolite of DDT which presumably might be found in the mallards' diets.)

[23]Bitman, J.; Cecil, H.C.; Harris, S.J.; Fries, G.J., "DDT Induces a Decrease in Eggshell Calcium," *Nature* 224, pp. 44-46.

[24]Stickel, "Bald Eagle Pesticide Relationships," *Transcript of the 31st North American Wildlife Conference*, 1966, pp. 199-200.

[25]Claus and Bolander, *Ecological Sanity*, op. cit., p. 399

[26]Scott, et al, "Effects of PCBs, DDT and Mercury Compounds Upon Egg Production, Hatchability and Shell Quality in Chickens and Japanese Quail," op. cit. See also G.S. Stoewsand, et al, "Shell-thinning in Quail Fed Mercuric Chloride," *Science* 1273, pp. 1030-1031.

[27]Scott, et. al, op. cit., pp. 350-368.

[28]Anderson, Hickey, Risebrough, Hughes, and Christensen, *Canadian Field-Naturalist*, Vol. 83, 1969, pp. 91-112.

[29]Leonard Axelrod, "Review Based on Scientific Evidence of the Decision Banning the Use of DDT," op. cit.

[30]"Deaths by Cause and Demographic group, 1990," *World Development Report 1993, Investing in Health*, p. 224.

[31]Vector Biology Control Project, U.S. Agency for International Development.

[32]Wolf, et al, "Blood Levels of Organochlorine Residues and Risk of Breast Cancer," *Journal of the National Cancer Institute*, op. cit.

[33]Kreiger, et al, "Breast Cancer and Serum Organochlorines: A Prospective Study Among White, Black and Asian Women," op. cit.

[34]Carlsen, E. et al, "Evidence for Decreasing Quality of Semen During Past 50 Years," *British Medical Journal*, Vol. 305, 1992, pp. 609-613.

[35]Dr. Gordon Gribble, "Natural Chlorine? You Bet!," *Priorities*, Vol. 6, No. 2, American Council on Science and Health, New York, 1994, p. 11.

[36]National Acid Precipitation Assessment Project Report, cited by Sen. John Glenn, *Congressional Record*, March 27, 1990, S-3254. The NAPAP report, which took ten years and cost $500 million in Federal funds received only a one-hour hearing in the Senate, and was never presented in the House at all. Senator Glenn said, "We spend over $500 million on the most definitive study of acid precipitation that has ever been done in the history of the world, and then we do not want to listen to what [the experts] say."

[37]Quoted by Warren T. Brookes of the *Detroit News*, "Acid Rain: The $140 Billion Fraud?" which originally appeared in that newspaper. It was reprinted in *Consumer Alert Comments*, Vol. 14, No. 6, November 1990.

[38]See Michael Bennett, *The Asbestos Racket*, Free Enterprise Press, Bellevue, Washington, 1991.

[39]Jon Franklin, "Poisons of the Mind," the keynote address to the 1994 convention of the Society of Toxicology, March 16, 1994, Dallas,

TX. Franklin is a Pulitzer-prize winning journalist who covered the Agent Orange story for the *Baltimore Sun*. He now teaches in the School of Journalism at the University of Oregon.

[40]Bruce Herbert, "Agent Orange, a Media Myth," *Chicago Tribune*, March 31, 1983.

[41]Dr. Elizabeth Whelan, "Deadly Dioxin?" *Toxic Terror*, Jameson Books, 1985. Reprinted in Lehr, *Rational Readings on Environmental Concerns,* op. cit., p. 223-246.

[42]Elizabeth Whelan, op. cit.

[43]Gary Lee, "Dioxin Study Prompts Intervention Plea," *Washington Post*, October 14, 1994, p. A8.

[44]Whelan, Elizabeth, *Toxic Terror*, Jameson Books, Ottawa, Illinois, 1985, p. 104.

[45]Richard Stone, "Environmental Estrogens Stir Debate," *Science*, Vol. 165, 1994, p. 310.

[46]Richard Stone, op. cit.

[47]Kenneth Smith, "The Media's War on Essential Chemicals: Targeting Chlorine," *Priorities*, Vol 6, No. 2, American Council on Science and Health, New York, 1994, pp. 6-9.

7

Do the Rat Tests
Mean Anything?

MYTHMAKERS SAY:

". . . [I]n 1969, Dr. Malcolm M. Hargraves of the Mayo Clinic said: 'Since the advent of pesticides in 1947, I've seen and taken inquisitive personal histories on 1,200 cases of blood dyscrasias and lymphoid diseases. Every patient at some time or another had great exposure to a pesticide, an herbicide, a paint thinner, a cleaning agent, or the like."
Quoted by Frank Graham, Jr., *Since Silent Spring*, Houghton Mifflin, Boston, 1970, pp. 147-48

"I read with amazement Dennis Avery's . . . article in the *Star* November 25. His bashing of worldwide efforts to make environmental progress is unconscionable. . . . To say don't worry about use of pesticides and chemical fertilizers is to step back 30 years before Rachel (Carson's) alarm. We do not really know how many pollutants we can spread over the globe and what the cumulative effect will in the next 75-100 years—the years in which our children and grandchildren will live."
William F. Steinmetz, letter to the editor of the *Indianapolis Star*, November 27, 1993

"When I read the extensive list of organochlorines, organophosphates, dioxin-containing sprays and other chemicals used as weedicides, fungicides, herbicides, pesticides and fertilizers (in cotton production) I was shocked. . . . Then someone told me that women with tiny babies are advised to wash new cotton garments three to four times to remove chemicals adhering to the cotton fibers before they use the clothes."
Helen Caldicott, anti-war and environmental activist, *If You Love This Planet*, 1992

REALITY SAYS:

"The standard carcinogen tests that use rodents are an obsolescent relic of the ignorance of past decades."
    Science editorial by Dr. Philip Abelson, "Testing for Carcinogens With Rodents," Vol. 249, September 21, 1990, p. 1357

"The current practice of feeding animals massive doses of chemicals to determine whether they might cause cancer in people has been attacked as misleading by two reports in today's issue of the scientific journal *Science*."
    Larry Thompson, "High-Dose Chemical Tests on Animals Overestimate Cancer Risk, Critics Say," *Washington Post*, August 31, 1990

"We feed rodents 'all-you-can-eat' buffets every day, yet we know that caloric intake is the single greatest contributing cause of cancer. In fact, we found you can modify the cancer-causing impact of one of the most potent carcinogens from 90 percent down to 3 percent just by cutting rodent caloric intake 20 percent. This means high-dose feeding skews the results."
    Dr. Ronald Hart, director of the National Center on Toxicological Research, 1990[1]

The rat tests mislead the public. They may communicate some useful information to the experts, but they have misled the public on the real cancer risks in our lives.

For the last 20 years, we have tested compounds for cancer by exposing rats to what we call the Maximum Tolerated Dose (MTD). In other words, we see how much of the stuff we can cram into their diets without either killing them or triggering a dangerous tumor. Some of the rats have successfully tolerated 100,000 times the maximum expected human exposure (MHE) to certain chemicals. If they developed tumors at 101,000 times the MHE, however, the compound went on the "cancer list."

The case of the sweetener saccharine illustrates how the high-dose tests can mislead. In the saccharine tests, male rats developed bladder tumors after eating a daily lifetime dose of saccharine totaling a relatively huge 5 percent of their *total diets*. We now know that at such high exposures, saccharine crystals formed in the rats' bladders and caused constant irritation. Female rats didn't get the cancers—because their bladders don't form the crystals.

In this case, the cancer clearly seems to result from the crystals, not the chemical compound. Nevertheless, saccharine went on the cancer suspect list.

Typical MTDs (Maximum Tolerated Dose) and Human Equivalents

Chemical	Lab Animal Dose	Comparable Human Dose
cyclamates	5% of diet	138-522 12-oz sodas per day
saccharin	5-7.5% of diet	500 times typical consumption of sweeteners
Alar	0.5-1% of diet	28,000 lbs. of apples daily for 10 years

Source: *From Mice to Men: The Benefits and Limitations of Animal Testing in Predicting Human Cancer Risk*, American Council on Science and Health, New York, 1991

Half of all the compounds tested by MTD produce tumors. Is it really possible that half of all the chemical compounds in the known and natural worlds cause cancer? Two thirds of the compounds now on the National Toxicology Program cancer listing are there because of the MTD tests. Virtually all of the public pesticide scares have likewise come from MTD tests. The first was the original Thanksgiving cranberry panic (over a compound named aminotriazol) in 1959. The latest was the Alar scare in apples.

Now, we're finding that the rat tests didn't tell us anything accurate about the real human risks from the chemicals. Instead, they frightened us about safe compounds and foods. They pushed our priorities in the wrong directions. As an example, the Alar scare reduced fruit consumption—especially among kids—when we should have been raising it.

In cancer as in almost everything else, the dose makes the poison.

MYTHMAKER:

"Environmentalists argue that since it is not known whether cancer-causing substances have a threshold, i.e. whether a certain amount need be in the body before it triggers uncontrollable cell proliferation, it is foolish to try to find a 'safe' exposure level."

"Priorities," *Sierra*, Sierra Club, January/February 1994, p. 43

VOICES OF REALITY:

"We believe that the MTD (Maximum Tolerated Dose) should be converted to the minimally toxic dose . . . or the highest subtoxic dose."

C. Jelleff Carr et. al., "A Critique of the Maximum Tolerated Dose in Bioassays to Assess Cancer Risks From Chemicals," *Regulatory Toxicology and Pharmacology*, 1991, Vol. 14, pp. 78-87

"This (MTD) approach requires certain assumptions that the Advisory Review Report now finds *invalid*. What are they?

"1) that the rates at which a substance is absorbed, distributed and eliminated by the body are the same regardless of the dose;

"2) that when maximum tolerated doses produce cancers in animals, the same cancers will be produced in proportion to smaller doses, no matter how small;

"3) that the rate at which the body repairs toxic genetic damage is unaffected by the dose of the toxic substance absorbed;

"4) that the likelihood of developing cancers is not influenced by the age of the animals;

"5) that the maximum tolerated dose can be higher—hundreds or thousands of times higher—than the likely human doses.

"There is now ample evidence and widespread consensus [that these assumptions] are scientifically untenable. . . . Yet . . . they have been the basis of far-reaching regulatory actions costing the U.S. economy billions of dollars. They have created many of the myths by which the media and advocacy groups have been able to foment the visceral fear of cancer now pervading all segments of society."

Dr. Gio Bata Gori, in a commentary on the editorial page of the *Wall Street Journal*, August 22, 1992, about the Advisory Review Report by the National Toxicology Program's Board of Scientific Counselors. Dr. Gori was formerly deputy director of the Division of Cancer Cause and Prevention in the National Cancer Institute

"Environmental policy has too often evolved largely in reaction to popular panics. . . . As a result, many scientists and health specialists say, billions of dollars are wasted each year in battling problems that are no longer considered dangerous, leaving little money for others that cause far more harm . . . for instance, thousands of regulations were written to restrict compounds that had caused cancer in rats or mice, even though these animal studies often fail to predict how the compounds might affect humans."

> Keith Schneider, "New View Calls Environmental Policy Misguided," *New York Times*, March 21, 1993, p. 1

We know a great deal more now about both cancer and pesticides than we did in 1962. We know, for example, that less than 3 percent of our cancers are caused by the environmental factors outside our own smoking habits, heredity, and dietary choices (mainly too much fat and too few fruits and vegetables). We know that we have spent billions of dollars trying to chase down the "cancers" which the high-dose rat tests say are lurking in pesticide residues.

We also know we have not found them.

We have found that the pesticides currently approved for use in the Western World are toxic only at fantastically high levels of dosage, to laboratory animals which are highly prone to develop tumors. The lab animals are especially prone to develop cancer of the liver in pesticide toxicity tests—but we humans have developed no increased level of liver tumors in any of the countries heavily relying on pesticides for food production.

Just to put the dietary skewing of the rat tests into perspective, a big recent Finnish study of beta-carotene in human diets may have been thrown off by just a fifteen-fold increase in dosage. A $43 million test, in which beta-carotene was added to the diets of 29,000 smokers, was supposed to reduce cancer rates. Instead, it raised the lung cancer rate by 18 percent. The researchers were astounded—and suggested as one possible cause that they had had the respondents take too much beta-carotene. They ate three times as much beta-carotene as they would have gotten from a diet rich in fruits and vegetables. The synthetic beta-carotene they consumed was also five times more readily available to the respondents' systems than normal beta-carotene. The resulting levels were enough to produce skin yellowing in more than one-fourth of the men.[2]

And then we assume that giving rats 100,000 times a "normal" exposure will give us a useful measure of toxicity!

The dose certainly causes the cancer in the case of gray asbestos. Canadian asbestos workers have had a higher risk of lung cancer than the general population. Their wives, living near the mines, do not have more cancer. Thus, the fibers of gray asbestos (the type used in virtually all building insulation applications) are toxic—but only at the high doses suffered by asbestos miners and installers working in air filled with floating fibers. There are no cases of passive non-workplace asbestosis.

Our state and local governments apparently have spent some *$20 billion* of public money to remove the gray asbestos from schools and public buildings—with no public health gain! (Blue asbestos, used in World War II ships, is far more deadly—but it was never used in buildings.)

The dose also causes the cancer in the case of dioxin. Workers in chemical plants where dioxin concentrations are high have a somewhat elevated cancer risk—but only if the dioxin concentrations in their tissues are *500 times the levels of the average citizen.* These results directly contradict the guinea pig tests. Dioxin was the most carcinogenic substance ever tested on an animal! Researchers thought they had uncovered our most vicious environmental killer. We evacuated the town of Times Beach, Missouri. Vietnam veterans have even been given disability payments for their Agent Orange exposures—dioxin was the so-called "danger" in Agent Orange.

But it turns out that people aren't very sensitive to dioxin. After one of the most thorough studies ever conducted on an environmental risk, researchers found no elevated risk of cancer or other pesticide-related dangers among any Vietnam veterans. The sole exception was a moderately elevated risk of the rare non-Hodgkins lymphoma among sailors who served on the ships offshore.

DIOXIN DOUBTER:

"You can imagine my horror when [the Agent Orange] story, the biggest of my life, began to slip through my fingers. . . . Nothing checked. . . . Scientists, all off the record, were telling me the whole thing was hysteria. . . .

Ranch Hand was the code name for the squadron that sprayed Agent Orange. Well, flyers are pretty macho. . . . They developed an initiation rite in which all new arrivals had to drink a cup of Agent Orange. They were supposed to wear protective clothing; they wore boxer shorts and tennis shoes, and were commonly covered with Agent Orange. . . . Well, these guys were obviously prime targets . . . and their health, ten and fifteen years after exposure, was very normal. No excess cancer, heart disease, alcoholism. . . . Most newspapers didn't run this story."

> Jon Franklin, journalist and two-time winner of the Pulitzer prize, in "Poisons of the Mind," keynote address to the Society of Toxicology, March 16, 1994[3]

DNA testing is also testifying against the rat tests.

Researchers say the examination of frozen DNA sections from the test animals give another good secondary test for suspicious symptoms. With it, researchers can sometimes distinguish between problems brought on by the heavy dosage and those triggered by the compound itself. The DNA tests say saccharine is safe—unless you're a male rat consuming 100,000 times the expected maximum human exposure of that compound.

As this is being written, a panel of experts is drafting a report for the National Institute of Environmental Health Sciences (a division of the National Institute of Health). The panel has already agreed that our rat testing procedure for "cancer-causing substances" has been a mistake from the beginning.[4] The panel says that deliberately stuffing rats with more and more of the test compound until they die was never a realistic way to assess human risks. The members are trying to outline a more effective cancer screening system for the future.

Twenty years ago, we weren't sure that the dose *did* make the poison in cancer. We opted for the most drastic test. Today, we can develop a more realistic set of cancer risk tests. We can figure out the maximum expected human exposure to the test compound, and test at a safety multiple of that. (One hundred times Maximum Expected Human Exposure? One thousand times? Certainly not 100,000 times.)

Western Europeans use a more realistic test. They look for the level where the animals begin to develop symptoms of stress such as weight loss, or other symptoms which show up in autopsies.

A more realistic set of animal tests would be truly more useful in guiding our lives and our choices—instead of being used primarily as a scare tactic to drive us away from our most healthful foods.

Ranking Cancer Risks

This is a ranking by a top cancer expert of the relative risks posed by pesticides and food additives *if the rat tests were an accurate guide to human risk:*

Source and daily exposure	Risk factor
wine (one glass)	4,700.0
beer (12 oz.)	2,800.0
cola (one)	2,700.0
bread (two slices)	400.0
mushroom (one, raw)	100.0
basil (1 gram of dried leaf)	100.0
shrimp (100 grams)	90.0
brown mustard (5 grams)	70.0
saccharin (in 12 oz. diet soda)	60.0
peanut butter (one sandwich)	30.0
cooked bacon (100 grams)	9.0
water (one liter)	1.0
additives and pesticides in food other than bread and grains)	0.5
additives and pesticides in bread and grains	0.4
coffee (one cup)	0.3

Source: Bruce Ames, et al., "Ranking Possible Carcinogenic Hazards, *Science*, Vol. 236, April 17, 1987, p. 271

The OECD/European Union guideline for carcinogenicity studies states the following:

The highest dose level should be sufficiently high to elicit signs of minimal toxicity without substantially altering the normal life span due to effects other than tumors. Signs of toxicity are those that may be indicated by alterations in certain serum enzyme levels or slight depression of body weight gain (less than 10 percent).

In contrast, the 1987 EPA position document on MTD from the Office of Pesticide Programs states the following:

> The highest dose to be tested in the oncogenicity study should be selected below a level which resulted in significant life-threatening toxicity in the subchronic study. *The level should not be selected too far below a life-threatening level.* . . . [emphasis added]

Europe has had no epidemic of cancers from using its milder form of testing. In effect, we've had a 30-year experiment in whether the dose makes the cancer or not, using a milder test in Europe and a more radical test in the U.S. The MTD has flunked. It has not delivered lower cancer rates. Worse, the MTD results have been widely used to frighten consumers away from the one major positive behaviour change they can make to cut their cancer risks substantially—eating more fruits and vegetables.

The MTD results also identify so many "carcinogens" that the public simply shuts off the results. If everything causes cancer then nothing causes cancer. This is surely a dangerous attitude, because some things *do* cause cancer, and some other things help *fight* cancer.

The EPA is currently being sued by the government of Peru for classifying chlorinated drinking water as a carcinogen. Peruvian officials saw the classification, removed chlorine from their drinking water—and caused a cholera epidemic which cost an estimated 5,000 lives.

The clincher: Researchers have found evidence that most of the known human carcinogens can be detected in animals at dose levels well below the MTD. Thus, reduced doses would show up the important health hazards without flagging the trivial.[5]

Reforming the Delany Amendment

We also have a major problem with the famed Delany amendment, which says the government cannot permit *any tolerance* for "carcinogens" in processed foods.

This was unrealistic when it was passed, when regulators were dealing in parts per million. It is horrendous when regulators are now dealing in concentrations a million times weaker—parts per trillion. If Delaney is administered honestly, with the advancing frontiers of detection, there soon may not be many processed foods which American consumers will be allowed to buy.

In fact, it should not be legal—right now—for us to buy the canned, frozen, or boxed forms of the foods that contain natural compounds which have produced tumors in high-dose rat tests!

That would mean

- no coffee or cocoa
- no apples, bananas, broccoli, Brussels sprouts, cabbage, cantaloupe, carrots, cauliflower, celery, cherries, eggplant, endive, fennel, grapefruit, grapes, honey, honeydew melons, kale, lettuce, mangoes, mushrooms,oranges, parsley, parsnips, peaches, pears, pineapples, plums, potatoes, raspberries, strawberries, or turnips

The processed food we were allowed to buy would also taste different, because most of the commonly used spices also contain known "carcinogens": basil, caraway, cinnamon, cloves, dill, horseradish, mace, mustard, nutmeg, black pepper, rosemary, sage, sesame seeds, tarragon, and thyme.

The lists were compiled by Dr. Bruce Ames, the noted cancer expert from the University of California/Berkeley. Dr. Ames says that if the full roster of natural food compounds were given the high-dose rat tests, almost every plant product in the supermarket would flunk the Delany Amendment. Many of them have simply not been tested yet.[6]

That's why even Carol Browner, President Clinton's appointee as administrator of the Environmental Protection Agency and a foe of farm chemicals, proposed replacing Delaney with a more reasonable standard of "minimal risk."

The courts rejected the proposal, saying that the Delany language is clear, and any change will have to be passed by Congress.

The environmental groups are opposing Delany changes, of

course. If "minimal risk" becomes the national standard for regulating pesticides, they would lose most of their food scare headlines and billions of dollars in fund-raising power.

What About the Circle of Poison?

The Circle of Poison is another of those brilliant public relations ploys invented by the environmental movement.

We've already seen that pesticides don't kill people, unless farmers or farmworkers are careless with the few compounds that are truly dangerous to handle. We've already noted that currently approved U.S. pesticides don't threaten wildlife except when misused, and that the dangers are declining rapidly as we get more of the safer, low-volume pesticides. We've just detailed the exaggerations in human risk introduced by the rat tests.

But all of that rational thought pales beside a menacing, provocative phrase like "Circle of Poison."

That phrase vividly conveys the impression the environmental movement wants to create: an America beset on all sides by foreign farmers using vile chemicals banned in the U.S., to grow unsafe food that will then be smuggled into U.S. supermarkets past the unseeing eyes of the Food and Drug Administration.

In the first place, few countries dare to use much in the way of pesticides that aren't legal here to grow food for the U.S. market. Any country thinking about slipping us Circle of Poison pesticides on their exports has surely noted what happened a few years ago when two grapes from Chile were found to contain small amounts of cyanide. Chile's huge fresh fruit and vegetable trade with the U.S. was virtually shut down for the rest of the season. The country, its farmers and farm workers lost hundreds of millions of dollars. (Later, tests indicated that if the cyanide had been put in the grapes in Chile, the grapes would have rotted before their arrival in the U.S. It is almost certain that the cyanide was injected on the docks in Philadelphia. That would also explain the telephone tip-off to FDA inspectors.)

But what if we can't detect the residue? If we can't detect it, given today's gas chromatography and parts-per-trillion technologies, then it is almost certainly because there *is* no significant residue.

Of course, if the dose makes the poison then residues that can't even be detected at parts per billion will be far too weak to overwhelm our natural defenses.

POLITICAL MYTHMAKER:

"If we are going to have tougher pesticide standards at home, it makes no sense to allow American companies to use a loophole in current law to dump unsafe pesticides abroad. . . . I am pleased the Administration is willing to do more to close the Circle of Poison loophole."
> News release from the office of Sen. Patrick Leahy, D-VT, then chairman, Senate Agriculture Committee, January 25, 1993

REALITY:

"First, there may be situations in which a hazardous pesticide is essential for control of a major pest, as in the case of fungicides used to control late blight in Ecuadorian potato production. . . . There are no effective substitutes for fungicides and farmers who understand the health risks of fungicide exposure may choose to use these materials because their (food production) benefits are commensurately high."
> John Antle and Susan Capalbo, invited paper for the 1994 annual meetings of the Allied Social Sciences Association, Boston, January 4, 1994[7]

*R*eality Comment: Note that Antle and Capalbo are talking about pesticide risks to Third World farmers, not First World consumers. There is no evidence that particular pesticides are being exported to foreign countries and coming back (past our FDA inspections) to afflict U.S. consumers.

Are We Poisoning the Rest of the World?

Then there is the matter of making pesticides in the U.S. that aren't needed here. We don't grow bananas, for example, or coffee. Should American companies be forced to make good coffee and banana pesticides overseas rather than providing the jobs here? (The banana pesticides, considered relatively dangerous, are a problem to the applicators, not to consumers or factory workers.)

Asia is also using some harsher pesticides (as measured by

applicator risk) on their rice paddies, but they don't sell rice to the U.S. Moreover, they are making their own decisions about the relative risks of applicator health versus running out of rice. What about a grass herbicide that was approved more rapidly in Argentina than in the U.S.? Should Argentina be denied the right to use it? Or again, should the company have to relocate its production and jobs outside the U.S. because our chemical approval process is too slow?

NEEDED—A CANCER TEST THAT TELLS THE TRUTH:

". . . High dosing may falsify the experiment in one of two ways: It can either poison the cells and tissues so severely as to prevent a carcinogenic response that might otherwise have been found, or it can 'overload' and change metabolic processes so as to cause a carcinogenic response which would not normally occur. . . . "

Edith Efron, *The Apocalyptics*, New York, Simon and Schuster, 1984, p. 248

America needs a better cancer testing system than the current high-dose rat tests. The system needs to incorporate these facts which we've learned about cancer over the last 30 years:

- Cancer is fundamentally a degenerative disease of old age.
- The doses and repetition of the insult are critically important to the risk.
- Smoking and our own heredity are the biggest risk elements in cancer, not the external environment.

The biggest flaw of the current testing system is that it leads us to fear and avoid our most potent weapon against cancer—fruits and vegetables. The Alar scare was perhaps the most vicious swipe at America's health the environmental movement has ever perpetrated. It led parents and school administrators to take apples away from their kids, pour healthful apple juice down the drain, and ban apples from our schools. By implication, every mother and father in the country was forcibly reminded of the message the Natural Resources

Defense Council wanted to convey—that non-organic fruits and vegetables were dangerous.

Nothing could be farther from the truth.

And nothing could be farther from the message we need to send to kids, parents and grandparents:

> Eat twice as many fruits and vegetables as you've been eating, regardless of whether they were grown with pesticides. The EPA, the FDA, and the USDA are doing their jobs, and making sure there's no harmful pesticide on that attractive apple or potato. You can eat produce in full confidence that it will add to your health, not subtract from it.

Virtually every cancer scare we've ever had has come from the high-dose rat tests. If there were no high-dose rat tests, there would be no scare material. We could then use the billions of dollars wasted on the high-dose tests on things that *would* improve public health. It is past time to make the tests a more realistic reflection of actual human risks.

If the rat tests are left as they are, they will continue to be used for blatant fearmongering which will actually undermine our health—and could ultimately endanger wildlife.

Science editorial, September 9, 1994

"Risk Assessment of Low-Level Exposures"

"In one example, 11 chemicals known to cause cancer at high doses were administered at low levels. With 8 of 11 substances. . . . Instead of damaging the rodents' livers, the low doses were apparently beneficial to them. . . . In the above instances, safe (diminished cancer) levels of exposure exist for substances known to cause cancer at higher doses. . . .

"The use of linear extrapolation from huge doses to zero implies that "one molecule can cause cancer." That assertion disregards the fact of natural large-scale repair of damaged DNA. . . . Adult humans are internally exposed to about 500 [grams] per day of oxygen—a relentless known destroyer of DNA. . . . Creatures ranging from microorganisms to mammals could not survive if they did not have mechanisms to respond to challenges from their environments. . . .

"The current mode of extrapolating high doses to low-dose effects is erroneous for both chemicals and radiation. Safe levels of exposure exist. The public has been needlessly frightened and deceived, and hundreds of billions of dollars wasted. . . . "

Source: Philip H. Abelson, *Science*, Vol. 265, p. 1507

Notes

[1]Dr. Ronald Hart, quoted in Warren T. Brookes, "Pesticide Phobia a Dangerous Health Threat," *Detroit News*, April 16, 1990, p. 7A.

[2]Kathleen Meister, "Antioxidants and Lung Cancer: What the Conflicting Reports Mean," *Priorities for Long Life and Good Health*, American Council on Science and Health, Vol. 6, No. 3, 1994, New York, pp. 7-11.

[3]Jon Franklin is currently professor of Journalism, University of Oregon, Eugene, Oregon.

[4]Joel Brinkley, "Animal Tests As Risk Clues: The Best Data May Fall Short," *New York Times*, March 23, 1993.

[5]A. Apostolou, "Relevance of Maximum Tolerated Dose to Human Carcinogenic Risk," *Regulatory Toxicology and Pharmacology*, Vol. 11, 1990, pp. 68-80.

[6]Ames and Gold, "Environmental Pollution and Cancer: Some Misconceptions," *Phantom Risk: Scientific Inference and the Law*, Edited by Foster, Bernstein, and Huber, MIT Press, Cambridge, Massachusetts, 1993, pp. 153-181.

[7]Antle and Pingali, "Pesticides, Productivity and Farmer Health: A Philippine Case Study," *American Journal of Agricultural Economics*, August 1994, Vol. 76, No. 3, pp. 418-430.

8

There Is Lots Less Hunger Than We've Been Told

MYTHMAKERS SAY:

"A lifetime of malnutrition and actual hunger is the lot of at least two-thirds of mankind."

Lord Boyd-Orr, director-general, UN Food and Agricultural Organization, 1950

"If present trends continue, the world in 2000 will be more crowded, more polluted, less stable ecologically and more vulnerable to disruption than the world we live in now. Barring revolutionary advances in technology, life for most people on earth will be more precarious in 2000 than it is now. . . . [T]he number of malnourished people in the LDCs could rise from 400-600 million in the mid-1970s to 1.3 billion in 2000. . . . In the developing world, the need for imported food is expected to grow."

Major Findings and Conclusions, *Global 2000 Study*, Carter White House, 1980

"Does human society want 10 to 15 billion humans living in poverty and malnourishment or 1 to 2 billion living with abundant resources and a quality environment?"

David Pimentel et al., "Natural Resources and an Optimum Human Population," *Population and Environment*, Human Sciences Press, 1994, p. 348

REALITY SAYS:

"During the last quarter of the 19th century perhaps 20 to 25 million died from famine. If an adjustment for population increase is made, a comparable figure for the third quarter of this century would be at least

50 million. . . . For the entire 20th century to the present, there have probably been between 12 million and 15 million famine deaths, and many if not the majority were due to deliberate governmental policy, official mismanagement, or war, and not to serious crop failure."

D. Gale Johnson, University of Chicago, *World Food Problems* and Prospects, American Enterprise Institute, 1975[1]

"Approximately 600 million people in the developing countries do not have access to enough food to meet their nutritional needs. Only a small portion of those people are clinically malnourished. The preponderance of them are mildly to moderately undernourished. Others are poorly nourished on a seasonal basis. Still more are at the margins of adequacy such that major illness, increases in food prices or decreases in real income could force them into nutritional deficit."

USAID policy statement, 1984

There is a great deal of good news on population and hunger in today's world. In the first place, we now know that we don't have an upward population spiral. Thanks to affluence, contraceptives, and TV, we have a fighting chance to peak the world's population at 8 billion rather than 10, 12, or 25 billion.

Furthermore, the latest evidence shows that the Third World countries which have done best in raising their crop yields have also done best on bringing down birth rates! That means we don't have to watch people starve in order to restabilize the world's population at a sustainable level.

Bread for the World, a charitable organization, is even telling the public that we have the capacity to eliminate hunger in the world.[2]

They are probably correct.

To eliminate hunger quickly, however, we will have to press forward on two fronts with more effort than we have mustered thus far.

We must, first, make larger investments in high-yield farming for the Third World. Those investments are not currently being made, in large part because eco-activists have been crusading against the high-yield seeds, the fertilizers, and (yes) the pesticides that will need to be part of the high-yield packages.

Second, we must simultaneously upgrade the skills of third world workers and instill the necessary concern for honesty and human rights in the governments of Third World countries. Virtually all of the world's famines since World War II have been due to "mistakes of government" such as government grain monopolies and shooting wars (especially civil wars).

There Is Lots Less Hunger Today Than Most People Think

Even *with* these limitations, the world has made enormous progress against famine. The biggest factor in that achievement has been high-yield farming. The resulting high food production has been backed by rapidly spreading public health services such as clean water, waste treatment, and vaccinations. These cut down diarrheic and other diseases which prevent people from taking full nutritional advantage of their food supplies.

With the notable exception of Africa, the world has come perhaps 90 percent of the way to eliminating famine since the Rockefeller Foundation started the Green Revolution some 30 years ago. Consider just a few dramatic facts:

- The threat of severe hunger no longer stalks perhaps two-thirds of the world's population on at least a periodic basis, as it did within living memory. Today, the threat of severe hunger affects perhaps 5-7 percent of the world's people in any year when Africa is *not* having one of its big continent-wide droughts.
- *Per capita* calories in the Third World have risen by 28 percent since 1960.[3]
- Asia, with about three-fourths of the world's population, has raised its per capita food intake by about one-third since 1960, in a region that many experts thought would suffer mass starvation.

The accompanying figure demonstrates graphically how sharply increased food productivity and rising consumer incomes have reduced hunger and malnutrition in recent years. Again, only in Africa has added food production *not* begun to break the back of the malnutrition problem.

Figure 8.1. Percentage of population with inadequate diets.

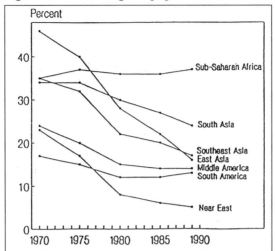

Source: *The Potential Role of Biotechnology in Saving Food Pro-
duction and Environmental Problems in Developing Countries.*
Presented to the ASA-CSSA-SSSA annual meetings, Cincinnati, Ohio,
November 1993

Astonishing Gains Against Hunger

In 1970, the world gave the Nobel Peace Prize to Dr. Norman
Borlaug—the plant-breeder who developed the Green Revolution
wheat varieties. Back then, the Green Revolution's "miracle" wheat
and rice varieties seemed one of the outstanding achievements in
human history. In the years since, however, some people have been
having second thoughts. They worry that saving 500 million people
from famine might just give the world a bigger famine—with even
more deaths—later on.

But famine is not inevitable. (Even the famous Dr. Thomas
Malthus came to realize this later in his life, and the tone of his later
writings was far different than the Malthusian gloom for which he is
famous.)

We now know, for example, that populations in affluent countries do not rise rapidly. And we know that agricultural production
can be intensified far more effectively than Malthus could have imag-

ined. Moreover, since we know that the world's population is simply in the final phase of a onetime surge, we also know that we need only to find the food productivity for this one last redoubling of human numbers.

In 1950, the world produced 692 million tons of grain. This represented the key food supply for what was then a population of 2.5 billion people. That was the period when the FAO director-general was estimating that two-thirds of the world's population suffered from food deprivation. The world had just suffered a major famine in Bengal (1943) and was about to suffer another in China.

In 1950, Americans were eating around 3,200 calories per day. The average resident of China was getting about 2,100 calories per day. In India, the average was estimated at 1,700. In Indonesia, the caloric average was 1,750, and virtually the entire population lived in abject poverty. Bolivians were eating 1,760 calories. No one was even *looking* yet at the calories available in sub-Saharan Africa.[4]

By 1992, the world produced 1,952 million tons of grain for 5.7 billion people. That's a 24 percent gain in per capita grain supplies.

In fact, total food supplies in the world's *poor countries* have increased even faster than that! Per capita calories in the Third World have increased 27 percent since 1963, and probably a full one-third since 1950. That's enormous progress when one thinks of helping billions of poor people lift themselves over the threshold from hunger to food sufficiency.

It is true that there are still many people with inadequate diets.

Figure 8.2

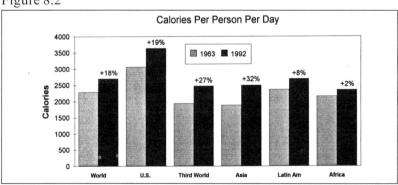

Source: FAO Production Yearbooks

In fact, the FAO estimates a slight *increase* in the numbers of the developing world's underfed, from around 540 million in 1979/81 to about 580 million in 1989/90.[5] Two points about this increase, however, must be made.

First, roughly 90 percent of the "hungry" in the estimates are within 10 percent of having fully adequate calories for good health.[6] In fact, many of the so-called hungry lack "adequate" calories because they prefer to spend part of their food budgets for higher-quality calories such as milk and fruit, rather than increasing their consumption of low-cost calories such as cassava flour.[7]

Second, there has been a 23 percent increase in world population during those years—nearly 1 billion people—so the increase in per capita food supplies represents a major productivity triumph.[8] Meanwhile, further progress beckons as better seeds and farming systems reach into such remote regions as Ethiopia, Ecuador, and Mongolia.

Per Capita Food Gains Accelerating Now

In fact, now that population growth rates are tapering off, progress against malnutrition is *really* picking up speed. (See Fig. 8.3.)

Figure 8.3

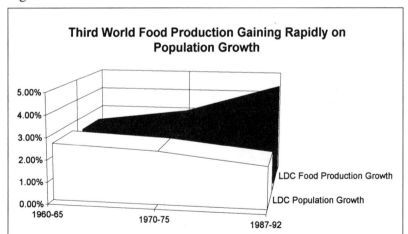

Source: FAO Production Yearbooks; Index of Total Food Production, All Developing Countries, *FAO Production Yearbook*, 1992, pp. 43-44

Figure 8.4

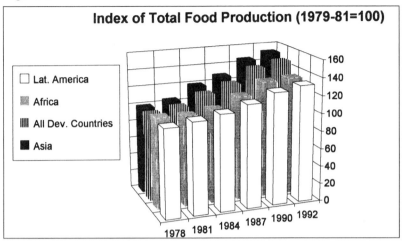

Source: Index of Total Food Production, FAO Production Yearbooks

The rate of increase in the Third World's food production in recent years has been more than double its population growth rate. Progress in the *next* decades should be even more rapid, since the Third World population growth rate over the next decade will be declining from 1.6 percent. Nor has there been any *slackening* in the rate of food production gain, contrary to some highly publicized reports. (See Fig. 8.4.)

Per capita food supplies, as well as production, have continued to gain (again, with Africa as a modest exception). (See Fig. 8.5.)

It is important to remember that Sub-Saharan Africa, where the remaining hunger is concentrated, contains only 7 percent of the world population. Asia, where the success has been concentrated, represents the huge majority of the Third World's population, and *three fourths* of the total world population. Latin America, which has also registered increases, accounts for 6 percent of the world's people.)

The African Exception

Africa is today the outstanding exception to the good news on hunger. There are several reasons why this is true. Moreover, Africa should be able to do far better at food production in the future:

Figure 8.5

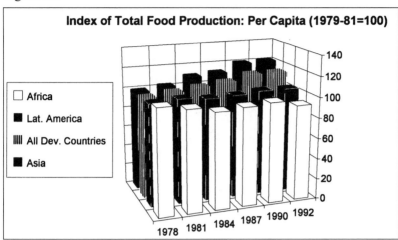

Source: Index of Total Food Production Per Capita, FAO Production Yearbooks

- First, Africa was until recently a sparsely populated continent with ample room for a low-yield/low-cost farming system called bush fallow. As a whole, the continent has probably never planted even 25 percent of its good cropland in any one year, because most of it has been in bush fallow, recovering its fertility without benefit of fertilizer.
- Second, the early Green Revolution scientific efforts were targeted at Asia, because our fear in 1960 was that billions of people would starve there first. Africa was considered a distant second in urgency.
- Third, when attempts to raise African farm productivity did begin, researchers were startled to find that almost none of the productivity results from other regions could be transferred successfully to Africa. The research on Africa had to start from square one, and that delayed the results by many years. Now, however, high-yield seeds and systems are beginning to flow from the African research stations.
- Fourth, Africa's dramatic drop in food security since 1970 reflects a real decline in living standards. But it also reflects the decline of African *crop reporting* systems. Many post-

colonial governments have lacked the jeeps and gasoline to
send their crop estimators out into the countryside. What is
not seen is not counted.
- Finally, African countries had little experience with self-gov-
ernment in 1960 when most of them began to get their inde-
pendence. As an additional handicap, many African nations
were advised in the 1960s to try fairly radical socialist and
even communist solutions to their organizational problems.
These organizational experiments did not succeed.

There is little question that Africa will be able to feed itself successfully in the long term. That ability will require broad application
of the high-yielding seeds and farming systems which research is
now beginning to release. The continent will also need a lot of fertilizer, and ways to finance it. African governments will need more
political competence and stability than they have yet been able to
muster.

Until the continent achieves high yields and political stability, it
will remain highly vulnerable to droughts and wars.

Recent Famines Were Due to Shooting, Not Food Failure

Most of the world's recent severe hunger has been due to shooting wars, with wrongheaded policies of the hungry countries' own
governments ranking as the second most frequent cause.

The last major famine in the non-Communist world was in Bengal in 1943, when 1.5 million people died of starvation after severe
flooding destroyed their crops. Communist China suffered a much
larger famine during Mao Tse-tung's Great Leap Forward in the late
1950s. (The Chinese government took so much grain from the communal farms to feed the cities that the countryside was devastated.)
Outside estimates range from 16 to 30 million deaths during Mao's
Great Leap disaster.[9]

Civil wars have been the key in the recent hunger events in Somalia, Ethiopia, Liberia, Angola, and most of Africa's other recent
famines. Thus, in a real sense, the world's recent famines could have
been avoided.

They have also afflicted a tiny fraction of the world's population.

The civil strife and resulting hunger in Somalia in 1992 involved only 0.001 percent of the world's total population and a few thousand deaths. The hunger in Sudan in 1994 involves perhaps 0.002 percent of the world population—and is occurring because the Sudanese government is actively trying to prevent food from reaching their rebellious South. In both Somalia and Sudan, there was enough food available to prevent deaths from famine.

The fact that our famines now are small doesn't make them unimportant. But we must not let our anguish over small-scale suffering blind us to the fact that we have found successful strategies to stop the large-scale famines. As D. Gale Johnson notes in the opening quotes of this chapter, famine caused 20-25 million deaths in the last quarter of the 19th century. A com- parable number of famine deaths for the current quarter-century would be 50 million.

Realistically, the famine death toll for 1975-2000 is likely to be 1 million or less, rather than 50 million or more.

Virtually all of the recent famines have featured the same deadly combination.

First, *they all occurred in African countries* which had not yet developed high-yielding agricultures. Africa got a late start

World Vision International Photo by E. Mooneyham

THE FAMINE-STRICKEN FEW—Newspapers are fond of publishing photos of famine victims like these Ethiopians beset by civil war and drought in 1981. Fortunately, rapid gains in the Third World's per capita food production are making it harder and harder to take such photos.

on agricultural research, in large part because it was land-rich (or sparsely populated) until recently. As mentioned earlier, high-yielding seeds and farming systems are only now beginning to become available to African farmers, 30 years after the Green Revolution began in earnest and 60 years after U.S. farmers got hybrid corn.

Second, *All of the famine countries' governments had agricultural policies which discouraged their farmers from planting high-yielding seeds and trying to meet rising food needs.* Such policies as low fixed prices for grain, government grain monopolies, and export taxes amount to powerful disincentives, which drive farmers back into the subsistence mode they know so well.

Most important, *all of the recent famines featured shooting wars,* which made it impossible for farmers to raise and market food normally. Combat turns problems (like ethnic tensions, poverty, and drought) into full-blown disasters.

Has there been any recent famine attributable to lack of food production potential? Only in the Sahel, the "edge of the desert" region south of the Sahara Desert, which suffered severe and extended drought both in 1973-74 and in 1983-84. But the entire population of the Sahel is about 25 million people, *one-half of one percent* of the world's population. The Sahel can support most of them most of the time, but not during the deep, extended droughts which occur there. Even high-yield farming research has been unable to break the grip of aridity on the Sahel to date.

(Incidentally, however, archeologists say the Sahel has been unpopulated for centuries at a time in the past, apparently because it was too dry even for pastoral grazing.)

Nor does all of the progress to date mean that the next big African drought will not produce almost as much suffering as the last one. We have not yet drought-proofed Africa the way we have India. But the solution is not to let more Africans die. The fastest, most humane solution is to breed more high-yielding seeds for African farms, build new fertilizer plants there, provide consistent, realistic incentives for farmers, and support them with political stability, roads, and storage silos.

USDA

A MOUNTAIN OF EXTRA GRAIN—For the past 25 years, we have been told to expect massive famine, but we have had surplus grain piled on the ground instead of famine victims in the streets.

Nearly All Countries Could Now Produce Adequate Diets

Other than the Sahel, there are few countries or regions which could not readily produce their own base calories today, using their own natural resources and the high-yielding seeds and farming systems of the continuing Green Revolution. Base calories are the fundamental calories—usually root crops and cereals—needed to supply minimum nutrition requirements in a poor country. Wealthy countries substitute quite a few "affluence calories" from meat, milk, eggs, and fresh fruits and vegetables.

Meanwhile, of course, the affluent countries of the world are struggling with surpluses and deliberately *trying* to limit food production gains; their low rate of increase, combined with troubles in the agriculture of the former USSR, kept the world average of grain production increase down to less than one percent in 1986-91.[10]

Ironically, Lester Brown of the Worldwatch Institute has been claiming that the world is now headed for famine, because per capita grain supplies have been declining since 1984. What he does not mention is that the slump has all been in the First World—

and has no hunger implications at all.

This does not fully answer the question of how densely populated countries can provide their consumers with high-quality diets rich in fruits, vegetables, meat, and milk. However, when countries can afford such high-quality diets, they can afford to import foodstuffs, meat, and the other items they prefer. (Generally, densely populated countries would be able to import these at less cost than producing them in-country.)

The Mismeasure of Food—And Famine

Feeding agencies like CARE and Bread for the World, no matter how well-meaning, are staffed by activists who want more food to distribute.

Organizations like the United Nations cite very large numbers of "hungry people"—but many of these organizations have both a legitimate concern for hunger and a vested interest in maintaining hunger donations.

Dr. Thomas Poleman of Cornell University pioneered the effort to achieve more accurate food estimates. His work suggests that we have typically underestimated food supplies by 10-15 percent, especially in the poorest tropical countries.[11] His on-the-ground research found a whole series of mistakes in food estimation which have led us to the erroneous (and rather astonishing) conclusion that most of the world's people have failed to provide themselves with their own first requirement—adequate food. For example:

- Few studies take into account the hunting and gathering which are particularly important for people in marginal economies—and which often supply 15 percent of their calories.
- There is a strong tendency to under-report food output. Farmers look at the crop reporter as a tax assessor and governments often choose to justify more aid rather than less.
- Food surveys typically leave out the "street foods" which are part of virtually every culture. The street foods are particularly important for protein, because much of the frying in poor countries is done on the street. (It seldom pays to heat frying fat for one family, whether it be French-fried potatoes at an American

fast-food restaurant or fried ants in Zambia.)
• In the tropics, you can't tell what's growing in the inter-cropped fields unless you crawl through the fields virtually on hands and knees.
• The poorer the country, the less of its food moves to market; most of it is eaten where it's grown. Few Third World countries spend their scarce dollars on good crop reporting systems.

Few Hunger Deaths

Most of the world's so-called "hunger" deaths—especially among children—are actually caused by untreated water, lack of sewage systems, lack of vaccinations, and contaminated food.

In fact the most effective method ever found for cutting child-hood malnutrition and death doesn't involve food at all. It's a cheap, simple treatment for diarrhea. The UN Children's Fund (UNICEF) says one-third to one-half of all infant deaths in the world are due to diarrhea. UNICEF is saving millions of lives a year by distributing packets of *oral rehydration salts*. Given to kids with diarrhea, the salts quickly restore body fluids and also help them digest some of the food available to them. Food distribution programs have seldom demonstrated any lifesaving capability except in genuine famine situations.[12]

Meanwhile, despite such evidence, many in the affluent West cling firmly to our belief in widespread hunger. I constantly find people who have traveled in Third World countries who "know" there is hunger because they have seen emaciated people, and even occasional wasted corpses. They have simply assumed that emaciated people were emaciated because they were hungry. In most places, however, it is far more likely that they are sick.

My wife, Anne, contracted both typhoid and amoebic dysentery while living in Ethiopia, and became a walking skeleton before the diseases were diagnosed—and she was an American attached to our embassy. (While working at a clinic, Anne also had tiny children die in her arms, after repeated bouts of diarrhea due to local infection sources.)

We Don't Know How Much Food People Need
—So We Overestimate It

Most of the nutrition studies in the world have been done with college kids in rich countries—a practice that helps guarantee that the
world's "nutritional requirements" are overestimated. There is little research on the *real* food needs of small-but-otherwise-healthy people
whose ancestors have been coping with hunger for generations.

Dr. David Seckler, who has worked with USAID and the Ford
Foundation, suggests that a child's body responds *first* to a food
shortage by limiting its own growth. Seckler followed up by checking a sample of young Indian men who had been medically screened
and found healthy. When he surveyed their food consumption, more
than 90 percent of them were "malnourished."[13]

Seckler's idea seems to be strongly backed by a USAID-spon-
sored nutritional assessment of children in 14 countries: The studies
found lots of "malnutrition". Ninety percent of it, however, was kids
who were short for their ages (by the standards of the World Health
Organization). They had normal weight for height. They were short
but not malnourished.

It would certainly be better if these children had fully adequate
diets—but being short certainly beats being dead from starvation or
mentally retarded by malnutrition.

The World Hunger Problem Doesn't Involve Much Food

Food aid has been donated liberally by the rich countries in recent decades. More often than not, so much food aid arrives in the
hungry countries that some of it sits in storage and depresses the
local farmers' price for the *next* crop.

Even this ample amount of food aid has required a smaller share
of the world's rising grain production. The total has averaged about
10 million tons per year for the last two decades. That means world
food aid has dropped from 0.8 percent of the world's grain production to 0.5 percent. Meanwhile, the world's annual grain carryover
has ranged between 200 to 400 million tons.

On top of the stored grain, there's enough good cropland diverted from production in just the U.S. and Argentina (because

of government policies) to feed another 1.5 billion people a calorie-adequate diet.

MYTHMAKER:

"It is unconscionable in a world with so many going hungry that we aren't doing more to prevent unwanted children from being born."
Jane Fonda, appointed by President Clinton as U.S. special good-will ambassador to the UN Population Fund, 1994[14]

Reality Comment: Most of the children born in the Third World are wanted. And relatively few of them are urgently hungry, except where there are shooting wars and government mismanagement.

What about conditions in the United States itself? It shouldn't be too surprising that few of our citizens are really hungry. The federal government alone is spending more than $33 billion per year on such feeding programs as food stamps, school lunches, women with infants, and special programs for pregnant mothers. Since 1961, federal spending on the food stamp program has expanded from $825,000 (for 50,000 recipients) to $22 billion, with the free food being offered to more than ten percent of the population of the richest nation on earth.

This expansion has not occurred because of increasing hunger in America, but because of Congressional logrolling. The city Congressmen voted more money for farm price supports, and the Agriculture Committees—in a direct exchange—budgeted more money for food stamps.

By the 1970s, we had essentially conquered America's hunger problem with school lunches, food stamps, and the other targeted feeding programs for infants and nursing mothers. In addition to the Federal effort, there were and are hundreds of well-organized and effective feeding programs run by organizations like Second Harvest, the Salvation Army, churches, cities, and local charities.

• Childhood anemia, one of the diseases most closely linked with malnutrition, has been cut in half in American children during recent years. At the same time, the percentage of poor children considered underweight has dropped below that in the general population.[15]

- A high proportion of our homeless have been found to be substance abusers and/or suffering from chronic mental illnesses such as schizophrenia. Hunger for these people is rarely a food problem but more accurately a consequence of substance abuse or illness.[16]

But in America, we count missed meals as hunger. Or the kids having to eat rice and beans rather than meat. This is not hunger, though it certainly is not affluence either.

So the food stamp program continued to expand, rising from 21 million recipients to 27 million between 1980 and 1993.[17]

Why So Much Mythology About Hunger?

Hunger is one of our strongest emotional "hot buttons." All of us have *felt* hungry. The emotion triggers age-old frantic responses, like a hungry kitten pouncing on anything that moves.

Hundreds of organizations have found it to be a key fund-raising appeal. Many charities tie their campaigns to hunger themes. Even the groups claiming we are threatened by global warming have tried to put in a famine-fear component—even though any global warming that occurred would likely *increase* world food output. (The global warming scenario offers a world with higher levels of CO_2 and more rainfall—essentially plant heaven.)[18]

High-yield agriculture is a huge success against hunger. Without it, we would have seen people die of starvation by the billions, and/or destroy most of the wildlife habitat in Asia and Latin America already. With high-yield farming, we have had small, terrible and unnecessary hunger spasms in a few remote corners of the world—most of them caused by civil strife.

Which do we want for the future?

Notes

[1]D. Gale Johnson, *World Food Problems and Prospects*, Foreign Affairs Study No. 20, American Enterprise Institute, 1975, Washington, D.C., 20018

[2]Bread for the World Institute, 802 Rhode Island Ave., N.E., Washington, D.C., 20018.

[3]"Food Supply: Calories Per Caput Per Day," *FAO Annual Production Yearbook Series*, FAO, Rome.

[4]"Calories Per Capita," *FAO Annual Production Yearbook Series*, FAO, Rome.

[5]UN Administrative Committee on Coordination, Subcommittee on Nutrition, and International Food Policy Research Institute, *Second Report on the World Nutrition Situation*, World Health Organization, Geneva, 1992.

[6]Poleman, Thomas T., *Quantifying the Nutrition Situation in Developing Countries*, Cornell Food Research Institute Studies 18, No. 1, 1981.

[7]Cheryl Gray, *Food Consumption Parameters for Brazil and Their Application to Food Policy*, International Food Policy Research Institute Research Report No. 32, Washington, D.C. 1982.

[8]Urban and Trueblood, *World Population by Country and Region, 1950-2050*, U.S. Department of Agriculture, Washington, D.C., 1993.

[9]Ansley Coale, *Rapid Population Change in China, 1952-82*, National Academy Press, 1984; and Ashton et al., "Famine in China, 1958-61," *Population and Development Review*, Vol. 10, December 1984, pp. 613-645.

[10]"Cereal Production," *FAO Annual Production Yearbook* series, op. cit.

[11]Poleman, *Quantifying the Nutrition Situation in Developing Countries*, op. cit.

[12]Taylor and Greenough, "Control of Diarrheal Diseases," *Annual Review of Public Health*, 10: 221-44, 1989. See also *Proceedings of the Third International Conference on Oral Rehydration Therapy*, Sponsored by the U.S. Agency for International Development, The UN Children's Fund and the World Health Organization, Washington, D.C., 1989.

[13]Dr. David Seckler, "Malnutrition," *Western Journal of Economics* 5, no. 12, December 1980, pp. 219-26.

[14]Jane Fonda, "High Time for Some Population Intelligence," *E, The Environmental Magazine*, Vol. V, No. 1, January/February 1994, pp. 22-24.

[15]Carolyn Lochhead, "Data Don't Back Claims of Activists," *Washington Times*, July 27, 1988, p. F5.

[16]Christopher Jencks, *The Homeless*, Harvard University Press, Cambridge, 1994. Jencks finds that about 25 percent of the U.S. homeless are suffering from mental illness, 33 percent from alcohol abuse, and many more from other dysfunctions such as schizophrenia. He says "the

spread of homelessness among single adults was a by-product of five related changes: the elimination of involuntary [psychiatric] commitment, the eviction of mental hospital patients who had nowhere to go, the advent of crack cocaine, increases in long-term joblessness, and political restrictions on the creation of flophouses. Among families, three factors appear to have been important: the spread of single motherhood, the erosion of welfare recipients' purchasing power, and perhaps crack." Cited in a book review by Douglas Besharov, "Book World," *Washington Post*, July 10, 1994.

[17]Budget Office, Food and Nutrition Service, U.S. Department of Agriculture, September 1994.

[18]R. Adams et al., "Global Climate Change and U.S. Agriculture," *Nature*, 345:219-244, 1990.

9

Organic Farming Can't Save the Environment

MYTHMAKERS SAY:

"Shouldn't we . . . having concluded that we are being asked to take senseless and frightening risks . . . no longer accept the counsel of those who tell us that we must fill our world with poisonous chemicals; we should look about and see what other course is open to us."

Rachel Carson, *Silent Spring*, p. 278

". . . [T]he choice we have as consumers is not between chemically treated fruits and vegetables and no food at all, as some would have us believe. The choice before us is between chemically treated food and produce grown without the use of toxic chemicals. Alternative agriculture is a promise for the future. We have excellent evidence that it is efficient, productive and profitable."

Susan Cooper of the Coalition Against the Misuse of Pesticides, "Do Farm Chemicals Pose 'Unnecessary Risks?'", *Global Food Progress*, Hudson Institute, 1991

"We need a second Green Revolution that will focus on the needs of the Third World's poor, increase the productivity of small farms with low input agricultural methods, and promote environmentally sound policies and practices."

Vice President Al Gore, *Earth in the Balance*, Houghton Mifflin, New York, 1992, p. 322

REALITY SAYS:

"When the first organic wheat is harvested next year, Mr. Lister expects a yield of around 4 tonnes a hectare. Conventionally grown

milling wheat . . . yields 8-9 tonnes a hectare."
> David Blackwell, "Green Field Site in Essex," *Financial Times*,
> December 5, 1991, Commodities and Agriculture page

"The United States has about 28 percent of the *organic* nitrogen needed to sustain current farm production."
> Conclusion from Gilbertson et al., *Animal Waste Utilization on Cropland and Pastureland*, U.S. Department of Agriculture, 1979

The secret is out. On any broad basis, organic farming is unsustainable.

Environmental activists have focused worldwide discussion on the issue of "sustainable" food production. They have charged that high-yield farming's high-powered seeds are more susceptible to pests than the traditional "landrace" varieties; that irrigation water supplies are running out; that soil erosion is stealing fertility from the

PEST DAMAGE—Few of today's consumers have ever seen the sort of damage that pests can inflict on crops. After this corn borer weakens the cornstalk it falls over, and the ear of corn it would have produced is lost.

fields; that pesticides cannot continue to cope with the insects and diseases; and that chemical-based farming will ruin soils and increase cancer rates among consumers.

None of these charges against high-yield farming is true. That's fortunate for the world, because organic farming offers no solution to the world's food or environmental problems.

Organic farming uses no manmade chemicals. It not only does without synthetic pesticides, but also foregoes manmade fertilizers. The organic producers believe that pesticides are dangerous to humans and the environment. They say manmade nitrogen is bad for soils—though all nitrogen is elemental and chemically identical.

Organic farmers *do* use pesticides. They allow themselves the use of "natural" pesticides such as sulfur, a natural biopesticide called *Bacillus thuringiensis*, and pyrethrins (a chlorinated pest killer that is the natural product of a plant flower). Most organic farmers spray more pesticide, more often, than non-organic farmers.

Mainstream farmers use large amounts of both pesticides and manmade fertilizers. In the U.S., pesticide use has increased from a little over 300 million pounds of active ingredient in 1964 to more than 800 million pounds per year in the latter 1980s.

Insecticide use has actually dropped in recent years, from more than 100 million pounds in 1964 to about 70 million pounds in the 1980s. New low-volume compounds and relatively lower crop prices have both had an impact in the decline.

The use of herbicides (chemical weed killers) has expanded, however, from only 70 million pounds in 1970 to nearly 500 million pounds per year in the late 1980s.[1] Since then, the level of pesticide active ingredients has remained roughly stable.[2]

The chemical intensity of mainstream farming has unquestionably been raised by the government's price support and cropland diversion programs. These programs have had the effect of taking some of the land inputs away from farmers, at the same time raising price incentives for more output.

The big recent increase in farming's chemical intensity, however, has been due to the increased use of herbicides in new conservation tillage farming systems—which radically reduce both costs and soil erosion. The new tillage systems are being used on perhaps 100 million acres of U.S. cropland, including a high proportion of the most erodible crop acres.

Degrading the Environment with Organic Farming

The day may come when we'll understand biology and ecology well enough at the level of cells and molecules to make organic farming a high-yield success. The new science of molecular biology is beginning to peel away some of the layers of mystery now. But that in-depth knowledge is still at least decades away.

Until then, organic farming will produce far lower and far more erratic yields of many crops than science-based high-yield farming. Because of its lower yields, organic farming will thus force tillage of more crop acres to produce a given quantity of food.

With present knowledge levels, no responsible authority or organization should recommend either organic farming or traditional low-yield farming systems as a broad-gauge alternative to high-yield agriculture. In fact, slashing farm chemical usage is likely to produce more soil erosion, more human cancer, and less wildlife habitat. At present, organic farming could not even sustain the fertility of our existing cropland, or protect it effectively from erosion.

Nor do the organic farming boosters offer *any* plan to feed the expanded world population of 2050. That alone makes it a nonstarter, because the rest of the world definitely plans to feed itself one way or another.

Lower Yields on Organic Farms

The yields of field crops from organic farming are only about half as high as those from mainstream high-yield farms—on a total-farm basis. Because of the low yields, any serious global attempt to rely on organic farming would force us to plow down millions of additional square miles of wildlife habitat for crops, legumes, and pasture.

Organic farmers and their advocates often claim to get "yields as good as their neighbors." In fact, the yields from an individual field of organically grown crops *can* be high—if productivity has been "borrowed" in the form of rotation with green manure crops (like clover) or spreading animal manure. I say "borrowing," because the high-yield organic acres are either lowering the cropping intensity or taking manure from feedlots or pasture acres. One famous "low-input" farm uses 18 tons of manure and municipal sludge per acre—plus some commercial fertilizer!

A set of organic and low-input farms was presented in *Alternative Agriculture*, a book published in 1989 by the National Research Council. Two points made there were particularly illustrative. First, the book's Iowa corn-soybean farm (The Thompson Farm) had corn and soybean yields comparable to those of other farms in the area—when it grew corn and beans. But two years out of five each field was in oats or meadow and thus virtually out of effective crop production. Second, the California rice farm in the book had high yields—but could produce them only every other year. During the off year the land was put in a combination of legumes and fallow to build fertility.

A South Dakota Organic Farm

I recently talked with an organic farming consultant who stated that he could point me to a number of organic farms with high yields. The first of these farmers I reached was in South Dakota. He reported a number of telling points:

- His first year of normal rotation would be a crop of oats interseeded with red clover. He reported his oats yielded about 60 to 100 bushels per acre. (Surprisingly, the state's average oat yield average was only about 50 bushels.) Mainstream farmers would probably rotate corn and soybeans, regarding oats as too low-yielding and low-value to claim field space.
- His second year, the farmer harvested two cuttings of hay, and plowed down the third cutting to provide nitrogen. (Mainstream farmers would take three cuttings of hay and might add some chemical nitrogen the next year.)
- The third year, the organic farmer would plant popcorn. He got nearly as much popcorn per acre as the neighboring farms (about 50-60 bushels). He said he'd given up growing field

corn, because his yields were only about half as high as his neighbors'. (The world needs only a small acreage of popcorn.)

- The fourth year was the most profitable in the rotation. The organic farmer grew soybeans, got yields comparable to those of his neighbors—and got double the price (from a maker of organic tofu).
- The farm produced "natural" beef (meaning the farmer did not use drugs to treat any animals that got sick). He did not produce "organic" beef, he said, because that would have forced him to raise his own low-yielding organic field corn. This way, he could feed his cattle the cheaper chemically supported corn and soybeans from his neighbors' farms.

Over and over, we find organic yields, measured over time and over the whole farm, run far less than the yields from mainstream farms.

Organic Farming Needs a Crop Yield Breakthrough

If, as organic farming advocates sometimes claim, we could grow high yields of the crops the world demands without expensive off-farm inputs, all farmers would want to do it. They would save money and increase their profits. Presently, however, we cannot.

It makes little sense to applaud an organic farmer who gets county-average yields by importing huge amounts of animal manure and/or urban sewage sludge onto his acres. We already don't have enough organic nitrogen to go around.

If that organic farmer isn't doubling county-average yields, he isn't part of the wave of tomorrow, because the best mainstream farmers are doubling county averages. Or the new-wave organic farmer could be matching the county average with half the organic nitrogen. Otherwise, he's not part of the organic breakthrough we need.

Of course, organic farmers *can* make money. They get vastly higher prices. Their chemical costs are lower than those of mainstream farmers (even though, as mentioned above, they do use sprays, and quite a lot of them). However, their labor and management costs per acre are almost certainly higher, and often their labor constraints confine them to low production volumes.

But we're not worried here about organic farm incomes. The question is how to insure high and efficient yields per acre which can meet the needs of tomorrow and leave room for as much wildlife as we have today.

I freely concede that mainstream farmers have often used chemicals more heavily than was really necessary. They were encouraged in their prophylactic pesticide use by a poorly conceived set of government subsidies. That's not the key point either.

The key point is that mainstream farmers can safely step up their intensity and yields as the world needs it. Can organic farmers?

To be part of the solution, organic farmers need a productivity breakthrough. They need to produce more food with fewer natural resources and less erosion than organic farming would today produce if it was extended to the less ideal lands.

Our natural resources are scarce. We have alternative ways to get yields, but we have no alternative on wildlife.

Until now, organic farmers haven't thought yields were that important. To many organic producers, the important thing is how few chemicals they can use and still produce *something*. To many others, the size of the price premium they can get from frightened consumers is the key.

But the amount of land we use to produce food in the world governs how much land is left over from farming for forests, wildlife and other nonfarm uses. That's why minimizing the amount of land needed for crops is *far* more important to maintaining wildlife and the natural ecology than eliminating chemicals.

The Shortfall in Organic Plant Nutrients

Low yields are only one disappointment about organic farming. Its biggest shortcoming is the global shortage of "natural" nitrogen fertilizer.

Experts at the U.S. Department of Agriculture have calculated that the available animal manure and sustainable biomass resources in the U.S. would provide only about one-third of the plant nutrients needed to support current food production.[3]

Most of the world has far less pasture and manure per capita than the U.S. Globally, we may have less than 20 percent of the organic plant nutrients needed to sustain current food output. The only visible way to make up the shortfall would be to displace much more wildlife for legume crops.

There is no precise way to calculate the food shortfall or the wildlife encroachment which organic farming would force on the world, but it would be massive—hundreds of millions of tons of grain per year, and/or millions of square miles of wildlife.

This shortfall in plant nutrients should come as no great surprise. Organic farming deliberately does without the off-farm inputs used in most high-yield farming. Instead, organic farmers deliberately put a heavier burden on farming's "natural" resources.

MYTHMAKER:

"Farm Achieves Natural Balance: Earthworms, Songbirds, Profit Abound After Chemicals Forsaken."
                    Washington Post headline, March 1, 1987, p. A3

Reality Comment: The accompanying article was written by Ward Sinclair, who left the *Post* to become an organic farmer. The body of the story reveals that the farm's yields have gone down sharply with the "natural balance"—but the farmer is getting much higher prices, from consumers frightened of chemicals. It is almost certain that there were songbirds on the farm even when it used chemicals, since virtually all farms have songbirds.

Organic fans reassure us that "lots" of organic fertilizer is being wasted. But they apparently don't realize the magnitude of the challenge they face. Where, for example, might we find additional organic fertilizers?

Is there any animal manure that's being stored away in silos?

No. Hundreds of millions of tons of manure are produced in a year, but it's already being spread on fields either by farmers or by the animals themselves.

What about all the crop biomass that's left on the fields; couldn't that be turned into high-quality compost?

Yes, but that biomass is already being incorporated back into the soil with the current farming systems—quickly. Incorporating it into the soil probably captures more of the biomass' value than would composting (because nitrogen generally escapes over time and during the composting process).

Nor would composting and redistributing maintain all of the soil erosion benefits we currently gain from incorporating the crop residue under conservation tillage systems.

What about using urban sewage sludge more broadly on crops?

It would take 50 times the nation's current total of sewage sludge, all dedicated to farm application, to replace the nitrogen currently provided by chemical fertilizers. All of the urban sewage in the country equals only 2 percent of the nitrogen currently being applied in commercial fertilizers.[4]

The EPA's National Sewage Sludge Survey for 1988 indicates that perhaps 25 percent of the nation's sewage sludge is already being used for agricultural fertilizer.[5] Perhaps another 20-40 percent could be retargeted for agriculture, but at a cost. First, it is expensive to transport the sludge, and many big cities are not near major farm production centers. Transportation costs can be very high for wet sludge. Second, the sludge is "perishable;" the nitrogen quickly dissipates into the air if it isn't handled quickly. Third, unless the city has a strong industrial pretreatment program, the sludge will carry high concentrations of heavy metals. Thus, overuse of sludge can result in food crops with abnormally high levels of the heavy metals. Liming the fields correctly can prevent much of the heavy metal uptake, but this takes careful management and a good deal of cost. Otherwise the food grown could carry harmful levels of heavy metals into consumers' systems—a far worse risk than chemically derived nitrogen.

It remains a puzzle how the eco-activists can be so fearful of pesticides and so casual about the use of human waste as fertilizer. Some organic farms are reportedly using as much as 50 tons per acre of sewage sludge *on vegetable crops*! When both the disease potential and the heavy metals are taken into account, sludge looks, if anything, more dangerous than pesticides. (Neither, of course, ranks with highway accidents as a life threat, but both need to be handled properly.)

Environmentalists claim they can gain 30 million tons of compostable materials from current urban landfill waste. Won't that help?

Thirty million tons of compost sounds like a lot—until you compare it with the 2 billion tons of manure, corn cobs, and other farm waste already being spread annually on American farms.[6] Then the compost just looks like an expensive way to add 1.5 percent to our agricultural biomass.

A recent New Jersey recycling report indicates this "free" compost will cost perhaps $100 per ton just for gathering the compostable material (with the heavy metals still in it) and getting it to the recycling site. We then have to take out the heavy metals (hand sorting?), make it into compost, and haul it to the field. (Separation alone adds $44 to $260 per ton to New Jersey's recycling costs.)[7]

Nor are the costs much offset by savings on landfilling. Even in densely populated New Jersey, the cost of building and maintaining a modern landfill that meets all standards is often less than $10 per ton.[8] Neither New Jersey nor the rest of the U.S. is short of rough wasteland on which to put landfills. The only problem is political—the "Not in My Back Yard" syndrome.

It's hard to see how this major increase in costly off-farm biomass would make us environmentally better off than using commercial fertilizers.

A recent issue of the *Amicus Journal*, published by the pro-recycling Natural Resources Defense Council, highlighted some of the key constraints in using compost.[9]

- "Until the late 1980s, composting was set aside as a costly, impractical solution, but over the past few years it has gained new appeal."
- "We are luckier than most urban regions. If the market for the compost is not within 50 to 100 miles, the costs will not pencil out" (according to a local recycling manager).
- ". . . the remainder, which is composted, is likely to contain heavy metals, especially lead from batteries, watches, calculators, TVs, oil filters and wine bottle wrappers, according to a study by Cornell University."
- "The 30 million tons of compost we eventually make will have to go to agricultural and . . . (forest) lands, so it makes sense that we go for the cleanest compost possible. . . ."

More Soil Erosion from Organic Fields

Why would organic farming mean a major increase in soil erosion? Organic farmers have always claimed they care *more* about
soil preservation than the average mainstream farmer. Unfortunately
for the organic enthusiasts, however, organic farming now carries
huge and inevitable soil erosion penalties.

Due to its low yields, organic farming would force us to plow
millions of additional acres that are generally more fragile than those
where our farm production is currently concentrated.

During the 20th century, mainstream American farming has radically increased its crop yields. Average U.S. corn yields, in fact,
have increased about sixfold. For most crops in prime farming regions, crop yield potentials have at least tripled. This tripling of yields
has let us take those millions of acres of steep, erodible land out of
crop production.

The environmental movement has failed to grant credit for these
erosion reductions. But if we shifted to organic farming systems as
the bases for all of our food production, we would see big tracts of
erodible soils put back in crops to replace the lost productivity. The
streams of my Shenandoah Valley might run red again with the clay
stripped from its steep hillsides.

Organic farmers' second erosion disadvantage is that they deliberately ignore modern weed-killing chemicals. Organic farmers don't
use conservation tillage or no-till farming, the soil-safest farming
systems ever devised, because both systems depend on herbicides
for weed control.

They leave themselves only mechanical tillage for weed control.
Hoeing and cultivating can kill weeds, but they inevitably leave the
soil open to erosion. These are "bare-earth" farming systems. Organic farming leaves far more of its soil bare to wind and water far
more of the time than the best modern high-yield farming systems.

The Thompson low-input farm in Iowa uses ridge tillage to minimize weed competition and selects soybean varieties that are tall and
fast-emerging to get canopy shading as quickly as possible. Still, the
farm has to rotary hoe its crops at least twice, which means a long
window of opportunity for soil erosion.[10]

Organic farmers are trying to surmount these obstacles. They

have always paid close attention to soil tilth, which has helped mod-
estly to reduce their erosion rates. They also tend to use conservation practices like contour farming and strip cropping to minimize
their erosion losses.

Try as they will, however, organic farmers have nothing to offer
that is nearly so powerful against soil erosion as the new conservation tillage and no-till farming systems. Organic farmers' mainstream
competitors—armed with herbicides—have made a quantum leap in
sustainability. A 90 percent reduction in erosion on the 39 million
U.S. acres farmed with no-till systems represents a *huge* cut in soil
risks. So does a 65 percent cut in soil losses on the 66 million American acres farmed with conservation tillage.

The Government Bias Against Organic Farming

Admittedly, the U.S. government helped to rig the game against
low-input farming: government subsidies offer high price supports
for corn, and no price support for legumes like alfalfa and clover.

The organic fans claim they can make up the difference between
their crop yields and the chemically supported fields with high yields
of "total digestible nutrients" from legumes like alfalfa and clover.
But the government doesn't offer a legume price support, so the
organic farms are less profitable.

South Dakota State University researchers say that organic rotations produced more total digestible nutrients per acre in their comparison tests than either conventional or ridge-till systems.[11] (Much
of the legume production was irrigated, however.)

These researchers say that the legumes could have supported
more beef production than the chemically assisted corn in the other
systems, and that the legumes could provide most of the diet for
gestating sows and 25 percent of the diet for market hogs.

It is true—in America—that we could use a lot more legumes in
our livestock feeding than we do. But we don't seem to have a market for the legumes. Even in America, the livestock industries are
hooked on corn. It may be the government's bias toward corn, or
the extra processing/transport costs for legume feeds, or the high
energy value of corn. Whatever the cause, it is a bias that cannot be
overlooked. Even the South Dakota State researchers who offer the

prescription admit that the nation's livestock industries would have to be radically reconfigured to use the added legumes; the animals would need to be fed closer to where the legumes are produced.

If there were no corn price support, it is entirely possible that American farmers would use more legume rotations and thus have less need for pesticides and chemical fertilizers. They might even feed the legumes to more livestock on their own farms or their neighbors', and thus recover a substantial part of the role now played by big cattle feedlots (and increasingly by hog hotels). But why is my South Dakota organic farmer fattening his cattle on purchased corn instead of his own clover or alfalfa?

Nor will alfalfa feed the rest of the world. The only countries which use any significant tonnage of feed grains that alfalfa might displace are the U.S., Western Europe, and Japan. There's also serious question about the potential role for legume rotation in hog producing countries that depend on multiple cropping each year, like China and India. Finally, the legumes take lots of moisture, and many countries have neither the rainfall nor the irrigation.

What About Low-Input Sustainable Farming?

LISA ("low-input sustainable agriculture") is the latest catchphrase in agricultural research policy. It is called low-input to differentiate it from both organic farming and from the mainstream farmers' heavy use of off-farm inputs.

LISA is attempting to find a middle ground between the chemical intensity of mainstream farming and the organic farmers' total rejection of manmade chemicals. LISA farmers try to minimize chemical use by doing more crop rotation, making fuller use of integrated pest management systems, and by using more crop scouting and banding of chemicals. They stop short of a full organic commitment.

Few farmers actually follow LISA currently because they would sacrifice income from Federal price supports and deficiency payments to do so. For example, South Dakota State researchers compared two adjoining farms from 1985-89. The conventional farm was significantly more profitable, but most of the difference was due to Federal farm payments.[12]

LISA is more productive than organic farming, and may well be more efficient than much of the high-chemical farming which has been stimulated by price supports and setaside. In the long term, however, even LISA will have to be critically examined in terms of its output per acre, and thus its ability to preserve wildlife habitat.

At the present time, neither animal manure, nor compost, nor crop rotation, nor integrated pest management nor LISA can feed tomorrow's world and still preserve its wildlife—without chemistry.

Integrated pest management is also a fine thing and should be used as widely as possible. A high percentage of our farms are using some form of IPM. But even IPM is dependent in the long term on pesticides to knock out the big pest infestations which eventually and inevitably occur. The true advantage of IPM is that it can cut the cost of producing crops, not that it cuts pesticide use.

Higher Cancer Risks from Organic Farming?

Organic farming's final big shortcoming is in the production of fruits and vegetables.

Produce crops look just as succulent and delicious to pests as to people. A wider variety of insects, disease organisms, fungi, and microorganisms attack fruits and vegetables than any other crops. Most organic fruit and vegetable production is barely able to cope with these pests, even though virtually all organic growers spray their crops with "organic pesticides."

Organic producers manage quite well with *some* produce crops. Red raspberries, for example, have relatively few pest problems. Some grape growers apparently manage effectively most of the time with mainly organic methods. Some Florida citrus producers, whose fruit is headed for processing rather than the fresh market, are using organic methods to cut production costs; they can accept fruit that is less attractive on the outside.

Organic techniques are used effectively by dedicated gardeners on small garden tracts all over the country.

Generally, however, organic production of fruits and vegetables means lower yields, higher labor costs, and/or less attractive produce.

This is the logical outcome. After all, if there were no yield/cost benefits from putting expensive chemicals on the crops, *no*

China's Organic Farming Disaster

China attempted to follow an organic farming system in the 1960s under Mao Tse-Tung. Mao wanted to increase food production without investing in fertilizer production or paying for food imports.

Under his direction, the Chinese intensified their traditional efforts to collect all animal manure and nightsoil. They also gathered as much biomass from their hillsides as they could to add mulch to the rice and wheat fields. This organic farming effort was implemented with all of the intensity that one of the most coercive regimes in world history could muster—and with 600 million pairs of hands. The major result of this intensive organic effort was to strip the hillsides of their vegetation, generate a massive increase in soil erosion—and produce an agonizingly small increase in food production.

The FAO Production Yearbooks show the story in stark black and white: Food production per capita rose only 5 percent during the decade of the 1960s, and increased only 1 percent annually during the whole 1960-76 period. By 1970 China offered its consumers only 1,984 calories per day, compared to a developing-country average of 2,103. Much of that (millions of tons of wheat in most years) had to be imported.

China had suffered a major famine (30 million deaths) in 1959/60 due to its poor farm policies. By the late 1970s, China still had 200 million malnourished citizens (its own estimate). Grain production per capita had virtually stagnated. Soil erosion was on a collision course with population growth.

The Chinese Communist government was shaken to its core by the unrelenting pressure to deliver more grain. The country lacked the exports to pay for heavy food imports on a continuing basis.

In 1978, China began one of the most dramatic shifts in agricultural policy the world has ever seen. The first change was a decision to make massive investments in chemical fertilizer. Chinese fertilizer applications, which had risen slowly from 4 million tons to 7 million in the 1970-77 period, jumped to more than 17 million tons in the following seven years.[13] The second major change was to scrap China's big communal farms and lease its farmland back to families. (Mao was dead by this time; he probably would not have

Continued on next page

farmers would use them. (The power of chemical-company advertising simply isn't great enough to sway businessmen with sharp pencils—and that is what the surviving farmers certainly are.)

Organic and non-organic farmers also tend to have big differences in their labor and management costs per acre. Though the organic farmers seem to discount their labor, they are often confined to smaller acreages of crops, which limits their incomes.

If organic costs were not higher, then the price premiums that organic production commands would bring forth a much larger stream of organic output.

Overall, organic farmers have *not* demonstrated that they can produce the rising commercial quantities of reasonably priced, attractive fruits and vegetables needed for a growing world population.

THE MYTH OF ORGANIC PEST CONTROL:

"As steward of a self-sustaining garden, your first job is to recognize that the forces in your garden will never be in 'perfect' balance. There will always be some plant damage, itself from severe damage from most pests most of the time. Such natural defense is

---

permitted such a radical departure from the Communist precept of state farm ownership.)

The result of the two changes was the biggest surge in food production ever seen, anywhere in the world. Grain output soared from 242 million tons in 1976 to 283 million tons in 1980 and 389 million tons in 1990!

Because China increased its grain yields from an average of 2.4 tons per hectare in 1970 to 4.2 tons in 1990, it produced this massive gain in food without a major increase in grain plantings. China used 88 million hectares for grain in 1970, 104 million in 1979, and had cut grain plantings back to 93 million hectares by 1990.[14]

Today, China's high yield farming sustains its population with a fully adequate diet—for the first time since at least the Communist takeover in the 1950s.

promoted by four major factors: sun, water, soil, and air circulation.

Pest	Organic Remedy
Colorado potato beetle	1. Use row covers in early season.
	2. Handpick immediately when sighted and crush adults and egg masses. Very effective control.
	3. Apply thick organic mulch to impede movement of overwintered adults to plants. Beetles walk more than fly during early season.
cabbage maggot	1. Use row covers early in season.
	2. Maggots don't like alkaline environment. Circle plants with a mixture of lime and wood ashes, moistened to prevent blowing.
aphid	1. This may be a symptom of too much nitrogen or pruning.
	2. Use row covers.
	3. Control aphids . . . with sticky bands, sticky yellow traps, or yellow pans filled with water."

Tanya Denckla, *Gardening at a Glance: The Organic Gardener's Handbook on Vegetables, Fruits, Nuts, and Herbs,* Wooden Angel Publishing, Franklin, West Virginia, 1991. Recommended by Bob Thomson, host of the PBS-TV "Victory Garden" show

Reality Comment: Squashing potato beetles by hand is very effective, in the sense that the squashed bugs are certainly dead. But there can be a million beetles and egg masses per acre in a potato field; catching and squashing so many is not cost-effective. Nor does the ring of lime and wood ash have a strong history of providing cabbage heads free of

RUBES ®   By Leigh Rubin

While environmentally friendly, pesticide-free crop dusting has proven to be extremely labor-intensive.

maggots from the ubiquitous cabbage moth. Few urban consumers have shown a willingness to shake out the maggots and eat the cabbage.

Poisoning Topsoil?

Dr. Sharon Ingham, an associate professor in botany and plant pathology at Oregon State University is one of those who claims that farm chemicals poison soils. She recently said, "We can keep dumping fertilizer and chemicals on farm land, but at what cost to the rest of the ecosystem?" (She is trying to set up a "sustainable" farming research program at her university.)

She says both her own research and that of other scientists has shown that the concentration of nutrients in chemical fertilizers kills many of the bacteria and other organisms in soils. Such biologically "dead" soil, she says, is less able to hold agricultural chemicals that are applied to it later. Fertilizers, herbicides, and pesticides then leach more quickly into surrounding land and water.

She says organic fertilizers would be preferable to chemical ones. In her view, just focusing on yields is "simple-minded."[15] Dr. Ingham is apparently worried that we will have too few soil microbes and earthworms under our crop fields. But the problem is self-limiting. If too much fertilizer kills too many useful soil organisms, crop yields will decline. Expensive fertilizer will be wasted. Farmers will change their systems.

In fact, one reason why conservation tillage and no-till farming systems are sweeping the mechanized agricultures of the world is that they *encourage* more soil microbes and more earthworms. These farming systems don't disturb the lower soil profile with plowshares, and provide year-round supplies of nutrients from decomposing cover crops and crop residue. The killed sod in no-till fields makes especially fine habitat for earthworms and soil microbes. The farmers get yield gains as a result.

Oddly, Dr. Ingham seems not at all worried about a much more serious problem: The fact that the world has far too little of the organic fertilizers she favors to support world food needs.

Due to the short supplies of animal manure and crop biomass, we might not feed even *half* of the world's current human population without a radical world diet change or a sharp reduction in wildlife habitat.

Dr. Ingham is not thinking globally.

If the yields in chemically supported fields were going down, Dr. Ingham would have a powerful argument. If high-yield farming was creating serious dangers for our groundwater or wildlife populations outside the crop fields, she would have an important argument.

But hers is a relatively minor quibble, not an argument. Fostering soil microbes for their own sake ranks far down the world's list of food and farming priorities.

What About Biological Controls?

The world has been searching for biological controls to suppress noxious pests for more than 100 years. (The boll weevil was an early target.) Some successes have been achieved:

• The biggest success to date has been in West Africa, against the cassava mealybug and the green spider mite. The two cassava pests emigrated from South America and

---

The Long-Term Record of the Morrow Plots

The Morrow Plots at the University of Illinois have been farmed since 1876.

The University says, "The Morrow Plots are the oldest agronomic research plots in the United States, and include the oldest continuous corn plot in the world."

They have been farmed with a variety of crop rotations and fertilizer regimes. The plots received no fertility treatments between 1888 and the mid-1930s, and their yields gradually declined. In 1955, most of the plots began to receive annual applications of liquid nitrogen, phosphorus, and potassium. Corn yields have roughly tripled since.

The continuous corn plot which has received no fertilizer is still today producing just about the 50 bushels per acre which it produced in 1888—despite the higher yield potential of the modern seeds now being planted on it. The nutrient constraint is holding firm.

Another plot recently grew 200 bushels per acre because it received adequate fertilizer—and despite the fact it has now grown corn continuously for over a century. Putting it another way, the yields quadrupled during a century of continuous intensive cropping.[16]

---

became serious threats to Africa's key root crop. Researchers from the International Institute for Tropical Agriculture (IITA) in Nigeria led the attack, searching out, propagating, and distributing a set of natural predators to suppress the mealybug and mite. The effort won the King Badouin international agricultural research prize in 1990. It was particularly important in Africa because cassava growers there could not afford to use pesticides, even to protect one of their most important food sources. It was relatively easy to do because there were highly developed predators of the two pests in their South American home territories.

• In America, biological parasites have been introduced to control the alfalfa weevil. They work, but only well enough to *reduce* the amount of spraying the growers must do, not eliminate it.

Unfortunately, it is not very likely that biological controls can substitute for very much of the pest control currently provided by pesticides. Biological controls are generally too narrowly targeted to give broad, cost-effective pest control, according to Leonard Gianessi of Resources for the Future. Gianessi recently addressed that problem in the National Academy of Science quarterly, *Issues in Science and Technology*.[17]

Gianessi notes that a pathogenic fungus is likely to be effective on a single weed species, while an herbicide can sometimes control hundreds of kinds of weeds.

East Coast apple growers can use one fungicide to control nine significant diseases of apples. Even if successful biological controls were developed for eight of these diseases, the apple growers might still have to use the fungicide to control the ninth.

Gianessi says just in the United States thousands of pest species infest 80 to 100 crops in many different regions. Thus, there are hundreds of thousands of possible combinations of pest, crop and region that researchers would have to target to replace any particular deployment of one of the roughly 200 active pesticide ingredients now in use.

There is also a problem with releasing and encouraging new biological controls. They too can have side effects on the local ecologies. Dr. Francis Howarth of the J. Linsley Grassit Center for Research in Entomology believes that introduced biological control organisms have themselves led to the extinction of nearly 100 species worldwide.

Being "natural" is obviously not enough.

MYTHMAKER:

"The Hyper-Expansionist scenario seems to be the route our society is now traveling. HE is a path by which the agri-food industry could further increase its control over the natural world and one where nature's long-term reliability would be replaced by clever technologies promising unparalleled abundance at merely the cost of computerized vigilance. This path implies systems that will demand the monitoring of fallible sensors by bored humans serving the giant corporations that control the food system. . . . We are not feeding the world, we are robbing the world. *I believe that localized agriculture is needed in order to make agri-*

culture more sustainable, but also because I simply can't imagine how we can teach people to protect the resources that produce their food unless somehow those resources are closer to home" [emphasis added].
Dr. Joan Dye Gussow, professor of nutrition at Columbia
University in New York City, interviewed in *Safe
Food News*, Winter 1993, pp. 8-10

Reality Comment: Dr. Gussow may be a very competent nutrition-ist. She does not, however, seem to understand much about how food is produced.

First, she implies that big corporations produce our food, when the truth is that ninety-plus percent of America's farm output is produced by family farms. (Many of the family farms have incorporated under the subchapter S rules for small businesses, mainly for inheritance tax reasons.)

Second, (and more embarrassing for a nutritionist) Dr. Gussow's local-production option would severely restrict our access to fresh fruits and vegetables for about 90 percent of the year.

Third, her "local and organic" production preference would mean famine for billions, stunted children for the survivors, and the loss of huge tracts of wildlife.

Fourth, she gives no indication how having city folks observe their neighborhood farms is going to result in better farm resource use.

Finally, how is her concrete island of New York going to feed itself on her model? Will New York use its own sewage to fertilize former parking lots, re-plowed for vegetable gardening? Will multistory park-ing garages be converted to feedlots, with the waste collecting in the subbasements for recycling?

Viability of High-Yield Versus Landrace Seeds

Opponents of high-yield farming claim that modern high-yield-ing seeds are such tender, exotic plants that they will be wiped out by natural disasters, leaving mankind to wish it had hung onto the old seed varieties.

The truth is that the high-yielding varieties are tougher than the old seeds. Much of their yield advantage comes from having pest resistance and stress tolerance that the old seeds lack. (American farmers have harvested good corn crops recently in years which would have been too dry to produce good yields before World War II, because of the added drought tolerance of the seeds.)

The old farmer-saving-the-best-seeds selection process had its good points. It might even have come up with the breeds we have now—but not very quickly. The real impact of modern seed breeding has been to speed the selective breeding process. Instead of tripling yields over 1000 years, we have done it in 35. That has been rapid enough to prevent the massive famines that the skeptics have been predicting for so long.

It is also true, however, that we need to preserve the genes in the old seeds. And we can't expect them to survive in the wild; they're just as dependent on man as the high-yielding varieties. That's why there is a major effort underway to save the landrace varieties in seed banks around the world. (And these efforts, too, need more funding!)

The Global Perspective on Organic Farming

It may be difficult for America's urban residents to understand why organic farming could not feed the current human population, let alone the one expected in 2050. They are continually hearing about farm surpluses and setaside cropland. But bringing back America's setaside cropland would equal only two years of the average increase which world farming must achieve in each of the next 40 years if the global food challenge is to be met. And bringing back the setaside would be a onetime gain!

The United States is one of the few countries in the world that could provide a quality diet for its expected population in 2050 *with* organic farming. But even the land-rich U.S. would have to rein in the 40 percent of its farm production which is now exported to countries less richly endowed for agriculture.

We are thus left with the same major question about both organic and LISA farming: How much land can we spare for low-yield agriculture?

The answer is that we can spare a *small* amount of land for organic farmers and chemical-free experiments—if we continue to pursue high-yield research and technology at the same time.

By way of analogy, we can also spare *some* farming resources to produce a few ranch-mink coats. (The mink eat lots of fishmeal and soy protein which we would otherwise need for human nutrition.)

With present knowledge, neither organic farming nor mink coats can be supported except as part of a much larger, more powerful *chemically assisted* farming system.

AFRICAN REALITY:

"Mr. Norman Borlaug, a prominent agriculturalist . . . told a meeting of the Overseas Development Institute yesterday: 'Some people say that Africa's food problems can be solved without the application of chemical fertilizers. They're dreaming. It's not possible.' He said that the environmentalists advocating traditional farming methods failed to recognize the rapid growth in population expected in the continent. . . . Sub-Saharan Africa had the lowest use of fertilizer in the world and soil nutrients were so low that other efforts to raise crop productivity would not be successful until fertility was improved."

Financial Times, June 10, 1994, p. 26

MYTHICAL REALITY:

"In Germany, 10,000 farmers have converted to organic methods and 2.4 percent of the country's agricultural land is cultivated without the use of artificial fertilizer and pesticides. However, the German government pays the equivalent of [$400] a hectare for farmers to produce in this way, which costs up to 30 percent more than conventional methods."

Financial Times, May 20, 1994, p. 26

Reality Comment: Western Europe, ironically, is paying for this shift to organic farming *because it does lower production*, thereby reducing the farm surplus induced by its high price supports!

Needed: A Radical Middle Ground

For years, I've argued that neither organic farming nor chemically intensive farming as we've known it deserves to dominate our agriculture. Organic gives up too much productivity for a purism that can't be justified by any of the risks we can identify. High-chemical farming, for its part, has high production costs.

What we need is the *radical middle ground*, in which farm-

Biosphere Reality

The crew of the Biosphere 2 recently emerged from two years in their self-contained ecosystem near Tucson, AZ. They had originally planned to spend half their time raising their own food and the other half on scientific experiments.

They never got the chance to do much science.

Insects and plant diseases found their way into the biosphere, and the crew had pledged to fight them without manmade chemicals. Mites ate the beans and potatoes. Powdery mildew shriveled the squash. The natural oils which were supposed to control insects attracted cockroaches, which also infested the living quarters. The sweet potatoes did well—and the crew ate so many that the beta carotene gave some of them orange-tinted skin. Even though 20 percent of the food they ate had been stored in the biosphere before the mission began (for emergencies) the crew lost about 25 pounds each. Hunger was a constant companion, they reported, dominating their thoughts.

---

ers use all of the most effective inputs they can get to get high yields at the lowest economic and environmental costs. What is reasonable? The lowest that will get the job done. How do we discover that? Through open competition, among systems, farms, and countries.

What we truly need is to abandon the old farm subsidies and international farm trade barriers. In America, the subsidies have tried and failed for 60 years to guarantee high net incomes for farmers. Eliminating the price supports and allotments would eliminate the artificial incentives for using chemicals.

Ending the farm trade barriers would also let American farms help provide the extra food that will be needed in an Asia nine times as densely populated as North America.

I think we would also see other benefits—more crop rotation, lower per-unit costs of production, and quite a lot less soil erosion. We might even see more family farmers than we get with price supports that encourage big, debt-leveraged one-man farms.

Free-market, low-cost, high-yield farming is the truly radical middle ground.

But the overriding consideration for the decades ahead will be a rapidly rising level of world demand that will overwhelm the capacities of organic farming, and very likely LISA as well.

Notes

[1]Osteen and Szmedra, *Agricultural Pesticide Use Trends and Policy Issues*, USDA Agricultural Economic Report No. 622, Washington, D.C., 1989.

[2]Arnold Aspelin, *Pesticide Industry Sales and Usage: 1992 and 1993 Market Estimates*, EPA Washington, D.C., June 1994.

[3]Van Dyne and Gilbertson, *Estimating U.S. Livestock and Poultry Manure Nutrient Production*, U.S. Department of Agriculture, ESCS-12, March 1978; and *Animal Waste Utilization on Cropland and Pastureland*, Environmental Protection Agency, Washington, D.C., 1959, EPA-600/2-79-059. The information in these studies is being updated by an expert panel of the Council for Agricultural Science and Technology of Ames, Iowa, led by Dr. A. L. Sutton of the Animal Science Department at Purdue University; Dr. Sutton says the preliminary results indicate that the new CAST findings will be similar to those of the earlier studies. (Personal interviews, 1993 and 1994.)

[4]Calculation by Dr. Steven Graef, director of technical services, Western Carolina Regional Sewage Authority, Greenville, South Carolina, based on "Estimated Mass of Sewage Sludge Disposed Annually," Table I-1, *Federal Register* Vol. 58, No. 32, February 19, 1993, p. 9257.

[5]Estimated by Dr. Steven Graef, op. cit. from *Regulatory Impact Analysis of the Part 503 Sewage Sludge Regulation*, Table I-2, "National Estimates of Number of POTWs and Sewage Sludge Quantity Used or Disposed in 1988 by Use or Disposal Practice," EPA Office of Water, EPA 821-R-93-006, March 1993.

[6]James DeLong, *Wasting Away: Mismanaging Municipal Solid Waste*, Competitive Enterprise Institute Environmental Studies Program, Washington, D.C., May 1994, p. 4. DeLong is a Washington lawyer and consultant. He has served as the research director of the Administrative Conference of the U.S., and on the staffs of the Federal Trade Commission and the U.S. Bureau of the Budget.

[7]Grant Schaumberg and Katherine Doyle, *Wasting Resources to Reduce Waste*: *Recycling in New Jersey*, CATO Institute, Policy Analysis Report No. 202, January 26, 1994, p. 13.

[8]Op. cit., p. 11.

[9]Beth Hanson, "Pass the Humus," *Amicus Journal*, Natural Resources

Defense Council, Vol. 15, No. 3, Fall 1993, pp. 38-42.

[10]"The Thompson Farm," *Alternative Agriculture*, National Research Council, National Academy Press, Washington, D.C. 1989, pp. 308-323.

[11]*Agronomic, Economic and Ecological Relationships in Alternative (Organic) Conventional, and Reduced-Till Farming Systems*, South Dakota State University Bulletin 718, September 1993.

[12]Dobs, Smolik, and Mends, "On-Farm Research Comparing Conventional and Low-Input/Sustainable Agricultural Systems in the Northern Great Plains," Ch. 15 in *Sustainable Agriculture Research and Education in the Field* (G.J. Rice, editor), National Academy Press, Washington, D.C., 1991.

[13]Dr. Bruce Stone, *Chinese Fertilizer Development 1990: Status and Prospects*, International Food Policy Research Institute, Washington, D.C., January 1991.

[14]"Total Grains: Area Yield and Production," *FAO Annual Production Yearbooks*, FAO Rome.

[15]David Wheeler, "Expansion of Agricultural Research Said to Have Fueled Dramatic Increases in Yields of Corn, Rice and Wheat," *The Chronicle of Higher Education*, September 22, 1993, p. A10.

[16]*The Morrow Plots: A Century of Learning*, Agricultural Experiment Station Bulletin 775, University of Illinois, Champaign, Illinois, 1974. Updated through 1992.

[17] Leonard Gianessi, "The Quixotic Quest for Chemical-Free Farming," *Issues In Science and Technology*, National Academy of Sciences, Fall 1993, p. 31.

10

Who Has a Soil Crisis?

MYTHMAKERS SAY:

". . . [E]very ton of fertile topsoil unnecessarily washed away, every hectare claimed by desert sands, every reservoir filled with silt further drains world productivity and spells higher costs for future gains in output."

> Erik P. Eckholm, *Losing Ground: Environmental Stress and World Food Prospects*, Norton, New York, 1976, p. 181

"The long-term social threat posed by uncontrolled soil erosion raises profound questions of intergenerational equity. If our generation persists in mining the soils so that we may eat, many of our children and their children may go hungry as a result."

> Lester Brown and Edward C. Wolf, *Soil Erosion: Quiet Crisis*, Worldwatch Paper 60, Worldwatch Institute, Washington, D.C., September 1984

REALITY SAYS:

". . . If current rates of (U.S.) cropland erosion prevail for 100 years, crop yields will be from 3 to 10 percent lower than they would be otherwise. Yield increases (resulting from technology) that are modest by historical standards would much more than compensate for such a loss."

> Pierre Crosson, one of the world's top soil erosion experts, reported in a special issue of *Scientific American* on "Managing Planet Earth," September 1989[1]

". . . [P]ractices such as mulching, manuring, low tillage, contour cultivation and agroforestry can frequently reduce surface runoff of water, sediment loss and erosion by 50 percent and more. These techniques are not yet widely used."

World Bank, Development and the Environment,
1992 World Development Report

"Satellites Expose Myth of Marching Sahara"

Heading of article in Science News, July 20, 1991

High-yield farming is producing a triumph over man's age-old enemy, soil erosion.

For centuries, man has accepted relatively high levels of soil erosion as the price of growing food. That trade-off is no longer necessary. Modern farming systems are radically cutting soil erosion on farms around the world—by raising yields so less land has to be open to erosion, and by using herbicides to kill weeds instead of plows and cultivators. These new farming systems preserve topsoil, encourage soil microorganisms and build organic content in our soils better than any previous mainstream farming systems in history.

Research is also providing new low-erosion farming systems like tied ridges and alley cropping for the Third World as well.

An impressed agronomist said it well: "Do you realize that now, for the first time in ten thousand years, people can grow crops without destroying the land?"[2]

These technical breakthroughs will permit the world to sustainably produce record-high yields of food and fiber from its best and safest cropland—with record-low losses to soil erosion. In the future, we should even be able to *increase* topsoil depths on our best farmlands, while carrying forward intensive, high-yield farming.

Remember, soil erosion *is* an inevitable, ongoing natural process. It has already shrunk the elderly Appalachian Mountains into a tiny vestige of the towering peaks they once were. Over millions of years, it will turn the Rocky Mountains into a set of foothills. And it will take all of today's topsoil off our fields.

What no one is telling our children is that the same unstoppable processes that *erode* topsoil also *create* topsoil. Sunlight, bacteria, moisture, and earthworms are just as powerful as wind and water. They're just more subtle.

The question is not whether erosion is occurring. It is. But topsoil *creation* is also occurring.

The real questions about erosion?

First, is topsoil eroding faster than it is being created on a particular surface? Second, are we creating problems downstream from the erosion that could be solved by reducing soil erosion upstream (such as silting up lakes or reservoirs)?

High Yields Cut Soil Erosion

High yields cut soil erosion in and of themselves.

A field of corn which produces 150 bushels of corn per acre with high plant populations—protected by pesticides from weed competition and corn borers—will probably suffer less than half as much erosion as two acres of organically grown 75-bushel corn. Not only will the organic corn present double the land area to erosive forces, but it will have less leaf canopy to moderate the effects of thunderstorms and high winds. The organic field will also have a much longer window of erosion potential; the organic farmer will need to combat weeds with mechanical tillage well into the growing season, while the chemically assisted farmer uses herbicides that do not disturb the soil surface.

After we factor in lower topsoil losses and the redoubled number of bushels, the *soil loss per bushel* on the 150-bushel field should be perhaps one-third of the soil loss per bushel on the low-yield field.

This soil erosion differential may not be a serious problem so long as organic farming is concentrated on top-quality, level land. If organic farming were extended into more difficult conditions, however, even its present yields would prove far harder to sustain.

Reduced-Tillage Systems for Mechanized Farms

Now, in addition to their high-yield advantage in soil conservation, the chemically assisted farmers have gotten another enormous advantage—conservation tillage systems that use chemical weed-killers instead of bare-earth farming systems like traditional moldboard plowing.

"Conservation tillage" cuts soil erosion *by 65 percent* compared to moldboard plowing.[3] It leaves a heavy layer of crop residue in the upper soil profile that radically slows runoff and soil loss. Nor does it disturb the microbes and earthworms below the top 3-5 inches of earth. (The formal definition of conservation tillage is at least a 30 percent residue cover on the soil after planting.) [4]

"No-till" farming is an even better soil-saver. It keeps a layer of sod on the field virtually throughout the entire year, cutting erosion by as much as 98 percent compared to plowing.[5]

Conservation tillage swept across the crop production areas of America during the late 1970s and early 1980s, and is now cutting erosion on roughly 100 million acres by 1994 in America alone. Reduced-tillage systems were used on nearly another 100 million acres— and on low-erosion fields the reduced-till can be enough to control erosion effectively. Thus more than 50 percent of America's cropland in 1994 was farmed under low-erosion farming systems.[6]

No-till is now displacing conservation tillage all across America— the second sweeping wave of revolutionary farming systems in as many decades. No-till was used on more than 39 million U.S. acres in 1993—an increase of 11 million acres in 2 years.

The Conservation Technology Information Center notes that soybeans have just completed their sixth successive year of dramatic increases in no-till. Cotton no-tilling got off to a slower start, but it has tripled since 1991.

Both conservation tillage and no-till are also being extended in such places as Western Europe, Brazil, Paraguay, Kenya, Australia, and New Zealand. It seems likely that low-till farming systems will become the global norm.

Lowest Erosion Rates in Farming History

If you doubt the triumph of new low-erosion farming systems, remember how primitive farming was—and is—carried out:

- Ancient farmers controlled weeds in grain fields with "clean fallow"—keeping half of their land bare of all vegetation for the entire year. Any weed seeds which sprouted were uprooted before they could set new seed. But the price was enormous, in terms of high wind and water erosion rates and lost soil moisture.

- Row crops such as the turnip came to Western civilization about the 12th century. They represented a big gain in food production, because farmers could then produce crops from their fallow land—by hoeing the turnips to control weeds. (The extra food and feed from turnips and other root crops helped support the emergence of medieval cities.) *But row* crops also permitted almost as much soil erosion as clean *fallow.*
- As recently as the 1960s, modern American farmers plowed their land in the fall and left it open to erosion throughout the winter's storms. Plowing was such a slow process that it couldn't wait until spring. (That would have sacrificed too much of the growing season and cut yields.)

AMERICA'S EXPANDING CONSERVATION TILLAGE
Tillage System Usage by Percentage

Figure 10.1

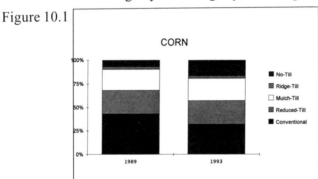

Figure 10.2

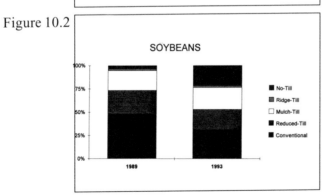

Source: Annual surveys of the Conservation Tillage Technology Information Center, reported in *Successful Farming*, December 1992, p. 44.

- Organic farmers still plow and cultivate. Contour plowing and strip cropping help reduce their erosion, but they cannot match the current low erosion rates of mainstream farmers.

The University of Minnesota Soils Department has done one of the most thorough and complete studies of U.S. soil erosion, based in part on the 1982 national soils inventory. The study concluded that Corn Belt soil erosion was far lower than the doomsayers (and the Soil Conservation Service) had been telling us.[7]

They estimated that America's 1982 soil erosion rates meant productivity losses of only about 0.03 to 0.1 percent per year. That means that if the 1982 soil erosion rates continued unabated for 100 years, soil productivity would decline only 3 to 10 percent. With crop yield rising by 3 to 5 percent annually, such productivity losses are almost trivial.

Today's reality is even better than that, since low-till farming systems have continued to spread—and further reduce erosion rates—in the years since 1982.

Frank Lessiter, a pioneering no-tiller and founder of *No-Till Farmer*, says the tillage revolution is succeeding because the new systems accomplish all the following goals:

- cutting soil erosion
- cutting surface water pollution
- cutting air pollution (dust)
- conserving water
- improving soil tilth
- increasing earthworm numbers
- providing more cost-effective weed control
- adding organic matter to the soil
- cutting soil compaction
- saving time
- saving fuel
- cutting machinery costs
- increasing farmers' management flexibility

FARMING WITHOUT THE PLOW—The crop residue stays in place to prevent soil erosion. At planting time, the tough no-till planter slices right through the old cornstalks to plant the new seeds.

How Conservation Tillage Works

Farmers had long known they could prepare a seedbed faster and with far less fuel using a disc plow. (A disc plow is a gang of concave steel discs dragged across the ground at an angle).

Disc plowing also halved soil erosion by leaving most of the crop residue on the surface of the soil and/or in its top few inches. However, disc plowing had never controlled weeds effectively.

Herbicides came into wide use in the 1960s. But they didn't deal effectively with the whole range of broad-leafed weeds and grasses until the 1970s. Also in the 1970s, OPEC sharply raised the price of oil (and tractor fuel). New herbicides and the opportunity to save on fuel costs combined to drive a rapid tillage revolution.

How No-Till Works

Under no-till, the farmers plant a heavy grass sod in the fall. In the spring they spray it with a vegetative killer and plant right through the killed sod. Later in the growing season a new crop of grass is interseeded to protect the soil after the harvest removes the crop canopy. It will be killed in its turn the next spring.

No-till eliminates soil erosion almost entirely. Soil is virtually never exposed. No-till is especially useful on steep slopes and problem soils.[8]

No-till ought to gladden the hearts of conservationists and environmentalists all over the globe. Not only does it reduce erosion to near-zero levels, but due to the year-round sod cover creates an especially hospitable home for earthworms and soil microbes. The improved tilth validates the tilth emphasis of traditional organic farmers—but boosts yields far higher than they have been able to do.

No-till farmers start out with yields comparable to plowed fields—and talk about a further yield gain after about the fifth year of the system.

Purdue University agronomist Peter Hill documented this longer-term yield gain in the histories of Indiana fields signed up in the 1992 MAX record-keeping program. Note that the yields *slumped* after the second year, but then moved up to a higher plateau than they reached the first year.

No-Till Corn Yields[9]

Years	Yields
1-2	167 bu.
2-5	158 bu.
6 and up	172 bu.

ELECTED MYTHMAKER:

"My earliest lessons on environmental protection were about the prevention of soil erosion on our family farm, and I still remember clearly how important it is to stop up the smallest gully. When I was a boy, there were plenty of examples elsewhere in the county of what happened when gullies got out of control and cut deep slashes through the pasture. . . . Unfortunately, little has changed . . . ."

Vice President Al Gore, *Earth in the Balance*, pp. 2-3

Reality Comment: According to the Tennessee Agricultural Statistics Service, the use of conservation tillage in Mr. Gore's home state increased from 17 percent in 1987 to 50 percent in 1992. Happily, this cut Tennessee's soil erosion by an estimated

8 million tons per year.

Fortunately for the Vice President and the rest of us, a great deal *has* changed.

Soil-Conserving Systems for the Third World

Alley Cropping

Alley cropping is a farming system designed for tropical regions like West Africa.

The farmer interplants rows of leguminous trees with his rows

---

Can No-Till Rehabilitate Chernobyl?

"Remember the tremendous explosion at the nuclear power plant in Chernobyl, Russia, back in the 1980s? It left over 11 million acres of Russian soils so badly radioactively contaminated that none of this cropland is now being farmed.

"'Unfortunately, research tests indicate Chernobyl area soils still show radioactivity and thus can't be used to grow crops for human consumption or used as feeds for livestock,' says Elmer Stobbe, University of Manitoba weed scientist. . . .

"Stobbe believes a combination of no-till with an entirely new set of industrial-grade oil crops could help Russian farmers bring much of these 11 million acres back into production.

"'The biggest concern is erosion which would wash the radioactivity off the ground and into streams,' he says. Stobbe is working with Russian ag officials to set up a trial with several thousand acres of no-tilled crops on these radioactive soils.

"'I think the ground could be no-tilled with industrial style crops, such as industrial grade rapeseed which could be used [for] manufacturing grade oil . . . but it will take a long-term study with a serious technology transfer to make it work.'

". . . [R]apeseed . . . has the ability to extract heavy metals from the soil and leave them in the residue. . . . [T]his gives the crop a potential role in aiding long-term remediation of the soil. . . .

"Around Chernobyl, no-till just might be the environmental and economical solutions to a 11 million acre nightmare."

Source: Frank Lessiter, editor/publisher, *No-Till Farmer*, December 1994, p. 3

---

of crops. The trees shade the young seedlings for part of the day, hold down soil temperatures, and reach deeper than the crop plant roots to bring up nutrients and moisture. Later in the growing season, the trees are pruned, and the nitrogen-rich leaves are used to mulch the crop plants, raising yields.

Alley cropping is the first fully stable farming system ever available to much of West Africa. The farmers who use it do not have to practice shifting cultivation, and they do not have to buy fertilizer. The system was developed under the auspices of the International Institute for Tropical Agriculture in Nigeria. It is spreading significantly where population pressures have shortened the fallow periods (and cut yields) for the traditional bush fallow system.[10]

Kudzu Cropping for the Rain Forest

The Amazon rain forest currently has about 3 million people attempting to subsist on shifting cultivation in its harsh environment. The subsistence farmers burn an acre or so of rain forest in the dry season, and the ash from the burned trees provides enough fertility for perhaps two years of crops before the farmer has to move on to another plot and let the first one rest. Over time, this means large areas of the rain forest are impacted by even a small population of farmers.

Recently, researchers have discovered that one crop of a legume called kudzu does as much for soil fertility as 14 years of bush fallow! (Kudzu is a noxious weed in the southeastern U.S. because it develops a storage root that is almost impossible to kill; it does not develop the storage root under Amazon conditions.)

This means that the 3 million people who are currently attempting subsistence farming there could be supported on about 10 percent as much rain forest land as they now occupy with their slash-and-burn system.

However, kudzu is a double-edged sword. It means that Amazon subsistence farming can actually *succeed*. Thus, if the Brazilian government's economic policies continue to discourage the creation of off-farm jobs, more and more discouraged people might migrate to the Amazon.[11]

Tied Ridges in Burkina Faso

In Burkina Faso, much of the annual rainfall runs off before the hard crust on the soil softens and lets the rains soak into the soil. A technique called "tied ridges" which uses animal traction to till a grid of soil ridges about a yard apart across the fields before the rains start is being extended. These interlocking or "tied" ridges trap the early rainfall. That extra moisture makes fertilizer a paying proposition. The combination of more water and fertilizer gives a fourfold yield increase.

The adoption of tied ridges will be slow, however, because it means the adoption of animal traction in regions which have no animal tradition, and a restructuring of traditional village land allocations and farming systems. Still, it holds important promise for both raising food production and reducing soil erosion.[12]

MYTHMAKER AS HUMANIST OF THE YEAR:

"Is an economic system that leads to the loss of 24 billion tons of topsoil from our cropland each year environmentally 'sustainable'"?
Lester Brown and Werner Fornos, "The Environmental Crisis: The 1991 Humanists of the Year Speak to One of Today's Most Serious Concerns," *The Humanist*, November/December 1991, pp. 26-30

Reality Comment: Here is Lester Brown at his best—or worst. He takes a phony number on soil erosion . . . and misuses it. There is *no* solid estimate of worldwide soil erosion, but Brown has "constructed" one. Then he uses it as though modern capitalism was to blame for a problem that has been threatening since man scratched the first seedbed with a stick. In reality, the world's severe erosion problems are in the poorest Third World countries and regions, where *tribalism*—not capitalism—is the dominant system of government.

Lester Brown has been forecasting famine, desertification and soil erosion crisis nearly every year since 1965. The predicted famines, as we saw in earlier chapters, have never appeared. The soil erosion crises, for their part, have been largely confined to poor countries extending low-yield farming onto fragile soils.

During the big African drought of 1983-84, Brown claimed that the African climate had been changed by cattle grazing and the clearing of forests. Climatologists, however, firmly rejected Brown's theory. They noted that the 1983-84 African drought was nearly continent-wide—too large an event to be triggered by a relatively modest set of regional factors. Moreover, Africa has always been subject to periodic major droughts.

Meanwhile, the years since Brown's African calamity forecast have brought more moisture rather than less, and Africa's great Sahara Desert has been receding since 1985, not expanding. In fact, most of Africa's severe grazing and deforestation problems have been confined to the Sahel region that contains few of its people.

The World Bank 1992 Development Report, *Development and the Environment*, states rather flatly, "Desertification in the form of advancing frontiers of sand that engulf pastures and agricultural land, as so often depicted in the media, is not the most serious problem in dryland areas, although it occurs locally."

But then, Lester Brown had already blown *his* credibility on soil erosion in 1980. He announced in that year that the U.S. was in a "soil erosion crisis" just when the new conservation tillage was being adopted on millions of acres, and reducing erosion to all-time lows.

Lester Brown and his Worldwatch Institute have been among the most prominent soil erosion crisis-mongers. They have frequently warned that the rich rolling fields of the Corn Belt will eventually look like the mountain slopes of Nepal if we don't stop population growth.

However, Brown doesn't command much respect among soil erosion professionals. Pierre Crosson, one of the top world experts on soils and erosion wrote a 1993 paper on "Future Supplies of Land and Water for World Agriculture." He noted the following:

> Brown provides no evidence to support his 24 billion ton estimate (of world soil erosion), nor for his assertion about the cumulative yield effects of the erosion. . . .
>
> [Brown and Wolf's] global estimate of 25.4 billion tons of excessive erosion annually is in fact based for the most part on erosion estimates for the United States and on a rule of thumb . . . adopted for [Soil Conservation Service] technicians to use in advising farmers which land should be treated

with soil conservation measures . . . I know of no soil scientist in or out of SCS who considers the standard to have scientific merit as an indicator of the land to which erosion in fact poses a significant threat to long-term productivity.

For China, Brown and Wolf note that although the drainage basin of the Yellow River is much smaller than that of the Ganges, the Yellow carries a much heavier sediment load. . . . They infer from this that erosion in China must be . . . 30 percent higher than in India. From this they derive an estimate of excessive erosion in China.

(They) assume that excessive cropland erosion per hectare in all countries is the same as in the "big four."

The boldness of Brown and Wolf in developing their global estimate commands a certain admiration. But that the estimate should be taken seriously is highly dubious.

THE WORLD'S MYTHICAL GRAIN CRISIS

"Between 1950 and 1984, world grain output climbed from 624 million tons to 1,645 million tons, a prodigious 2.6-fold gain. Since [1984], world output [of grain] per person has declined each year, falling 14 percent over the last four years. In part, this fall measures the unsustainable use of soil and water. . . . This grim process of eroding soils is leading the world into a period of agricultural retrenchment."

Lester Brown, "Reexamining the World Food Prospect," *State of the World 1989*, Worldwatch Institute, Washington, D.C., pp. 41-58

Recently, Brown has been claiming the world has been suffering a grain production "slump" since 1984. This is his latest turning point. *Now*, he says, the famines will occur.

Unfortunately for Brown, and fortunately for the rest of us, most of the slowing in world grain production gains in the mid-1980s has been in rich countries, not poor ones. It has been the result of the U.S., the EC, and Japan *trying to suppress surplus grain production*. In addition, the grain output in the former USSR has declined sharply with the collapse of its old command-style economy. That has nothing to do with soil erosion or Third World famine.

True, India did have a monsoon failure in 1987. But India *always* has a monsoon failure about one year out of five. This time, the country had some 26 million tons of grain in storage from record crops in the early 1980s. Thus, India only had to import about 2 million tons—to make up for its worst monsoon failure of the 20th century. (And India has since rebuilt its grain stocks from still-larger record crops.)

No reputable agriculturists agreed with Brown's forecast of food production retrenchment in 1989, and no such retrenchment has in fact appeared. Instead, world grain production potential has continued its escalation. For example:

- Grain yields in the developing countries rose 32 percent in the 1981-92 period, outstripping their population growth of 26 percent.
- As a result of the recent food output gains, per capita calories in the Third World rose to an all-time high of 2,473 in 1990. That compares with 2,117 calories in 1960 and 2,129 in 1980.
- Grain yields in the industrialized countries rose 25 percent from 1981 to 1992.
- World grain production in 1993 was 108 million tons higher than in 1984, with most of the gain in the developing countries.
- *Total food production* in the developing countries rose 3.9 percent annually during the 1984-to-1992 period, nearly double their population growth rate of 2.1 percent! Lester Brown's "grain crisis" depended on some carefully selected numbers.

If soil erosion rates haven't visibly slowed the gains in world food production, how can the anguish about soil erosion be so high?

In part, the soil erosion anguish has been manufactured—as an excuse to demand population suppression and/or reorganization of the world's "wasteful" socioeconomic systems.

One of the most startling moments of my recent career came in 1992 at an environmental workshop for a group of affluent urbanites in northern Indiana. I had come from my steep, rocky hills in the

Shenandoah Valley to one of the most favored agricultural regions of the world. The huge, level Corn Belt fields stretched as far as the eye could see, with rich loam topsoil six feet deep.

I was astounded to find that my audience *wanted* to believe that soil erosion was a serious problem in their area. They *wanted* to spend more resources fighting soil erosion, though northern Indiana has no serious soil erosion problem. They were terribly offended when I said their greatest contribution to soil conservation might be to release their Federal soil conservation funds to regions that really needed them (like the steep Tennessee foothills).

The Real Soil Erosion Crisis

The history of such long-term farming experiments as the Rothamstead test plots in England and the Morrow Plots at the University of Illinois proves that we *can* keep cultivating farmland for hundreds of years with *rising* crop yields.

The rice paddies of Asia, in fact, have been producing high and rising yields of rice for 4,000 years. Agricultural researchers have found no reason why they should not continue to do so. Much of the world's agriculture could achieve similar gains in the long term, if given continuing investments in research, inputs, and infrastructure.

Development and the Environment, the World Bank Development Report for 1992, goes out of its way to politely put the soil erosion crisis into perspective. Essentially, the Bank says that modern farming systems have reduced the soil erosion problem to manageable proportions in the U.S. and throughout the temperate-zone agricultures of the whole world. For example:

> The few comprehensive analyses of soil erosion that have been done in temperate areas indicate that the consequences are not large for aggregate agricultural productivity, although they are a concern locally for susceptible soils.
>
> . . . [S]tandard measurements of gross soil erosion from test plots typically overestimate the consequences for productivity, since the eroded soil can remain for decades elsewhere in the farming landscape before it is delivered to the oceans.

The Bank report also offers strong hope for erosion reduction in the rest of the world; as the quote from the Bank's 1992 World Development Report noted at the beginning of this chapter, most of the world's farms are not yet using the mulching, contour farming and low-till systems that can cut erosion by more than 50 percent.

Pierre Crosson, of Resources for the Future, notes that the scary erosion estimates for other parts of the world haven't held up under close examination, even without the best farming systems:

> The U.S. is the only country in the world that has reasonably accurate and comprehensive estimates of soil erosion and its effect on productivity. . . . Global estimates must be taken with more than a few grains of salt. . . . Experts who have examined these estimates . . . concluded these evaluations have little scientific merit. There is no question that erosion and the resulting loss of productivity is significant in some regions, including Nepal, parts of India, the highlands of East Africa and parts of the Andes.

As Crosson notes, however, these risky regions don't contain much of the world's cropland or people.

The world still has a potential soil erosion crisis, but as the World Bank properly notes, it is in tropical developing countries, where the soils and rainfall patterns are different, and where soil conservation has so far relied mostly on bush fallow. With the population surge, tropical areas will now have to use more intensive farming systems. That means they will also have to use more aggressive soil conservation systems, such as kudzu crop rotations, alley cropping, ridge tillage, and mulch cropping. And eventually, they will use no-till.

Fortunately, there are only a few regions where the agriculture cannot be sustainably modernized to provide the base calories for the population growth expected. Even Nepal could provide its own base calories safely if it achieved the high yield potential of its Churai lowlands.

There are also some "edge of the desert" regions like Africa's Sahel where farming and herding will always be precarious. But the Sahel and the Nepalese highlands contain only about 0.01 percent of the world's population. If the ultimate answer in such regions involves people emigrating, it will produce only a small number of emigrants.

America's Soil Erosion History

Soil erosion has been an emotionally charged issue in the U.S. at least since the 1930s. The droughts of the 1930s coincided with—and aggravated—the Great Depression. The USDA's Soil Conservation Service was created after a dust storm from the Midwest blew over Washington and frightened the wits out of the Congress in session there.

Without question, American farming had extended crops onto some droughty and erosion-prone soils in its move westward. The experience of the 1930s made it clear that some of this land had to be returned to grass.

Since the 1930s, the Soil Conservation Service has spent $18.6 billion to encourage soil conservation on American farms, 55 percent of it since 1980. SCS has fostered such laudable techniques as contour farming, farm ponds, filter strips to protect waterways, and rows of windbreak trees to reduce wind erosion on the Great Plains.

Ironically, the 1930s also led to price supports for U.S. farmers—which worked in direct opposition to soil conservation programs. Price had the unintended side effect of stimulating many farmers to push more crops onto erodable soils, cut down woodlots, and drain wetlands.

In the 1990s, U.S. farm price support programs have belatedly begun to include environmental safeguards. The programs now require farms with highly erodable land to have farm conservation plans approved by the Soil Conservation Service. "Sodbusters" who plow drought-prone soils and "swampbusters" who drain wetlands risk losing their eligibility for farm program payments.

These new environmentally oriented provisions of the farm subsidy programs have added to the already-strong momentum of conservation tillage in America. The impact has been so strong, in fact, that even Lester Brown has been pushed to take favorable note.

MYTHMAKERS HAVE TROUBLE STOPPING:

"Between 1985 and 1990, U.S. farmers cut their losses of topsoil from wind and water erosion by more than one third. This reduction, the result of an innovative national program incorporated in the 1985 farm bill, is the first major breakthrough in the effort to stem the heavy world-wide losses of soil."

Lester Brown, "U.S. Soil Erosion Cut," *Vital Signs*, 1992, Worldwatch Institute, p. 96

Reality Comment: Trust Lester. Even when he has to note progress, he credits it to the wrong source. He wants you to believe that we're saving more soil entirely because of the legislation, and not because we developed improved technology (with chemicals).

Because of the swampbuster and sodbuster provisions in the 1990 law, America's soil conservation effort has thus gotten a little more consistent and coherent. Nevertheless, the price support programs continue to have important negative side-effects for the environment.

Fighting the Good Fight

Erosion is inexorable. But so is topsoil creation.

With high-yield farming, the world should be able to support its expected human population *with less soil erosion than we have to-day*. In fact, with high-yield farming extended to the best land, the world can *build* topsoil depth on many of the best farmlands.

Other putative "solutions" miss the mark. "Population manage-ment" cannot solve the Third World's soil erosion problems. Third World populations are already too high to be supported on the low-yield farming systems its farmers have used to date. Can we shoot the "extra" people? Can we forcibly sterilize young couples by the millions? If we leave people to starve in "benign neglect," how much of their local forests and wildlife would they destroy before accept-ing famine as their fate?

Obviously, we can accept none of these policies.

Moreover, we have a real and proven solution for the whole world. It is to help people apply the best soil-saving farming system on the best and safest land. Then they *will* be able to feed their higher populations, and still have their most fragile soils in grass or trees—and indigenous wildlife.

Resource reading: Charles E. Little, *Green Fields Forever: The Conservation Tillage Revolution in America*, Island Press, Washington, D.C., 1987.

Notes

[1]Pierre Crosson and Norman J. Rosenberg, "Strategies for Agriculture," *Scientific American, Special Issue on Managing Planet Earth*, Vol. 261, No 3, Set. 1989, pp. 128-135.

[2]Greg Schmick, agronomist and farm equipment executive in Spokane, WA, speaking of "no-till" agriculture in the mid-1980s. Quoted in the frontispiece of Charles E. Little's *Green Fields Forever*, Island Press, Washington, D.C. 1987.

[3]Jerry Hytry, executive director, Conservation Technology Information Center, West Lafayette, Indiana.

[4]Op. cit.

[5]Flinchum, "Producing Soybeans Under a Highly Erodable Situation," *Proceedings of the 1993 Southern Soybean Conference*, American Soybean Association, St. Louis, 1993.

[6]1993 National Crop Residue Management Survey, Conservation Technology Information Center, West Lafayette, Indiana.

[7]F. Pierce, R. Dowdy, W. Larson, and W. Graham, 1984, "Soil Productivity in the Corn Belt: An Assessment of Erosion's Long-term Effects," *Journal of Soil and Water Conservation*, vol. 39, No. 2, pp. 131-136.

[8]Flinchum, "Producing Soybeans Under a Highly Erodable Situation," op. cit.

[9]John Walter, "Better With Experience," *Corn Farmer*, Harvesting Issue, 1993.

[10]B.T. Kange, G.F. Wilson, and T.L. Lawson, *Alley Cropping, A Stable Alternative to Shifting Cultivation*, International Institute for Tropical Agriculture, Ibadan, Nigeria, 1984; see also IITA Annual Report 1989-90, Ibadan, Nigeria, 1991.

[11]Pedro Sanchez, "Low-Input Cropping for Acid Soils of the Humid Tropics," *Science* 238 (December 1987, pp. 1521-27; also see Pedro Sanchez, Testimony before the U.S. House of Representatives Committee on Science, Space and Technology, February 23, 1989.

[12]John Sanders and Michael Roth, *Field and Model Results from Burkina Faso for Tied Ridges and Fertilization*, Purdue University Department of Agricultural Economics, April 1985.

11

Is High-Yield Farming Sustainable?

MYTHMAKERS SAY:

"Pesticides often leave the most resistant pests behind. . . . Then . . . the resistant pests multiply . . . soon, enormous quantities of pesticides are sprayed on the crops to kill just as many pests as were there when the process began. Only now the pests are stronger. And all the while, the quantity of pesticides to which we ourselves are exposed continues to increase."

Vice President Al Gore, *Earth in the Balance*, p. 52

"The second cause of slower food production growth is environmental degradation, which is damaging agriculture more than ever before."

Lester Brown, *State of the World 1993*, Worldwatch Institute

REALITY SAYS:

"The Food and Agricultural Organization reported Sunday that the percentage of people in the developing nations who are hungry fell to 20 percent from 36 percent between 1961-63 and 1988-90."

Paul Overberg, Gannett News Service, quoted from the Binghampton, N.Y. *Press and Sun-Bulletin*, September 21, 1992

". . . [P]ublic and private research institutions, commercial R&D enterprises and especially the various international agricultural (research) centers . . . are moving forward in concerted efforts to extend, redirect and fine-tune the original Green Revolution thrust. With the added impetus of biotechnology and other new scientific tools, we see clear indications that many of the problems and

constraints of the 1960s and 1970s have been surmounted."
                Dr. John R. Campbell, then-president, Oklahoma State University
                    and former dean of agriculture, University of Illinois,
                        Global Food Issues, Hudson Institute, 1991

"No doubt there is a [biological limit to yield] waiting for us somewhere, but the evidence says we don't seem to be there yet in farm yields."
                Dr. Donald Plucknett, in his farewell lecture as senior science
                        advisor to the international network of agricultural
                            research centers in 1993[1]

"Sustainable farms cannot be constructed by going back to traditional
farming systems. The success of traditional systems lay in their
nonextractive use of natural and human resources. Under intensification
. . . the systems collapsed. . . . [I]t is only in the unrealistic scenario of
reduced population pressure that these systems can be made to work."
                Lightfoot, Pingali, and Harrington, "Beyond Romance and Rheto-
                        ric: Sustainable Agriculture and Farming Systems Research,"
                        NAGA, The ICLARM Quarterly, International Center for
                            Living Aquatic Resources, 1993[2]

One of the key charges of the environmental activists is the claim
that high-yield farming is "unsustainable." This has resonated with
the public, probably because it implies a lurking, hidden threat.

Actually, as we saw in the preceding chapter on soil, high-yield
farming is *more* sustainable than organic farming. The best new high-
yield farming systems have much lower levels of soil erosion, the
key long-term constraint on farm production since ancient times. We
also have strong evidence that high-yield farming can continue producing higher and higher yields on into the future.

Every serious study of the world's food production potential has
concluded that we have more than enough resources to support the
current surge in population, and sustain the larger-but-restabilized
population expected in the future. The latest work to confirm the
world's huge "carrying capacity" is by Dr. Paul Waggoner, distinguished scientist at the Connecticut Agricultural Experiment Station.
His study, entitled *How Much Land Can 10 Billion People Spare
for Nature?* was published by the Council for Agricultural Science
and Technology (CAST).

Waggoner concludes that the current globe's cropland could provide a vegetarian diet for 10 billion people right now, and with current yield levels (if we converted the land that is currently in pasture for draft animals to crops instead). Waggoner further concludes that if we continue to pursue new research and technology, we might well be able to feed 10 billion people in 2050 at affordable prices with *less cropland* than we need today.

From the *Encyclopedia Britannica*: "SOYBEAN. Surely one of the most depressing statements ever made is that the world could support a population of 16,000 million people if everyone ate soybeans instead of meat. An acre of these beans can keep a moderately active man alive (but not necessarily contented) for 2200 days, while the same acre could keep him for only 75 days if he lived on beef. The soybean is the richest natural vegetable food known to man—and one of the dullest."

Is There a Yield Limit?

Perhaps the strongest endorsement of the Green Revolution's continuing importance and potential has recently come from Dr. Don Plucknett. As senior science advisor to the Consultative Group on International Agricultural Research, the key international network for agricultural research, Dr. Plucknett may have the world's best overview of agricultural research potential.

Dr. Plucknett until recently was inclined to say that we didn't know where our next farm research breakthrough was coming from. But over the last five years, he has reviewed statistics from the UN's Food and Agricultural Organization for the world and for individual countries around the globe. He also reviewed historic—even archeological—evidence of yields in past centuries.[3]

Plucknett says that yield takeoff marks a transition point when a farmer stops expanding his fields and starts getting more from the land he is already using. He starts benefiting from scientific advice on how to boost yields.[4] Plucknett believes once a country's farmers begin "yield takeoff," their production potential *keeps going upward*.

Food Supply Systems in the Tropics

system	farming intensity	population density	tools used
gathering	0	0-4	None
forest fallow	0-10	0-4	Axe, machete, digging stick
bush fallow	10-40	4-64	Hoe, axe, machete, digging stick
short fallow	40-80	16-64	Hoe, animal traction
annual crops	80-120	64-256	Animal traction, tractor

Source: Pingali, Bigot, and Binswanger, *Agricultural Mechanization and the Evaluation of Farming Systems in Sub-Saharan Africa*, Johns Hopkins Press, Baltimore, 1987[5]

Dr. Waggoner says we've been looking at agriculture through the wrong lens. We've assumed that crop yields are governed by the law of diminishing returns. But he points out that high-yield agriculture has been cheerfully violating the "law" of diminishing returns for decades—and is still getting away with it!

Diminishing returns would mean that after a certain level, more fertilizer wouldn't produce more yield. Better seeds wouldn't raise yields much higher. Instead, we find that more nitrogen, for example, can add just as much yield at higher levels as at low ones—assuming such constraints as moisture and trace minerals are dealt with. Artificial insemination keeps adding more milk per cow, as long as we keep improving the cow's nutrition, comfort, and health care. Improved seeds keep pushing yields higher.

Waggoner thinks what is happening is that farmers are *removing limitations* on crop yield rather than moving out on a diminishing returns curve.

Let us review the past surges in farm yields:

- Mankind's first and most obvious crop yield limitation was weeds. We learned to do clean fallow, and then to plow and hoe.
- Adding nitrogen (at first with animal manure) removed a constraint on the plants' nutrient requirements.
- Adding phosphate as well as nitrogen removed another nutrition constraint, and yields surged again.
- Later we learned that the plants need up to 26 trace minerals as well, and removing the constraint of mineral deficiencies raised yields again.
- Breeding shorter stalks on wheat and rice plants removed two constraints: It allowed more of the plant's energy to go into the grain heads; and the plants could support the heavier grain heads produced by heavy fertilization without falling over.
- Using supplemental irrigation on rain-fed land can produce still another yield surge in dry years, without even requiring much additional water or water delivery cost.
- Blocking insect and disease attacks with pesticides and pest-resistant breeding removes another yield constraint; and so on.

Confidence in the sustainability of yield-enhancing technologies continues to be increased by new developments on almost a daily basis. One good example is the USDA's newest pest-resistant soybean for hot climates. The new soybean resists nematodes, leaf-eating insects, and stem canker, all of which have taken a heavier toll in hot climates than in regions with cold winters. Its yields, as a result of the pest resistance, match corn belt levels (45 bushels per acre) and double the yields of current Southern commercial varieties (21 bushels).[6]

Waggoner also asserts that science and technology should enable the developing countries to raise their crop yields fully as much as the rich countries already have, by removing their yield constraints over the long term.

Waggoner concludes that 10 billion people should need no more land for food production than they use today, assuming the world continues to support agricultural research and permit freer trade in farm products.[7]

RAISING CROP YIELDS SUSTAINABLY IN THE THIRD WORLD:

"Data from China's National Network of Chemical Fertilizer Experiments (during 1981-83) revealed . . . 74 percent of China's cultivated land was deficient in phosphate, . . . about 40 percent was severely deficient in P, and about 23 percent was deficient in potash. . . . This scenario of imbalance is, outside of the large alluvial plains and deltas, typical of most developing countries, and is one of the reasons for stagnating yields, poor quality crops, increasing incidences of diseases, and soil degradation. . . . With few exceptions, organic manures alone will not support the yield increases in crop production that are required. . . . "

World Bank staff members Richard Grimshaw, Christopher Perry and James Smyle "Technical Considerations for Sustainable Agriculture," *Agriculture* and Environmental *Challenges*, Proceedings of the 13th World Bank Agriculture Sector Symposium, 1993[8]

"Keeping the poor in their misery while protecting the environment and promoting economic growth is *not* sustainable development."
Ismail Serageldin, World Bank Vice President for Environmentally Sustainable Development, 1993[9]

Refueling the Green Revolution with Biotech

There were better excuses for predicting famine in 1974 than there are today. In 1974, we didn't know where our next research breakthroughs would come from. Today we know they should come from biotechnology—if we keep making the research investments:

- With biotech, research will move faster; we will be rifle-shotting our breeding programs instead of using the shotgun approach of making semi-random crosses. Instead of crossing two organisms with thousands of genes apiece to see what comes out, biotechnology takes a particular gene from a particular place in one organism and inserts it into the genome of a target organism to achieve a predicted result.
- Even more important, we will have a vastly broader pool of genes from which to draw. Biotech, in fact, offers the first pragmatic incentive to *save* species and their genes. Until now, breeders could use only closely related genes from

"cousins" (phytogenetically related species). An example: Rust diseases are one of the most destructive pests of wheat, worldwide. Now, researchers have found the strongest wheat rust resistance ever, in a wild relative of the wheat plant. Without genetic engineering techniques, the wild genes would be useless. The wheat plants would reject them. But biotechnology has already transferred the rust resistance to domesticated wheat lines. Breeders will be releasing wheats with more rust resistance to farmers within a few years.[10]

- Cloning and tissue culture have already shortened the breeding cycle in trees from decades to months. As a result, we are quadrupling the yields of palm oil, cocoa, rubber, and wood. Anything that can be produced from a tree will be dramatically cheaper and more plentiful in the decades ahead.[11]
- Biotech will thus be the best protection that tropical forests can have. We won't *need* tropical forests to produce food or forest products because of high yields from the few acres in plantation farming and forestry.
- We're already testing crop plants with bred-in pest-killing power. The first cotton and corn varieties with the gene for the pesticide (a protein) from the *Bacillus thuringiensis* bacteria bred into them are already in field testing. Over time, we will have crops with a wide variety of bred-in pest-killers that could sharply reduce the need for sprayed-on pesticides.

The first big results from biotech are—predictably—coming from single-cell organisms. For example, bacteria have been taught to reproduce bovine and porcine growth hormones, human growth hormone, insulin, and many other compounds that would otherwise be impossible or impossibly expensive to produce. Added bovine somatotropin yields a 10 percent gain in feed efficiency for dairy cattle. BST has already been approved in the U.S. and was already being used in countries that want more dairy output, such as Mexico and the former USSR.

The potential for biotechnology has recently gotten a strong endorsement—from Dr. Robert Herdt, director for agricultural sciences of the Rockefeller Foundation.

A longtime pessimist about ultimate Third World success against hunger, Dr. Herdt was asked to assess the potential of biotechnology to solve food and environmental problems for the ASA-CSSA-SSSA 1993 Annual Meetings.

"Biotechnology's greatest contribution . . . will come through environment-friendly technology giving higher farmers' yields," said Herdt. "With higher yields, the pressure to extend cultivation to land better suited to natural cover will be reduced, thereby reducing the threat of erosion and preserving a greater state of biodiversity."[12]

As a first payoff on biotechnology's Third World potential, Dr. Herdt noted, "Rice plants transformed . . . for resistance to rice tungro virus have been produced and are being evaluated at the International Rice Research Institute. Rice tungro virus is believed to be one of the most damaging diseases of rice, estimated to eliminate, in Asia, on average, over 7 million tons of rice output annually. . . . Potato varieties with resistance to serious viruses will soon be available in Mexico. These kinds of developments will both increase food output and reduce incentives to use insecticides. . . ."

True to his long-time pessimism, however, Dr. Herdt still fears First World countries will get most of the biotech benefits because they are doing most of the research. (The Rockefeller Foundation has made more than $50 million in grants for rice biotechnology research to help redress the imbalance.)

But think of the long-term potential of understanding how to control the blueprints of organisms directly, instead of through laborious and chancy crossbreeding.

Researchers are already trying a bacteria-suppressing gene from the chicken in the potato. They hope it will lead to a tropical potato free of the bacterial rot that prevents potatoes from becoming a major food source in hot countries. (Potatoes produce more calories per acre than any other major food crop.)

Other researchers have found that flower blooms don't die of old age; plants intentionally kill them. That insight into plant biology has permitted one laboratory to produce a carnation that lasts three weeks instead of three days. Other genetic remedies may be found for other limitations that can add important utility to all sorts of organisms.

The Boyce Thompson Laboratory at Cornell University says it thinks the nitrogen-fixing abilities of the legume plants can successfully be added to other types of crop plants. This would not eliminate the need for chemical fertilizer on the higher-yielding fields, but could be an important step forward for remote, low-income regions like the Andes or interior Africa. (They even hope they can raise the rate of photosynthesis in the plants to cover the added energy requirements for the nitrogen fixing, so as not to lose yield capability.)[13] The Institute staff believes it will take another 15 years of research to produce a field-competitive nitrogen-fixing package—*if they get the funding.*

Already, researchers have used molecular biology techniques to create drought-tolerant corn varieties. Researchers at the International Maize and Wheat Improvement Center in Mexico moved copies of desirable genes from one corn variety to another, creating new gene combinations that had never existed before. (And without transferring any of the undesirable genes that often are included in a normal crossbreeding operation.) The resulting corn varieties yield up to 40 percent more food under drought conditions, and up to 30 percent more than conventional breeds without fertilizer. (In 1993, drought cost Third World farmers an estimated 24 million tons of corn.)[14]

Opposition to Biotechnology

Eco-activists have raised concerns about BST, since the growth hormone survives for a short time in the milk. (It does *not* survive pasteurization.) However, there has *always* been BST in unpasteurized milk, and there is no extra BST in cows treated with extra hormones.

In 1989, I talked with the Food and Drug Administration division chief responsible for approving BST. He called it a "particularly safe" compound for two reasons:

- It is a protein and is digested like a piece of steak if it reaches the human stomach.
- Humanity has been exposed to the BST in cow's milk for thousands of years; either it causes no ill effects or we have long since become adapted to it.

The potential of pork somatotropin is even bigger than that of BST. PST will produce hogs with up to 60 percent less fat and 15 percent more lean, using one-third less feed grain[15]. By saving 33 percent in feed grain, PST could represent the global equivalent of 40 million tons of corn per year—produced from laboratory bacteria. At the current world average corn yields, that much corn would require about 25 million acres of cropland—equal to all the arable land in Mexico.

The environmental militants have vehemently opposed the breeding of herbicide-tolerant crop plants. They decry these new crop strains as "the chemical companies' way to keep the world addicted to larger and larger doses of crop sprays." The reality is that these herbicide-resistant strains are a relatively easy and logical interim step while we are still mapping the genomes of organisms and are not yet ready to actually transfer genes.

The herbicide-resistant plants will let us grow higher yields of crops using the environmentally safest pesticides, pending more powerful tools from biotechnology.

Rice for the 21st Century

In January, 1993, I visited the International Rice Research Institute in the Philippines. IRRI has the parents of the miracle rice for the 21st century growing in its test plots today.

IRRI's first strategy is to hybridize the rice plant, which has always been self-pollinating. IRRI thinks it will be able to mass-produce hybrids as we already do corn, sorghum, and sunflowers. The whole world's rice yields could gain an almost-immediate 25-30 percent.

The second IRRI strategy is to channel another 10 percent of the plant's energy into the grain head. They've designed a plant with fewer but larger stalks to support the bigger head with still less of the plant's energy.

Then IRRI will start genetically engineering the hybridized design. Resistance to the white-backed planthopper will be pulled from barley. Resistance to the yellow stem borer has been found in another host plant. The whole roster of natural genes will be screened to make the new rice plants as pest-proof as possible. IRRI also thinks it can find enough salt tolerance genes from halophyte plants to permit rice production on saline aquifers.

All told, IRRI thinks it can produce 50-75 percent more rice in

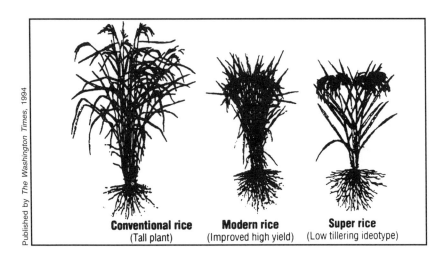

Published by *The Washington Times*, 1994

| **Conventional rice** | **Modern rice** | **Super rice** |
| (Tall plant) | (Improved high yield) | (Low tillering ideotype) |

2030 than the world raises today, on *fewer* acres of land.[16]

IRRI's major question, unfortunately, is whether they will have the funding to carry forward their research. IRRI's funding has dropped 23 percent in real terms since 1990 and the U.S. Agency for International Development budget is about to slash overseas agricultural research again.

Meanwhile, the U.S. wastes billions of dollars on such trivial environmental problems as acid rain, and such health non-problems as taking asbestos out of public buildings. Even our foreign aid programs have swung away from agricultural research—which can help in the short and medium terms to prevent famine and wildlife loss—toward "population management," which helps only marginally in the very long term.

SUSTAINABLE AGRICULTURE IN HIGH-BIRTH AFRICA:

"In the late 1930s, Machakos District, a semiarid area of East Central Kenya . . . was considered . . . to be degrading alarmingly and to be rapidly approaching, if not exceeding, its capacity to support its inhabitants and their livestock. Today the area has a population five times as great and the value of agricultural output per head is estimated to be three times larger than it was then. At the same time food production in the area is less susceptible to drought than before . . . the rate of erosion has been sharply reduced. . . . More than 200,000 hectares has been terraced in some way, most without external support. There are more trees than before and they are being actively managed by farmers. Projections made in the 1950s, the 1960s and again in the 1970s all foresaw severe fuel wood shortages, but there is no evidence that such have occurred. Initial emphasis was on coffee and cotton, with a subsequent shift over the past decade into fruit and horticultural crops. . . . Staple food production appears to have stabilized at about the level required for basic subsistence, about 200 kg of maize per head per year."

> John English, World Bank staff, "Does Population Growth Inevitably Lead to Land Degradation?" *Agriculture and Environmental Challenges*, Proceedings of the 13th World Bank Agriculture Symposium, 1993[17]

Making Wild Genes More Valuable

All over the world, expeditions are moving into the uncharted wilds in search of genes. Biotechnology is making the wild forests' genetic diversity usable for the first time.

Until now, the likelihood of finding a new "quinine in the rain forest"—a usable new drug or ready-for-market new product—were about a million to one against. Few of the genes in wild organisms were useful. Traditional plant and animal breeders could only marry "first cousins." Wide crosses between species, or even between distant cousins in the same species, were impossible.

Yet now, thanks to biotechnology, every gene on the planet is a potential lottery winner. We have no idea—yet—which genes can do what in the re-engineered plants, processes, and creatures of tomorrow. That knowledge will come slowly, as we map genes in each organism and learn about them bit by bit. But the world's forests, deserts, and odd corners have just gotten their greatest status boost in history.

The gene hunters are already hard at work:

- One California firm, appropriately named Shaman, talks with witch doctors about their traditional cures. Then Shaman analyzes the ingredients for potential modern medical uses.
- America's National Cancer Institute has contracted for access to genetic resources in Zimbabwe, Madagascar, Tanzania, and the Philippines.
- Costa Rica has created a National Biodiversity Institute to

identify its wild species. Merck, the pharmaceutical firm, is providing $1 million in "seed capital"—and gets to screen the gene collection for useful chemicals and extracts.[18]

The world is still fumbling toward an equitable set of arrangements to reward the regions that hold the genetic diversity, as well as the companies and institutions that can transform the genes into new products, processes, and services. The success of biotechnology will depend on both.

Activists claim they fear the Third World will be robbed on a wholesale basis. They are almost certainly wrong. It is far more likely, in fact, that many of the companies which invest in biotech research will lose money on this high-risk frontier.

Still, biotechnology is already among the most important pieces of knowledge that man has ever uncovered. No doubt it will someday rank with the wheel, the computer, combustion, electricity, telecommunications, and vaccines in reshaping the world. It may even overshadow them all.

And it will do enormous good for the environment.

Preserving Genetic Diversity with Gene Banks

The agricultural research institutions of the world are in a crash program to save the old landrace varieties along with their wild relatives by collecting their seeds and preserving them in gene banks.

The world really is in danger of losing these old "landrace" varieties of crop plants as they are being displaced from the fields by higher-yielding modern seeds.

The "Green" solution to this risk of gene loss would be to eliminate the new varieties. Essentially, they would turn the whole Third World into a gene museum, without the productive power to feed humans or protect wildlife from encroachment.

Nor does having a primitive rice plant in a Burmese farmer's field make its genes available, say, to a rice breeder trying to defeat the brown planthopper in Indonesia.

The International Board on Plant Genetic Resources (IBPGR) is leading the gene bank effort. IBPGR is part of Consultative Group on International Agricultural Research (CGIAR) whose researchers launched the Green Revolution. (The Green Revolution was probably founded by the Rockefeller and Ford Foundations when they established a plant breeding program in Mexico in the 1940s; it later became the International Maize and Wheat Improvement Center, now a key part of CGIAR.)

CGIAR encourages and coordinates national and multinational gene preservation efforts all over the world.[19] These gene banks now have more than 500,000 plant "accessions" representing hundreds of plant species and thousands of varieties. The board has working relationships with more than 120 countries and 600 research institutes.

The IRRI rice collection alone has 41,000 seed samples of landrace rice from Asia, and another 6,000 from Africa. The CIP potato collection has more than 5,000 accessions of domesticated potatoes, plus 1,500 from wild potatoes, covering 90 percent of the variation in about 100 wild species.[20]

One payoff already has been the discovery of resistance to the bean weevil. A search of *all* the field bean varieties in the world's gene banks had failed to turn up such resistance. Now, bean varieties are being bred for the whole world which can protect themselves from this voracious pest.

Creating Genetic Diversity

Other dramatic potentials for genetic power abound. We can probably recreate the American elm and chestnut trees, each one gene different to foil the Dutch Elm Disease and chestnut blight. Researchers are also developing more powerful bacteria to break down various toxic wastes, including oil spills. Dairy cattle, to cite another example, have already been given genes that turn their very milk into innovative medicine. The genes are taken from other organisms, and the cow's system orders the production of the new products as easily as it signals the production of the proteins and components in natural cow's milk.

These are just early examples of ways in which biotechnology can *add* diversity to the wild species that already exist.

Unfortunately, there has been a good deal of public controversy and apprehension about biotech and what it might create. Lawsuits have been filed in attempts to stop some types of biotech research.

Field tests have been picketed and sabotaged.

The approval for bovine growth hormone in dairy cattle was delayed for several years by political maneuvering in America, even though Food and Drug officials call it "a particularly safe compound." In Western Europe, a seven-year delay has been under consideration—mainly because the dairy farmers fear it might endanger their *subsidies*.

I do not doubt that biotechnology can be misused—as airplanes and wheels and dynamite can be misused. But on balance, both humanity and the environment would be far worse off without modern technology's advances.

In fact, genetic engineering is probably less likely to produce dangerous crosses than with standard selective breeding strategies. Standard plant breeding crosses two plants with thousands of genes apiece, and there is no way to know which ones will transfer or what impact they will have. With genetic engineering, the breeders will have gene maps of each organism (they're being mapped now). They will take exactly the genes needed for selected purposes, and the resulting organisms will be required to pass careful testing before they're allowed into the open atmosphere.

Less Spraying with Biotech

Biotechnology is also the best new knowledge we have for reducing our reliance on the chemical sprays which some people find so abhorrent.

- Biotech is allowing us to cost-effectively copy the complex protein coatings on disease viruses to produce fully safe vaccines.
- We can copy insects' own sex pheromones, so we can suppress some by attracting them to traps rather than spraying the entire field.

What About Soil Compaction?

Another charge leveled at high-yield mechanized farming is that it leads to soil compaction. It often does. But this is another problem that will lead to its own solution.

LOW-PRESSURE TIRE—The huge footprint of this combine tire sharply reduces soil compaction, even with big machines.

The first piece of good news is that low-till farming produces less compaction. Smaller tractors and fewer trips are needed. Moreover, soil compaction quickly becomes a yield factor in no-till, so farmers are trying more aggressively to correct it.

One technique is to use the same set of machinery tracks year after year, so the soil between the tracks is never compacted.

Farmers can put dual or triple tires on their machines, or tires with lower pressures per square inch.

Another technique is being proposed by Caterpillar, which is aggressively marketing its new rubber-tracked tractors. Tracked machines radically reduce soil pressures per square inch compared to wheeled machines of the same weight. Until now, however, most mainstream farmers have not seen soil compaction as a big enough problem to warrant the higher costs and transport disadvantages of tracked equipment. (Steel-tracked equipment is not allowed on most public roads, forcing farmers to load it on transporters to move from farm to farm or to fields with access only from public roads.)

Caterpillar says its new tractors are cost effective, and can travel public roads at more than 18 miles per hour. Caterpillar also offers

QUAD-TRAC—It's not a lunar lander, but the latest effort to provide farmers with a cost-effective way to prevent soil compaction. It is pulling a tool that breaks up compacted subsoil layers.

track systems for use with spray tanks, wagon beds, and other towed equipment—and it has just set up a marketing agreement with a manufacturer of big no-till planting drills.[21]

Another major tractor maker has also just entered the rubber-tracked field. Case-IH is now offering a *four-tracked* rubber track system for its tractors.[22]

We can expect to see a major new emphasis on combatting soil compaction in mainstream farming over the years ahead.

The Role of Integrated Pest Management

Integrated pest management is a vital element in maintaining the sustainability of high-yield agriculture. It will probably become even more important as more of the Third World intensifies its farming; Third World farmers will have the same need to avoid building up pest tolerances to pesticides, and they also have less cash to spend on pesticides in the first place.

However, integrated pest management is more important for

ensuring that costs are kept low; and that our pest control technologies continue to work well than as a way to eliminate (or even reduce) the use of pesticides.

Analyzing even the successes of IPM points up how complex it is, as the following example shows.

The Case of Pakistan's Mangoes

Mangoes in Pakistan are attacked by four major groups of insect: mealybugs, fruit flies, scale insects, and leafhoppers. During the 1980s, the International Institute of Biological Control worked with the mango growers, who were spraying about five times per year and still not getting good insect control.

Research showed that the mealybugs laid their eggs in the soil at the base of the trees, and moved up to the leaves in the spring. They were preyed on by ladybird beetles, but the ladybirds didn't build up their populations until late in the season.

Research offered two inexpensive solutions.

First, the farmers were told to hoe around the bases of the mango trees in the winter, to expose and kill the eggs.

Second, the ladybirds were having to overwinter on other trees because the bark of the mangoes isn't rough enough to shelter them. Simple bands of rough sacking around the mango trunks let the ladybird beetles overwinter right on the trees and start effectively preying on the mealybugs sooner in the season.

Fruit flies were the reason for most of the insecticide use, because their maggots, laid in the mangoes, ruined the fruit. As an alternative to spraying, attractant traps were set up using imported fruit fly attractant (methyl eugenol). The traps cut fruit fly infestation rates from 35 percent to 3 percent.

Mango hoppers still needed spraying—but a study of hopper distribution on plants revealed that the growers could spray just the lower part of the trees (up to 5 meters) and still get control. This cut the amount of spray used.

Cutting the other sprays also eliminated the scale problem, because beneficial insects now controlled the scale. (They had been killed by the pesticides.)

Overall, research cut the mango growers' spray program from

five applications to one, with a 14-fold reduction in chemical costs. About 25 percent of Pakistan's mango growers currently use the IPM program.[23]

The IPM programs are highly complex and extremely site-specific.

The biggest success for IPM to date is against the brown planthopper in the rice fields of Indonesia. The miracle rice varieties of the Green Revolution were being increasingly attacked by the hoppers during the 1970s and 1980s—despite subsidized pesticides and additional varieties bred for planthopper-resistance.

Research in the 1980s indicated that cutting pesticide applications didn't reduce yields. The pesticides had been killing many beneficial insects, and the hoppers had developed enough resistance to the approved pesticides that they offset the impact of the chemicals. (Too many farmers had also focused too long on a few favorite rice varieties that brought high prices.)

In 1986, a Presidential Instruction banned 57 insecticide formulations from the rice fields, It also ordered that only resistant varieties be grown in affected areas and that the rice industry be trained in IPM. Most farmers now spray once a year instead of four times. The amount of pesticide used has been cut by 50 percent, while yields have risen.[24]

Leonard Gianessi, a pest control expert with Resources for the Future, says the U.S. alone has thousands of pest species infesting 80 to 100 crops in thousands of microclimates. Thus, as we saw earlier, there are hundreds of thousands of possible combinations of pest, crop, and region for researchers to struggle with in replacing the 200 active pesticides ingredients now in use. Yet only a small and declining fraction of pesticide uses appear to threaten human or environmental health.

Preserving Wetlands

Amazingly, the United States is now *gaining* wetlands.

High-yield farming and the environmental movement share the credit for this development. The environmental movement gave wetlands a far higher priority in the public mind than they had ever had before—and a priority much more in keeping with their ecological importance. High-yield farming provided the high farm productivity so that we could spare these important ecological assets.

America has recently undergone a dramatic shift in its attitude toward wetlands, as Jonathon Tolman notes in his important report for the Competitive Enterprise Institute, *Gaining Ground: An Analysis of Wetland Trends in the United States.*[25]

At the turn of this century, as Tolman writes, the U.S. Supreme Court characterized wetlands as "the cause of malarial and malignant fevers," and said "the police power is never more legitimately exercised than in removing such nuisances." It is no wonder that America has lost half of its original wetlands.

Currently, however, the conversion of wetlands has been slashed from roughly 450,000 acres per year in the 1960s and 300,000 acres per year in the early 1980s to a current conversion rate of perhaps 100,000 acres per year.[26] Farmers' conversion of wetlands has been slashed dramatically, from a rate of more than 350,000 acres per year in the 1960s to less than 30,000 acres annually today.[27] Meanwhile, nonfarm conversions of wetlands for development have remained constant at about 80,000 acres per year.

The biggest factor in the reduction has been the change in the farm subsidy programs denying federal farm subsidies to farmers who drain wetlands. The credit for the "Swampbuster" provision goes to the environmentalists, not to farm organizations.

On the positive side of the ledger, says Tolman, more than 100,000 acres of wetlands have been gained in each year since 1991. These wetlands gains were recorded under the following auspices:

- The Partners for Wildlife Program of the Fish and Wildlife Service, which encourages private landowners to restore converted or degraded wetlands on their property (210,000 acres total).
- The Conservation Reserve Program of the farm subsidy structure administered by the U.S. Department of Agriculture's price-support agency (300,000 acres total).
- The Wetlands Reserve Program administered by the USDA's Soil Conservation Service, which secures permanent easements for restoring wetlands on cropland (125,000 acres).

These totals do not include the additional wetlands which have been restored on both Federal and private lands. The Fish and Wildlife Service, for example, restores 33,000 acres per year in its national wildlife refuge system, which is not included in the figures.

It is highly unlikely that today's public opinion of wetlands would have become nearly so positive if America were facing severe shortages of key foods—or rampant epidemics of malaria.

MYTHMAKER:

"The relatively cheap and abundant supplies of fossil fuel have been substituted for human and draft animal energy. . . . Per capita use of fossil energy in the U.S. is . . . 14 times the level in China. . . . As our population continues to grow, we will inevitably experience resource shortages similar to those now being experienced by China and other nations."

Pimental et al., "Natural Resources and an Optimum Human Population," *Population and Environment*, 1994[28]

Does High-Yield Farming Require Too Much Fossil Fuel?

Environmentalists like to claim that use of fossil fuels makes high-yield farming unsustainable.

Farming, however, is not a big energy user compared to other sectors of a modern economy. In the U.S., farming takes only about 2 percent of our energy use for both its direct and indirect needs. The oft-cited need for petroleum in pesticide manufacture is truly trivial.

Farming's *direct* use of energy has *declined* by almost 30 percent since 1978. About half of agriculture's total energy use today is for fertilizer (and the small mount used in pesticides). We have already established the overriding importance of the fertilizer and pesticides in raising yields and thus protecting wildlife habitat.

How much more loudly would the environmental activists be complaining if today's farms were powered—like yesterday's—with draft animals? A grass-powered agriculture would take far more land. In the U.S., *the shift from draft animals to internal combustion engines released 30 million acres of prime arable land for crops*! (Moreover, that horse and mule pasture couldn't be shifted out to marginal acres in Wyoming; it had to be on the margin of each farm, so it put a lot of prime cropland into pastures in top farming regions like Indiana and Iowa.)

Modern farming derives its basic energy pattern from the larger economy. Farmers didn't invent the internal combustion engine, but were quick to see its potential in adding "horsepower" to the farm. Farms today use diesel fuel and electricity because they are the low-cost energy sources.

If the rest of the economy shifts to other energy sources, farmers probably will too.

No one concerned about the planet and its wildlife should be eager to see the return of draft animals and their huge land requirement. Instead, we should be working for sustainable and economic energy use throughout the world.

There are several alternative sources of energy for human society which could be used if CO_2 and/or methane turn out to be truly dangerous to the planet. (There is still a fierce scientific debate about this, which the eco-zealots would like to ignore in favor of immediate drastic suppression of economic growth.) Note the following:

- Hydroelectric dams make sense if the world is truly at immediate risk from a dangerous global warming. However, environmentalists oppose them.
- The fusion reactor seems promising, but its promise has remained temptingly beyond our technical grasp for decades now. (Environmentalists say it would produce too much heat anyway, and thus contribute to "thermal pollution.")
- Hydrogen could supply our need for liquid fuels, and hydrogen is one of the most abundant elements; the whole weight of the earth is nearly 1 percent hydrogen.[29] But we would need energy to isolate and extract the hydrogen.
- The world has huge sources of tidal power. (Franklin D. Roosevelt was fascinated with harnessing the power of the huge 60-foot tidal flows in the Bay of Fundy.) There's a location problem, of course, because few cities are located near big tidal flows.
- There are enormous temperature differences between the oceans' surfaces and 300 feet below the surface. This could

be harnessed, much as we harness energy for houses and buildings now with heat pumps. Again, there are locational advantages and disadvantages.

Dr. Jesse Ausubel of the Rockefeller University points out that the world has been moving for 200 years toward less carbon and more hydrogen in its hydrocarbon energy mix. Coal has one hydrogen atom for each carbon atom. Oil has two hydrogens for each carbon, and natural gas has four. Ausubel suggests that the ultimate solution is to move toward pure hydrogen in the energy system. It can be made from water, and its burning produces only energy and water. He suggests high-temperature gas-cooled nuclear reactors as "an appealing line for development" to generate the hydrogen from the limitless supply of water.[30]

There are probably at least three major problems with shifting from fossil fuels to *any* of the visible alternatives.

First, the direct economic costs for any of the alternatives would probably be higher than the direct costs of the fossil fuels we are currently burning. Higher fuel costs mean lower living standards for the poor and elderly, and less new job creation.

Second, any change so massive will require equally massive amounts of capital. This is capital that won't make our lives any more comfortable, or raise any impoverished people out of destitution. It will simply go toward replacing the energy system we already have. That may become necessary, but we shouldn't consign the world to more poverty until we know it is necessary.

Third, the eco-activists oppose every energy alternative, including their own. (Windmill farms, for example, make too much noise, and chew up birds in their high-speed propellers.)

We cannot protect our current lifestyle if we all go back to growing our own food with hand hoes and squashing potato beetles by hand. Even the champions of the low-petroleum-use alternative admit that China's current hand-powered low-protein diet costs 16 times as much human labor as America's.[31] America's current diet might take 30 times as much human labor.

MYTHMAKER STILL DOESN'T GET IT:

"The use of more land to produce food reduces the total energy inputs necessary for crop production and would lead to greater solar energy dependence and sustainability in agriculture. This of course assumes the availability of sufficient land, halving crop yields per hectare. . . ."

Pimental et al., "Natural Resources and an Optimum Human Population," *Population and Environment*, 1994

Reality Comment: How does Pimental protect the wildlife if he needs twice as much land per person? He says we can only support 2 billion people on his system. Three billion people must be subtracted so we can give up the fossil fuels now used in agriculture. Who gets to choose the survivors?

Agriculture is the crucial industry for people *and* wildlife. It should not be the place where we casually *start* our energy-change experiments. Rather, it should be the place where we implement tested-and-successful strategies. Maybe we should listen to Dr. Pimental after his University (Cornell) has banned autos for its students and faculty.

Unfortunately, his work so impressed the American Association for the Advancement of Science that Pimental was invited to address their national meeting in the spring of 1994. His fearful conclusions were reported to the whole country by the Associated Press.

The Sustainable Reality

If and when the rest of the world shifts to non-fossil energy sources, its agricultures will shift too. It is highly unlikely that humanity is going to go back to living on a diet of oatmeal and onions. It is even less likely that the world's population will magically and painlessly pare itself down to 2 billion or 500 million people. If we cannot reach practical sustainability through minimal lifestyles and slashing birth rates, then we must reach it through practical improvements in food production. Through still-higher yields.

It can be done, and quickly. In many cases, the improvement in sustainability will even pay for themselves.

How much longer will the activists and vegetarians continue to pat themselves on the back for coming up with failed strategies?

How much longer will they continue to stand in the way of the higher-yielding farms and forest plantations that can truly protect the wildlife and nature we all cherish?

Notes

[1]*Chronicle of Higher Education,* September 22, 1993.

[2]Lightfoot, Pingali, and Harrington, "Beyond Romance and Rhetoric: Sustainable Agriculture and Farming Systems Research," *NAGA the ICLARM Quarterly*, International Center for Living Aquatic Resources Management, Manila, Philippines, January 1993, pp. 17-18.

[3]Bob Holmes, "A New Study Finds There's Life Left in the Green Revolution, *Science*, op. cit.

[4]Dr. Donald Plucknett, "Science and Agricultural Transformation," IFPRI Lecture, September 9, 1993, International Food Policy Research Institute, Washington, D.C.

[5]Reprinted in Keck et al., *Population Growth, Shifting Cultivation and Unsustainable Agricultural Development: a case study in Madagascar*, World Bank, Washington, D.C., 1994, p. 7.

[6]U.S. Department of Agriculture, Agricultural Research Service, *Quarterly Research Bulletin*, December 1993, Washington, D.C.

[7]Dr. Paul Waggoner, distinguished scientist at the Connecticut Agricultural Experiment Station, New Haven, CT, *How Much Land can Ten Billion People Spare for Nature?* Council on Agricultural Science and Technology, Task Force Report No. 123, Ames, Iowa, February 1994.

[8]Grimshaw, Perry, and Smyle, World Bank, "Technical Considerations for Sustainable Agriculture," *Agriculture and Environmental Challenges, Proceedings of the 13th World Bank Agriculture Sector Symposium*, Washington, D.C. 1993, p. 19.

[9]Ismail Serageldin, World Bank vice president for environmentally sustainable development, *Agriculture and Environmentally Sustainable Development: Thirteenth Agriculture Symposium*, Washington, D.C., 1993, p. 6.

[10]"Wild Genes May Tame Leaf Rust," *Successful Farming*, August 1992.

[11]Cloning means slicing the tissue of an organism into tiny micro-thin slices and then using tissue culture to grow out many identical copies of the organism from these "starter cells."

[12]Dr. Robert Herdt, "The Potential Role of Biotechnology in Solving Food Production and Environmental Problems in Developing Countries," ASA-CSSA-SSSA Annual Meetings, Cincinnati, Ohio, November 1993.

[13]Personal communication from Ralph Hardy, director, Boyce Thompson Institute, March 24, 1994.

[14]Boyce Rensberger, "Building a Better Ear," *Washington Post Science Section*, June 27, 1994, p. A3.

[15]R. D. Goodband et al., 1990. "The Effects of Porcine Somatotropin

and Dietary Lysine on Growth Performance and Carcass Characteristics of Finishing Swine," *Journal of Animal Science,* vol. 68:3261-3276.

[16]International Rice Research Institute, *Rice Research in a Time of Change: A Medium-Term Plan for 1994-98*, Manila, Philippines, IRRI, 1993. See also IRRI, report of the *Fourth External Programme and Management Review of the International Rice research Institute*, Manila, Philippines, IRRI, 1993.

[17]John English, "Does Population Growth Inevitably Lead to Land Degradation?" *Agriculture and Environmental Challenges, Proceedings of the 13th World Bank Agriculture Symposium*, Washington, D.C. 1993, pp. 46-47.

[18]Simpson and Sedjo, "Contracts for Transferring Rights to Indigenous Genetic Resources," *Resources*, Fall 1992.

[19]See Erich Hoyt, *Conserving the Wild Relatives of Crops*, International Board for Plant Genetic Resources, International Union for Conservation of Nature and Natural Resources, World Wide Fund for Nature, Rome, Italy, 1988.

[20]*Partners in Conservation: Plant Genetic Resources and the CGIAR System*, Consultative Group on International Agricultural Research, International Board for Plant Genetic Resources, IBPGR Secretariat, Rome. See also *IBPGR Annual Report for 1992,* Rome, 1992.

[21]"There's a Major New Player in No-Till," *No-Till Farmer*, December 93, p. 5.

[22]"A New Generation of Horsepower," *Successful Farming*, January 1994.

[23]Jeff Waage, Director, International Institute of Biological Control, "Making IPM Work: Developing Country Experience and Prospects," *Agriculture and Environmental Challenges, Proceedings of the 13th World Bank Agriculture Sector Symposium*, Washington, D.C., 1993, pp. 119-133.

[24]Waage, op. cit.

[25]Tolman, Jonathan, *Gaining Ground: An Analysis of Wetland Trends in the United States*, Competitive Enterprise Institute, Washington, D.C., May 1994.

[26]Dahl and Johnson, *Status and Trends of Wetlands in the Coterminus United States, Mid-1970s to Mid-1980s*, U.S. Department of Interior, Fish and Wildlife Service, Washington, D.C., 1991.

[27]USDA Soil Conservation Service, *1991 Update of National Resources Inventory, Wetlands Data for Non-Federal Rural Lands*, Iowa State University Statistical Laboratory.

[28]Pimental, Harman, Pacenza, Pecarsky, and Pimentel, "Natural Resources and an Optimum Human Population," *Population and*

Environment, Vol. 15, No. 5, May 1994, pp. 347-269.

[29]*Encyclopaedia Brittanica.*

[30]Jesse Ausubel, "Energy and Environment: The Light Path," *Energy Systems and Policy*, Vol. 15, 1991, pp. 181-188.

[31]Giampetro and Pimental, "The Tightening Conflict: Population, Energy Use and the Ecology of Agriculture," *The NPG Forum*, Negative Population Growth, October 1993, Teaneck, New Jersey, p. 2.

12

Seeds of Success

MYTHMAKERS SAY:

"The famines which are now approaching will not . . . be caused by weather variations and therefore will not be ended in a year or so by the return of normal rainfall. They will last for years, perhaps for several decades, and they are, for a surety, inevitable. Ten years from now parts of the undeveloped world will be suffering from famine. In fifteen years the famines will be catastrophic and revolutions and social turmoil and economic upheavals will sweep areas of Asia, Africa, and Latin America. . . . I *know* the food possibilities in these countries. I *know* that future food increases, based on today's techniques, are limited and can only change slowly. . . . Herewith is the principal of triage [emphasis in the original]."

> William and Paul Paddock, *Time of Famines*, 1976, pp. 8-10[1]

"Serious technological constraints are limiting the rapid expansion of food, particularly beef and soybeans. All four of the major resources used to produce food—land, water, energy and fertilizer—are now in tight supply."

> Lester Brown, *By Bread Alone*, 1974[2]

"Three historical trends are converging to make it more difficult to expand world food output. One is the growing scarcity of new cropland and fresh water that affects most of the world. The second is the lack of new technologies, such as hybrid corn or chemical fertilizer, that can dramatically boost output. And the third is the negative effects of planetary environmental degradation."

> Lester Brown, *State of the World* ,1990[3]

"Yet the demand for basic food grains could double by 2020, and the ability of agriculture to keep pace with the demand is being called into question. Some neo-Malthusians insist that mass starvation is on the horizon, while some economists counter that human ingenuity will come through as it always has. Even some who have brought the Green Revolution about, however, acknowledge that it has made its biggest and easiest gains, and that the challenge ahead appears formidable."

> William K. Stevens, *New York Times*, May 5, 1992[4]

REALITY SAYS:

"There are now six times as many people as there were when (Malthus') unsinkable essay was written. On average, the world's people are better fed. And clothed. And housed. And transported. What happened? Science happened. Science and technology made two blades of grass grow where one grew before. More than two blades. . . . Two hundred years ago, few people were aware that a scientific revolution had started right before their eyes. They assumed that the 'carrying capacity' of the earth . . . would not change."

> Garret Hardin, *Insight*, December 20, 1993[5]

"*In World Agriculture: Toward 2000*, Nikos Alexandratos of the Food and Agriculture Organization (FAO) of the United Nations reports that only 34 percent of all seeds planted during the mid-1980s were high-yielding varieties. Statistics from the FAO show that at present only about one in five hectares of arable land is irrigated, and very little fertilizer is used. Pesticides are sparsely applied. Food output could drastically be increased simply by more widespread implementation of such technologies."

> John Bongaarts, Vice President, Population Council, writing in
> "Can the Growing Human Population Feed Itself,"
> *Scientific American*, March 1994, p. 36-42

The Paddock brothers wrote a frightening book in 1967 titled *Famine 1975!* They predicted widespread famine throughout the Third World, and they urgently and sincerely recommended that the First World practice triage—selecting those countries which could be saved and letting the others suffer their self-induced famines without aid.

The Paddocks republished the same book in 1976, under a new

title, *Time of Famines*—even though the famines they predicted in 1967 had not occurred. "The basic facts have not changed," they insisted in the preface for the second book. "The world is far less able to cope with famine today than in 1967, when this book first appeared." As of 1994, the major food shortfalls they have predicted have *still* not occurred.

The 1990 quotes from Lester Brown at the beginning of this chapter make the same arguments for predicting famine that Brown had made in 1974—even though the famines he had predicted in 1974 did not occur. Unfortunately, whole new generations of journalists and readers were too young to know that Brown had made the same arguments before, and been wrong for the same reasons.

About the only thing that Lester Brown and I have agreed on over these years is that we can't harvest much more wild seafood from the oceans. But that doesn't mean we can't have more seafood; the additional seafood we want can be raised in ponds and sea cages, and fed rations based on grains and oilseeds. Most of our growing shrimp harvest already comes from such sources.

David Pimental of Cornell University makes a common mistake when he attempts to tie human well-being to a natural resource base. Natural resources are no longer the key to human well-being. Poverty-ridden Brazil has enormous natural resources, and wealthy Japan has virtually none. In China, since that country has begun to liberalize its centrally planned economy, agricultural output and per capita incomes have both doubled without the help of major new discoveries of natural resources.

Virtually every country in the world has adequate farming resources to produce adequate calories for its projected population in 2050—if high-yield farming systems are pursued.

The doomsayers like Lester Brown charge that our gains in world farm output come from mining groundwater and destroying topsoil. They dismiss the power of agricultural research and technology. They continue to claim that the world is headed for famine and farming disaster.

Nothing could be farther from the truth.

Even a gifted observer like Garret Hardin, who gives such a cogent explanation of why the new Malthusians were wrong that this chapter puts him in the "reality" section, then betrays his own

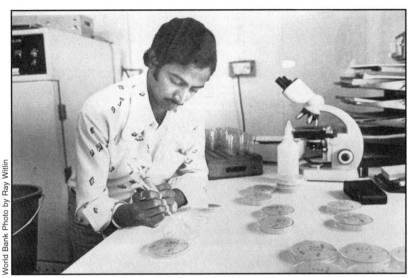

World Bank Photo by Ray Witlin

KEEPING THE GREEN REVOLUTION GOING—This research center in India is one of more than 20 internationally funded farming research units for the Third World. A leading example of the phrase "big bang for the buck," their existence is currently jeopardized by cutbacks in funding from wealthy countries.

observations and joins the doomsayers in predicting disaster. (Hardin was the *originator* of the "lifeboat ethic" of the 1970s and still claims that we will run out of farming research before population restabilizes.)

We shall now examine *why* the world is far more likely to eat *better* in the years of population growth that lie ahead.

Genetics Lead the Green Revolution

The Green Revolution has gotten its primary stimulus from genetics. The simple process of crossbreeding plants, animals, poultry, and fish has driven the most dramatic changes ever seen in the world's food supply.

The genetics work has also been strongly reinforced by enormously important breakthroughs in new farming systems, fertilizer technologies, mechanization, and pest-control chemistry. Major productive investments have been made in irrigation and infrastructure (roads, silos, etc.).

But the real success story starts with genetics.

The following improvements have been achieved since 1950:

- Crop yields and yield potentials have been tripled or more.
- Pests have been foiled with bred-in resistance.
- Poultry feed efficiency has been doubled.
- Extra crops have been added to the calendar with short-season seeds.
- Artificial insemination has been adding 2 percent each year to the milk yields of millions of dairy cows.

These are not isolated examples of onetime successes. They are all part of a general upward trend in food production potential.

Genetics has produced more productive strains in virtually every crop, domesticated creature and region in the world. More new strains continue to flow from the labs and test plots with no sign of a slow-down. Such a continuing flow is particularly important; we need to continue a sizeable set of breeding programs to keep from sliding backwards as pests and diseases continue to mutate and adapt.

Higher-yielding, shorter-strawed, pest-resistant, cold-tolerant, daylength-insensitive, higher-protein seeds have come from the plant breeders in profusion.

American corn breeders started the plant breeding revolution with hybrid corn in the 1920s. U.S. corn averaged about 27 bushels per acre in the 1920s[6] and more than 138 bushels per acre in 1994.[7] U.S. corn yields gained about half a bushel per acre annually in the 1930s, and are gaining 2 bushels per acre per year today.

The best farmers in most countries are still out-producing their neighbors two or three to one, indicating that there is still lots of potential for increase. The Green Revolution continues spreading to more and more countries, and to more and more commodities.

Chinese rice yields averaged 2.2 tons per hectare in the 1940s and have recently averaged 5.7 tons per hectare—an increase of 250 percent.[8] In the 1980s, Chinese researchers were the first to success-fully hybridize rice, achieving another 25 percent yield gain.[9] China's top rice yields have soared to more than 16 tons per hectare![10]

French wheat yields have more than tripled, from less than two tons per hectare in the 1940s to the current average of 6.3 tons.[11]

France is now planting the Green Revolution's short-strawed high-yielding wheat varieties in cold-tolerant winter strains, which get off to a stronger and earlier start in the spring than its old spring wheats. French farmers top-dress their wheat with repeated small applications of fertilizer for maximum yield stimulus, and use multiple fungicide treatments to prevent crop loss in its humid climate.

Corn yields in the Ivory Coast currently average 0.8 tons per hectare—but the potential yield is 7 tons per hectare. Consumer demand is so weak that additional corn production would drive corn prices below the cost of production. Because of the weak demand, farmers rarely use fertilizer or hybrid seed (which must be bought each year from a seed farm.)[12]

Indian sunflowerseed yields have begun to explode recently. India has just begun to adopt hybrid sunflowerseed. Yields have doubled (to 0.6 tons per hectare) in the past 8 years, and new strains with the potential for 3 tons (under irrigation) are being released. Sunflowerseed production has already increased sixfold, to more than 2 million tons, and is still rising.[13]

Shorter-season corn varieties have pushed the world's Corn Belt 250 miles north in recent decades, into central Canada, northward in the former Soviet Union and in China and further south in Argentina. We have moved corn from tropic Mexico to Central Canada over the centuries, and have cut a month off the growing season in the last 40 years.[14]

(I saw the short-season corn march northward as I grew up. When I was a kid, central Michigan was a bit chancy for corn. There was a lot of wheat, barley, and oats. As I grew older, the land went increasingly to corn and soybeans, with small grains grown only often enough to break pest cycles.)

Shorter-season rice varieties have cut the length of the growing season from 180 days to 110 days, permitting more double and triple cropping all over Asia. At the same time, researchers have made the rice plant more responsive to fertilizer and given it resistance to such pests as the brown planthopper, green leafhopper, gall midge, blast, blight, and grassy stunt.[15]

A redesigned rapeseed plant has produced a whole new product in addition to raising crop use value. Canadian plant breeders took out the natural chemicals which made rapeseed's oil bitter and its protein meal toxic to animals. They renamed the new plant "canola," and it now produces the most highly recommended vegetable oil for health-conscious consumers. Canola's protein meal is now a valuable addition to livestock and poultry feed supplies.

Kenya's new coffee tree, Riuru 11, has bred-in resistance to coffee berry disease and leaf rust, so growers can cut chemical sprays by one-third (and cash outlays by 60 percent).[16]

New cassava varieties for Africa are resistant to several endemic pests—and thus yield three to five times as much food.[17]

New high-protein corn has 90 percent of the food value of non-fat dry milk. The high-protein genes should help to overcome chronic protein shortages for people (and especially children) in regions where white corn dominates the diets of the poor. These include the Andean countries, remote regions of India and parts of Africa. The high-protein varieties are also being bred into yellow corn varieties, to increase their feed value by about 2 percent.[18]

Cloned cocoa trees and high-density planting will permit Malaysian cocoa growers to more than triple their production per acre. The new cloned hybrids by themselves triple yields. The new high-density planting system (3,300 trees per hectare instead of the conventional 1,000) adds further yield gains.[19]

Chickpeas resistant to root rot—and planted in a new broadbed-and-furrow farming system—produce 50 percent higher yields in Ethiopia.[20]

Wheat plants redesigned for more grain-bearing spikes per acre have been bred at the international research center in Mexico. The new plant structure will take spring bread wheats to a new yield plateau over the coming decade.[21]

Disease-resistant bananas and plantains will apparently prevent the near-total loss of these key starchy foods to the dreaded Black Sigatoka disease. Black Sigatoka, first noticed in Fiji, has already spread through much of Latin America and is now established in Africa as well. Researchers at the Fundacion Hondurena de Investigacion Agricola and the Institute for Tropical Agriculture in Nigeria led the breakthrough in a scientific "first."[22]

Wait a minute! Are you telling me that all the world's bananas and plantains were at risk? My kids' bananas? Fruit salad? We were going to lose the major starchy staple for the whole Southern Hemisphere?

That's correct. A new disease, produced by natural evolution, emerged from the Fiji Islands and began attacking the banana (Musa) family worldwide.

Why haven't I heard about this?

Probably because it wasn't an immediate threat to Americans. Bananas are just a variety of fruit to us. The big food losses would have been in Latin America and Africa.

Why didn't I hear the good news when the "cure" was found?

The *Atlantic Monthly* had a small feature story. Mostly the media doesn't hype good news—though they frequently write about Lester Brown's latest famine claim, or Paul Ehrlich's complaint that we've got too many people to feed.

Did anybody get a medal?

No. And the U.S. Agency for International Development is cutting its aid for the international research center where much of the work was done.

MYTHMAKER:

"Imagine driving the plants to uniform prodigies of production with fertilizers and hormones while simultaneously eliminating their competitors with weed killers and destroying their insect and disease pests with appropriately structured biochemicals. . . . Mother Nature bound, gagged and blindfolded, helpless at last."

Dr. Joan D. Gussow, *Chicken Little, Tomato Sauce & Agriculture,* 1991[23]

Good-bye to the Bull

My personal experience with the power of genetics goes back to my boyhood on the dairy farm. When I was very young, we always had a young bull, penned away from the cows except when one of them was in heat.

My father was *very* careful to tell me how dangerous the bull was; that the animal was completely untrustworthy no matter how tame he might seem. It was all right to pet the cows, horses and hogs, he said, but *never* get into the bullpen. Our bull was always young, because old bulls were even more dangerous than young ones.

Whenever a neighbor was gored by his bull—which happened fairly often—Dad would reinforce his message.

When I was about 10, we got rid of the bull. We started using artificial insemination instead. By that time, I was old enough to keep an eye on the herd, and note if any of the cows was coming into heat. (Dad was a county agent and often didn't get home during daylight.) If a cow was ready for breeding, we had to pen her up and call the artificial inseminator.

We also joined the Dairy Herd Improvement Association. To me, that meant sharing my bedroom one night a month with a young man who would weigh every cow's milk night and morning, and test it for butterfat content.

I didn't realize at first that this periodic hospitality was part of a much larger concept. All the data from all the member herds' cows was being fed into a central information bank.

The point was to know which bulls added more production to their offspring and which ones *didn't*.

The result of artificial insemination and record analysis has been better bulls that have added 2 percent per year to the milk of all the cows in America, each year since I was 10. This has increased average milk per cow from about 5,000 lbs. to 15,000 lbs.[24] (The world milk production record is now held by a Holstein cow in Missouri which produced 59,300 pounds of milk on twice-a-day milking in 365 days.)[25]

At the time, all I knew was that I didn't have to be afraid any more of Dad going into the bullpen.

Twinning Calves and Pest-Resistant Soybeans

In 1974, Lester Brown scoffed at the potential for higher food production in the future. He specifically noted that research had not produced higher-yielding soybeans or consistent twinning in cattle. It took a while, but research has now done both.

Mississippi State University and the USDA's Agricultural Research Service have announced a new pest-resistant soybean for America's southern states. This region has long been plagued by low yields, in large part due to heavy pest pressure. The new soybean resists soil nematodes, stem canker and several leaf-eating insects.

In three years of tests, a check variety averaged 21 bushels per acre, and the new variety 45 bushels![26]

There's your higher-yielding soybean, Mr. Brown.

Genetics have also produced perhaps the biggest potential breakthrough in raising the productivity of the world's cattle herds—twin calves. An American cattle breeding service has started selling bull semen that is predicted to produce 40 percent twins, and their cow embryos 30 percent twins. Cows from the standard popular beef breeds produce about 1 percent twins.

In exchange for giving the "twinners" top-quality feed, cattle breeders can likely cut their per-pound costs of production by up to 30 percent. That's because twin calves represent almost twice the usual 70 percent of the cow's body weight "harvested" through the calf. Twins yield a far more efficient use of pasture, fencing, cow health costs, etc.

The new germplasm is from an experimental herd at the USDA's Clay Center, Neb. cattle research station. Breeds used in the twinning project include Hereford, Angus, Shorthorn, Simmental, Charolais, Brown Swiss, Holsteins and a number of others.

Other Key Farming Technologies Waiting on the Shelf

- Hybrid rice, developed in China, offers potential yield gains of 25 percent for virtually all of the world's rice plantings. Currently, China is the only country using the hand labor required for pollination. However, the International Rice Research Institute thinks it can use temperature sensitivity and apomixis to get male-line sterility and mass-produce new hybrids.[27]
- High-yielding wet rice farming systems could take advantage of 500 million acres of inland wetlands in mid-Africa. Africa could be self-sufficient in rice by planting only a small proportion of these wetlands. Most of Africa's current rice production is on low-yielding uplands better suited to trees.[28] Human diseases in the past have kept farmers out of the wetlands, but the diseases can now be controlled.
- Infrastructure also raises the effective yields of crops. In Bangladesh, a new farm-to-market road is associated with a

one-third increase in crop yields. Better transport makes inputs less costly and the crop more valuable. Storage silos and grain dryers cut crop losses after harvest. Processing plants turn harvest-time gluts into year-round supplies. India's food processing industries have attracted 300 billion rupees of investment in the last two years, but the country still estimates that 20 percent of the country's farm output is wasted because of inadequate storage, refrigeration and roads.[29] All it takes to provide more infrastructure is capital, and the world's capital resources are growing more rapidly than ever before.

Creating New Cropland

We shouldn't *need* much additional cropland if we continue to raise yields. However, it may be comforting to know that there is a great deal of good land which *could* be used for farming if more were needed—without threatening biodiversity:

- Acid-tolerant corn, rice, and forage crops have recently been developed in Brazil and Colombia which can be planted successfully on the world's 1 *billion* acres of acid savannah. These savannahs have hitherto been tropical wasteland. They do not even have much genetic diversity beyond stunted brush and a few coarse grasses. Now they have the potential to protect other more environmentally valuable land for wildlife. One-third of this acid savannah is in Latin America, one-third in southern Africa and the rest in Southeast Asia.
- The upper Nile valleys offer major tracts of unplanted arable land. A high-yielding hybrid sorghum has already been bred for the area—but civil war in Sudan is preventing its widespread use.
- In the upper Euphrates valley, the big dams are already filling for Turkey's Greater Anatolia project. The dams will create a replica of California's famed Central Valley. Eventually, some four million hectares of low-yield dryland crops will give way to fruits, vegetables, cotton, and other high-value irrigated crops. Half of this will come into production in the next five years or so. (Such dams are also currently the most environmentally

responsible way to expand the world's power capacity.)
- Saudi Arabia test-planted 2,500 acres of a new salt-tolerant crop called salicornia in 1993. Salicornia has been bred up from a ubiquitous saltwater weed. Green-chopped before maturity, it makes a rich livestock forage like alfalfa. If allowed to mature, it yields an oilseed with a 70 percent meal proportion, like the soybean. *Most remarkably, it can be grown on the desert and irrigated with seawater.* Any coastal desert within 5-7 kilometers of the sea (so the irrigation water can flow back into the ocean without contaminating groundwater aquifers) is now a potential site for "saltwater soybeans." Saudi Arabia thinks it has 400,000 acres of suitable desert. Other Middle Eastern countries are watching the results, along with such coastal-desert countries as Chile, Australia, and Morocco.[30]

High-Yield Farming and Forestry—Even for Africa

As we have seen, Africa is almost always the fearsome example held up to show the unsustainable pressure being put on natural resources by population growth. It is even offered as an example of the dangers or inadequacies of high-yield farming.

But Africa is the one continent where we have yet to *deploy* the power of high-yield farming and forestry. It is the only continent still trying to sustain rising populations on low-yield farming and wild harvest of trees nobody owns. The continent got a late start on high-yield farming. Africans didn't worry about raising farm yields during the 1960s because their land was still sparsely populated.

When agricultural researchers did begin to focus on Africa during the Sahel famines of the 1970s, they found that almost nothing developed for other continents worked on Africa's farms. The miracle rice varieties of the Green Revolution worked everywhere *except* Africa. Cassava bred for other continents did poorly in Africa. African farmers couldn't afford hybrid corn or fertilizer.

Nevertheless, strong reasons for optimism emerge from conversations with such experts on African agriculture as Nobel prize-winner Norman Borlaug; Dr. David Seckler, director of research for the Winrock Foundation; Dr. John Sanders of Purdue Uni-

---

Higher-Yielding Fish

For centuries, farmers have been breeding better cattle, hogs, chickens, grains, and oilseeds. Little has been done to improve fish genetics—until lately.

The Nile tilapia is a fast-growing, sweet-tasting fish from Africa that is renowned for its rapid growth and tolerance of tough conditions. High populations, murky water, high temperatures—the tilapia can take everything except severe winters. The tilapia converts feed efficiently. It will even grow in both fresh and salt water!

As a result, the tilapia has been fish-farmed widely for decades throughout much of Africa and Asia.

In 1988, the new International Center for Living Aquatic Resources Management (ICLARM) in the Philippines began the laborious task of breeding a still-better hybrid tilapia. It's not hard to understand why fish genetics have been slow to take off. A typical ICLARM experiment involves 500 cages, and the individual tagging of 25,000 individual little juvenile fish. (ICLARM got important help from Norway, which has already done a major breeding improvement on its high-value Atlantic salmon.)

By 1992, ICLARM's improved tilapia were growing up to 60 percent faster and with 50 percent better survival—on farms—than the commercial tilapia most commonly farmed in the Philippines.

It looks as though the increased productivity already developed in livestock and poultry can be developed for fish farming as well.

(From ICLARM Report, 1992)

---

versity; and Dr. Gebisa Ejeta (now at Purdue), who has bred some of the outstanding new crop varieties for African farmers.

Dr. Borlaug, who bred the original Green Revolution wheat varieties, is now leading an African farm productivity effort called Global 2000. The project is proving that the seeds and farming systems already available can double the yields of African grains and can repay the costs of fertilizer and pest control several times over. Global 2000 says its sorghum farmers in Ghana are tripling their yields with Africa's first short-season, short-stalk white sorghum.

Dr. Seckler returned from mid-Africa several years ago saying his biggest surprise was finding that high-yielding new seed varieties were already widely distributed on the region's farms. I asked why we weren't seeing the impact of the seeds in rising African grain production. He answered that consumers in African cities are so poor they're eating mainly root crops. Additional corn production at high cost would simply drive down the price to ruinous levels. (The best seed breeding advances *reduce* per unit production costs.)

"Africa's farmers are using their high-yielding seeds to reduce the amount of land they clear for subsistence," Seckler told me. That is a benefit, even an environmental benefit. But it is far less than the seeds could do if Africans could achieve economic growth and higher incomes.[31]

Seckler is worried about how African farmers can get and afford fertilizer, but agrees that fertilizer and soil-safe cropping systems offer substantial yield gains for that continent.

John Sanders has worked for a decade on Purdue University's animal-traction project in Burkina Faso. With animal traction, he says, farmers there can increase their grain yields fourfold, and their family farm output by sixfold by tilling "tied ridges". The key is breaking the encrusted soil surface before the rains start—and this cannot be done with feeble hand tools. But only a few of the community's farmers can become "commercial" farmers with oxen. That would leave the rest without a farming role. Sanders knows that until Africa has nonfarm jobs for more of its people, the dominant pattern of African agriculture will remain subsistence farming.

Dr. Ejeta has bred the first high-yielding hybrid sorghum for Africa (aimed at the Sudan). He is now working at Purdue to breed crops that resist Striga, a parasitic weed that is one of the key crop constraints in all Africa.

With high-yield seeds and farming systems, feeding Africa should take less cropland than the continent uses today. The elephants and gorillas need not be displaced by people.

An Ultimate "What If" Game?

About ten years ago, when I was with the State Department, I had a personal discussion with Lester Brown. He was launching yet another of his annual predictions that "this year" we would start to see the famines.

This is my recollection of the conversation:

Brown asked if I didn't think that we were running out of farm technologies. I said I saw no sign of it; in fact, I saw more productivity on the horizon.

He asked if we weren't running out of cropland. I said that we *had* more cropland, but it was less costly to raise the yields on the cropland we already farmed.

Brown: "Yes, but don't we face a limit on agricultural water supplies?"

Avery: "We could triple the efficiency of our farm water use."

Brown: "Don't we face a limit on the rate of photosynthesis?"

Avery: "Researchers have even had some success with breeding corn for a higher rate of photosynthesis."

Brown: "But we have an ultimate limit in the amount of sunlight that falls on the earth."

Avery: "We're using only 1 or 2 percent of it now."

Brown: "Then you agree that we face ultimate limits on food production."

REALITY:

"One hundred years from now the earth may have 10 billion inhabitants. . . . [T]he human population will then be approaching a stable level as the industrialized countries already have. Will our species be able to feed itself when this steady state is reached? The short answer is probably yes.

"The long answer is not quite as simple. Not only must the food supply expand, it must expand in a way that does not destroy the natural environment. For that to happen, a steady stream of new technologies that minimize erosion, desertification, salinization of the soil and other environmental damage must be introduced.

"We are confident that if the strong system of agricultural research organizations already in place is provided with enough financial support and leadership, it will develop these techniques."

  Pierre Crosson and Norman J. Rosenberg, "Strategies for Agriculture," *Scientific American Special Issue on Managing Planet Earth*, September 1989, pp. 128-135. Crosson and Rosenberg are Fellows at Resources for the Future, a respected environmental think tank in Washington, D.C.

Notes

[1]William and Paul Paddock, *Famine 1975!* Little, Brown, Boston, 1967, republished in 1976 as *Time of Famines*, pp. 8-10.

[2]Lester Brown, *By Bread Alone*, Praeger, New York, 1974, p. 7.

[3]Lester Brown, "The Illusion of Progress," *State of the World 1990*, p. 11.

[4]William K. Stevens, "Humanity Confronts Its Handiwork: An Altered Planet," *New York Times*, May 5, 1992, pp. C6-7.

[5]Garret Hardin, "Limits to Growth Are Nature's Own," *Insight*, December 20, 1993, p. 23.

[6]Johnson and Gustafson, *Grain Yields and the American Food Supply*, University of Chicago Press, 1962.

[7]U.S. Department of Agriculture Crop Production Estimate, November 9, 1994.

[8]*FAO Production Yearbooks*, op. cit.

[9]*Hybrid Rice: Proceedings of an International Symposium*, International Rice Research Institute (IRRI), Manila, Philippines, 1988, pp. 1-21.

[10]Trip Report, Yunnan Province, China, by Gurdev Kush, Dennith Cassman and Shaobing Peng, IRRI, August 1993.

[11]FAO Production Yearbooks, op. cit.

[12]*Grain and Feed Annual Report*, Abidjan, Foreign Agricultural Service, U.S. Department of Agriculture, Washington, D.C., August 1992.

[13]USDA/FAS, *Oilseed Annual Reports, New Delhi*, 1992 and 1993.

[14]Corn breeding staff, Pioneer Hi-bred International, personal interview, 1993.

[15]Huke and Huke, *Rice Then and Now*, International Rice Research Institute Manila, 1990.

[16]USDA/FAS, *Kenya: Coffee Annual Reports*, Nairobi, 1987-89.

[17]IITA, *IITA Strategic Plan 1989-2000*, pp. 59-61. See also *IITA Annual Report 1989/90*, pp. 42-44; and USDA/FAS *Grain and Staple Food Outlook for Nigeria*, Unclassified cable, July 19, 1990.

[18]*Quality Protein Maize*, Board on Agriculture, National Research Council, Washington, D.C., 1988.

[19]"World Cocoa Bean Production," *World Agricultural Production*, U.S. Department of Agriculture, WAP 10-94, Washington D.C., 1994, p. 38.

[20]*ICARDA Annual Report for 1993*, International Center for Agricultural Research in the Dry Areas, Alleppo, Syria.

[21]Based on a presentation by CIMMYT, the International Maize and Wheat Improvement Center, at International Centers' Week, Washington, D.C., October 26, 1993.

[22]Rowe and Rosales, "Diploid Breeding at FHIA and the Development of Goldfinger (FHIA-01)," *INFOMUSA, the International Magazine on Banana and Plantain*, Vol. 2, No. 2, December 1993, pp. 10-11.

[23]Joan Gussow, *Chicken Little, Tomato Sauce & Agriculture*, The Bootstrap Press, New York, 1991, p. vii.

[24]FAO Production Yearbook series.

[25]"New World Milk Record," *Successful Farming*, December 1993, p. 38.

[26]Agricultural Research Service Quarterly Research Report, USDA, December 1993.

[27]"Hybrid Rice," in *Proceedings of the International Symposium on Hybrid Rice*, Hunan, China, October 1986, by IRRI, Manila, Philippines, 1988. See also TAC Secretariat, Food and Agriculture Organization of the United Nations, *Report of the Fourth External Programme and Management Review of the International Rice Research Institute*, New York: FAO 1992.

[28]*IITA Annual Report*, 1989/90, p. 66.

[29]Jimmy Burns, "Sweet Fruits of Sufficiency," *Financial Times* Special Section on India, November 8, 1994.

[30]Glenn, O'Leary, et al., "Salicornia Bigelovii Torr: An Oilseed Halophyte for Seawater Irrigation," *Science,* March 1991, 1065-7. See also, "A High-Grade Fodder and Seed Crop Which thrives on Seawater," *Arab World Agribusiness*, Vol. 2, 1986, No. 7/8.

[31]Dr. David Seckler, Winrock Foundation, personal communication, 1989.

13

Drink Up, the Water's Fine

MYTHMAKERS SAY:

"The river systems that sustain terrestrial life and provide fresh water to 90 percent of the world human population are losing their life-giving capacity. . . . In developed countries like ours, toxic rivers illustrate dramatically the unimpeded destruction of the planet's lifeblood."
Letter to the editor, from Owen Lammers and Juliette Majot of the
International Rivers Network, Berkeley, CA, printed in *E, the
Environmental Magazine*, February 1994, Vol. V, No. 1

"This book has been written in response to increasing fears that nitrate from agriculture has found its way into drinking water, causing cancer, cyanosis in infants, the growth of toxic algae in rivers and seas, and untold mayhem in otherwise balanced, natural ecosystems. What is worse (so we are told) is that much nitrate has not yet had these effects but is waiting to do so, moving unseen in underground waters, sinking slowly, insidiously and inexorably towards our taps. In short, a nitrate time-bomb."
Addiscott et al., *Farming, Fertilizers and the
Nitrate Problem*, preface[1]

"Agricultural groundwater pollution seriously threatens public health and welfare. Recent data from USDA indicate that 36 states have documented instances of well contamination with pesticides. Contamination with fertilizer nitrates has been detected in 30 states. These are troubling findings as most residents of rural American obtain their drinking water from underground sources."
Blueprint for the Environment: A Plan for Federal Action, the
report of a task force of 19 environmental organizations including

the Sierra Club, the Natural Resources Defense Council, The
Audubon Society, and Zero Population Growth, 1989[2]

"The growing use of chemical fertilizers is causing another more
localized but hazardous problem: the chemical pollution of drinking
water. Nitrates are the main worry, since they have risen to toxic levels
in some communities in the United States. Both children and livestock
have become ill, and some have died, from drinking water that contained
high levels of nitrates."
                Lester Brown, *By Bread Alone*, Overseas Development Council,
                                                                New York, 1974, p. 50

REALITY SAYS:

"We're safer and healthier than ever—and also more afraid of what
we eat, drink and breathe. Why the reality gap? Too often, critics say, the
media's coverage fuels our fears."
                David Shaw, column one of "Living Scared," a *Los Angeles Times*
                series of stories on why Americans are safer and more frightened
                                        in their daily lives than ever before[3]

"Results from the U.S. EPA's National Pesticide Survey indicate that
less than 1 percent of either rural domestic wells or community water
system wells contain any pesticides in excess of lifetime (health advisories)."
                                                                U.S. EPA, 1990[4]

". . . [A] continuing saga . . . began with EC Directive 778, which laid
down a mandatory limit of 11 parts per million of nitrate-nitrogen in
drinking water. Previously, the UK had been working to a limit of 22
parts per million with no ill effects on consumers. The reason for restrictions of any kind are based on the belief that excessive nitrates can
cause blue babies and stomach cancer. The facts show, however, that the
last 'blue baby' in the UK was 30 years ago. . . . And the incidence of
stomach cancer in eastern England, where nitrate levels are highest—is
below that of the rest of the country."
                David Richardson, "The Case Against Nitrates is Far from
                                        Watertight," *Financial Times*, June 25, 1991

"Nationwide, the total number of (pesticide) detections is a few
percent of the total (water) analyses done, and in most cases the

concentrations found are very small fractions of levels that are believed to be harmful to humans and aquatic life."
Pesticides in Surface and Ground Water, Council for Agricultural Science and Technology, Issue Paper No. 2, April 1994[5]

Environmental zealots—and perhaps even agencies of the U.S.
government—want us to end the use of farm chemicals and/or spend
billions of government dollars to make our drinking water "safe."
They are seemingly immune to the recently rechecked reality that
our drinking water is *already* safe.

The zealots believe—apparently because they want to—that fertilizer and pesticides are threatening our lives through our drinking
water. That gives them another "reason" to condemn high-yield farming. In addition, "contamination" is a proven fund-raiser for an environmental organization no matter what the "contaminant" or its real
danger. Even rural areas have succumbed to the tempting idea that
Federal money for studying their "water problems" comes free.

The Blue Baby Scam

Let's deal first with nitrates.

There *are* nitrates in many of our wells. Some of them come
from natural sources like legume plants and animal manure, and some
from commercial fertilizer.

The EPA and the environmentalists call these nitrates "contamination." That implies danger. In reality, the small amounts of nitrate
found in our wells have not been tied to *any* health threat. But nitrates are nevertheless considered contamination, and listed as such.

The average U.S. farm well contains 5-7 parts per million of
nitrate. This is only a trace level. Hardly any Americans are exposed
to high enough nitrate levels to represent real threats to their health.[6]
Only about 1.5 percent of the U.S. population is exposed to anything
above the recommended lifetime Maximum Contaminant Level, even
seasonally. And the U.S. health limit is set far below the real danger
level.

Environmental activists have searched hard and long to find some
significant health threat that they can link to these trace levels of

nitrate. Though they haven't found a real nitrate threat so far, this hasn't slowed their efforts very much.

In the European Community, nitrate tolerances were cut in half in 1980 with NO scientific basis for the change. The EC is now suing Great Britain to comply with the standard, even though it will wreak havoc on British farming—and produce no public health gains.

"Blue baby" is a real condition. (It is also known as methaeglobanemia or cyanosis.) However, it attacks fewer and fewer babies each year. The problem is so rare that no national statistics are kept on it. The U.S. has apparently had only one blue-baby death in recent decades—one that occurred because of a large spill of nitrogen fertilizer near a farm well in North Dakota, which drove the nitrate level in the well up to 116 parts per million. (Even then, the baby should have been saved.)[7]

Doesn't it seem strange that we are considering massive Federal mandates on one of our key basic industries for a problem so rare that no health statistics are even kept?

The same pattern is found in other countries. Great Britain has not had a blue baby fatality since 1950. (Back then, incidentally, British farmers used hardly any fertilizer.) No blue baby case has even been *reported* in the UK in 20 years, despite the fact that British farmers have radically increased their fertilizer use to levels far higher than those in the U.S.[8] (UK farmers began to get lavish EC farm price supports in the 1970s, which greatly increased their use of fertilizer.)

It usually takes nitrate levels of over 200 ppm to put even small infants at risk from blue baby syndrome—unless the well is contaminated with bacteria as well. With bacterial contamination, the blue baby syndrome can be triggered at about 100 ppm.[9] The radical difference between the current 5-6 ppm nitrate levels in our water supplies and the 100-200 ppm levels which trigger "blue baby" explains why the syndrome is so rare.[10]

The blue baby cases that occur are almost always traced back to a leaking septic tank, a badly sited manure pit, or an old shallow well; not to fertilizer spreaders.

In Indiana, a farm wife recently brought a well sample to Purdue University technicians that tested 164 ppm! Asked how deep the well was, she answered, "Twelve feet." It was an old hand-dug well that had never made anybody visibly sick, so it was still in use. The odds are that it was also downhill from a livestock herd that had grown radically in numbers since the turn of the century.

Water and Cancer

Health professionals have looked carefully for any link between nitrate in water and stomach cancer. There *are* theoretical reasons for suspecting linkage. But a British study of 229 urban areas found a *negative* correlation between nitrate concentrations and stomach cancer.[11]

Longtime workers in fertilizer plants *do* show higher concentrations of nitrate in their saliva—but show no elevated risk of stomach cancer.[12]

Meanwhile, stomach cancer rates have been dropping rapidly in the very areas and countries where fertilizer use has increased! Stomach cancer used to be the top cancer killer among U.S. men, and third among women. The rate has dropped by roughly three-fourths, and the U.S. now has one of the lowest stomach cancer rates in the world.[13]

Doctors think refrigeration and year-round consumption of fruits and vegetables are the major factors reducing stomach cancer.[14] Nitrate in the water seems to have no offsetting effect.

REALIST ON THE RIVER:

"I am an old Calvert County farmer who has lived and farmed for the last 71 years. I have loved the old river both for its bounty and for its aesthetic qualities. The Patuxent is the largest river entirely within Maryland and a major contributor of water to the Chesapeake Bay. . . . Treated effluent now adds 55 percent of the river's fresh water. . . . During the recent ice storm, thousands of tons of urea (46 percent nitrogen) were used on airports, sidewalks, etc., all impervious surfaces. As the ice melted, I wonder where the nitrogen went?"

John A. Prouty, Huntingtown, MD, letter to the *Delmarva Farmer*,
March 8, 1994

Pesticide Contamination—Or Traces?

Trace amounts of pesticides have been found in many groundwater and surface water sources. A few pesticides are both persistent and weakly bonded to soil particles, so they can be leached out of the soil by rainfall. Examples include aldicarb on potatoes; a nematode pesticide called DBCP which was formerly used in California; and atrazine, a corn herbicide widely used in the Midwest.

The public is easily frightened about these pesticide traces, because they have been told so often that all pesticides are "killers." What pesticides are designed to kill, however, are not humans, but weeds and insects, pest rodents, etc.

In pesticides as in virtually every "poison," danger requires a combination of 1) a substance toxic to the recipient organism and 2) enough exposure to cause damage.

Fortunately, we are long past the days when mainstream farmers tried to kill their pests with such compounds as lead arsenate and copper sulfate—which can be deadly to virtually all living organisms. We have also left behind the days of persistent pesticides like DDT—regardless of safety or efficiency. Modern pesticides are deliberately designed to have minimal impact on humans and beneficial wildlife. Most are also designed for rapid breakdown, in days or weeks.

The pesticide traces found in water supplies represent even smaller risks than the pesticide residues in food—which are trivial.

It would be nice to be able to flatly say that trace contamination of water poses *no* threat, but we can't prove that negative. Any more than we can say that walking across the street (with the traffic light) poses *no* risk.

What we *can* say is that our well water supplies are safer than they've ever been. We no longer spread typhoid or cholera through our water. We are more careful now about having wells near our septic tanks or having them downhill from livestock pens.

The water experts working with rural wells say they check first for sources of bacterial contamination like the barnyard and the septic tank. They also look to make sure that the farmer isn't loading or rinsing his sprayer near the well. Those are by far the largest risks to farm water supplies.

The Ohio Example

Ohio typifies the relative freedom from pesticide "contamination" in the U.S. Corn Belt. And remember, the Corn Belt features the heaviest use of pesticides among non-irrigated U.S. farms.

A survey of Ohio water sources indicates that pesticide residues were *below the detection limits* in more than 90 percent of the private wells.[15]

Only a tiny proportion of its residents (about half a percent) are consuming water-borne pesticides in excess of their recommended lifetime risk standards. These at-risk consumers are almost all drinking from a few particularly vulnerable sources: surface springs and shallow wells.

The EPA's 1991 National Pesticide Survey indicates that less than 1 percent of either rural domestic wells or community water system wells contain *any* pesticides, even seasonally, above the lifetime health advisories.[16]

Surface water sources occasionally have peak concentrations above the level of the lifetime health advisory after springtime run-off events. However, this involves only a few surface waters (mainly smaller rivers) and short periods of time.

The major "problem" chemical is atrazine—and the EPA itself has recently decided that atrazine is about seven times safer than has been reflected in our water health advisories. If the EPA raised its Maximum Contamination Limit for atrazine to reflect its new safety rating, it would be hard for even the most dedicated fear-monger to instill much terror over American well water.

Further Cleanup

More good news: Monitoring of wells in the Midwest strongly suggests that little of the pesticide traces currently found in ground and surface waters get into the water supply from farmers' field applications. Virtually all of the contamination has come from *point sources*—where the pesticides have been accidently spilled or where the mixing and rinsing has been done carelessly in the past.[17]

In Iowa, over 80 percent of the water well systems in which pesticides were detected (other than atrazine) had known point sources—usually the local agricultural chemical dealer—near one of the town wells.

In Illinois, the state environmental agency randomly monitored more than 300 wells for pesticides and found *none*. Disbelieving, they then targeted more than 400 "high-risk" wells, testing for 34 pesticides with a *highly sensitive detection limit of 20 parts per trillion*. Only three of the wells were positive for pesticides and all three were near known point sources.[18]

These outcomes make it relatively easy to reduce further the current traces of pesticides in the water:

- A major campaign is already warning farmers not to mix pesticides or rinse their application equipment near wells or surface waters.
- Farm chemical dealers now virtually all have covered storages, concrete rinsing pads and holding tanks for rinsate, and their facilities are now surrounded by impermeable dikes.
- Chemical companies are increasingly delivering their products as dry compounds (which can be cleaned up if they are accidentally spilled).
- When the compound *has* to be delivered as a liquid, it increasingly comes in a reusable sealed container that locks onto the applicator rig to prevent spillage. The empty container is returned to the factory for reuse. Millions of plastic jugs that used to go into dumps and landfills have been eliminated as a side benefit of the reusable lock-on containers.
- Or the companies sell their liquid products in pre-measured water-soluble pouches (so there is less spillage danger, and no container to rinse).

Since 1985, the government has frozen the farms' yield histories for price supports and begun to require much more stringent farm conservation plans on all farms. Chemical manufacturers have also come out with new compounds that require very little active ingredient because they are so narrowly targeted at the pests' vulnerable points, such as key enzymes.

As a result, the amount of pesticide used by farmers has dropped significantly since 1976. Insecticide application rose from 117 million pounds (active ingredient) in 1964 to a peak of 130 million pounds in 1976—but by 1982 usage had declined to 71 million pounds.

Herbicide use, fostered mainly by the expansion of soil-conserving tillage systems, rose from 71 million pounds in 1964 to 456 million in 1982.[19]

That doesn't mean, of course, we can't further reduce pesticide traces in our groundwater. A new USDA research study combined no-till farming and ultrahigh populations of corn plants per acre. They used very narrow rows, and planted 52,000 plants per acre, compared with a normal "high" population of 26,000. *Because the high plant populations quickly shaded out weeds*, the researchers got equally high yields—150 bushels per acre—with one-fourth as much herbicide.

About 200 million pounds of herbicides are used on U.S. corn annually, and especially on no-till corn. Atrazine (used to control broadleaf weeds in corn) and metolachlor (for grassy weeds) are widely used preemergence chemicals that are often found (at low levels) in ground and surface water. But, as we shall see in Chapter 22, these pesticides do not present human danger.

Eco-Economics: Billions to Fix Something Not Broken

Despite this picture of safe wells and drinking water, alarmists are sounding their cries about water contamination all over the country.

The Federal government is spending billions of dollars on grants, pilot projects and demonstration efforts aimed at "making our drinking water safer."

REALIST VALUES CLEAN WATER:

"Purer drinking water, cleaner rivers and less polluted beaches have clear attractions. But what is the price of delivering them? Too high according to Mr. Ian Byatt, director-general of OFWAT, the economic regulator of Britain's water industry. Meeting European Community environmental commitments agreed by the government since . . . 1989 will lead to an extra ($3 billion) a year in capital investment over the next five years on top of the [$7 billion] currently being spent.

"For the average customer, the full programme would mean an extra [$108] a year. . . .

"Nor is there much evidence that better standards would improve public health. Mr. Byatt argues that the new sewage measures would mean that a town with a population of 10,000 produced the pollution equivalent to 27 pigs, while the drinking water provisions would result in pollution equivalent to one aspirin in an Olympic-size swimming pool."

From an editorial in the *Financial Times*, London, July 14, 1993

Notes

[1]Addiscott, Whitmore, and Powlson, *Farming, Fertilizers and the Nitrate Problem*, CAB International, Wallingford, UK, 1991.

[2]Alan Comp, ed., *Blueprint for the Environment: A Plan for Federal Action*, Howe Brothers, Salt Lake City, 1989, p. 13.

[3]The David Shaw "Living Scared" series ran in the *Los Angeles Times* on September 11, 1994.

[4]U.S. Environmental Protection Agency, *National Survey of Pesticides in Drinking Water*, Washington, D.C., 1990.

[5]Available from CAST, Ames, Iowa.

[6]Environmental Protection Agency, *Another Look: National Survey of Pesticides in Drinking Water Wells*, Phase 2 Report, EPA 570/9-91-020, January 1992.

[7]Dr. Mark McClanahan, National Center for Environmental Health, personal interview, September 1994.

[8]Addiscott et al., *Farming, Fertilizers and the Nitrate Problem*, CAB International, Wallingford, UK, 1991, p. 8.

[9]Addiscott et al., op. cit.

[10]Addiscott et al., op. cit.

[11]Addiscott et al., op. cit.

[12]Addiscott et al., op. cit.

[13]American Cancer Society, *Cancer Rates and Risks*, 1985, pp. 114-115.

[14]*Cancer Rates and Risks*, op. cit.

[15]Dr. Robert M. Devlin, "Herbicide Concentrations in Ohio's Drinking Water," *Rational Readings on Environmental Concerns,* Van Nostrand-Rheinhold, New York, 1992.

[16]EPA, *Another Look: National Survey of Pesticides in Drinking Water Wells,* op. cit.

[17]Dr. Richard S. Fawcette, "Pesticides in Ground Water—Solving the Right Problem," *Rational Readings on Environmental Concerns*, op. cit., pp. 73-78.

[18]Fawcette, op. cit.

[19]USDA ERS data.

14

If We Stop Wasting the Water . . .

MYTHMAKERS SAY:

"At international meetings about resources we have frequently heard the statement that even in the 1990s, some countries or regions will have to stop their growth or go to war, or both, because of shortages of water."
Donella Meadows, Dennis Meadows, and Jorgen Randers, Beyond the Limits: Confronting Global Collapse, Chelsea Green Publishing, Post Mills, Vermont, 1992, p. 54

"'Irrigation is not likely to expand much faster than one percent per year during the 1990s, while population rises at 2 percent,' Postel said. 'This raises a red flag for the food supply.' Postel said the imposition of new population controls . . . is necessary to avoid a 'collision' between population growth and water scarcity."
Quote from a Washington Post story on Water for Agriculture: Facing the Limits, by Sandra Postel of Worldwatch, December 10, 1989, p. A4

"The pressure of rapid population growth, especially in the Third World, represents the fifth major strategic threat to the global water system. . . . One of the main reasons for this is the growing reliance on irrigation for agriculture. . . . "
Vice President Al Gore, Earth in the Balance, pp. 110-111

AND SOMETIMES THEY GET IT RIGHT:

"Farming accounts for some 70 percent of global water use. Much of the vast quantity diverted by and for farmers never benefits a crop: worldwide, the efficiency of irrigation systems averages less than 40

percent. The technologies and know-how exist to boost that figure substantially; what is needed are policies and incentives that foster efficiency instead of discouraging it."

> Sandra Postel, "Saving Water for Agriculture," *State of the World
> 1990*, Worldwatch Institute, Washington, D.C., pp. 39-40

One of the favorite new predictions of the eco-zealots is that the
world is running out of fresh water. Those claims are false. Most of
the world has ample supplies of fresh water to meet the expected
human and environmental needs—if we stop wasting it.

The world's farmers use 70 percent of the water consumed, virtually all of it for irrigation. The vast majority of this irrigation water
is wasted.

Worldwide, farmers' irrigation water efficiencies *in the field* average less than 40 percent, and perhaps less than 30 percent. (No one
really knows accurately.) Even before the water gets to the farm field, a
great deal is lost from evaporation and from seepage out of unlined
canals. Once at the farm, most of the irrigation water is applied to poorly

USAID Photo by Chapellas

CAMEL PUMP—The typical Third World farmer wastes most of his
irrigation water. The camel isn't too fond of the system, either.

leveled fields with inherently wasteful flood irrigation systems. (The parts of the field near the water source *have* to get too much water, so that enough will flow to the more distant parts to support a crop.)

Other factors also encourage inefficiency. Most governments offer the water to the farmers virtually free, leading them to overuse it. All too often, the irrigated fields have inadequate or nonexistent drainage systems, so that overuse of water and poor drainage lead to salinization and ruined soils.

It was probably poor drainage that ruined the Hanging Gardens of Babylon, one of the Seven Wonders of the ancient world.

Bad examples of *current* water usage:

- Saudi Arabia is using eons-old fossil water to produce millions of tons of gritty desert wheat which it dumps at giveaway prices in poverty-stricken Mideast markets under the label of "economic diversification."
- California farmers use underpriced government water to produce rice (one of the thirstiest crops) on semidesert where it is ill-suited. Some of the rice is even surplus (given the trade barriers).
- Indonesia is using heavy doses of irrigation water, pesticides, and even plant growth stimulants to boost the yields on its domestic rice, while shutting out lower-cost rain-fed rice from nearby Thailand.

Solutions to the Water "Shortages"

There are relatively simple and cost-effective solutions to all of these problems. However, they are unlikely to be implemented until the problems reach crisis proportions because water is always a highly sensitive issue that affects pocketbooks and property rights.

(I remember a brief assignment working on a national water resources report in 1968. New Mexico's state report announced that it would need to import millions of acre-feet of water in the future to fully develop its desert crop potential. Washington state was equally fervent in saying it wouldn't be able to export any water in the future because it would be needed to irrigate timberlands! Neither was remotely realistic; both parties were just trying to stake out water claims.)

California stands as a good example of how we could resolve seemingly intractable water problems.

Californians could double the amount of water available for non-farm use with virtually no public cost and without losing the jobs or earnings from agriculture: They would only need to give the farmers who currently own water rights *actual title to the water*. The farmers could then sell their surplus water to the cities, use the money to pay for more efficient irrigation systems, and suffer no loss of farm production.

But a vocal minority of the citizens opposes giving the farmers with their current limited water rights a "windfall."

Many Californians want to shut down irrigated agriculture altogether, on the misunderstanding that it is despoiling the environment. But the irrigated land would support little wildlife if it *weren't* irrigated. Much of California's irrigated land would go back to virtual desert, with the rest probably in grassland lacking much biodiversity.

Dams and Fees

Even the land inundated by the dams is usually steep and erodible, and using it to hold water for high-yielding irrigated land protects much larger stretches of wildlife habitat downstream.

The biggest real environmental problem caused by a dam is probably the stream flow for fish below the dam. For important fisheries like the salmon, this is a major difficulty. For most dams, it probably is far less important—despite the eco-activists' past solicitude for the snail darter.[1]

There are also some important dam sites which still *should* be developed for other important reasons. Noteworthy among these are sites for high dams in the mountains of Nepal:

- Dams in Nepal would inundate little wildlife and displace practically no people, because of the awesome steepness of the valleys.
- The dams would prevent much of the downstream flooding which helps make life so desperate and precarious in Bangladesh.
- Such dams would produce huge amounts of energy without

CO_2, which could provide nonfarm jobs in both the highlands and lowlands of Nepal and in neighboring India.

• The dams would also provide irrigation water for Nepal and India to increase crop yields and avoid expansion of low-yield agriculture onto more wildlife habitat.

• Water needs to be priced at its real value, so farmers will use it efficiently. Worldwide, farmers probably don't pay even 10 percent of the real water cost. If farmers have to pay the real cost of the water, they will actually irrigate more land with the same water supply, for much longer spans of time, with far fewer environmental problems. And if the water recipients have to pay the real water cost, only the best irrigation projects will be built.

• Pricing irrigation water at its real value would also encourage us to produce our farm needs on rainfed land—without the high capital costs and environmental risks related to irrigation. (Existing irrigation projects, of course, should continue to be used as efficiently as possible.)

• Irrigation must shift toward more efficient water application systems.

Relative Water-Use Efficiency

flood irrigation	35-60 percent
center-pivot sprinklers	70-85 percent
trailing tube pivots	85-90 percent
drip irrigation	85-90 percent

• The latest in irrigation systems is a dual-level system pioneered at Iowa State that has virtually no evaporation or leaching.[2] The system uses two different levels of perforated pipes, one at the crop root zone and the other a foot or so below it. Any water and plant nutrients that get below the root zone are recirculated back to the upper pipes. There is virtually no loss to evaporation, runoff or leaching. (The initial capital cost is high.)

• The world's farm trade rules need to be liberalized along the lines of its nonfarm trade. The current pervasive use of farm

FAO Photo by G. Tortoli

TRIPLING WATER EFFICIENCY—A pressurized sprinkler system uses its water up to three times as efficiently as the flood irrigation systems typical of poor countries. That means more crops from the same water, with less salinization and water logging.

trade barriers encourages well-off countries to misuse water and build expensive irrigation systems in dry regions instead of importing low-cost farm commodities from rainfed agriculture.

The Future of Irrigation

Most of the best irrigation sites *are* already developed, at least by current standards. Most irrigation systems in the world today *are* troubled with waterlogging and salinization, which threaten their long-term viability. However, the environmental zealots are wrong to contend that we should turn our backs on irrigation and quietly accept famine or food aid for poor arid countries.

There is nothing inherently unsustainable about irrigated agriculture. The technologies and policies to support long-term productivity from irrigated fields are simple, straightforward, well-known to water experts—and politically difficult.

As water continues to become more valuable, it is virtually

certain that urgent needs will overcome political reluctance and that the key technologies and policies will eventually prevail.

MYTHMAKER:

"We have also fallen victim to a kind of technological hubris. . . . We dare to imagine that we will find technological solutions for every technologically induced problem."

Vice President Al Gore, *Earth in the Balance*, p. 206

A Global Warming Incentive for Irrigation?

If global warming *is* occurring, then the world should rush to build many more dams for clean power that emits no CO_2. (Surely even the eco-activists would want to build dams rather than bringing on the ravages they have prophesied from global warming.) If we have global warming, the comparative advantage in farming will swing toward places with power dam sites. It will make sense to use the dams for both power and irrigation.

In that case, raising the efficiency of farm water use will become even more important. We don't know where these places are going to be, however, because the global circulation models (GCM) tell us even less about future precipitation patterns than about temperatures. The big GCM model in the UK Meteorological Office, for example, now projects the same midyear rainfall in 2050 for the Sahara Desert and Ireland, currently one of the wettest places on the planet.

Raising California's Water Efficiency

California *can* have the water it needs for urban uses, and at relatively low cost.

California's farmers currently use antique flood irrigation. This has low capital costs, but wastes lots of water. If the farmers are given incentives to conserve water, they can invest in low-pressure pipelines, center-pivot sprinklers, drip irrigation, trailing tubes, and other delivery systems that use water more efficiently.

Numerous technologies are available to stretch an acre-foot of water on a farmer's field. They range from low-pressure pipes and small temporary earth "damlets" to computerized center-pivot sprinklers with low-pressure rubber tires.

Farmers can also save water by changing their crop mixes—if they have a financial incentive to do so. Alfalfa is one of the major crops grown in California's irrigated valleys today. But alfalfa is a very thirsty crop. Rice, as mentioned, is another thirsty crop of questionable real value in today's California—except where it is grown in such naturally wet locations as the Sacramento Delta.

The change would make an enormous difference. California uses 35 billion of the 339 billion gallons of water America withdraws from its water sources daily. That's more than 10 percent of one of the biggest water bills in the world. California also applies 20 percent of America's irrigation water.[3]

California-based water experts suggest that farm water savings of 10-15 percent can be readily achieved. Experts who have worked in California—and then transferred out of the line of political crossfire—suggest that even bigger water savings (20-25 percent) are possible.

Because agriculture now represents more than 80 percent of the state's water consumption, a 15-20 percent savings in agricultural water would roughly double the water available for non-farmers. A 1984 water market modeling effort directed by Dr. R. E. Howitt and Dr. Henry Vaux of the University of California/Davis says agricultural water savings of 8-12 percent would be enough to satisfy urban needs to the year 2020.[4]

How and for How Much Cost?

Saving water isn't free, although it would be far less expensive than big new water transfer projects. (Just the environmental lawsuits involved in a new water project might make it prohibitive.)

It would require many farmers to convert from flood irrigation by setting up pressurized water systems and buying a lot of new irrigation equipment.

A 160-acre farm might need to dig a two-acre pond ten feet deep and line it with clay and bentonite. A big electric pump and a center-pivot sprinkler system (essentially a water pipe on wheels with sprinkler heads along its length) might cost $55-60,000. The total investment might well be $70-75,000, and the machinery has an expected useful life of 7 years. Thus the effective cost for cutting the farm's water needs might come to about $60 in annual costs per acre of land. If water needs were cut from three acre-feet to 2.5 acre-feet per acre, the water saving cost would be $120 per acre-foot.

The actual costs of water saving will vary widely between farms and localities. But with a water market, the farmers who could convert at lowest cost would be the first to save and sell water. Those with high conversion costs would not need to make any change.

Key to Water Savings: A Real Market

The key to successful water shifts is the creation of an effective market for water. At the moment, water rights have no off-farm value to farmers. They get water to put on crops, but have no right to resell any surplus. Thirstier crops may even be grown to "use it up." Hardly any money is spent on water-saving equipment because there is no incentive to do so.

Most of the farmers use flood irrigation and most flood irrigators put on more water than the crops need, to make sure the whole field gets at least enough.

The extra water even aggravates drainage and salinity problems. Contaminated water and salinity are already significant and costly problems for large parts of the state's irrigated farmland.

California farmers have had little enthusiasm for water-efficient systems in the past, but then it was hard to see how water-efficient investments would pay off for them. Much of the new water technology was invented in places like Nebraska and Israel, where each acre-foot saved meant lower costs or more crops for the farmer. But now the center-pivots, trailing tubes and drip systems developed in those water-scarce farming environments could be a key to continued economic growth and quality of life in the Golden State.

California and the World

California's water problems are scarcely unique in the world. The same sorts of water resource questions that face California are being faced in such diverse places as the upper Euphrates valley in Turkey, at a hotly contested new dam project in Hungary, and in the Senegal River valley of Africa.

With no more water than farmers use today, higher use efficiency will let us produce higher yields on more of the acres already in farming, while reducing the waterlogging and salinity problems that plague too many irrigated farms.

That's not Doomsday knocking. It is opportunity.

Notes

[1]The snail darter was an "endangered" small fish that was used by the eco-activists as an excuse to block the construction of the Tellicoe Dam on the Tennessee River. Because the darter was protected under the Endangered Species Act, they claimed the Tennessee was its last refuge. After the dam was built, it was amazing how many streams and rivers turned out to have snail darter populations. In environmental strategy, the snail darter was the first spotted owl. The comeback strategy that has evolved on the development side has been to offer bounties to anyone who can discover additional populations of such endangered species.

[2]"Subsurface Irrigation Systems: Water Management System Recycles Water," *The Grower*, Vol. 24, 1991, pp. 32-34.

[3]W.B. Solley, R.R. Pierce, and H.A. Perlman, *Estimated Use of Water in the U.S.*, U.S. Geological Survey Circular 1081, Washington D.C., 1993.

[4]Howett, Vaux, et al., "An Interregional/Interindustry Trade Model for California Water," *Water Resources Research*, Vol. 20, No. 7, July 1984, pp. 785-792.

15

Sustaining Our Water Quality

MYTHMAKERS SAY:

"Agricultural runoff alone impairs or threatens over 100,000 river miles and almost 2 million acres of lakes. Little progress has been made to address the pervasive source of pollution."
　　　　　　　　　Bob Adler, "Clean Water Alert," *Amicus Journal*, Natural
　　　　　　　　　　　　　　　Resources Defense Council, Fall 1993[1]

REALITY TRICKLES IN:

". . . [In a] detailed rebuttal to last week's report by the Environmental Working Group, dubbed 'Tap Water Blues,' which charges Midwest drinking water contains up to 30 times the acceptable Federal level of cancer-causing herbicides, . . . David Barker of the Water Quality Laboratory at Ohio's Heidelberg college . . . *using EWG's math*, calculates the additional risks pose a likelihood of one quarter of one additional cancer case per year for Illinois' 11.4 million people."
　　　　　　　　　　David Judson, Gannett News Service, sent to
　　　　　　　　　　　　　　　　Gannett papers October 28, 1994[2]

"Dual-Purpose Ponds: You can call them wetlands or you can call them watering holes, but the cows and the wildlife that use them won't care which."
　　　　　　　　　Headline and subhead, *Successful Farming*, January 1994

Critics fear that agriculture harms the quality of our surface waters. Their evidence is weak and spotty—as is our data on surface water quality nationwide.

The awful truth is that we don't have any national water quality data that are worth looking at twice. In most cases, we don't know how dirty our rivers and lakes were when we started cleaning them up 20-plus years ago. Often, we don't know how much we've reduced the loads of key pollutants. We don't know the current pollution loads with any accuracy, or very much about where they come from.

The search for answers has been set aside for politics.

The cities feel they've done a big cleanup job on their sewage treatment plants and on their industrial wastes. The city governments are facing budget deficits proportionally as tough as the federal government's (and for many of the same reasons, due to the unfunded federal mandates handed down by Congressmen). And yet the rivers, lakes, and bays have still not been fully restored to health.

Something additional must be done. The public knows this and wants action. In this politically flammable moment, it has become fashionable to call agriculture "the leading source of pollution remaining in the country," or "the greatest single threat to the nation's groundwater quality."

Guess who's being set up for the next big hit?

No sensible person would contend that agriculture has no impact on water quality. All of those cattle and broilers and fields full of crops are visible and large and part of the modern ecosystem.

But in trying to assess just how much blame agriculture should bear, and what we can reasonably do about it, I was defeated by the lack of even semi-accurate data.

One exception, I found, is my own locality. Virginia has better water data than many states, and there is very good water quality data for the Shenandoah Valley.

Moreover, conditions in this particular region are important to the nation, because our "local" situation is the Potomac River watershed, feeding directly into the Chesapeake Bay.

The Potomac is the "nation's river," not least because it flows within sight of Capitol Hill. Moreover, the Chesapeake Bay may be the single largest threatened water resource in America, with more than 5,000 miles of shoreline. It is fed by famous rivers like the Susquehanna, the Patuxent, and the Rappahannock, flowing through one of the country's most intensively developed landscapes (the

Baltimore-Washington-Richmond-Norfolk corridor).

The Chesapeake's major problem is apparently over-fertilization. It gets too much nitrogen and phosphorous. These encourage too much algae growth. As the algae die, the decay process steals too much of the dissolved oxygen which should be in the water to sustain marine creatures. Algae also shade out the eelgrass that originally was a major feature of the bay bottom. Both problems may play a role in the sharp declines in such bay resources as oysters and striped bass. (There are other important problems too, such as a virulent virus attacking the oysters.)

The Potomac watershed also faces typical water quality problems: lack of information about massive and complex realities, enormously expensive alternatives, and no money available from any willing government.

Yet the most common bumper sticker in the region says, "Save the Chesapeake Bay."

The political tea leaves say that someone is going to get stuck.

As it happens, I've had a ringside seat on this drama through a personal friend. Dr. Rick Halpern was until recently in the Rockingham County (Virginia) Planning Department. (He is now a private consultant in Harrisonburg, Virginia.)

Rick originally got into the water quality business because the Shenandoah Valley is a major production center for chickens and turkeys, and the poultry industry underwent a massive expansion in the 1980s. Big new poultry houses sprang up on the hillsides, generating large amounts of poultry waste, and sending their birds to big new processing plants that produced additional waste of their own.

In addition, the Valley was—and remains—home to a large number of dairy farms. Rockingham County alone has 300 dairy farms milking 25,000 cows.

Rick, as the representative of the county, played a key role in developing legislation for nutrient management plans for Rockingham County's poultry and dairy producers. The Rockingham County plan has been regarded as a model for the state of Virginia, and more widely across the country. His expertise caught the attention of Virginia Senator John Warner, and he was asked to advise the senator on key parts of the Clean Water Act and its administration.

What follows is an inside look at the water/politics/economics complex, as seen through the correspondence between various players:

June 11, 1993

To: Richard N. Burton, Executive Director,
Virginia Department of Environmental Quality

From: James Couch, Chairman,
Rockingham Country Board of Supervisors

Rockingham County is a leader and innovator in nutrient management planning and local water resource protection. We hope we can also be enthusiastic partners in the effort to improve water quality in the Chesapeake Bay through the Virginia Tributary Strategies program. Following the May 17 public meeting, however, we do have questions and concerns which we would like addressed by your Department.

Rockingham, the leading agricultural county in the Commonwealth, and other counties in the Valley as well, have a vital interest in the regional impact the program will have on agriculture. . . . We wish to be sure that the data and assumptions used in the process are appropriate, accurately reflecting the real situation. . . .

It was announced at this meeting that a nutrient reduction target of 40 percent had already been set for the Potomac. . . . This was done without any consultation with local government, sharing of basin-specific data . . . or explanation of the process by which this target was determined.

Rockingham County is also concerned about the reliability of nutrient loading data that has been presented in various documents.

First . . . it is widely assumed that failed septic systems contribute significantly to non-point source nutrient loading. This is alluded to in the Chesapeake White Paper published by the Alliance for the Chesapeake Bay (and) distributed at your May meeting. . . . Yet in all the charts that assign shares of nutrient loading . . . no share is ascribed to this obvious major source. We must wonder if agriculture is being asked, tacitly, to bear a larger share of accountability than is justified by the facts.

Second, we have recently become aware that certain data contained in VWCB's 1992 305(b) report to the Environmental Protection Agency . . . are grossly inaccurate. The report states that livestock waste produced (in the North River watershed) annually yields 22,000 tons of nitrogen to meet total crop needs of 5,434 tons. The correct figures . . . indicate annual nitrogen yield of 2,659 tons and crop needs of 6,605 tons—a very different picture indeed. Have these data been incorporated in the watershed modeling?

The Department of Environmental Quality and the Chesapeake Bay Commission should be aware that two-thirds of Rockingham County's poultry farmers and one-third of its dairies are operating under locally sponsored nutrient management plans. Are the impacts of this nutrient management process being credited against estimates of nutrient loading?

Finally, the County would like to have a better understanding of the relationship between the computer modeling and the actual situation in the field. The White Paper . . . states that the Bay models are too general to be used for local-level management decisions and do "a poor job of predicting water quality in the tidal tributaries." The County wishes to understand in what ways and to what extent these models have been refined in order to develop tributary strategies. . . .

August 5, 1993

To: James V. Couch, Chairman,
Rockingham County Board of Supervisors

From Richard N. Burton, Director,
Virginia Department of Environmental Quality

Thank you again for your letter of June 11, 1993. As I indicated in my initial reply, we will need the support of all local government officials to complete our Tributary Strategies. . . .
Mathematical modeling has shown that a 40 percent

reduction in the flow of nutrients from the Potomac and rivers to the north will result in a 20-25 percent improvement in the low dissolved oxygen problem of the main Bay. Such a reduction will significantly improve conditions for the living resources in the Bay. . . .

What we are concentrating on now is an exploration of how the 40 percent Potomac basin reduction can be achieved and maintained in a cost-effective, practical and equitable manner. At this point we have no specific proposal in hand for meeting that goal and are seeking information and ideas that will help us develop a realistic strategy. . . .

The reduction estimates may be viewed as conservative because they undoubtedly under-represent reductions in agriculture. (T)hey do not include voluntarily installed agricultural Best Management Practices or local programs. . . . We recognize the need to account for all local programs.

The Potomac Strategy is being developed to determine how best to meet the nutrient reduction target of 40 percent which was set to improve the mainstem of the Bay. It is not dependent on model improvements. In order to achieve the necessary overall reductions, regions above the fall line such as Rockingham County . . . need to participate.

September 1, 1993

To: Mr. Keith Buttleman, Deputy Director
Virginia Department of Environmental Quality

Rockingham County appreciates the opportunity to review the Discussion Paper, *Reducing Nutrients in Virginia's Tidal Tributaries: the Potomac Basin* (August 1993) because the authors of the paper attempt to indict our agricultural community as a major contributor to the pollution in the Chesapeake Bay. A careful reading of Dr. Halpern's report to me, copy enclosed, clearly shows that such is not the case.

[The following are excerpts from Dr. Halpern's report]
It is my opinion, with all due respect, that Mr. Burton . . .

does not seem to take the County seriously. In the letter from
DEQ, we are told again that "mathematical modeling has shown
. . . etc." and that we will simply have to gird up our loins and
do what is required of us. Also, DEQ's summary dismissal of
the septic issue shows a distressing lack of familiarity with the
basic realities of ground/surface water interaction in karst (limestone) areas such as the Valley.

A substantial body of water quality sampling data from the
Shenandoah basin are available, and [they] do not support the
assumptions or conclusions published with such confidence in
the Potomac basin discussion paper. [T]he controllable source
nitrogen and phosphorous loadings contributed by the Shenandoah River are a minimal factor, if a factor at all, in determining
the quality of life in the Bay. The quality of the water entering
the Potomac River from the main stem Shenandoah River, with
the exception of PCB contamination from Avtex, is excellent.
The nutrient loads attributed to the Shenandoah basin . . . are
just not there. . . . Nutrient concentrations are low, and net
contributions of controllable nitrogen and phosphorous from
nonpoint sources . . . are inconsequential—approximately 1
million pounds of nitrogen per year and 200,000 pounds of phosphorous per year.

Actual field data make it clear that . . . nutrient concentrations . . . in the upper watershed of the South Fork Shenandoah are significantly diminished by the time the river reaches
Luray and Front Royal (well above Washington). Trends for
nutrient concentrations at these sampling locations are down-
wards, not upwards, and water quality in the main stem of
the South Fork improves as the river flows north.

The river totally supports the Clean Water Act swim-
mable goal, and only PCB contamination from a clearly identified industrial point source prevents full support of the Clean
Water Act fishable goal.

The total annual controllable nonpoint source nitrogen
load from the Shenandoah is approximately 1.16 million
pounds. The total annual controllable nonpoint source phosphorous load is approximately 200,000 pounds. If all this
nitrogen and all of this phosphorous could be kept from

entering the Potomac, the net impact on the Chesapeake Bay would probably not be measurable.

There is no jurisdiction in the state, and perhaps no county in the country, that has done as much on its own initiative to sponsor watershed projects to assess and address water quality issues. I do not believe it is helpful or responsible to create and present in an official paper a scenario in which agriculture is singled out to bear the preponderance of blame for poor water quality in the Shenandoah River, and by implication in the Bay, without presenting a substantial and specific database to support these claims.

[T]he discussion paper states that nutrient concentrations in the entire South Fork Shenandoah subbasin are generally high, and that these concentrations are "attributable to the intensive agricultural operations." However, the concentrations . . . are low not high . . . and it is certainly not an established fact that intensive agriculture . . . plays a dominant role.

[W]hile the lower South River watershed does have the highest maximum and median nitrate concentrations . . . it is far from the most intensively farmed watershed. . . . The North River watershed, which has lower . . . values for nitrates is far more intensively farmed. The majority of the nitrogen and phosphorous loading in the lower South River watershed is much more likely to be attributable to very substantial municipal and industrial discharges upstream from the monitoring station.

At two places in the discussion paper, a rather bold claim is made that "relatively large amounts of phosphorous in the Shenandoah reflect both the large size and extensive agricultural production" in the watershed. . . . Aside from the fact that concentrations of phosphorous in the main stem . . . are the same as in the [unpolluted control stream], elevated phosphorous readings in the North Fork have, in fact been traced through local DEQ sampling to the [Harrisonburg-Rockingham regional sewage treatment plant].

. . . [Regarding] discussion with DEQ on the interaction of ground and surface water in the Valley. There seems to be little appreciation of the fact that in karst (limestone) geology, the

connection between ground and surface water is immediate
and direct. If, as is assumed by every health official, geologist
and soil scientists operating in the region, there are significant
numbers of septic systems in the Valley which have failed, then
untreated wastes are most assuredly entering our groundwater . . .
depositing both nutrients and fecal coliform that are compromising
water quality. . . .

The 305(b) report estimates that some 50,000 people in
the North River basin are using septics. The average life of a
septic drainfield in this area is estimated by the Health Department at about 20 years. It seems highly likely that nutrient loadings from septics play a major role in nutrient loadings and as a nonpoint source, then a significant additional
burden is indeed being shifted to agriculture.

Finally, with regard to the assumption . . . that a high
proportion of pasture land in a watershed implies high animal populations and significant nonpoint source pollution,
let us observe . . . [that] a high percentage of pasture land,
by itself, suggests very low intensity of agriculture and low
rates of nutrient input.

Despite our request for clarification of the statistical assumptions on which the tributary strategies are to be based, the
County still has no idea where the inputs for the . . . model are
coming from, who developed them or how, or what level of
accuracy is claimed for them based on what verification.

What has emerged with considerable clarity, however, is
that the numbers being generated by this model bear little
resemblance to the numbers that can be generated from field
data collected over a ten-year period. The field data, in fact,
suggest very different conclusions. . . .

It is cheaper, and perhaps easier, to go after agriculture,
which the paper describes as the "dominant controllable
nonpoint source of pollution in the Chesapeake Bay Basin."

DEQ may regulate agriculture in the Shenandoah, but if
the 305(b) data mean anything at all, the State and the Bay
will get no significant nonpoint source nutrient reductions
from us—they just aren't here to be had.

(Richard A. Halpern)

September 23, 1993

To: Keith J. Buttleman, Deputy Director
Virginia Department of Environmental Quality

From: Mark B. Graham, Professional Engineer
Vienna, Virginia

In response to your request for comments on [reducing nutrients in Virginia's tidal tributaries]. . . . I believe it is important to recognize how little is understood about urban storm water management facilities. . . . I remain unconvinced that they really work for nitrogen removal. . . . The reason is rather simple.

The National Urban Runoff Program data for this area indicate that up to 70-80 percent of the nitrogen in highly urban storm water results from atmospheric deposition, primarily as a resulting pollutant from combustion engines. Almost none of this nitrogen is in the form of ammonium ions which readily adsorb to sediment, and most is in the form of NO_2, which is highly soluble.

Urban storm water facilities work through settling of particulates. . . . If the nitrogen is in the form of nitrates or nitrites, these [storm sewer facilities] would be almost totally ineffective. It is unfortunate that no one appears to have examined this question.

I would recommend that more efforts be made with regard to source reduction strategies, including education, for reduction of urban storm water pollution runoff. The programs for proper disposal of motor oil are a good illustration that this type of effort can be effective. . . . I believe source reduction strategies bring to life the realization that people's everyday activities are a source of the problem for the Chesapeake Bay. Arlington County . . . recently completed a survey of perceptions among residents with regard to sources of water pollution. In the study, people consistently identified industry as being the largest source of pollutants in Arlington County. This is despite the fact that Arlington County essentially has no industry.

*   *   *   *

Rick Halpern concludes his doleful assessment of the water "cleanup" process by noting that by DEQ calculations the Shenandoah River contributes 3,000 tons of total nutrients per year to the Potomac's nutrient loading.

Meanwhile, one sewage treatment plant (Blue Plains, below Washington) contributes 7,000 tons, one hundred miles closer to the Bay, because of the treatment process chosen for the plant. It is required to eliminate ammonia—which it does by taking out the hydrogen molecules and leaving the nitrogen dissolved in the plant's effluent to flow down the river!

Strategies for Keeping Water Cleaner

Fertilizer Runoff
The problem of fertilizer runoff from farmlands is the most valid charge laid against high-yield farming. Fortunately, the problem does not need to be nearly so serious as we have made it.

Fertilizer has gotten a bad reputation in the rich countries, in large part because their farm subsidies have encouraged farmers to use too much of it. High price supports always mean heavy fertilizer applications to get maximum yields. Too often, some of the surplus fertilizer has leached or run off, and then stimulated algae growth in downstream surface waters. This elevated algae growth results in oxygen starvation in ponds and lakes.

The runoff problem has been aggravated by the trend toward intensive feeding systems for livestock and poultry, too often without adequate systems for containing and disposing of the wastes.

Fortunately, the situation can be sharply improved, and steps are already under way.

Perhaps the biggest remedial step is being taken in farm price support structures: The rich countries are phasing them out. Europe and the U.S. are both moving rapidly toward direct farm income payments instead of price supports. This is helping to lower fertilizer intensity—something very difficult to do when fertilizer is too cheap compared to crop prices.

As Figure 15.1 shows, the industrial world has actually reduced its

---

Federal Agencies Joining Forces to
Clean Up the Chesapeake Bay

by Sandra Sobieraj, Associated Press writer, published in the
Staunton News Leader, July 15, 1994

Washington—Senior officials from 25 Federal agencies and departments signed a historic agreement Thursday to restore the Chesapeake Bay's ecosystem.

The agreement, which Environmental Protection Agency Administrator Carol M. Browner called the first of its kind, aims for better coordination of ongoing federal and state efforts to clean up the bay's 64,000-square-mile watershed that spans five states and the District of Columbia.

"The 13 million people who live in the Chesapeake Bay watershed understand that the health of the bay is vitally important to our own health, the health of our natural resources, and the health of the economy," said Browner. "This agreement shows our willingness to work across agency and department lines in order to move forward."

The federal government, through various agencies and departments, spends on estimated $374 million annually on bay restoration.

The Chesapeake agreement will serve as a model for cleanup efforts in other basins, including the Great Lakes, Gulf of Mexico and San Francisco Bay delta, Browner said. . . .

---

fertilizer intensity somewhat in recent years, while Asia has nearly doubled its fertilizer use per hectare. Latin America's fertilizer use is still modest, while Africa's is almost nonexistent.

Better policies on farm trade liberalization and reduced use of farm price supports—along with new farming systems approaches—should lead to a more moderate and even use of fertilizer around the world.

Still, the world must continue to use fertilizer, and some regions will probably have to use it more intensively.

Asia, for example, has radically increased its use of fertilizer. If it continues to pursue food self-sufficiency, it will have to radically escalate fertilizer per acre again. However, Asians have a good alternative—they could rely more heavily on farm imports in the future. Given the strong economic growth trend in the region, Asia will certainly have the foreign exchange to import farm products. Exporters

Figure 15.1

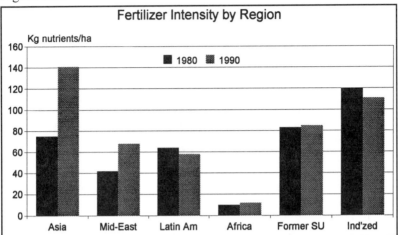

Source: *The Potential Role of Biotechnology in Solving Food Production and Environmental Problems in Developing Countries.* Presented to the ASA-CSSA-SSSA annual meeting, Cincinnati, Ohio, November 1993

such as the U.S., Argentina, Turkey, Australia, and Thailand would be willing and cost-effective sellers.

Improved Fertilizer Application Systems
The world can also make important improvements in fertilizer application systems, as the following examples illustrate:

- Conservation tillage and high yields are minimizing runoff and erosion.
- Less and less fertilizer is being put on fields in the off-seasons when there is no plant growth activity to take it up (and thus when it is most likely to leach and/or be carried off with eroding soil particles).
- More farmers are fertilizing in several small applications rather than one heavy one, to increase effectiveness and further reduce leaching and runoff.
- More rice fertilizer is being applied in large slow-release

granules, which give more yield per ton of fertilizer applied.
- More and more fertilizer is being knifed into the soil rather than left on the soil surface.
- More farms are planting "filter strips" of grass along waterways to catch runoff from fields and filter out both soil particles and nutrients.

Precision Farming

One of the most promising new runoff-reduction developments is called "precision farming," or "site-specific management." The aim of precision farming is to put on just exactly the right amount of seeds and chemicals for each square yard of the field.

The basis of precision farming is a computer microprocessor right on the farmer's tractor at planting time. The tractor is located within inches of its true position on the planet by using global positioning satellites (GPS) and radar. The on-board computer reviews seeding and chemical rates seven times a second, based on intensive sampling of soil type and acidity, slope, hydrology, plant population, past yields, nearness to waterways and any other important factors. (Researchers eventually hope to have instantaneous soil sampling right on the tractor, but to date they rely on intensive soil sampling, guided by GPS satellite.)

In the fall, the computer processor is moved over to the combine, where it automatically updates the yield information for the next spring.

Ted Macy is a young Illinois farmer who developed the hardware and software for precision farming. Using the new gear on his own farm, Macy says he not only improved his yields, but saved $13 per acre on chemicals during his first season.[3]

The importance of precision farming is that it should let us put on as much chemical input as the plants need—and not an ounce more. We can use less chemical per acre without losing yield.

Limiting Phosphorous Runoff

Phosphorous from livestock operations is another element in the fertilizer runoff causing downstream problems. About 6 percent of the phosphorous used in high-yield U.S. farming has reached surface waters as runoff.

Hogs apparently produce about 20-25 percent of the excess phosphorous. Hog producers until now have had to add phosphorous to

Sample computer printout of
precision farming data

their hog feeds, aggravating the problem. There is phosphorous in the grain and oilseeds that make up the feeds, but it has not been biologically available to non-ruminant creatures such as hogs and poultry.

Recently, however, research has produced a genetically enhanced microbe that can produce commercial quantities of phytase, the enzyme in rumen bacteria needed for phosphate release and uptake. Using this phytase, producers are able to cut back the normal phosphorous supplement in their feed rations, and let the hogs and poultry get more of their phosphorous from the plant sources.

The new phytase product is already in wide use in Europe, Canada, and Australia, where it is cutting phosphorous excretion from pigs and poultry by 30 to 50 percent.[4] Marketing is beginning in the U.S.

Notes

[1] Bob Adler, "Clean Water Alert," *Amicus Journal*, Fall 1993, Vol. 15, No. 3, Natural Resources Defense Council, p. 27.

[2] Barker's detailed study of the Environmental Working Group's report is available from the National Council of Farmer Cooperatives in Washington, D.C.

[3] Ted Macy, Applications Mapping, Inc., Frankfort, Illinois.

[4] P.P. Hoope, *Review of The Biological Effects and the Ecological Importance of Phytase in Pigs* and F.J. Schoner, *Review of the Biological Effects and the Ecological Importance of Phytase in Broilers and Layers*, presentation at the 4th BASF Animal Nutrition Forum, November 4-5, 1992, BASF Corp., Ludwigshafen, Germany.

16

More People *and* More Trees: Saving Forests with Technology

MYTHMAKERS SAY:

"The projections indicate that by 2000, some 40 percent of the remaining forests in the [developing countries] will be gone."
Major Findings and Conclusions, *Global 2000 Report*,
Carter White House, 1980, p. 2

"Every day, some of these human beings move into places on the planet where only plants and animals used to live. Forests are cut down. Wetlands, oceans, ice caps and prairies are invaded."
Russell Train, World Wildlife Fund, quoted in *50 Simple Things You Can Do To Save the Earth*, Earthworks Press, Berkeley, California, 1989

"We must explore other building materials, such as mud bricks, that are made from soil adjacent to the building site and dried by solar power. They are widely used in Australia and New Mexican adobe houses, with beautiful results."
Helen Caldicott, *If You Love This Planet*, W.W. Norton, New York, 1992, p. 59

REALITY SAYS:

"The whole world's expected industrial wood needs for the year 2000 could be met sustainably from less than 200 million hectares of forest plantation—just 7 percent of the world's closed forest land area."
Roger Sedjo, Resources for the Future, *The Comparative Economics of Plantation Forests: A Global Assessment*, Johns Hopkins University Press, Baltimore, 1983

"Annual growth in U.S. forests exceeds harvest by more than 55 percent."

U.S. Forest Service, *The Condition and Trends of U.S. Forests*, 1991

A New Era in Forestry

Most people have been taught to think the world is being stripped of trees. They think more and more forests will inevitably be cut as the world's human population doubles again.

They are wrong.

We no longer need to sacrifice trees for people. Nor must we sacrifice the habitat of wildlife to get paper or timber. The doomsayers' link between the number of humans born and the number of trees lost is disappearing:

- If cities in 2050 occupy less than 4 percent of the earth's surface;
- If we use no more land for farming then than we do today; and
- If the forest products for 10-12 billion people can be produced from a few acres of forest plantations with 15-20 times the yield of today's forests;
- Then where is the danger to wildlife?

More than half of the world's forests are in the temperate zones. These First World forests are expanding in area. They are increasing *dramatically* in the number of trees per acre and speed of growth. They are no longer being cleared for crops, as they were 100 years ago, because farmers are boosting the crop yields on existing acres instead. Fewer temperate-zone trees are being cut for fuel. Far fewer trees are being lost to fire and pests. A rising percentage of the world's people are concentrating themselves in cities where their impact on trees is minimal.

In addition, First World residents now put a higher value on saving trees and especially on reforestation.

Consider the following benefits from new technology and better forestry management which is already achieving success in temperate zone forests.

USDA

MANAGEMENT MAKES A DIFFERENCE—These two red pines were the same age at harvest. The bigger one was in a well-managed tree plantation.

Better forest management is minimizing tree losses to fires and pests in temperate forests. As a result, the U.S. forest acres logged today produce 30 percent more timber per acre than they did without management. That means more acres can be left as untouched wildlife habitat if we choose not to log them.

Tree plantations can produce far more forest products per acre than wild forests, using the best tree species for a given area. These tree monocultures are not the same as wild forest habitat. Even so, they are excellent wildlife habitat. (The lush forests shown in the frontier movie, *Last of the Mohicans*, were actually a 35-year-old tree plantation in the Carolinas.)[1]

Tree breeding breakthroughs from biotechnology are giving us the first real high-yield forestry. Genetically enhanced trees are already yielding up to 15 times as much timber and pulpwood per acre as wild forests.[2]

New chemistry and engineering breakthroughs that produce more forest products from less wood are radically increasing the efficiency of forest production. That means more forest products from each tree, and fewer trees harvested to meet a given level of need.

Not surprisingly, given the new technologies, the northern hemisphere offers dramatic examples of forestry success:

- The growing stock in Europe's forests rose 30 percent between 1971 and 1990. This information contradicts the commonly held view of European forest decline (and the myth
  that acid rain has devastated these forests).[3]
- Timber volumes in North America, Europe, and the former
  USSR together are increasing at about 700 million cubic
  meters per year—due to better management.[4]

REALITIES OF LOGGING:

"East Perry Lumber Company began its harvest of the Fairview timber sale in the Shawnee National Forest . . . four long years after being
awarded the sale. Police arrested 17 people, four of them on Federal
charges. . . . The arrests were more orderly than last year, when several
protesters buried themselves in the ground and one chained himself to a
logging skidder."

Greenspeak, National Hardwood Lumber Association, Memphis,
Tennessee, September 1991, Issue 24., p. 1

"If one were to project deforestation in the U.S. based on the logging rate of the late 1800s, the last tree would have fallen years ago. But
the projections based on the logging and growth rates of the late 1900s
would show forests covering every square inch of America in the next
century. Obviously, 'if present trends continue' is misleading; the current trends never do continue."

Dixie Lee Ray, *Environmental Overkill*, Regnery Gateway,
Washington, D.C., p. 111

"The fires . . . have come to northwestern Montana. Today, 150 fires
are burning, from 100 acres to 5,000 each. . . . A senior fire-fighting
'hot shot' . . . says he's never seen fires behave like these conflagrations.
He would have if he had been in Lincoln County in 1910, when 3 million
acres went up in flames in a matter of days. It is not just coincidence that
the life span of a Lodgepole Pine—80 years or more—is the amount of
time that has passed since the devastating fires of 1910. For years now,
the trees of the Kootenai National Forest have been ready for harvest—

either by mankind, or by nature. Using appeals and litigation, environmentalists made sure that it wouldn't be mankind."

William Perry Pendley, *Summary Judgment*, Mountain States
Legal Foundation, Denver, Colorado, September 9, 1994

Temperate forests *are* being logged, but logging seldom means losing the forest. Logging is the harvest of mature trees. Without logging, the trees will eventually fall down and rot—or burn. The wildlife in a logged forest may actually benefit from the logging if it is done properly. Forest wildfires due to too many overage trees can be prevented.

Mature trees have already done most of their carbon storing. Taking them away to make houses, furniture, paneling, etc. means that the forest-stored carbon will *stay* stored. If the trees are *not* harvested, they die, rot, and release their carbon quickly.

Virtually all of the forest's wildlife stays in the forest if the cutting is done soundly. If clear cuts are not huge, they need not threaten wildlife species. Forest regrowth can take decades, but these are the decades in which carbon storing is most rapid. That's a "global warming" advantage. The regrowth period is also when that acre of forest supports the most wildlife. Only a few temperate-zone woodland species prefer or "need" old growth forest.

LOCAL MYTHMAKER GETS LOCAL FAME:

"Some trees in the George Washington National Forest targeted for a timber harvest early next year are falling under the watchful eye of Steve Krichbaum. Krichbaum, a director for Preserve Appalachian Wilderness Network, filed an appeal protesting the 88-acre timber sale near the village of Headwaters in Deerfield Ranger District . . . because a number of the chestnut oaks in at least one stand are 183 years old. 'As far as (Virginia) goes, that's really old,' Krichbaum said."

"Preservationist Wants to Save Old Trees from Timber Sales,"
Daily News-Leader, Staunton, Virginia, October 14, 1993, p. B1

Reality Comment: The only reason Krichbaum offers for trying to prevent the logging is that the trees are "really old." How much longer are they expected to live?

Eighty-eight acres may not sound like much. But 221 million board feet of timber and 1.1 million cubic feet of pulpwood would be lost from these acres, turned back into CO_2. And we'd get nothing in return—no extra wildlife, because the trees are standing in the midst of a forest already full of wildlife; and no extra environmental quality, because the trees are in the midst of a heavily forested and sparsely populated area that already has an abundance of natural beauty.

Krichbaum got his name and picture in the local paper, and no doubt lots of "attaboys" from his colleagues in PAWN. But, we, the public, would get higher wood prices. And, the forest creatures would get a higher risk of a major fire when these aging trees die.

The trees would not be preserved. They are not antique rocking chairs to be admired in our living rooms. Nor are they old buildings which can be restored. They are living organisms with a basic life span, and they are near the end of it. The question is whether they will die uselessly or whether their timber (and stored carbon) will be harvested. We do not have the ability to maintain old trees as they are.

Why is this called "preservation"?

(Postscript: Krichbaum later filed a lawsuit to block the harvest. Now we, the public, have to pay the salary of another government lawyer on top of losing the lumber, risking the fire, and gaining no wildlife.)

USDA

WILDLIFE HABITAT REBORN—This reforested slope in Oregon offers fine habitat to most of the forest wildlife species.

MYTHS OF THE NORTHWEST:

". . . the harvesting of edible mushrooms . . . could well become a major incentive for preserving rather than clearcutting mature forests in the Pacific Northwest."

Larry Evans, "Life in the Fungal Jungle," Buzzworm, the Environmental Journal, August, 1993, p. 28

"One of North America's last great forests is being cut down and turned into telephone books. . . . Twenty years ago when directory

---

American Forests Thriving

Americans seem to think that the country is losing its trees.

Weyerhauser's Charles Bingham says, "Images of disappearing rain forests are shaping the way Americans think about forestry. The public has concluded that what is happening in some Third World rain forests is what is happening here in America. For many, saving forests has become a religious experience."

The fact is, America is *not* losing its forests. The U.S. Forest Service itself says that after 500 years of harvesting, America's forest land base is still two-thirds as large as it was when European settlers arrived in the 1600s.

The big dip in North American and European forests occurred during the mid-19th century—the early days of the iron industry, when iron ore was crudely refined in small wood-fired smelters and wood was still a major fuel source.

Most of the forests on America's Eastern Seaboard were logged in the late 1800s, including the Adirondacks and the Alleghenies. After Pittsburgh began using big coal-fired Bessemer steel furnaces, the forests were largely allowed to regrow. Coal became the fuel of choice for our cities. Thus, forest area in the U.S. has been stable since 1920. Thanks to good forest management, we now have 30 percent more standing timber per acre in U.S. forests than we had in 1952. Moreover, timber production is already forbidden on 70 percent of national forest lands.

(These facts are taken from the U.S. Forest Service's publications, *1992 RPA Assessment* and *The Condition and Trends of U.S. Forests*, 1991.)

assistance was provided free . . . phonebooks were optional. When phone companies began to charge a fee for directory assistance, however, phonebooks became a necessity."

from "Turning Forests Into Phonebooks," Sierra, Sierra Club,
January/February 1994, p. 28[5]

Southern Industry Protects Western Forests

Richard Haynes, program manager for social and economic research at the U.S. Forest Service, reports that the total timber volume from the U.S. Northwest dropped from 13 billion board feet in 1988 to 7.2 billion board feet in 1992. In the South, the total volume grew from 12.7 bbf in 1988 to 14.4 bbf in 1992. Haynes says the trend is continuing.[6]

Privately owned forests in the Southeastern U.S. are profitably producing a rising share of U.S. forest products. Meanwhile, the huge National Forests of the Western U.S.—which frequently produce at a net loss—are harvesting less timber.

The Southern softwood expansion and new restrictions on cutting in national forests have radically shifted the timber and wood products market.

But What About the Spotted Owl?

Listen to Dr. Louis Oliver of the University of Washington. He says we can encourage more spotted owls and other old-growth species, more understory plant species and generally a higher level of biological diversity—with just some modest changes in the way we manage our forests.

Oliver notes, for example, that the spotted owl likes to nest in old-growth, but likes to hunt in more open territory. (The owls eat mostly wood rats, which like more open woods better than old-growth.)

Oliver's forest management suggestions:

• Keep doing modest-sized clear-cuts, but leave a small island of old growth in the center of each section. Leave five or six trees per acre (some live, some dead) for habitat variety.
• Make small clear-cuts in dense forests to open up spaces for

wildlife species that need them. Old-growth forests don't let much light into their understories. In fact most species *avoid* the dark old-growth forests.
• Thin out millions of acres of reforested trees, not only to get timber, pulp, and chips but to let the remaining trees get to their full size. Otherwise, the stands will need early harvesting to prevent most of the trees from dying young.
• Prune some of the older trees—or even girdle a few—to create dead snags for cavity-nesting birds.
• Set small, controlled fires to get rid of dead wood that might later cause a major wildfire.

Another forest economist, Dr. Peter Koch of the Wood Science Laboratory at Corvallis, Oregon, says the spotted owl reserves are resource-costly. It would take another 6 billion gallons of oil (and add another 62 million tons of CO_2 to the atmosphere) if we made up for the number of trees that would have been put off-limits by the first spotted owl forest reservation recommended by the U.S. government's interagency committee on the spotted owl by using more steel, aluminum, brick, and concrete.

Replacing timber products from the spotted owl preserves from *other* forests elsewhere in the world might have even bigger environmental costs. Bruce Lippke, Director of the University of Washington Center for International Trade in Forest Products, says that replacing the fast-growing trees on *each 100,000 acres of Pacific Northwest forest* by cutting Siberian forests would take *1.5 million acres* of slower-growing Siberian trees. (Nor are there any laws mandating reforestation in the former USSR.)

If the "spotted owl" timber products came from wild tropical forests instead, how many species would be endangered there?

MYTHMAKER REDEFINES CAPITAL:

"Old-growth forests are a form of natural capital that has taken centuries or millennia to accumulate; 'sustainable logging' of these nonrenewable resources is, strictly speaking, an oxymoron."
                Sandra Postel and John C. Ryan, "Reforming Forestry," *State of the World 1991*

Reality comment: What kind of "capital" do old-growth forests represent if they harbor little biodiversity—and then burn up or rot? The key to preservation is good management.

Technology and Forestry

A huge re-engineering in timber products is radically increasing the efficiency of forest product conversion. We're getting more forest products from fewer trees—more product from each log.

In 1948, one acre of U.S. Douglas fir logs produced 17,900 cubic feet of timber. See Figure 16.1 for that timber's typical yield.

Figure 16.1. Wood Use Efficiency, 1948.

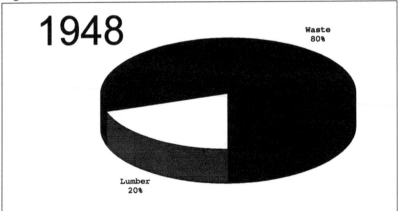

Figure 16.2. Wood Use Efficiency, 1973.

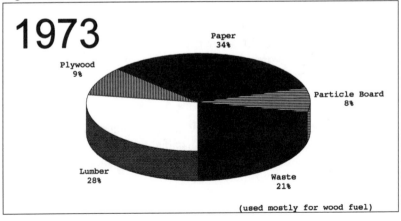

See Figure 16.2 for what the same quantity of raw materials yielded in 1973.

Numerous new forest-product technologies have made this higher yield possible:

- The retractable chuck lathe, in the 1960s, made it possible to economically peel small logs for veneer. It gave birth to the southern pine plywood industry.
- The chipper-canter, introduced in the 1960s, raised the efficiency of turning smaller logs into lumber.
- Computerized log positioning, introduced in 1971, sharply improved lumber yields per log.
- Particle board, waferboard, and hardboard now make important use of cellulose and wood fibers which used to be wasted because they were in pieces too small to make standard lumber.
- Parallel strand lumber (parallam) was introduced in 1986 and became an immediate competitor in structural lumber. Parallam is made from narrow strands of clipped veneer that are dried, blended with resin, and compressed with heat in a continuous press into solid wood billets. It calls into question the future need for large sawlogs.
- Pressure-treated lumber, which lasts 20 years or more in open outdoor applications, has replaced kiln-dried lumber which lasted only half as long before it needed replacement.
- Lightweight coated papers have been developed which take less pulpwood per page.
- Prefabricated roof trusses use small-dimension lumber and patented fastenings to do a job which used to take large timbers and nails. In the process, they radically reduce labor costs. Such trusses have taken about 80 percent of the building truss market since 1960.
- Laminated veneer lumber is an alternative to higher-priced and less ecologically sound steel production. The major use of LVL is in flanges for wooden I-beams.
- Plywood I-beams and stronger modern adhesives are a far more efficient way to produce load-bearing joists and other structural pieces than waiting for a tree to grow big enough

to produce 2 by 10 inch planks. The I-beams also produce a higher-quality floor system.

• Louisiana Pacific Corporation is producing weatherproof chipboard from fast-growing aspen trees. The products use a new adhesive system with a stronger, weather-tight bond. The aspen trees regrow rapidly from their cut stumps, taking advantage of their existing root systems.

• Plywood manufacturers in Taiwan, using more expensive equipment, are producing veneer sliced to 1/80th of an inch, compared with the longtime U.S. veneer standard of 1/26th. That produces three times as much valuable veneer from each hardwood log.[7]

Dr. Brian Greber of Oregon State University estimates that the average yield of lumber from 1000 board feet of logs increased 14 percent just in the 1970s, and says utilization rates have continued to rise rapidly since.[8]

My Airtight Wood Stove

Technology has also improved the efficiency of wood fuel.

I have an airtight wood stove in my home. It is a wonderful device, which provides most of the heat for our home (except the basement office) during the winter. It does this with three to four cords of wood per winter.

At the nearby Museum of American Frontier Culture, the curators tell me that the imported and rebuilt English farmhouse (from the 1600s) probably burned 30 to 40 cords of wood per winter due to its poorly designed fireplaces and lack of insulation—even in the mild English climate!

We harvest our firewood from the fast-growing locust trees that would otherwise take over our pastures. Locust is not a famous firewood like oak. It snaps and pops when burning—a major disadvantage in an open fireplace, but no disadvantage at all in a closed stove. The locust wood is as dense and hot-burning as oak, and the locust trees grow much more rapidly.

The locust is also harder to split, but most people split their firewood now with hydraulic rams.

My stove even has a catalytic converter which virtually eliminates any emissions that might be harmful to the environment.

Now, when my oak is ready for harvest, I can sell it for timber instead of burning it up. Technology deals new cards—and winning hands all around.

Tree Plantations to Protect Forests and Wildlife

Farmers everywhere are producing more crops for more people on fewer acres. Foresters are starting to do the same thing with trees. That leaves more land for wilderness and recreation.

Forest plantations let us produce lots of timber products from a few acres. For example, less than one percent of Latin America's forests are tree plantations—but those plantations already produce more than one-third of the region's industrial wood output. By the year 2000, the plantations are expected to produce *half* of Latin America's expanding wood requirements from less than three percent of its forest area![9]

Major forest plantations have been started in Brazil, Chile, Venezuela, South Africa, India, Indonesia, the Philippines, Australia, New Zealand, and a host of other tropical and southern hemisphere countries.

In the mid-1970s, developing countries had 6.7 million acres of plantation forest. Five years later, they had 9.1 million plantation acres. The projection for the year 2000 is *21 million* acres.[10]

Other major gains have come from putting existing tree species in new settings where they maximize yields:

- Eucalyptus is thriving in semiarid areas all over the world, and producing more wood per tree and per acre than native species.
- A brushy leguminous tree called *Leucaena leucocephala* (from Central America) is helping to fertilize crops in the new alley-cropping system of West Africa; provide dry season cattle forage in India and Ethiopia; and helping stabilize rice paddy dikes in Southeast Asia—even as it provides more firewood for the farm families in all these countries.
- A U.S. company is investing $15 million to replant Costa Rican

forests cleared by homesteaders 90 years ago. It is planting 27 million *gmelina arborea* trees, native to India, which will soar to 90 feet in five years. (The project has already created 1,300 jobs in the small country—even before the first harvest has begun.)[11]

MYTHMAKER CAN'T SEE THE FOREST FOR THE TREES:

"By 'permanent forest,' I assume Mr. Phillips means the 30,000 acres of gmelina, a nonnative monocrop. If this is a forest, then so is an Iowa cornfield."

"Costa Rican Rights and Wrongs," *E. The Environmental Magazine,* February 94[12]

Reality comment: Apparently, if it can't be the way it was 20,000 years ago the eco-activists believe it's wrong. But the gmelina trees will protect the other forests in Central America from being logged or cleared—*much as an Iowa cornfield can protect fragile acres in China from being plowed.* Is this not worthwhile?

MORE MYTHOLOGY:

"When diverse populations of trees are replaced with genetically uniform stands, future timber harvests are put at risk."

Sandra Postel and John C. Ryan, "Reforming Forestry," *State of the World 1991,* p. 82

Reality comment: Tree plantations *ensure* future timber harvests without risking either wild forests or wildlife. Is that why Worldwatch is trying to discredit them? Will more forest loss make population suppression more politically acceptable?

Their claim is that the plantations would risk big disease losses, but in reality the risk is no greater than depending on wheat fields for our bread. (If a disease does hit a forest, you can harvest the trees as they stand, and replant with another variety, just as we do in wheat. The only difference is that the pace is slower.)

The World's First Truly High-Yield Forestry

Now biotechnology takes a hand, producing improved tree varieties that will yield even more wood products per acre of plantation.

Cloning and tissue culture have radically shortened the tree breeding cycle. Tree breeders used to think in decades. Now, they think in months. China says it can produce a new rubber tree variety—complete with thousands of new seedlings—in four years!

An explosion in tree productivity has been touched off. The USDA's agricultural attaches from Indonesia, Malaysia, Thailand, and Kenya in recent years have reported two to sixfold increases in the yields of tree crops like teak, pine, cocoa, and palm oil due to genetic engineering.

In Brazil, a genetically enhanced plantation of Georgia yellow pine (an exotic species there) is producing 50 cubic meters of pulpwood per hectare per year, compared with 15 cubic meters for the same trees in a Georgia plantation and 3 cubic meters of pulpwood for a natural forest in Sweden. Each acre of such plantations can effectively protect as many as 14 acres of forest from being logged.[13]

Of course, this leaves each nation with the question of how best to manage its forests. In the U.S., if we don't harvest the wood from a forest, we'll need to invest management dollars in burning it up—under controlled conditions so we don't get the big, too-hot forest fires from which the forests take too long to recover.

My wife remembers as a girl driving through Oregon's huge, infamous Tillamook Burn—millions of acres of devastated woodlands still barren and untenable for wildlife more than 20 years later. (It has since been reforested.)

THE REALITY ABOUT "SUSTAINABLE" FOREST MANAGEMENT: NO PROFIT = NO JOBS:

"The Collins Pine Company has been trying to manage its 92,000 acres of California forest in the best traditions of the Sierra Club and Earthwatch since the 1870s. But the company has run into trouble.

"Leaving the healthiest and most vigorous trees and cutting only those that were diseased or fully mature turns out to be expensive. It takes a troop of foresters who analyze which trees to cut, harvesting many different size trees slows down the sawmill, and fewer trees per acre are cut. (Collins harvests less than 2 percent of its standing timber each year, against an industry average of 2.5 to 3 percent.) Collins' trees grow more slowly as well—partly because they are older.

"The result: In 1993, Collins made no profit on sales of $100 million worth of wood molding, windows, doors, and furniture. Now the company has had to fire its sawyers and lumberjacks and farm that work out to contractors."

Bill Wagner, "Not Business as Usual," *Business Ethics*, September/October 1993 p. 14[14]

Should We Use More Wood, Not Less?

"In the emerging global economy, nations should be *increasing*, not *decreasing*, their dependency on wood fiber because wood is renewable, recyclable, biodegradable, and far more energy-efficient in its manufacture and use than are products made from steel, aluminum, plastic or concrete."

So says Dr. Robert Bowyer, who is president of the Forest Products Society and a professor at the University of Minnesota. "Furthermore," he adds, "trees and the wood-turned-into-lumber they provide are both capable of storing large amounts of carbon dioxide that would otherwise escape into the atmosphere, adding to the potential for global warming."

REALITY:

"Wood, an energy form that is relatively abundant and renewable, is where we should be looking for a continued energy supply."

Mollie Beattie, now director of the U.S. Fish and Wildlife Service, before a Vermont natural resources conference in 1990[15]

Reality Comment: Other experts at the same conference as Beattie said even *wood-fired electrical generation* could actually help diminish the greenhouse effect and global warming trends—without forest loss. Norman Hudson of the Vermont Department of Forests, Parks and Recreation, said that the two-thirds of Vermont in forest is "vastly underused." He suggested that simple—and healthful—thinning of tree stands could produce 50 tons of wood chips per acre. The CO_2 produced by burning the wood would be offset by the trees' absorption of gases and release of oxygen during their growing years—and less fossil fuel would be released into the atmosphere.

CHAINSAWS CONFUSED WITH ASSAULT RIFLES?

". . . [A]t one of the conferences, I suggested that chainsaws be banned . . . and governments pay a bounty of $5,000 for each such machine turned in. . . . What will nations and the world do about the factories where these machines are made and about the people who work there? We cannot allow those employed in such places to remain hostage to destructive and poisonous inappropriate investment and production."

Richard Grossman, author of *Fear at Work*, in a letter to the editor of *Earth Island Journal*, Winter 1993-94[16]

REALITY AT WORK:

"I'm CEO of a company that owns and develops timberlands and am a board member of the Alaska Forest Association. . . . You offer the opinion of some (in your January 17 article) that there has been overcutting in the Tongass (National Forest). . . . The facts are that, of the 17 million acres in the Tongass, only one-tenth of 1 percent will be harvested each year. Over the 100-year rotation cycle, 10 percent will be harvested. Forty percent of the Tongass is in land-use designations that are either wilderness or limited access. Twenty-three percent of the Tongass is designated for intensive uses (which include logging) but less than half of that area will be used for logging.

"Those of us who live and work here . . . care more than any political advocacy group that our harvest practices leave the land fertile and able to support a new crop. We obey the law, monitor the health of fish streams, build roads to specifications that control runoff, leave buffers around water bodies, avoid steep slopes, elevate logs over stream beds and generally take good care of the land. The difference between those in the timber industry and those referred to as 'environmentalists' is a matter of politics and values, not husbandry.

"This is good timber-growing country. Rain and moderate temperature offer the opportunity. . . . The salmon streams are productive. The areas cut are in sustainable proportion to the forecast demand. The other species here have viable habitat. The world demand for fiber will be supplied from some source. . . . "

Letter to the editor of the *Wall Street Journal* from Ernesta Ballard, Ketchikan, Alaska

Notes

[1]"The Competition for Albertan Wood Fiber," speech by Roger Sedjo of Resources for the Future, before the Conference on International Competitiveness of Canadian Forest Products, University of Alberta, Edmonton, October 23, 1991.

[2]Roger Sedjo, Resources for the Future, interview by the author, 1992.

[3]Kaupi, Mielikanen, and Kuusela, *Science*, Vol. 256, pp. 70-74.

[4]UN Food and Agriculture Organization (FAO)/Economic Commission for Europe (ECE), *Forest Resources 1980*, Rome, 1985.

[5]Jay Letto, "Go East Young Timberman," *E, The Environmental Magazine*, February 1994, Vol. V, No. 1, p. 27.

[6]Dr. Peter Koch, Wood Science Laboratory, Corvallis, OR, before the "Wood Product Demand and the Environment" conference, Vancouver, British Columbia, November 1991.

[7]Dr. J. L. Bowyer, "Successes and Failures in Process and Product Technology," University of Minnesota Department of Forest Products; see also Bowyer, "Analysis of Growth of Competing Materials," op. cit.

[8]Mark McQueen, "Pondering the Environmental Advantages of Wood," *Evergreen,* Summer 1993, p. 18.

[9]InterAmerican Development Bank (IDB), *Forest Industries Development Strategy and Investment Requirements in Latin America*, Technical Report No. 1, prepared for IDB conference on Financing Forest-Based Development in Latin America, June 22-25, 1982, Washington, D.C., p. 17.

[10]Lanly and Clement, "Present and Future Natural Forest and Plantation Areas in the Tropics," *Unsylva*, 1979, Vol. 31, No. 123, pp. 12-20.

[11]"Global Consequences of U.S. Environmental Policies," *Evergreen*, Summer, 1993, p. 15.

[12]Andre Carruthers, "Costa Rican Rights and Wrongs," *E, The Environmental Magazine*, Vol. V, No. 1, February 94, p. 7.

[13]Sedjo, personal interview, op. cit.

[14]Jim Petersen, "Think Globally, Act Locally," *Evergreen*, Summer 1993, p. 4.

[15]Sylvia Dodge, "Chipping Away for Alternative Energy," *Vermont Business Magazine*, 1990, Vol. 18, No. 6, p. 46.

[16]Richard Grossman, author of *Fear at Work*, letter to the editor of *Earth Island Journal*, Winter 1993/94, Vol. 9, No. 1, Earth Island Institute, San Francisco, p. 2.

17

Can We Rescue the Rain Forests?

MYTHMAKERS SAY:

". . . [B]illowing clouds of smoke regularly blacken the sky above the immense but now threatened Amazon rain forest. Acre by acre, the rain forest is being burned to create fast pasture for fast-food beef."

Vice President Al Gore, *Earth In The Balance*, p. 23

"The world's forests declined . . . between 1980 and 1990 . . . by an area larger than Peru. Tragically, much tropical forest is being cleared in order to cultivate soils that cannot sustain crop production for more than a few years. Yet the species extinguished in the process are gone forever."

Sandra Postel, "Carrying Capacity: Earth's Bottom Line," *State of the World 1994*, p. 12

"At the present, frantic rate of deforestation, all the world's tropical forests will within twenty-five to fifty years be destroyed, along with 15 to 24 million species, and the land will be desert. . . . The Club of Earth maintains that species extinction is 'a threat to civilization second only to the threat of nuclear war.'"

Antiwar activist Helen Caldicott, in her new "environmental" book, *If You Love This Planet*, p. 51

REALITY SAYS:

"Today, we know that the 1984 . . . deforestation estimate was too high. David Skole, an ecologist at the University of New Hampshire, and Compton Tucker of NASA examined in 1993 satellite photos of the Amazon rainforest to determine how much deforestation occurred between 1978 and 1988. After painstakingly examining 210 such photos, they concluded that the average rate of rainforest loss was [just 1.5 million hectares] per year. If deforestation in Brazil accounted for half of all rainforest deforestation in the world, as is generally assumed, then the new estimate means the global rate of rainforest deforestation was . . . less than a tenth of 1 percent."

> Bast, Hill, and Rue, *Eco-Sanity*, Madison Books for the Heartland Institute, Lanham, Maryland, 1994, p. 84

"Emphasize this point at the beginning and throughout your chapter. Deforestation is not the same as timber extraction. . . ."

> Douglas Southgate, author of *Economic Progress and the Environment: One Developing Country's Policy Crisis*, commenting on a draft of this book, November 17, 1994

"The Amazon does not serve as the lungs of the planet; the forest consumes as much oxygen as it produces. It is not being cleared to produce fast-food hamburgers; the region is a net importer of beef. Experts disagree about the extent of deforestation (reasonable estimates vary between 8 percent and 12 percent, mostly along the edges of the jungle) but it is clear that the rain forest will not 'disappear' any time soon."

> Jon Christensen, a Pacific News Service correspondent, then-recently returned from a year on assignment in Brazil, writing in the *Baltimore Sun*, December 10, 1989, p. 13-14

Let's be grateful to the naturalists for warning about the need to save the rain forests.

Let's commit ourselves to saving them.

But let's *not* take the naturalists' advice on how to do it. Their advice is too often unworkable and sometimes needlessly inhumane.

The Bad News on Tropical Forests

Trees *are* being cut in the Third World. Although relatively little of the tropical wet forest has been cleared and converted to other uses, substantial parts of it are being logged. Hardly anyone lives in the wet rain forests, and there is little point in clearing them. Most of the logged forests will simply be allowed to regrow, their species largely still in place.

Some of the logged rain forests are actually cleared, mostly for slash-and-burn agriculture. This low-output farming provides only a bare subsistence living, but the people clearing the land lack better economic alternatives. However, the most serious tree losses have so far been in the dry tropics. There, the trees are being cut mainly for firewood and charcoal for cooking and heating.[1]

Firewood scarcity is an important cause of woodland loss and degradation in sub-Saharan Africa and India.[2] Places like Kenya and the Sahel are facing wood crises. That is a tragedy on two counts; not only is the tree-cutting unsustainable, but the carbon is being inefficiently turned into CO_2 and released into the atmosphere. More efficient cookstoves can double firewood efficiency. But the real problem is not that trees are being cut. It is that no one is replanting any new ones.

United Nations agencies and the World Bank say tropical forests are currently being "deforested" at the rate of about 0.9 percent of total tropical area each year. This is substantially higher than the 0.6 percent estimated a decade earlier. Asia is thought to have the highest rate of cutting (1.2 percent), with Latin American cutting at 0.9 percent and Africa at 0.8 percent.[3]

The naturalists are afraid that the losses are so high and will mount so rapidly—with population and economic growth—that they will quickly doom thousands of tropic wildlife species.

The picture is certainly better than that, though concern is warranted. The fact is that our data on forest losses have been poor. It's hard enough to get data on *logging* in a remote wild forest. It is harder still to keep track of land converted from forest to other uses. Even satellites have trouble distinguishing between a cut-over forest and an interplanted tract of crops and oil palms. And how do you assess the smoke from the slash-and-burn farmers, who clear another field every two or three years and let the old one regrow?

It is a vacuum that scary forecasts have come to fill. Yet the history of such unsupported forecasts should make us wary. The latest satellite data, for example, shows that the Amazon has lost about 12 percent of its original rain forest area. The rate of loss in the Amazon has now been reduced to 0.3 percent per year, with even lower rates of loss probable as Brazilians become more affluent and environmentally sensitive.[4]

And Some Good News

Dr. Ariel Lugo, one of the top U.S. experts in tropical forestry, says that only about half of the virgin tropical forests being cut annually are actually lost; the rest simply become secondary forests. Such secondary forests are still good wildlife habitat. In addition, says Dr. Lugo, replanting and natural regeneration have been producing additional secondary forest equal to another ten percent of the forest cut.[5]

Forest *loss*, then, is almost certainly lower than the environmental activists claim. More important, the current rate of rain forest loss is unlikely to be the long-term trend—any more than America's surge of cutting Eastern forests to fuel little iron smelters in the 1850s was a long-term trend. We know now that there's no need to lose much more tropical forest.

- There is no global shortage of food, nor of additional farm production potential outside the rain forest. (Few of the rain forests even make very good cropland.)
- We have more cost-effective ways to increase our forest products supplies than rainforest logging.

Nor does saving the rain forest depend on the near-impossibility of stopping population growth immediately, or the brutality of "subtracting" live humans.

The rain forests being lost are largely victims of lagging economic growth and institutional arrangements in the Third World. The key problem is neither "greed" nor population growth; expanding populations have little impact on forests if the extra people live in cities and have alternative fuels to take the place of firewood.

The reality is that Third World residents are cutting trees "nobody owns" because they have no jobs and need free fuel and free cropland. Deforestation losses can be radically reduced by better institutional arrangements—along with the rapid economic growth and job creation already occurring in much of the Third World.

REALITY:

"Deforestation is really land use change; conversion to cropland and pasture. People do this for the reasons you identify in the chapter—weak property rights, perverse policy incentives, and (above all else) the low earning opportunities of unskilled rural labor. Clearing land for farming is basically a very unrewarding activity. Almost by definition, that means it is done by people with limited job prospects."

> Douglas Southgate, author of *Economic Progress and the Environment: One Developing Country's Policy Crisis*, commenting on a draft of this book, November 17, 1994

"Investment in fuelwood production and tree farming, on a large scale, by farmers and by community groups and private enterprises will not occur unless it is profitable. The incentives are gradually emerging. . . . But woodfuel markets are developing too slowly. . . . The pace of market development will accelerate if open-access sources of fuelwood are eliminated, cutting in protected areas is restricted, farmers are not restricted in marketing wood from their own land . . . and farmers have uncontested ownership of local forests and woodlands."

> Kevin Cleaver and Gotz Schreiber, World Bank staff, "The Population, Environmental and Agriculture Nexus of Sub-Saharan Africa," 1993[6]

Stealing What No One Owns

If population growth isn't stealing the forests, what is?

Let's look at a resource named the elephant. Africa is losing half of its elephants every eight years. Thus naturalists are (naturally) predicting the extinction of the elephant early in the next century.

Once again, the predictions will be wrong.

The reality is that elephants in some countries are doing just fine. Their offspring will undoubtedly be available to repopulate the game parks of those countries which are currently managing their game resources badly.

In most of Eastern and Central Africa, the governments have owned the elephants. The animals are "protected" by game wardens who are too few in number, poorly equipped, and poorly paid (so they are susceptible to bribes). In these countries, many farmers see the elephants as competitors who tear up their crops, destroy their trees, drink their water, and even trample houses and citizens.

The only way the farmers can profit from the elephant's existence is by poaching them for their ivory, hides, and meat. Or they see no reason to risk interfering with those who *do* poach. The elephants in these countries are declining rapidly.

Just the opposite is happening in Southern Africa, which already has 20 percent of Africa's elephants—and where the elephant count is rising.

Zimbabwe is one country that is creating incentives for local people to protect the elephants:

- Hunters are charged $25,000 for shooting a trophy animal, and the money is used to pay elephant costs—including damage to local farms and homes.
- The meat is given to tribes living in the game park areas.
- Rogue elephants outside the parks are shot by the Park personnel to minimize damage, and/or villages can sell hunting permits themselves.

Zimbabwe would also like to sell its legal ivory and elephant hides to help finance elephant management.

Once the elephants become an economic plus, *poachers* are shot rather than elephants. Enough people care so that the laws are fiercely enforced.[7]

The World Wildlife Fund is recommending that all of Africa adopt the failing policies which have reduced elephant populations in Kenya and Tanzania: giving the governments title to the animals and outlawing the sale of hides and ivory. If the elephants are lucky, the World Wildlife Fund's recommendation will be ignored.

In this light, it is interesting to note that the new director of Kenya's Wildlife Service hopes to move control and ownership of the national parks and surrounding areas from the county councils to the local communities. The Wildlife Service is relying on a recent court case which ruled in favor of local control of land and revenues. If he is successful in implementing this change in ownership direction, the eyes of the environmental world will be focused on the results.[8]

The same questions of ownership, incentives, and alternatives which plague the elephant apply to the forests. Here are two good rules of thumb for evaluating "conservation" proposals anywhere in the world:

- If the proposed "solutions" depend on people acting self-lessly, reject them. People always follow what they perceive to be their best interests. Get the incentives right.
- If the "solutions" involve government "saving" resources from greedy private citizens, reject them. The Third World cannot hire enough game wardens, or pay them enough, to defend environmental resources from the public if the incentives are wrong.

The key forest problem is the common ownership of resources. As environmental leader Garrett Hardin has noted in his famous essay on "lifeboat ethics," common ownership almost by definition leads to the rape of the resource.

Forests as Commons

The Third World is losing huge tracts of tropical forest, both wet and dry, because the land and the trees don't belong to anybody. The incentives lead the local people to exploit that local resource rather than sustain it.

Kenya is losing too many of its trees to charcoal.[10] Madagascar has been burning forest (habitat for some of the world's most unique and threatened wildlife species) because its socialist farming policies have been failing. India's governmental forest authorities effectively took title to huge tracts of forest which it could not defend from the goats and cattle of the local residents. The goats and cattle prevented the growth of young trees to replace the ones poached for firewood.

We can put more and more of the Third World's natural resources in "preserves" and suffer these resource losses while we wait for the currently weak governments to become strong. Or we can change the incentives for behavior by local people.

Changing the incentives can be as simple as it has been in Zimbabwe (and perhaps will be in Kenya) with the elephants: letting the local people help manage the resource in return for sharing in the profits.

The Commons Problem

Many of the world's natural resources are held "in common." That is, they have no direct owner. Air, flowing water, wild genes, and wild animals all fall into this category. Forests, fields, and pastures are often owned in common by communities or tribes. Natural resources "owned" by governments are effectively held in common.

The difficulty is that looking after a commonly owned resource is tough and unrewarding. Someone has to cover costs for everybody else. There are too many free riders. Too often, the common resource doesn't get saved.

The grasslands of the Sahel, the rain forests of the Amazon, the air over Los Angeles and the waters of the Chesapeake Bay are all "owned" by so many people that they have been difficult to protect. Many trees in the Third World lack owners, and so risk being cut by any passerby.

Natural resources owned by weak governments are often at risk, even when they are designated as national preserves, because the governments are unable to maintain effective protection.

Garrett Hardin made a dramatic impact on America's collective mind when he published his "lifeboat ethic" in 1974. It was based on an extremely realistic (and thus dismal) examination of commons ownership and what Hardin then concluded would mean vast starvation and wildlife loss. As one commentator put it:

"Garrett Hardin's article in *Psychology Today* on 'lifeboat' ethics electrified the general public. . . . Hardin had been the first to state clearly and convincingly 'the tragedy of the commons.' His study showed how rational human self-interest within a system of common ownership or usage results, ironically but foreseeably, in a loss to everybody within it."[9]

Unfortunately, Hardin is so committed to the myth of scarcity that he argued for limiting food aid (induced starvation) instead of changing the resource ownership structures!

MYTHMAKERS IN HOLLYWOOD:

"Displaying a 50 by 25 foot inflatable chainsaw bearing the message: 'Hollywood: Stop the Chainsaw Massacre,' Rainforest Action Network, Greenpeace and Earth First staged a mediagenic protest at the entrance to Hollywood's Paramount Studios on September 15. Eight demonstrators, handcuffed to cement-filled barrels painted to look like tree stumps, blockaded the studio entrance as activists negotiated with Paramount over the studio's use of plywood made from lauan, a wood harvested from Southeast Asian tropical forests."

Earth Island Journal, Winter 1993-94, Vol. 9, No. 1,
Earth Island Institute, San Francisco, p. 19

MYTHMAKERS' JOURNEY TO HARSH REALITY:

"In November 1989, I went to . . . Venezuela, hired a dugout canoe, and set off down the Orinoco River. We stopped at one of the (Indian villages). . . . The more I saw of these wonderful indigenous people, the less I thought our culture was at all civilized. They live in harmony and peace with the forest, protecting and respecting it, while we rape and destroy it for "economic" reasons."

Helen Caldicott, *If You Love This Planet: A Plan to Heal the
Earth,* W. Norton, New York, 1992. P. 46-47[11]

". . . only the left eye (of the river dolphin) is used in magic rituals and as a charm. . . . The Brazilian government has outlawed this trade, but it continues illegally."

"Rainforest Dolphin Trade," *Buzzworm's Earth Journal,*
January/February 1994, p. 19

"Fundraising concerts by Sting for his Rainforest Foundation have been successful in raising money to protect the forest home of the Kayapo people of Brazil's Amazon. But a problem has arisen. . . . Now it seems, the Kayapo have been prevented from selling off their mahogany trees . . . as a result of Sting and the others putting pressure on Brazil to stop the logging of mahogany. In case you're wondering, the Kayapo are suing for loss of income."

"The Eco-Mole," *Earth Island Journal,* Winter 1993/94, Vol. 9,
No. 1, Earth Island Institute, San Francisco, p. 4

Why Property Rights Were Invented

Property rights have been around so long and become so ingrained in Western society that we have evidently forgotten why they were invented.

Iceland in the 12th century was losing its eider ducks and other seabirds. Too many people were preying on the eggs. Not enough young birds were hatching to maintain the colonies.

Iceland solved the problem by declaring that the seabird eggs were henceforth the property of the landowner on whose land they were laid. The seabird colonies promptly recovered. Every landowner wanted big colonies of seabirds to lay lots of eggs on his land. So he made sure enough nests were undisturbed.

Despite the long record of resource conservation success established by ownership incentives, the tragedy of the commons is still far too typical of the Third World's forests today.

Third World societies have lacked the institutional structures to protect their forests and wildlife. The answer does not lie in returning to the old tribal customs, however.

CONSERVATIONIST'S REALITY:

"The old paradigm of conservation held that the best way to protect biological diversity was to mark off the territory, build a wall around it, and patrol it with a machete or machine gun. . . . In the old conservation paradigm, people were frequently seen as the enemy. There were two major problems. . . . First, the preservation model was increasingly seen as unethical. Conservation workers resisted the idea of pushing people off lands they may have occupied for centuries. And they began to oppose the vision of declaring national parks while rural families suffered malnutrition around its borders. The second problem was that it didn't work. In areas of the globe with the most biological diversity—the humid tropics—rural families ignored the signs around national parks, tore down the fences, and invaded the reserves."

James Nations, vice president for Latin American Programs,
Conservation International, 1993[12]

"It can hardly be a coincidence that virtually every serious environmental problem, historically and today, occurred or occurs in those areas where well-defined systems of property rights are lacking. Indeed, upon further reflection it becomes clear that this is the essence of pollution and wildlife problems: No one owns the resources involved, and consequently no one protects them."

Bast, Hill and Rue, *Eco-Sanity*, Madison Books,
Lanham, MD, 1994, p. 216

Tribalism Is Not the Answer

The American Indians are widely praised now in some circles because they did not "own" land. This is presumed to reflect their lack of greed and their respect for nature.

That gentle but misguided thought betrays a misunderstanding of the American Indian culture and economy.

It was almost impossible for the Indians to assign land titles for game animals and for their typical shifting cultivation of crops. So they owned their hunting grounds as a tribe rather than as individuals. At the same time, Indian tribes reacted *violently* to any intrusion on their tribal lands. A quick death was about the best that an intruder could expect; torture was common. [13]

When the populations of the American Indians became dense, they depopulated the forests of game, cleared more land, and put more pressure on the resources. Some of the Eastern American Indians sometimes hunted with fire, using flames to drive game to the hunters. Some early Plains Indians would drive a whole herd of bison over a cliff to get the meat they needed from a few animals. Famine is what limited the Indians' impact on nature and made the Indian culture look friendly to the environment—in distant retrospect.

Tribal and village landholding has suited the needs of indigenous peoples in Africa and Latin America in the past because they practiced the lowest-cost form of agriculture—shifting cultivation. (It is also called slash-and-burn or bush-fallow.)

Now, with rising populations and incomes, the shifting cultivation needs to give way to more intensive farming systems, such as tied ridges and alley cropping. The more intensive systems need fixed locations, and the farmers need clear title to a fixed piece of land so they can make the investments needed for the new systems.

Otherwise, both hunger and severe soil erosion will keep driving the expansion of low-yield farming into more critical wildlife habitat.

Tribal landholding and/or other forms of communal ownership have often failed to defend the ecology. They are failing on a colossal scale throughout the Third World today. We probably have to get rid of either the people or the commons ownership. I vote to get rid of the commons.

MYTHBREAKERS:

". . . [T]he Kayapo, handsome warriors of the [Amazon's] Xingo basin . . . [now] have a proper reservation, and contracts for their wild oils and essences with environmentally friendly companies such as The Body Shop, a cosmetics chain. But the Kayapo's land is also rich in gold and mahogany . . . about $33 million in mahogany alone in 1988. . . . Such money as they get is often pocketed by chiefs who spend it on ranches, cars and aeroplanes . . . In 1988, [one] village . . . collected $1 million in timber and mineral bounty, but still had a quarter of its children die in infancy. . . .

"Under pressure to give up logging, 88 Kayapo stormed into Brasilia with an ultimatum . . . either allow the tribe to go on cutting down its forests, or pay $50,000 per village per month for timber sales forgone. The government, which is broke, would not pay; the Kayapos' trees continue to fall.

". . . The Guajajare of Northeastern Brazil seized some government agents in a bid to make the government grant them logging permits. A group of Nambikwara, from Mato Grosso, having razed their own hardwood, began to poach on their neighbors'.

"It is an awkward time for the green movement. 'We are going through a phase of disenchantment,' says one supporter of Indian rights."

"The Savage Can Also Be Ignoble," *The Economist*,
June 12, 1993, p. 54

Stealing Biodiversity with Economic Stagnation

Bad economic policies in Third World countries have been another major factor in forest loss.

The environmental movements have freely criticized the governments of Third World countries—but often for the wrong reasons. Virtually never, for example, have the environmental critics complained that *most Third World governments have created too few off-farm jobs.*

In fact, Dr. Mostafa K. Tolba of the UN Environmental Program recently warned an international conference that there have been "loud complaints from a number of developing countries that the rich are more interested in making the Third World into a natural history museum than they are in filling the bellies of its people." [14]

And yet the failure to create good urban jobs stands at the heart of key tropical resource losses in the world today.

A logging road doesn't bring settlers to the Amazon if they have almost any other choice. The Amazon is a steaming jungle with enough dangerous snakes, biting insects, and pervasive diseases to frighten off any rational human being who wasn't born there.

Even the poorest Brazilians have mostly voted for a tin shack in a Rio slum where the sewage runs down the unpaved streets, rather than move into the jungle.

But Brazil (and most of Latin America for the last 400 years) has been caught in an economic time warp. The Spanish and Portuguese captains who conquered the Amerindians left a tradition of repressive and pervasive government control.

Since the beginning of the 19th century, Latin governments have veered back and forth from repressive right to populist left. Both sides, however, left in place the real economic culprits—a set of indomitable government officials who tied everything up in a web of red tape and graft. Anything not specifically titled to an individual person belonged automatically to the government. Land, forests, the right to sell fruit on the street, were all part of the bureaucratic empire. If you didn't pay off the officials, you couldn't run a bus line. Even if you *paid off* the officials, they wouldn't let you raise bus fares to match the inflation the government created. The buses lost money. So there were few bus lines, strangling economic growth.

Peruvian Hernando De Soto reveals in his important book, *The Other Path*, that he went through the process of getting the permits for a small clothing factory that would employ a dozen women and two sewing machines. It took 289 man-days, 19 bribe solicitations, and four bribes to get the government permissions to start the business! The same process in Miami, Florida, took De Soto four hours and the standard $25 fee for the permit.[15]

Population increase and economic growth *should* pose little danger to the rain forests. Few people want to live by subsistence agriculture in the jungle. If there are good jobs, schools and amenities in the cities, the jungle will be left to its primitive inhabitants. (If, indeed, even they choose to stay there.)

The real reasons for tropical rain forest loss include:

- Constraints on trade in farm products, due to farm subsidies in the rich countries and local farm politics in all countries.
- Ill-conceived government subsidies for forest clearing (as in the Amazon);
- Government policies that suppress economic growth, driving people to accept a short and desperate life as subsistence farmers in the rain forest; and
- Failure to invest in high-yield farming research, so that increasing populations drive the expansion of low-yield farming onto what once were forests. [16]

CASE STUDY IN THE PHILIPPINES

"Economic stagnation . . . (in the 1980s) created such massive unemployment and poverty that internal migration patterns drastically changed. Frontier migration, already present in both countries since the 1950s, accelerated while urbanward movements, which were dominant in the 1970s, declined. Most migrants could only turn to open access forest lands. . . . As much as 25 percent of total arable lowlands in the Philippines remain underutilized. Meanwhile, cultivated area in forest has expanded from 23 to 31 percent of total cropped area between 1980 and 1987."

Maria Concepcion Cruz, Environmental Department, World Bank, "Economic Stagnation and Deforestation in Costa Rica and the Philippines," 1993[17]

The Famous Rainforest Beef

The most famous (or infamous) government policy mistake on tropical forests was made in the 1970s by the military junta then running Brazil. The generals decided that if they didn't populate the Amazon, "invaders" might take it away. So they built roads, and offered a government subsidy for clearing cattle pasture in the rain forest. Fortunately, the rain forest made such lousy cattle pasture that the subsidy was paid on only 1.5 percent of the Amazon rain forest area over the 16 years it was offered.[18]

Ironically, while Brazil's generals were encouraging the misuse of tropical forest, agricultural researchers in Brazil and Colombia were developing new acid-tolerant grasses and legumes that would tolerate the highly acid soils of Latin America's big acid savannas. The new acid-tolerant forage crops can *sustain over the long term* ten times as many cattle per acre as would degrade the rain forest pastures. Even better, the new grasses are planted *outside* the rain forest on the big acid savannas which have far less biodiversity. Latin America has some 300 million acres of these acid wastelands, which are covered with stunted brush and coarse grasses.

(Brazil also has a successful "beef" industry in the lower Amazon, where Asian water buffalo have proven well-adapted. They thrive on jungle greenery that doesn't adequately nourish cattle. They defend their calves from the snakes and jaguars. And in the rainy season, when the cattle herd up on the dry ground and starve, the water buffalo simply swim to food. The Amazon water buffalo numbers have expanded from a few dozen at the end of World War II to more than a million.)

In truth, where rain forest has been cleared for cattle pasture, it has usually been due to government policies that devalued the trees. The rain forest makes such poor pasture it doesn't normally pay the cost of clearing the land. There's usually more profit in trees.

What Will Preserve Tropical Forests?

New Farming Systems

Science is already demonstrating its potential to preserve Third World forests through high-yield farming, high-yield forestry, and radical gains in the efficiency of forest product harvest and use. The Third World is already adopting these technologies broadly and rapidly. Even better, Third World researchers (in China, Indonesia, and Malaysia) are among the world's leaders in the field of forestry biotechnology.

In addition, the acid savannas also stand as a buffer against any need to clear forest for pasture. The new acid-tolerant forages mean there is less need than ever to cut rainforest for cattle pasture.

Free Food Trade

Asian forests are being sacrificed for government policies aimed at nation-by nation food self-sufficiency. The policy is designed to placate local farmers, not to feed consumers or preserve the environment. For example, the Indonesian government is planning to clear

1.5 million acres of tropical forest to grow soybeans—when at least 50 million acres of better soybean land are already cleared and lying uncropped in the U.S. Argentina.

The GATT is probably the only way to bring a swift and sweeping end to agricultural protectionism. The GATT rules already require member countries to dismantle their industrial trade protections. If the GATT also required openness to farm trade, most countries would still join, because they see the GATT and export manufacturing as the path to affluence. Bilateral efforts to open trade barriers in Japan and South Korea have dragged on for decades with little result—because the entrenched political power of farmers is not outweighed by the broader interests of the public and the environment.

Thus, the world should put a high environmental priority on another GATT round that will eliminate farm trade barriers as quickly as possible.

Better Institutions and Policies

Preserving the world's tropical forests will not only require more science and freer trade. It will also take better government policies—and strong economic growth in the Third World.

Institutional and policy reforms are now critical frontiers.

We urge First World observers to understand that the jungle is not America's Yosemite Park. It is not surrounded by an effective legal system, a tradition of respect for the law, or modern law enforcement personnel equipped with helicopters and two-way radios.

Incentives for preservation need to play a much more important role than they have to date, including at the recent Rio environmental summit. It may even help to privatize some of the forests in the Third World to give the protection of ownership or contract control—and thus the incentive for good management and reforestation.

This does not mean privatizing all the forests, or even a majority of the forestland. National forests and wildlife preserves should certainly be kept and protected. But where a government cannot afford to protect a forest at risk, a *well-regulated timber company given the right long -term incentives* might do enormous environmental good.

Making the Third World wealthier is also important because wealthier people can afford to care more about forest preservation.

Richer countries give their residents good economic alternatives besides logging and rainforest subsistence farming. They enforce their game laws and logging regulations. And they fund more science, which gives us more high-yielding forest crops on relatively few acres. America's national forests are surrounded by affluent citizens who can afford to be charitable about the competition for resources.

Preserving forests will take environmental sensitivity. But environmental sensitivity will do little by itself. Mere anguish will condemn many of the Third World's most important forest resources to death.

The "caring" urged by environmental advocates is not enough. It is only the beginning.

Notes

[1]Ariel Lugo, Institute of Tropical Forestry (Puerto Rico), U.S. Forest Service, presentation to the National Forum on Biodiversity, Washington, D.C., 1986.

[2]FAO, *Forest Products Yearbook 1988*, Rome, 1990.

[3]Forest Resources Assessment Project 1990, UN Food and Agriculture Agency, "Second Interim Report on the State of Tropical Forests," presented at the 10th World Forestry Congress, Paris, September 1991.

[4]USDA/FAS, *Brazilian Forest Products Annual Report*, 1992, p. 3.

[5]Ariel Lugo, Institute of Tropical Forestry (Puerto Rico) U.S. Forest Service, presentation to the National Forum on Biodiversity, Washington, D.C., 1986.

[6]Cleaver and Schreiber, "The Population, Environment, and Agriculture Nexus in Sub-Saharan Africa," *Agriculture and Environmental Challenges, Proceedings of the 13th World Bank Agriculture Sector Symposium*, Washington, D.C., 1993, p. 208.

[7]Elizabeth Larson, "Elephants and Ivory," *The Freeman*, July 1991, 261-263.

[8]"Kenyan Conservation Chief Finds Refuge in Communities' Support," *The Washington Times*, November 24, 1994, p. A12.

[9]Joseph Fletcher, "Chronic Famine and the Immorality of Food Aid," *Focus*, published by the Carrying Capacity Network, Vol. 3, No. 2, 1993, pp. 42-45.

[10]"Wood, Fodder and Soil-Fertility Problems in Western Kenya," *International Centre for Research in Agroforestry, Annual Report,*

1991, Nairobi, Kenya, 1992.

[11]Helen Caldicott, *If You Love This Planet: A Plan to Heal the Earth*, W.W. Norton & Co., New York, 1992.

[12]James Nations, "Does Conservation Condemn the Poor to Perpetual Poverty: A Nongovernmental Organization Perspective," *Agriculture and Environmental Challenges, Proceedings of the 13th World Bank Agriculture Sector Symposium*, Washington, D.C., 1993, p. 245.

[13]Alden Vaughn, "New England Frontier," *Puritans and Indians, 1620-1675* (Vaughn and Clark, eds.), Belknap, Cambridge, Massachusetts, 1981.

[14]Mostafa Tolba, before the Convention on International Trade in Endangered Species, Kyoto, Japan, 1992.

[15]Hernando De Soto, *The Other Path*, Harper & Row, New York, 1989.

[16]Southgate, Sanders, and Ehui, "Resource Degradation in Africa and Latin America: Population Pressure, Policies and Property Arrangements," *American Journal of Agricultural Economics*, December 1990, pp. 1259-1263. See also Southgate, *Tropical Deforestation and Agricultural Development in Latin America*, London Environmental Economics Centre, LEEC Paper DP 91-01.

[17]Maria Cruz, "Economic Stagnation and Deforestation in Costa Rica and the Philippines," *Agriculture and Environmental Challenges*, Proceedings of the 13th World Bank Agriculture Sector Symposium, Washington, D.C., 1993, p. 227.

[18]Dennis J. Mahar, *Government Policies and Deforestation in Brazil's Amazon Region*, World Bank, Washington, D.C., 1989.

18

Saving the Planet with Plastic?

MYTHMAKERS SAY:

"During the manufacture of plastic, large quantities of different chemicals are made as by-products. They constitute toxic waste that is emitted into the air through factory chimneys, poured into sewage systems, sent to garbage dumps, drained into streams, rivers and lakes, buried in landfills, or illegally dumped by the Mafia at night when no one is looking. The food chain concentrates many of these toxic organic chemicals, so the plastic we use every day may come back to haunt us as poisonous food, water, or air, or it stays in our garbage dumps for hundreds of years."

Helen Caldicott, *If You Love This Planet*, 1992[1]

"If brewers were forbidden to put plastic nooses on six-packs of beer, if supermarkets were not allowed to wrap polyvinyl chloride film around everything in sight, if McDonald's restaurants could rediscover the paper plate, if the use of plastics was cut back to those things considered worth the social costs (say artificial hearts or video tape) then we could push back the petrochemical industry's toxic invasion of the biosphere."

Barry Commoner, "Why We Have Failed," *Greenpeace*, 1989[2]

Naturally, this chapter title is an overstatement.

We will not save the planet with plastic. However, the title makes a key point: Plastic, too, is a vital element in the high-yield farming that *can* make room on the globe for both people and wildlife.

Far from being an insult to the environment, plastic can do a great deal of environmental good through agriculture. Plastic, too, can save wildlife by raising crop yields and cropping intensity.

Plastic Sheeting

The biggest use of agricultural plastics is for simple polyethylene sheeting.

Mulch. Primarily, plastic sheeting is used for mulch. Laid atop the ground, the plastic raises the temperature of the soil, so that tender young seedlings can be started and transplanted earlier in the spring. That promotes more rapid crop development and thus raises yields.

Plastic mulch can mean extending the ability to grow crops farther onto cool plains like those of Canada and northern China. In central China, it can mean an extra rice crop each year. In southern China, it can mean a crop of vegetables in addition to two rice crops from the same land.

The plastic sheeting has other virtues as well:

• It prevents weeds from competing with the crop plant, without either pesticides or hand weeding.
• It cuts water evaporation and makes the use of fertilizer safer and more effective. That can make the difference between 25 bushels of wheat per acre and 50 to 60 bushels in arid regions.
• It helps cut soil erosion wherever it is used on slopes or in windy areas.
• It can reduce losses to rot in crops like strawberries and tomatoes.

Soil Fumigation

Another major use of sheeting is for soil fumigation. Intensively farmed fields can build up high populations of destructive soil organisms like nematodes. To combat the nematodes and other subsoil pests, farmers sometimes have to fumigate the soils. Plastic sheeting seals in the soil fumigant, giving the soil pests a toxic dose while decreasing chemical usage.

Crop rotation is not be very effective against nematodes, because they can lie dormant in the soil for up to 20 years waiting for the right crop to be planted and emit the correct feeding signal.

STRAWBERRIES IN PLASTIC—The plastic film used in this strawberry field in California helps warm the soil, conserves water use, and eliminates weeds.

Greenhouse Covering

Millions of yards of plastic sheeting are also used to cover greenhouses. Stretched over a light framework, the plastic film is far less expensive than glass greenhouses with their costly glass and glazing. (It may also take more fossil fuels to produce that glass than the plastic.)

One of the big advantages is that if the plastic greenhouse is hit by a hailstorm, the farmer can simply stretch a new roll of plastic over the frames. With a glass greenhouse, a storm means a huge reinvestment in rebuilding and reglazing.

Greenhouses grow many of our fruits and vegetables, both for growing them to harvest in cold weather, and for starting seedlings early to fill gaps in the produce market. Thus they play a key role in supplying good nutrition year round.

Greenhouses are especially important in cold climates and dry ones. China, again, is a major user. China's internal transportation system is still underdeveloped, and most of its population centers have had to grow most of their own food. Chinese consumers still have to get their produce from their local region, simply because they can't get fruits and vegetables brought in from another climate zone.

In the Middle East, the latest greenhouse technologies are using seawater to help grow indoor crops. Forced air is blown through a mist of seawater and then into the greenhouse. The air picks up moisture but not salt. Some of the best designs get 90 percent of their crop moisture from the salt water.

Protecting Livestock Feed

Dairy cows and other ruminant livestock need huge amounts of forage year-round. In most climates this means storing food from the summer to provide for the winter. Plastic has been playing an expanding role in protecting these off-season feed supplies.

Plastic sheeting is widely used to protect silage, in both affluent countries and poor ones. Silage is simply a green forage (usually alfalfa, green corn, or high-value hay). The silage is chopped green at the peak of its total nutrient value and stored *without drying* in an airless environment where it cannot rot.

In the past, having silage meant building an expensive vertical silo, usually out of brick, cement, or cement blocks. Those silos were almost as much the hallmark of American farming as the barns they stood next to. In recent decades, big blue steel glass-lined silos have become landmarks in many farming regions. But such silos are expensive. They require natural resources to build and maintain.

With plastic, making silage can be as simple as digging a trench in the ground, lining it with plastic sheeting, and weighting a plastic cover down with old rubber tires to keep it from blowing off. It's cheap, effective, and good for the environment because it preserves productivity at low cost.

Plastic sheeting is also used increasingly to protect the big round hay bales that now dominate U.S. hay-making. Dairy farmers, cattle ranchers, sheep raisers, and horse farms store these bales in the open, instead of building more expensive barns.

Plastic sheeting is so effective that it has become one of the major farming inputs in the world's largest agriculture. Chinese farmers currently use some 400,000 tons of plastic sheeting per year.[3]

Plastic for Irrigation

One of the most water-efficient irrigation systems is called drip irrigation. It uses permanently installed plastic tubes to feed water directly to the roots of orchard trees and other high-value plants. A modified drip irrigation system can be easily rigged by laying plastic tubing on the ground with holes at the appropriate places where the plants or trees are growing.

A newer irrigation system, with even higher water efficiency, is called dual-level irrigation. Developed at Iowa State University, it is the closest thing to a closed irrigation system that can be achieved outside a greenhouse.

The first level of perforated plastic pipes is laid in the root zone of the crops to be grown. This is the feed piping. The second level of perforated piping is laid perhaps two feet lower, and works as the recycling level.

No water evaporates because the water is added below ground level, and no runoff occurs because any water and nutrients not used the first time are put back through the system. Without the low cost and inert character of PVC plastic pipe, the system could not be cost-effective.[4]

Chemical Containers

Virtually all of the chemicals used on the farm are transported in plastic containers.

Environmentalists see this as a major complaint, because they envision millions of plastic jugs full of dangerous substances lying around farms or being dumped into landfills all over the country.

But the only other material tough and inert enough to transport the chemicals is glass. If chemicals were delivered in glass jugs, the breakage in transit—and resulting spillage—would represent a much greater environmental threat than disposing of triple-rinsed plastic containers.

Secondly, the plastic containers for agricultural chemicals are increasingly the big, reusable kind that go back to the factory for reuse instead of into a landfill.

Handling spills have now been fingered as the major reason for the occasional high pesticide readings in farm groundwater sources. Now big containers generally have positive lock-on features to prevent any spills in the handling and loading process.

Third, the agricultural chemicals industry is making strenuous efforts to collect old pesticides and empty pesticide jugs. The pesticides are incinerated or put into hazardous waste sites. The plastic jugs are turned over to central facilities where they can be safely rinsed and some are turned into—fence posts!

The inert nature of plastic makes for wonderful fence posts.

Farmers need millions of such posts to keep livestock safely in their fields. These fence posts are a major highway safety plus for the public—as anyone who has ever driven in the Latin American countryside knows. Colliding with a horse or a cow can do enormous—even fatal—damage to highway travelers.

In the old days, the valley fence posts were typically cut from mountain locust trees. Locust yields a hard, insect-resistant wood that may last 20 years, but with today's labor costs they're expensive.

Presently, most of our fence posts are treated pine, also with a service life of perhaps 20 years. Or cheaper steel posts that aren't as strong and have a somewhat shorter service life.

Making waste plastic into fence posts takes it far away from any people who might be chemically sensitive or concerned about the plastic's previous condition of servitude.

Farmers love the idea of nearly permanent plastic fence posts, and the idea is spreading.

Biodegradable Plastics

Among the newer plastic developments are biodegradable plastics.

Farmers can now buy plastic sheeting that disappears from the environment. Ultraviolet light triggers a timed disintegration process in this new sheeting, which continues until the plastic has completely degraded. Once the sheeting has broken down into low-molecular-weight fragments, it is attacked by soil microbes that turn it back into carbon and water. The "timer" in the sheeting can be varied so the sheeting lasts as little as two weeks or as long as 12 months.

The biodegradable sheeting is more expensive, but eliminates the need to gather up the old sheeting and take it to a landfill.

Other types of biodegradable plastic use starch made from corn intermixed with the normal polyethylene molecules, so that the fragments break down under exposure to sunlight. Then the remaining flimsy polyethylene structure soon disintegrates.

ICI, a British-based chemical firm, is making small amounts of fully biodegradable plastic under the trade name Biopol. The firm uses bacteria that convert sugar (from corn or beets) into a natural polymer. Again, the biodegradable plastic is more expensive, and its use has been limited so far to shampoo and cosmetic bottles.

Environmentalists are not impressed. They view biodegradable plastics, including Biopol, as a red herring. They feel that they might give people the wrong message—that it's OK to throw plastics away—and distract from what they feel is the real need to recycle plastics. (So far, the biodegradables are a tiny part of the 100 million ton plastic industry.)

Nor have the environmental groups had much good to say about such efforts as turning chemical jugs into fence posts—a clear victory in recycling. (Approving the fence posts might seem to express approval for the pesticides.)

Meanwhile, researchers in the U.S. are working on plastics from lactic acid, a cheap by-product of the dairy industry.

Other Plastics for the Farm

Farmers use a wide variety of other plastics to perform necessary farm chores and to cut farming/food costs, including:

- Fiberglass shovel handles;
- Plastic seat covers for tractors and combines (machines that often sit out in the weather for extended periods);
- Plastic push broom bristles;
- Fiberglass watering tanks for livestock, that won't rust and leak water;
- Plastic insulators for the electric fences that are important for rotational grazing;
- Nylon livestock halters and lead ropes;
- Plastic non-rusting hoppers and nylon seed plates for crop planters;

- Plastic hoses and pipes for watering crops and livestock; and
- Fiberglass spray tanks for chemicals, that won't rust or corrode.

All of these products have strong, solid, functional reasons to be on our farms: to raise productivity and yield.

Growing Plastic Lumber?

An Iowa farmer and inventor named George Tyson has come up with a method of making hard, durable "wood-substitute composites" by combining agricultural biomass and discarded plastic. It's like being able to grow trees in a farm field—and reduce landfill requirements at the same time.[5]

His process uses superheated steam and chemicals to explode the cell fibers of wheat straw or other farm-produced biomass. The tiny fragments that are produced in these mini-explosions combine instantly with molecules of ground-up recycled consumer plastics. The resulting "Bondomass" is 40 percent stronger than wood, can be cut, shaped, drilled, and nailed like ordinary lumber—and is impervious to water, rot, and insects. (It can also be made flame-retardant.)

Tyson sees it being used initially for outdoor construction, highway signposts, porch furniture, insulation panels, playground equipment, and even low-cost housing. He expects the cost to be 10 or 15 percent less than pressure-treated lumber.

"The raw materials for this technology are relatively cheap and they're either already available or becoming available in abundant supply. . . . With the recycling programs that are going on throughout the country, all kinds of post-consumer plastics are looking for a home. We hope to offer that home," says Tyson.

The environmental zealots would prefer that we use virtually no plastic at all. But that is a vain hope unless you assume the world will revert to 1 billion people living in mud huts.

If we assume a realistic scenario, with 8-10 billion people living affluent-but-sustainable lives in coexistence with wild species, then we need plastic as well as pesticides—for their environmental contributions.

We need to use them carefully, but we need them.

PLASTIC BUCKETS FOR AFRICA:

"Half the population of Africa is under 15 years old. Children are everywhere: in the armies and the refugee camps, working in the fields and trading in the marketplaces. And at home it is the child who performs the most vital function of the family: fetching the water. At dawn, while so many are still asleep, small boys start up in the dark and hurry off to wells, ponds or rivers. The new technology has provided them with an essential instrument: a plastic bucket.

"The plastic bucket has revolutionized the lives of Africans. You cannot survive in the tropics without water; the shortages are always acute. And so water has to be carried long distances, frequently dozens of kilometers. Before the invention of the plastic bucket, water was carried in heavy vats made of clay or stone. The wheel was not a familiar aspect of African culture; everything was carried on the head, including the heavy vats of water. In the division of household labor, it was the women's task to fetch water. A child would have been unable to lift a vat. . . .

"The appearance of the plastic bucket was a miracle. To start with, it is relatively cheap, . . . costing around two dollars. And it is light. And it comes in different sizes: Even a small child can carry a few liters. . . .

"And now it is the child's job to fetch water. . . . What a relief for the overworked African woman! What a change in her life!. . . ."

Ryszard Kapuscinski, "Plastic Buckets and Ballpoint Pens,"
Granta, reprinted in *Utne Reader,* Jan./Feb.1995, p. 39

Notes
[1]Helen Caldicott, *If You Love This Planet: A Plan to Heal the Earth*, W.W. Norton & Co., New York, 1992, p. 63.

[2]Barry Commoner, "Why We Have Failed," *Greenpeace,* September/ October 1989, reprinted in *Learning to Listen to the Land*, Island Press, Washington, D.C., 1991, p. 165.

[3]*China Light Industry Handbook*, Beijing, 1991.

[4]"Subsurface Irrigation Systems: Water Management System Recycles Water," *The Grower* 24, 1991, pp. 32-34.

[5]"Straw + Plastic = Wood?" *The Furrow*, January/February 1994, Deere & Co., Moline, Illinois, pp. 20-21.

19

Conserving with Cows

JEREMY RIFKIN, MYTHMAKER EXTRAORDINAIRE:

It is remarkable for one man and one book to gather so much misinformation about any single topic in one place—so we are relying on Rifkin's 1992 book, *Beyond Beef*, for most of the Mythmaker quotes in this chapter.

We will list the quotes by chapter headings, because Rifkin's chapter titles are so creative. And then we will deal one by one with the issues he raises.

"Malthus and Meat"
"It seems disingenuous for the intellectual elite of the first world to dwell on the subject of too many babies being born in the second-and-third-world nations while virtually ignoring the overpopulation of cattle and the realities of a food chain that robs the poor of sustenance to feed the rich a steady diet of grain-fed meat. The transition of world agriculture from food grain to feed grains represents a new form of human evil, whose consequences may be far greater and longer-lasting than any past examples of violence inflicted by men against their fellow human beings."[1]

One of Rifkin's major charges in *Beyond Beef* is that poor people in the Third World are being starved so their countries can export grain-fed beef to the rich countries.

This claim is utterly false.

Rifkin's "advisor" on this book was a young man who grew up on a Montana cattle ranch. He apparently believed that Third World countries produced beef the same way that North America does—

with grain and oilseeds to fatten the animals in the final stage before slaughter.

As discussed earlier, most of the world's cattle eat little in their lifetimes except grass and crop residues which humans cannot eat. About 90 percent of the feed for the world's cattle consists of things that humans cannot digest. Most of this feed is grown on land which is too dry, too steep, too rocky, or otherwise unable to support crop production. In addition, the cattle are helping to produce the high-quality food protein that the world is increasingly demanding—and doing it from safe, renewable resources.

To forgo the production of beef would be to waste the world's grass resources and crop residue. In a world that is tripling its demands on farming resources in the short space of four decades, that alternative seems ridiculous.

The countries that *do* feed grain to cattle all have their own grain surpluses. Again, none of them import fed beef from rain forest countries. (Due to their tropical climates, few rain forest countries have access to the low-cost grain needed to *fatten* cattle.) Moreover, while the affluent countries have been feeding grain to cattle, the price of grain in the world has continued to decline in real terms!

The list of grain-feeding countries is short:

- the U.S.
- Canada
- the European Community (now the European Union), which includes France, Germany, the Netherlands, Belgium, Luxembourg, Italy, Spain, Portugal, Denmark, Greece, Great Britain, and Ireland
- Japan

You may recognize the U.S. and the EC/EU as the world's two largest grain exporters. Both typically have large grain surpluses, with the EC recently carrying about 25 millions tons of surplus grain and the U.S. holding anywhere from 100 million to 400 million tons of surplus. Both would prefer to be self-sufficient in meat, and they import meat only to fulfill international trade obligations.

Japan in most years has a surplus of rice, and has pushed large tracts of land not needed for rice into wheat production. Japan does import most of its feed grain, primarily from surplus-producing countries: the U.S., Western Europe, and Thailand. Japan has recently allowed some beef to be imported from the U.S. and Australia.

In practice, America imports only about 0.5 percent of its beef. Most of that is grass-fed beef, used primarily in canned meat products. Much of it comes from Latin American countries, but most of this is from Argentina and Uruguay which have no rain forest. We also import some better grades of beef from Australia and New Zealand, but this beef is also primarily grass-fed.

"Malthus and Meat"
"It takes 9 pounds of feed to make 1 pound of gain in a feedlot steer . . . cattle have a feed protein conversion efficiency of only 6 percent.[2]

Rifkin is correct when he notes that grain use throughout the world has changed dramatically. About 40 percent of the world's grain production is currently used to feed livestock and poultry.

This use of grain for high-quality protein foods has not aggravated hunger, however. In fact, as the accompanying table shows, both beef and dairy cattle produce a net contribution to human food supplies. The table actually understates the human nutritional return on animal production, because the calculations include everything that humans *could* have digested—including fish meal, rendered fats, and a bunch of other stuff that isn't found on the supermarket shelves.

Human-Edible Energy and Protein Returns (Inputs=100%)

	energy %	protein %
milk	101	181
beef	85	120
swine	58	86
poultry	31	75

(Source: Bywater and Baldwin, 1980, calculated on animal production practices in 1978. Beef cattle were raised on pasture until ready for final feeding.)[3]

Humans, in fact, consume less than half of the dry matter produced as "crops." However, much of the field residues and processing by-products can be converted to human food by animals. That
substantially raises the productivity of the crops, and the acres that
produced them.

Even in California, there is three times as much land that will not
support crops as can be cropped. Much of this land *can* be grazed,
however, and the soil erosion on most of the grazing land is as low—
or lower—than on forests and "waste land."

In addition, cows eat things like citrus pulp, the dried grains left
over from brewing, cottonseed (after the oil is crushed out), rice
straw, and corn stover. These "food sources" contribute millions of
tons of cattle feed that people are not going to eat (though much of it
is theoretically digestible in the human stomach.)[4]

The University of California's College of Agriculture (at Davis)
says even grain-fattened cattle actually consume only about two
pounds of grain per pound of beef created.[5] (Most of their growth
occurs before they go into the feedlot.)

"Tropical Pastures"
"Since 1960, more than 25 percent of the forests of Central America
have been cleared to create pastureland for grazing cattle. . . . Each imported hamburger required the clearing of 6 square yards of jungle for
pasture."[6]

Again, Rifkin has no factual basis for the forgoing claims.

I know of only one case in which tropical pasture has been deliberately cleared for beef production. That is the famous case of the
Brazilian government's subsidy for clearing cattle pasture in the
Amazon rain forest (discussed in chapter 16). When trees are valued
realistically, they are at least as valuable as beef pastures. Cattle
have been pastured on former tropical forestland that was cleared
for farming and proved unable to support crops. Very little of U.S.
beef is produced on such land, however.

Again, no fast-food hamburger is being marketed in the U.S.
from rain forest cattle. *Less than one-half of one percent of our beef
is imported from anywhere*, because we have such a vigorous and
productive animal agriculture of our own. Rifkin had no reason to

target his 1993 Beyond Beef campaign against the McDonald's chain of hamburger restaurants—except that it was the biggest and most visible *media* target.

JEREMY'S DESERTIFICATION MYTH:

"Hoofed Locusts"
"The destructive impact of cattle extends well beyond the rain forests to include vast stretches of the world's rangeland. Cattle are now a major cause of desertification. . . ."[7]

DESERTIFICATION REALITIES:

"Two-fifths of the earth's land surface . . . are drylands susceptible to desertification. However, . . . since the first desertification conference in 1977, the UN's own estimates of the areas affected have fallen dramatically, from about three-quarters of drylands to less than a quarter," says Professor David Thomas, director of the Sheffield Centre for International Drylands Research . . . in his recently published book *Desertification: Exploding the Myth.*"
"The 'Grass Roots' Strategy for Holding Back the Deserts,"
Financial Times, Oct. 14, 1994, p. 38

Grass protects fragile soils even more effectively than trees because of its dense root structure. That's why pasture is normally among the environmentally safest land uses. However, if too many animals are kept on too little grass, overgrazing can create environmental problems.

Rifkin suggests that "nearly 6 billion of the 7 billion tons of eroded soil in the U.S. is directly attributable to cattle and feed crop production" . . . and that America is suffering spreading desertification.

Both claims are unfounded.

Rifkin's major source of "information" here seems to be the Worldwatch Institute, an organization best known for its attempts to deplore the evils of population and prosperity.

Professor Thomas, on the other hand, says that about 20 percent of the world's soils are degraded according to the latest global survey. However, if the "light degradation" category is omitted be-

WE HAVEN'T LOST THE BISON—But the bison are too big and too hostile to be the basic grazing animal that turns our grasslands into meat.

cause it covers only minor changes that can be easily reversed, *the degraded proportion of the world's land is only 12 percent.*[8]

(Interestingly, Professor Thomas says Europe has a high proportion of degraded soils, mostly because of the semiarid lands around the Mediterranean.)

America has no soil erosion crisis on range *or* croplands. Our soil erosion today is the lowest in modern history. U.S. soil erosion has probably been cut by two-thirds since 1960, in part with the help of improved pasture management, weed killers and improved forage varieties.

NEW JERSEY MYTHMAKERS CLAIM THE GREAT PLAINS:

"Is the idea of turning 139,000 square miles of land across ten states in the Great Plains into a wildlife refuge one of the most farsighted, pragmatic and ecologically sound proposals in the history of the area? Or is it just another in the long line of misguided fantasies created by Easterners who do not appreciate or understand the geography and climate of the place?

"The idea of the Buffalo Commons occurred to (Frank and Deborah Popper) while stuck in traffic on the New Jersey Turnpike.

"Visitors to the Commons 'would see the heart of the continent as Lewis and Clark first knew it,' writes Matthews.

"The Plains are emptying on their own, [the Poppers] argue.

"Matthews . . . gives a balanced though finally sympathetic portrayal of the Poppers and their idea. The truth is, they win you over themselves. Their humility and seriousness and lack of pretensions make their moments of naivete or shortsightedness acceptable."

> From a book review of *Where the Buffalo Roam* by Anne Matthews, reviewed by Dallas Crow in the *Amicus Journal*, Fall 1993[9]

Reality Comment: Obviously, Rifkin is not the only environmental activist "beyond reality" on the grazing issue. The Poppers note that the human population of the Plains is declining—but they don't seem to understand that the land remains very much in use, for crops and grazing.

The Poppers obviously feel overcrowded. It seems unlikely that they will feel better after the people now on the Plains have been moved to New Jersey. Nor is North America truly in need of more bison. Let's resolve the *real* problem bothering the Poppers—being stuck in traffic in New Jersey.

What if we moved the Poppers and an appropriate percentage of New Jersey's humanity to North Dakota? They'd adapt quickly enough to the winter temperatures of 30 degrees below zero. Perhaps more important, they'd find a sense of community that is obviously lacking on the Jersey Turnpike. I'd recommend this seriously, except that I have too many friends in North Dakota.

In the Third World, there *has* been extensive desertification, and some of it has been due to overgrazing. This is mainly so for two reasons.

In some tribal cultures, a family's status is based on the number of animals they own, rather than on the animals' productivity in terms of meat, milk, wool, etc. This provides an artificial incentive to keep more animals than the pastures will support.

Many Third World pastures are replaying the tragedy of the commons. When the pastures belong to everyone, they belong to no one. In the African Sahel, for example, too many herdsmen build up herds in the wet years which cannot be maintained in the dry years. The heavy grazing can even prevent key forage species from reproducing.

The answer to the overgrazing problem in the Third World has little to do with population numbers, and a great deal to do with ownership of the pastures.

In ancient times, the Sahel was defended by swords, and then by rifles. Herdsmen that built their herds too large suddenly found some of their animals forcibly removed. A former minister of agriculture in the Sahelian country of Mali once told me that the Sahel's real problems had begun when the colonial governments disarmed the tribes. "The Tauregs (a dominant tribe) never shot nearly so many people as die now in the droughts," he told me. (See chapter 17 for a discussion of the commons ownership problem.)

Even in the Third World, however, neither overgrazing nor desertification are anywhere near as serious as environmental activists would have us believe. Lester Brown, for example, tried to tell us that Africa's major drought in 1983-84 was brought on by overgrazing, and that it would be followed by more and more severe drought conditions spreading across Africa. Instead, the Sahel has entered a relatively wet period, and since 1985, satellite data show clearly that the desert has been receding.[10]

Geographers say that some 2 million square miles on the edge of the Sahara have been moving back and forth from desert to grasses and back again over the centuries, depending on the rainfall cycles. Archeologists say the Sahel has been totally unpopulated for centuries at a time in the past because it was too dry to support any population. It is fortunate that only a few of the world's people and resources are affected by these marginal conditions. The entire population of the Sahelian region, for example, is probably only about 25 million people . . . 0.48 percent of the world's population.

America is unlikely to replay the tragedy of the commons on our own rangeland unless we put people like Jeremy Rifkin in charge of our grasslands.

"Marbled Specks of Death"
"Living atop the protein ladder has turned out to be very precarious. The affluent populations of the northern hemisphere are dying by the millions from grain-fed beef and other grain-fed red meat."[11]

Here Jeremy Rifkin reminds us forcefully, if not very precisely, that people should keep their fat intake moderate. However, he fails to make his case thoroughly—partly because he does not deal with the dairy products he himself consumes. I discovered his fondness for dairy products during a debate with Rifkin on Iowa Public Radio in 1992. I mentioned the potential problem of protein deficiency that goes with a vegetarian diet. He noted that he didn't worry about protein deficiencies because he and his wife ate plenty of dairy products.

But wait a minute! What is the environmental difference between a dairy cow and a beef cow? Both eat grass, trample things underfoot, drink water, and emit methane and bodily wastes.

Come to think of it, the *nutritional* impact of dairy products is essentially the same as beef. You can get just as big a dose of saturated fats from cheese and cream as from a piece of steak.

"Sacrifice to Slaughter"
"In order to obtain the optimum weight gain in the minimum time, feedlot managers administer a panoply of pharmaceuticals to the cattle, including growth-stimulating hormones and feed additives."[12]

Jeremy is right for a change. Ranchers and stockmen do use a panoply of medicines to protect their animals from sickness, and to cure them when they become sick.

Doing less would, rightly, bring a public outcry.

(It puzzles me that "organic" livestock producers claim credit for not using medicine on sick animals, or preventive medicines to prevent their becoming sick. Should we praise parents who refuse to get medicine for their children? A cattle herd is almost as likely to produce infectious diseases as a school full of kids.)

All livestock medicines have to be approved by the Food and Drug Administration, with full testing and full regard to their impact on both the animals and consumers. They must be used according to directions, or the animals may be rejected in the marketing system. Where appropriate, waiting periods are specified between the administration of the medicine and the marketing of the animal, to insure that there is no carryover of the medicine in the meat.

Some of the feed additives help to prevent the cattle from becoming ill. Here, too, their use has to be approved by the FDA and the producers must follow directions or risk having their animals rejected at the slaughter plant.

Jeremy is also correct that some of the feed additives are hormone treatments which help that cattle gain weight faster.

The original hormone used for cattle fattening was diethylstilbestrol (DES). DES was helpful not only in fattening cattle, but also—in massive doses—in helping many women prone to miscarriage keep their babies to term. Then a few cases were discovered in which the daughters of women who had taken DES to prevent miscarriage had come down with a rare form of vaginal cancer.

To match the DES exposure of the women taking it to prevent miscarriage, a consumer would have had to eat 25 tons of beef liver containing 2 parts per billion of DES—at one sitting. A woman would have had to eat 1 million pounds of DES-treated beef liver to match the synthetic estrogen in one "morning-after" contraceptive pill. No matter, DES was banned.[13]

The hormone treatments that are still used must be approved by FDA and used according to directions. Key among them is withdrawing the treatment well before the marketing date, so that the medication can pass out of the animals' systems.

In the case of livestock growth stimulants, America has been a good deal wiser than Western Europe. The European Community banned all such medications completely. The result has been a rampant black market in growth stimulants. Observers estimate that up to 90 percent of the cattle in Belgium, for instance, are illegally treated with hormones. This is done, not under the watchful care of veterinarians, but in the "dark of night" with under-the-counter drugs that may not even carry their correct names and the necessary safety precautions.[14]

The real environmental kicker on livestock pharmaceuticals is this: A recent survey of veterinarians in Western Europe indicated that to raise the current amounts of red meat without them, farmers would have to raise nearly twice as many cows and half again as many pigs. That would be the impact of death losses and sickly animals.

The veterinarians don't usually treat poultry, but chickens, ducks, and turkeys are even more susceptible to epidemic diseases than four-footed animals. It might well be that the only way to raise poultry without medicines would be in the little movable cages that my neighbor used to put out in his alfalfa fields. Labor costs and death losses would still be much higher. Even then, the birds would have no protection against avian tuberculosis.

"Quenching Thirst"
"Now, even the freshwater reserves of the planet are threatened by . . . droughts, overcultivation and overgrazing. Nearly half the grain-fed cattle in the U.S. are raised . . . on a single underground aquifer."[15]

Rifkin is correct that a lot of cattle are raised over the Ogallala Aquifer which underlies parts of Nebraska, Kansas, Oklahoma, Texas, and Colorado. However, it's not clear what his ominous-sounding sentence is supposed to mean.

Irrigation doesn't cause drought.

The current water use on the Ogallala may not be fully sustainable, but that is a relatively small and self-limiting problem. As irrigation draws down the water table in the Ogallala, farmers will react to the rising pumping costs by irrigating fewer acres and shifting to less thirsty crops. As the Ogallala produces fewer crops, the production can be made up fairly readily by better seeds, supplemental irrigation, or some other productivity investment on other farms in other places.

The reason there are so many cattle in the region of the Ogallala is that the rich prairie soils there produce a lot of feed grain and feeder calves. Some of the grain is irrigated, but most is not. Nor are the pastures irrigated.

During Rifkin's media campaign against beef consumption, he kept claiming that each pound of steak required huge quantities of water to produce.

Apparently, his water consumption number was based on the idea of the steer being raised and fed from irrigated land in some arid place like Southern California or Arizona. Few beef cattle are raised in such places, in part because water and feed *do* tend to be expensive there.

Despite Rifkin's insistence to the contrary, cattle production doesn't take much water. Cows drink only a few gallons of water per day apiece, and it is returned to the environment almost immediately, enriched to encourage plant growth. The grass cattle eat is overwhelmingly rain-fed. Most of our feedstuffs are grown on rain-fed land, and *all* of it could be if we were short of water and gave up irrigating feed grain.

The true water requirements of beef and dairy cattle are tiny.

"Warming Up the Planet"[16]

"The increase in the cattle and termite populations and the burning of forests and grasslands account for much of the increase in methane . . . of the past several decades. Methane emissions are responsible for 18 percent of the global warming trend."

Once again, Rifkin's zeal has outrun reality.

Methane does contribute an estimated 18 percent of the global warming gases. But domestic livestock contribute only about 14-16 percent of the methane.[17]

Thus, all of the world's cattle apparently contribute less than 2 percent of the global warming gases. The U.S. has 8 percent of the world's 1.3 billion cattle and buffalo, and 10 percent of *those* are dairy cows (which Rifkin *likes*).

The world may begin to experience global warming, though we haven't had any rise in temperatures yet. If the warming does begin, remember that each cow on the planet emits about enough methane to equal the global-warming impact of the average 75-watt electric bulb.

The real question is what happens if the grasslands of the world are *not* grazed.

The answer is that the grasses would grow lush and tall—and catch fire spectacularly when the inevitable bolt of lightning hit in the dry season. Early accounts of prairie wildfires in the Great Plains say they lasted for days, and drove all kinds of frightened wildlife before their flames.

The CO_2 that would be produced by the wildfires would dwarf the global warming impact of the methane from grazing animals.

GLOBAL WARMING REALITY?

"Savannah Grasses—the Missing Carbon Sink?"

"Pasture grasses planted to increase beef production in the South American savannas are countering the doomsday predictions of global warming, announced scientists at the International Center for Tropical Agriculture (CIAT) in . . . the September 15 issue of *Nature* magazine.

"'The deep-rooted grasses may remove as much as 2 billion tons of carbon dioxide—a "greenhouse gas"— from the atmosphere yearly,' says Dr. Myles Fisher, CIAT ecophysiologist.

". . . [T]he perennial grasses *Andropogon gayanus* and *Brachiaria humidicola* convert as much as 53 tons of CO_2 per hectare yearly to organic matter, Fisher says. . . . The storage of organic matter was not noticed earlier because the extensive roots of these grasses deposit it as deep as a meter in the savanna soil. . . . CIAT . . . introduced Andropogon and Brachiaria, originally from Africa, to the grassy savannas of South America in the 1970s.

"The ocean, tropical wetlands and green plants absorb some atmospheric CO_2. But scientists cannot resolve the fate of several billion tons.

"'Improved savanna grasses must explain part of this difference,' Fisher says. Brazil alone has at least 35 million hectares of introduced pastures—enough to fix 2 billion tons of CO_2 per year . . . because Andropogon and Brachiaria adapt well to acid soils, national programs have released one or both of the grasses to farmers in at least 12 Latin American countries."

from CGIAR News, Vol. 1, No. 1, Consultative Group on
Agricultural Research, October 1994, p. 1

"Meat and Gender Hierarchies"
"The beef mythology has been used over and over again to perpetuate male dominance, foster class divisions and promote the interests of nationalism and colonialism."[18]

No comment.

"Beyond Beef"
"Reconstructing our relationship to the bovine is a gesture of great historical significance. By making a personal and collective choice to go beyond beef, we strike at the heart of the modern notion of economics with its near-exclusive emphasis on 'industrial productivity,' a concept that has come to replace the ancient idea of generativeness. . . . Our changing relationship to the bovine, from one of revered generativeness to one of controlled productivity, mirrors the changing consciousness of Western civilization as it has struggled to define itself and its relationship to both the natural order and the cosmic scheme."[19]

This may be philosophy. Then again, it may not.
I think Rifkin is trying to say that he admires India, where they

don't eat cows, more than he admires America, where we do.

But how can that be?

India has 200 million cows and 75 million water buffalo, compared to America's 100 million cattle. That means that India's ruminants are producing three times as much methane to ruin the atmosphere and bring on global warming.

India also has much more severe water constraints than the U.S., so the cattle are probably ten times the water conservation problem that they represent in America. Overgrazing is another of the country's problems, as anyone who has seen a dusty Indian travelog can tell you. (Remember Rifkin's "hoofed locusts?")

And the Indians let the cows wander the streets, adding to *urban* pollution.

Could it be that Rifkin's real agenda has to do with animal rights, and not with the environment at all? The only significant difference between beef and dairy cattle is that we don't eat the dairy cattle (at least not until they're past their milking prime, and then only in processed form because the meat is quite tough). India sells its old cows to be slaughtered in Bangladesh.

Most people who are personally acquainted with cattle find them intellectually limited. But if Rifkin truly prefers cattle to people, I recommend he get his own cows and pastures. Then he can enjoy the revering generative relationship without fear of being invaded by McDonald's. He can also ensure that his ranch's neighbors are not afflicted by overgrazing and pollution of nearby streams.

Meanwhile, how do we evaluate cows on an environmental basis?

- Cows produce small amounts of methane, but grazing prevents big wildfires that would unleash large amounts of CO_2— on virtually an annual basis.
- Few cattle pastures could support crops. Most of the grasslands have been grasslands since time immemorial.
- Cows and grazing even help maintain a broader variety of forage species on the grasslands. (Without grazing, the tallest grasses shade out the others.)
- Cows help meet the world's need for high-quality protein from low-cost, renewable, and environmentally stable ecosystems.

As long as we need to graze the grasslands, we might as well make use of the meat they produce. Letting the wolves have it all doesn't seem to make sense when the world wants more protein.

And since we're going to have some grazing animals, take the advice of someone who has worked with large animals. It makes *good* sense to pasture cattle instead of bison. Cows weigh perhaps 900 pounds each, are fairly timid, and aren't very athletic. Bison weigh up to two tons apiece, have hostile attitudes, and can jump or go through a 10-foot anchor fence at will. I would not want to give worm medicine to a bison.

Notes

[1]Jeremy Rifkin, *Beyond Beef*, Penguin Books, New York, 1993, p. 160

[2]*Beyond Beef*, op cit, pp. 160-161.

[3]A. C. Bywater and R.L. Baldwin, *Animals, Feed, Food and People: Alternative Strategies in Food Animal Production*, Westview Press, Boulder, Colorado, 1980, pp. 1-29.

[4]R.L. Baldwin, K.C. Donovan, and J.L. Beckett, *An Update on Returns on Human Edible Input in Animal Agriculture*, Department of Animal Science, University of California, Davis, undated paper.

[5]Eric Bradford, director of the Animal Agriculture Research Center, and Edward Price, chairman of the Animal Science Department, letter to Dr. Richard Stuckey, executive vice-president, Council for Agricultural Science and Technology, April 14, 1994.

[6]Rifkin, op. cit., p. 192.

[7]Rifkin, op. cit., p. 200.

[8]Geoff Tansey, "The 'Grass Roots' Strategy for Holding Back the Deserts," *Financial Times*, October 14, 1994, p. 38.

[9]*Amicus Journal*, Fall 1993, Vol. 15, No. 3, Natural Resources Defense Council, pp. 46-47.

[10]Monastersky, "Satellites Expose Myth of Marching Sahara," *Science News*, July 20, 1991, p. 38. Also, Tucker and others, "Expansion and Contraction of the Sahara from 1980 to 1990," *Science*, Vol. 253, July 19, 1991, pp. 299-301.

[11]Rifkin, *Beyond Beef*, op. cit., p. 171.

[12]*Beyond Beef*, op. cit., p. 12.

[13]Elizabeth Whelan, *Panic In The Pantry*, Atheneum, New York, 1975, pp. 164-69.

[14]Rita Boone, *An Easy Mind on Meat Again,* Roularta Books, Research Park De Haak, Netherlands, 1993, pp. 46-47.

[15]*Beyond Beef*, op. cit., pp. 218-219.

[16]*Beyond Beef*, op. cit., p. 225.

[17]J.B. Smith and D.A. Tirpak, *Potential Effects of Global Climate Change on the United States*: Executive Summary, U.S. Environmental Protection Agency, 1989.

[18]*Beyond Beef*, op. cit., p. 286.

[19]*Beyond Beef*, op. cit., p. 287.

20

Farming's Radical Middle Ground

MYTHMAKERS SAY:

The crops we grew last summer weren't enough to pay the loan
Couldn't buy the seed to plant this spring and the
    Farmers Bank foreclosed
Called my old friend Schepman up to auction off the land. . . .

When you take away a man's dignity he can't work his fields
    and cows
There'll be blood on the scarecrow, blood on the plow. . . .
      from John Cougar Mellencamp/George M. Green, "Rain on the
          Scarecrow," copyright 1985, John Mellencamp

When there's one yard light in a Dakota night
    and one farmer waking in the morning sun
Then there by the grace of God went us
    and technology's logic is done.
         Tim Ralston, farmer from Petersburg, North Dakota,
               "The Successful Farmer"[1]

"The common thread is the worldwide tightening control of wealth and power over the most basic human need, food. Multinational agribusiness firms right now are creating a single world agricultural system in which they control all stages. . . . Once achieved, they will be able to effectively manipulate supply and prices . . . on a world-wide basis through well-established monopoly practices."
        Six Myths About Hunger, 1976, Institute for Food and
                     Development Policy[2]

ANOTHER VIEW OF REALITY:

"The rise of per capita farm income from one-third that of nonfarmers in the 1930s to more than 100 percent of nonfarmers is no statistical aberration but rather the culmination of a long-term secular trend. . . . Farm wealth is impressive. Net worth averaged $407,186 per farm in 1991 compared with median wealth of $78,807 for U.S. households headed by college graduates."

> Luther Tweeten and Lynn Forster, Ohio State University,
> *Choices*, 1993[3]

"The biggest flaw in Avery's analysis is that he offers no reasonable middle ground between a doomsday scenario of forced organic farming and today's practices. Many real farmers are ahead of him. . . . Our industry is moving toward using chemicals the way doctors treat illnesses—as a judicious last resort. Avery seems unaware of this sensible middle road. His shrill defense of the past only plays into the hands of the environmental extremists."

> Dan Looker, business editor, *Successful Farming*, in a column
> criticizing a briefing paper I wrote for Hudson Institute,
> "The Organic Threat to People and Wildlife"

FAMILY FARMERS AT WORK—America's family farms have not disappeared. They get fewer and larger as the nation generates more attractive nonfarm jobs. But the family farm remains the backbone of our agriculture, and the success model for the world.

As my former critic Dan Looker implies, there *is* a radical middle ground between the harsh constraints of organic farming and the heavily subsidized chemical intensity of the current farming pattern in the United States, Western Europe, and Japan.

The productivity of organic farming is too low. But the costs of price-support farming have been too high, both economically and environmentally.

The only way to avoid either extreme is to let the agricultural resources compete. Worldwide. The only way to know who can achieve the lowest costs and greatest environmental safety is to let everyone try within a competitive framework—without government subsidies and trade barriers to lend artificial incentives.

That means getting rid of the farm subsidies in all countries. They foster too much chemical use in the rich countries, and too little in the poor ones. They keep some low-quality acres in production in the rich countries and keep out some high-quality acres in the developing world.

Worst of all, the subsidies and trade barriers keep big chunks of the world's best land producing at far below capacity. For example:

- It is an environmental crime to keep perhaps 50 million acres of good U.S. farmland in setaside and "conservation reserve," thus, wasting the sunlight and rainfall which descend on them in the course of a year.
- It is environmentally foolhardy to keep 75 million acres of the Argentine Pampas in cattle pasture, while clearing millions of acres of Asian tropical forest for soybean production on low-caliber soils.
- It is both economically and environmentally wrong for India to risk the habitat of the Bengal tiger and the barking deer by raising price supports and trade barriers so high that farmers cannot resist the temptation to expand their cropland.

To date, the national governments of the world have been unwilling to let markets make the farm resource decisions. The results of this paternalism have been unfortunate.

Farm subsidies and the surpluses they stimulate have led people in affluent countries to believe that we already have too much farm productivity. Thus, they think, it's all right to mandate a shift to low-yielding organic systems. In addition, Americans and Europeans now undervalue the agricultural research that is man's greatest scientific achievement *and* the world's strongest defense against environmental degradation and species loss—because of subsidies.

Some of my scientific colleagues assume that higher yields are an unmitigated blessing. This optimism is also misplaced. If we invest in the wrong resources, or even if we invest too much in the right resources, the world becomes poorer than it should be.

A few examples should suffice to make the point:

- The affluent countries of the world are currently wasting $350 billion per year on farm subsidies that stimulate surplus production. This creates heavy taxes on their consumers and on job creation.[4] In the EC, the annual farm subsidy bill is $450 *per person*, in Japan $600, in the U.S. $360, and in Finland $910.
- Income transfers average $36,000 per farm in the U.S., $17,000 in the EC (for much smaller farms), $38,000 in Sweden, and $31,000 in Japan (for tiny farms).
- The Third World countries, worried about employment and political stability in their big farming populations, put up trade barriers to keep out the subsidized exports, even when they actually *need* such imports to maximize economic growth and well-being.

Why Farm Subsidies in the First Place?

Governments have been trying to help farmers since the spinning jenny opened the Industrial Age 200 years ago.

Historically, countries have regarded their farmers as hard-working, family-oriented, community-building good guys.

Moreover, farmers' average incomes *always* fall behind urban incomes when industrialization is in its early stages. Agriculture becomes no less important, but it does become a smaller and smaller part of the Gross National Product.

Typically, cities gradually bid away farm labor to make the refrigerators, hi-fi sets, and athletic shoes for the modern lifestyle.

The urban work force gradually swells, while the farm work force declines. Farms, therefore, get bigger, reflecting more than anything else the rising value of an off-farm job. Too often, rural communities shrivel as the farm labor force declines. Meanwhile, because farmers are so much admired—and usually so politically potent as well—that governments have tried to placate them with national farm policies.

For their part, farmers have consistently asked for price supports on commodities. They feel buffeted by the weather-driven variability in farm prices. They also feel the need to strengthen what they perceive as their weak bargaining power with big commodity buyers and input suppliers.

After Poland ended the Russian Army's 40-year occupation in the late 1980s, for example, the Rural Solidarity movement's *first request* was for price supports like the farmers got in the European Community. The Polish government was too broke to comply.

But most national governments, being more fortunate, *have* offered such price supports.

Governments from such widely varied countries as the U.S., Mexico, Ivory Coast, and India have made price supports a key element in their farm policies.

Hot debate continues on whether and how much these price supports and import barriers help farmers' incomes. (There has been a strong tendency for the subsidy benefits to become capitalized into farm land values—turning the intended income gain for farmers into a higher cost of production instead.)

However, there has been no doubt about the impact of price supports on farm trade. The minute a country has a price support, it must also have a trade barrier. Otherwise, it would have to support the prices for every *other* country's farmers in low-price periods.

Environmental Side Effects

In most countries, the higher prices supported by governments have stimulated heavier use of fertilizers (to raise yields) and heavier use of pesticides (to minimize crop losses.)

In most price-supporting countries, farmers have also done their best to bring additional land into production. In many cases, this has meant installing drain tile to dry out waterlogged soils, building field bridges to get to the last patch of land on the far side of creeks, and tearing out fencerows and hedges. Too often, price supports have also meant bringing in drought-prone land and clearing forest for crops.

Probably the worst environmental side effects from farm price supports have been inflicted on Western Europe. Europe has typically offered farm price supports roughly twice as high as those of the U.S.—very strong incentives for higher output. Since Western Europe is about twice as densely populated as the U.S., land-use pressures have been intense:

- Chemical use rates in Western Europe have become twice as heavy as in the U.S. Fertilizer application rates have been extremely high, with wheat crops often getting five top-dressings of nitrogen to urge every last bushel of yield. Due to the moist climate, farmers have also sprayed cereal crops with up to five fungicide applications as well. Then there have been the insecticides and herbicides to control bugs and weeds. Finally, stalk-stiffening sprays have been needed to keep grain plants from collapsing under the weight of their ultra-heavy grain heads.
- The European governments have not only subsidized crops, but livestock and poultry production as well. These subsidies have spawned a set of huge, highly intensive livestock and poultry "batteries" with concentrated odors and manure production.
- Because the European price supports for grain have been so high, many of these batteries have come to be located in the outskirts of Europe's port cities. There, they have had access to lower-cost feed imports such as Argentine wheat bran, American corn gluten feed, and Indonesian cassava. Manure storage and odor problems have thus affected lots of city folks.
- Europe's lakes, rivers, and coastal seas have been overfertilized by both commercial fertilizers and intensive livestock and poultry production. Big algae blooms have disturbed the streams and coastal waters.

- The Adriatic Sea, which gets little summertime flushing, has almost literally turned green with algae blooms as Italy's Po valley has become a prime production region for high-priced corn and soybeans in the last 15 years.
- Traditionally, Western Europe fenced fields with stone walls, or with hedge plants trained into living hedgerows. Over the centuries, these hedgerows had come to harbor populations of hedgehogs, birds, small rodents, and myriad other life forms. When the EC's farm price supports were at their zenith, the land became too valuable for hedgerows. Thousands of miles of these famous landmarks were torn out in Great Britain, France, and other West European countries. Erroneously, the public often blamed the decline in local bird numbers on pesticides, rather than on loss of hedgerows.)
- Ironically, about one-third of the farm products produced under these high subsidies—grain, flour, meat, dairy products, poultry, and processed foods—have been sold into third-country export markets at a severe economic loss! The Soviet Communist government was the biggest outlet for surplus EC beef and butter; the USSR got billions of dollars worth of almost-free meat, while Holland and Belgium were almost buried under in the manure from producing it. Wealthy Middle Eastern oil exporters also benefited heavily from subsidized EC foodstuffs.

Poisoning Public Opinion Against High-Yield Farming

Early in 1993, I was invited to serve on an advisory panel for the International Rice Research Institute (IRRI) in the Philippines.

IRRI, the reader will recall, is one of the two original international research centers that helped launch the Green Revolution. (The other was the International Maize and Wheat Improvement Center in Mexico). IRRI's high-yielding rice varieties have helped the world rice production more than double, while average world rice yields have risen by 85 percent.

IRRI also faces one of the toughest farm research challenges in the world over the next 40 years: The populations of the rice-eating cultures are likely to double again, *and* achieve high incomes. Asia will not only consume more rice, but high incomes will generate more demand for higher-quality rice varieties that have typically been lower-yielding. Meanwhile, most of Asia's good rice land is already in production and already using high-yield seeds and systems.

Unfortunately, in the midst of history's biggest surge in world rice demand, IRRI's funding has been cut sharply! IRRI's budget has been slashed by 23 percent since 1990, hundreds of trained workers have been fired, and more cuts seem likely. In our advisory panel meetings, I learned one of the important reasons why the world's funding for agricultural research is being cut—just as it faces the biggest demand surge in history.

Another of the panelists was farm science advisor to one of Scandinavia's foreign ministries. When I began to point out to the group the important role that high-yield farming had played in preserving wildlife habitat, he got visibly upset.

During a break, he told me I was making a valid point—but he was angry that I was "whitewashing" high-yield farming.

He had worked for five years in Netherlands agriculture. He had watched the massive increase in chemical use, the accumulation of livestock and poultry manure, and the loss of wildlife habitat. Not distinguishing between the good effects of science and the negative effects of subsidies, he had become an emotional opponent of high-yield farming.

It is obvious that rice cultures in general and Asia in particular have no good land to spare for low-yield farming. Still he argued in the discussions for lower-yield "sustainable" farming systems—for a region which is desperately short of land and which has been boosting yields on the same rice paddies for 2,000 years!

Thus, even the experts have enormous difficulty separating the impact of high-yield farm science from the environmental side-effects of farm subsidies.

The whole of Western Europe is already in the throes of a public backlash against high-yield farming:

• The Dutch government has set an official goal of cutting pesticide use in half by 1995. This goal has been set with no evidence that the pesticides are harmful to human health, or that they are threatening wildlife species.

- Dutch dairy farmers—who used to symbolize the country— are being told to cut by half the number of dairy cows they pasture.
- The country has a hugely expensive plan to build 200 million tons of manure-processing facilities in the country. These "factories" are supposed to take livestock wastes, turn them into odorless garden fertilizer—and export them overseas at a huge loss. There is serious doubt whether this "solution" can be financed.[5]

In Germany, a high proportion of the wildlife species are said to be endangered, and the public blames farmers.

European city dwellers are miffed that many little peasant homes and villages dotting the countryside are now boarded up and abandoned. Urbanites regard this as a loss in their "quality of life." They blame high-yield farmers for pushing out the peasants.

In reality, of course, hardly anyone wants to be a peasant. The villages are boarded up because many former farm workers have found better jobs in the cities; and because many of those quaint little homes were more attractive to the viewer than comfortable for the inhabitants

Setaside Side Effects

American farm subsidies have functioned a bit differently than Western Europe's subsidies. The U.S. government has offered price supports, but it has also relied heavily on taking cropland out of production to "balance supply with demand."

Cropland diversion was part of the original Agricultural Adjustment Administration program in 1933; cotton and other crops already planted were plowed down to cut back supplies and drive up prices. Cropland diversion has been an important element of American farm programs ever since.

In most years since 1960, the U.S. Department of Agriculture has been diverting up to 60 million acres of relatively good farmland to hold down production.

The exception to cropland diversion occurred in the late 1970s. The OPEC oil boom put billions of extra dollars into several countries with big populations and poor diets, including Mexico, Nigeria, Indonesia, and the USSR. The result was a sudden surge in farm export demand that pulled American setaside land back into production from 1973 to 1982.

After oil prices collapsed in the 1980s, however, so did the farm exports. Prices for both crops and U.S. farmland collapsed in turn. The USDA had to run its biggest cropland diversion in 1983 (78 million acres) on an emergency basis.[6]

One of the biggest problems was that by 1981, farmers had bid up land values to twice their 1971 levels. They thought the boom would last. Those farmers who bought land at too high a price couldn't pay back their loans and went bankrupt in droves during the "farm crisis" of the mid-1980s.

There was a rash of farm-family suicides, and even the shooting of hapless bankers who had had to foreclose. It was, in fact, the bursting of a real-estate balloon fundamentally brought on by the collapse of OPEC's oil prices.

Since 1983, cropland setaside has reemerged as a major element of U.S. farm policy. In fact, the government has not only diverted cropland on the usual year-by-year basis, but has also taken out more than 36 million acres of land on ten-year contracts under a Conservation Reserve Program started in 1984.

The stated aim of this long-term land retirement was to take high-risk land out of farming. In truth, however, it was a political reaction to the farm mortgage crisis brought on by the OPEC collapse.

Inevitably, much of the land in the CRP was bid in because of the owners' situation, not because of the risk of cropping it. Thus, for example:

- A friend who works in Arkansas and inherited a small farm in Iowa put it into the CRP.
- An Ohio State professor says he had trouble getting farm tenants who paid their rent on time—and the CRP payments come in as regularly as clockwork.
- My father had put his fine little Michigan farm into the original Soil Bank in the 1960s; he was getting too old to enjoy moonlighting on the farm.

As the result of motivations like these, over 60 percent of the land enrolled in the CRP falls in the top three soil capability classes— that is, those best-suited to crops.[7]

Meanwhile, some 40 million acres of highly erodable land was *barred* from the CRP. Congress was afraid that *too much* land would be enrolled in regions with poor land—and would disrupt the artificially based farm economies which the price supports had created there!

The Environmental Sins of Cropland Retirement

Cropland diversion has had major negative impacts on the environment, even beyond those incurred by price supports.

In effect, U.S. farm policies have tied about 25 percent of its farmers' land behind their backs. This land was not turned into wildlife habitat; most of it was simply planted to annual grasses, and many farmers put a different part of their farms into the setaside in different years.

Meanwhile, the government's high price supports stimulated farmers to seek new cropland and higher yields from the cropland that was planted. Inevitably, they plowed fragile lands and used extra off-farm inputs like fertilizer and pesticides to raise production. Heavy reliance on chemicals was a direct consequence of the setaside structure itself. One of the simplest and soundest ways to cut pest and weed infestations is crop rotation. If the 60 million acres of setaside had been available for rotation crops, farmers would have needed far fewer chemicals to achieve the same output.

Wetlands Drained. The U.S. drained 11 million acres of wetlands between 1955 and 1975, with about 80 percent of it for agriculture.[8] Drainage continued after 1975, though at a slower rate. Overall, we may have drained as much as 15 million acres of wetlands.

The disappearance of many of these wetlands was the direct result of the price supports and cropland setaside programs. The new land was used to produce crops (or gain payments for not producing crops) which were already in surplus. Adverse environmental consequences soon followed. For example, much of the wetlands drainage was in the pothole regions of the Upper Midwest, and many of the potholes drained had been prime duck nesting habitat.

There has also been substantial drainage of swamps on the sandy Eastern Shore peninsula of Delaware, Maryland, and Virginia. The reclaimed land has been planted primarily with corn and soybeans. Much of the fertilizer applied on those crops has leached through the Eastern Shore's sandy soils into the Chesapeake Bay.

Over-fertilization of the Chesapeake has produced more algae, reducing the sunlight reaching the eelgrass at the bottom of the bay. The eelgrass historically has harbored young game fish and crabs until they were able to fend for themselves. The marine harvests in the Chesapeake—oysters, rockfish, and other valuable seafoods—have dropped precipitously in recent years.

This recitation of the facts is not meant to excuse *urban* contributions to the pollution of the Chesapeake, including inadequate sewage treatment and overfertilizing of suburban lawns. It is simply meant to show that the subsidy system as it stands has produced its own serous negative effects on the environment.

Marginal Soils Plowed. Setaside has also encouraged too much erosion. Even after the Dust Bowl days of the Depression were over, and even after farmers learned to use windbreaks and strip-cropping, subsidies have kept steep and/or droughty high-risk land in crop production which should have been in forage, grazing, or forest.

Fencerows Gone. Price supports have also helped to eliminate thousands of miles of fencerows that used to harbor wildlife.

In the old days, farmers wanted to produce both crops and livestock to diversify their incomes because of volatile prices. Livestock was also important to earn winter labor income.

Price supports ended the need for farm diversification. Owners could project their crop yields into assured income—and take vacations in the winter instead of tending cattle or hogs. (They could also save money on fences.) Thousands of farms dropped livestock production and let the hogs and cattle be fattened in big "hog hotels" and hi-tech cattle feedlots.

As in Western Europe, wildlife that used to live in the fencerows disappeared, and the public blamed farm chemicals.

Heavier Use of Chemicals. Most activists would also rate the heavier use of chemicals virtually mandated by cropland setaside as a major environmental negative.

This point is debatable, because the wildlife implications of most modern farm chemicals are not very severe. As earlier chapters have shown, there is little impact on surrounding lands from the modern lower-volume, narrow-toxicity, faster-degrading chemicals now being used. Even farmers will agree, however, that setting aside 25 percent of the land they own and then paying for chemicals to offset the production loss makes little environmental sense.

Suspicion of Surpluses

For the past several decades, American farmers have been trying to justify high-yield farming systems on the basis of fighting hunger. But it is hard to sell "hunger" as an important policy rationale to the best-fed people in the history of the planet!

It is even harder to frighten the public about prospective food shortages when the government has 200 to 400 million tons of surplus grain in storage, *and* millions of acres of additional cropland just waiting for an opportunity to jump back into production.

When the argument that "we're saving you from hunger" fails to convince consumers, the farmers' fallback strategy has been to point out that Americans get their food for the lowest percentage of income anywhere in the world. (The USDA says American consumers spend only 11 percent of their incomes to support one of the world's highest standards of eating.)

Although this is true, it begs the question and ignores the following:

- The biggest factor behind the low percentage of income spent for food is that Americans have high incomes.
- The public knows that without farm price supports, food prices might be cheaper still.
- U.S. food prices are so low that most consumers aren't terrified of their rising a bit! Europe has charged its consumers twice as much as America, and Japan twice as much as Europe.

Surpluses and abundance seem to consumers a permanent part of farm landscape, like red barns and black-and-white cows.

This wasn't much of a problem as long as farmers wore halos

on Capitol Hill. But in recent years, eco-zealots have stripped these halos away. Now, instead of an environmental "son of the soil," the farmer is presented as the guy who's poisoning people with pesticides, despoiling wildlife, and cheering for soil erosion.

Farm Science Accused

Activist movements have stripped halos away from farm scientists as well. The Nobel Prize won by Dr. Norman Borlaug for launching the worldwide Green Revolution is long forgotten—and perhaps even regretted.

Now, agricultural research is said to be what gave us those "dangerous" pesticides, killed off the family farm, threatened the ancient, vital landrace seeds that nourished our forefathers, and like nonsense.

Many people apparently *do* fear that producing more food now will just support a larger catastrophe later, when people will starve by the billions. The result has been a slow starvation of agricultural research. The federal contribution to U.S. agricultural research has been about $1 billion in real dollars for 20 years.[9]

Meanwhile:

- The world's population and farming intensity have risen.
- The growing concern about wildlife preservation has escalated the urgency of high yields.
- The real cost of doing research has also soared as scientists have had to delve deeper into cells and molecules with supercomputers, gene machines, and electron scanning tunneling microscopes.

The U.S. and other First World countries have done or led most of the key "frontier" research on boosting food production for the whole world. But now they may be losing momentum.

Neither farmers nor agricultural scientists have wanted to admit it, but nothing undercuts the rationale for farm science more radically than farm surpluses.

Adding insult to injury, a growing share of the research funding is going to "sustainable" research projects that are essentially aimed at developing lower-yield farming systems.

In the Third World, the Western public's disdain for farm science research is producing a real funding crisis. The International Food Policy Research Institute recently published a study of the declining support for agricultural research and development, titled *Aid to Agriculture: Reversing the Decline*. The study notes that assistance to Third World agriculture has dropped from $12 billion in 1980 to $10 billion in 1990. Agriculture's share of total development funding fell from 20 percent to 14 percent during that decade.[10]

In September 1994, the World Bank had to bail the CGIAR centers out of a deep budget deficit, because almost every donor country except Japan had slashed its support for Third World farm research! The CGIAR centers were $55 million in the red on their tiny budget of $270 million.

At the same time, the U.S. and other donors were pledging $17 billion of aid dollars for "population management" at the Cairo population conference—when population management to date has had marginal effect on birth rates, and that only in the very long term.

A Global Food Surplus? No!

The world has no agricultural surplus.

Western Europe's surplus is not a surplus at all. As the EC shifts from farm price supports to direct farm income payments, and as environmental restrictions tighten, production will become less intensive. Much of the European food surplus will disappear and the rest could be usefully exported to Asia.

The United States *does* have a surplus. At current yields, bringing back diverted U.S. cropland would add about 90 million tons worth of grain production annually. This represents about two years' worth of the expansion the global food system will have to make *each of the next 40 years* to feed the expected population. And bringing back the setaside is a onetime move.

America's grain surplus is thus a drop in the bucket compared to food system expansion the world must achieve.

The biggest problem is that this surplus has blocked public perception of the need to fund high yield research—research that will be vital to averting both massive famine and a huge loss of wildlife habitat to food production.

The Environmental Future with Farm Subsidies

It is absolutely clear our future will need both farm science and a greater sensitivity to environmental impact than government subsidies have shown to date.

Most of the environmental movement was initially very slow to attack farm programs, despite their obvious environmental negatives. Recently, however, activists have taken a more direct interest in farm legislation. The 1990 farm bill was the first to include significant conservation requirements; it denied subsidy payments to "sodbusters" who plow drought-prone land, and to "swampbusters" who drain wetlands.

The 1990 Act also required subsidized farms to have conservation plans designed to minimize soil erosion and loss of wildlife habitat. The farm conservation plans have helped increase the popularity of conservation tillage and no-till farming systems—though these were sweeping across the countryside on their own merits before the plan requirement was installed.

The next American farm bill is likely to put much tighter environmental constraints on farmers. The activist movement has clearly now taken a seat at the negotiating tables which used to hold only farmers and government officials.

Activists are also talking up some radical ideas on reorganizing farming:

No one should buy food not grown within walking distance of their homes. The idea is to eliminate agriculture's "unhealthy" dependence on fossil fuels. (In reality, the U.S. food system is no more fuel-dependent than most American industries.)

Never mind that this local focus would restrict most Americans to an extremely narrow diet, and countermand recommendations from the health professionals to double fruit and vegetable consumption.

A licensing requirement for farmers and foresters. The Sierra Club and other groups already feel they have a good handle on America's public lands through lawsuits, demonstrations, media impact, and the public hearing process.

Until now, they have been unable to get the same degree of control over *private* farms and forests. The last thing they want is to spend the environmental movement's billions of donor dollars to *buy* private lands.

If they can set up farm licensing boards, however, they can pack the boards with their own people. Then any farmer who doesn't manage the way eco-activists want can be stripped of his license. They'll claim that farmer "abused" his land or the wildlife on it.

The new Wildlands Project of the Society for Conservation Biology calls for a network of wilderness reserves, human buffer zones, and wildlife corridors that might occupy as much as half of the North American continent! They think big carnivores like grizzly bears and mountain lions need enormous amounts of space to generate "an adequate genetic pool."[11] Obviously, this proposal would leave a lot less room for farming or ranching.

There is also a strong possibility that the environmental movement will demand a high price for their continued tolerance of farm subsidies.

American farm subsidies are being starved out by the federal budget deficit while new environmental mandates raise costs or reduce resources available.

Equally important, the vision of an Asia getting rich and upgrading its diet may finally persuade American farmers they have more to gain from exports than from Washington.

In Europe, the EC has begun to cut support prices, cut the quotas which now limit nearly every commodity's production, and shift to direct farmer income payments. If the EC is going to make direct income payments, it will have no need to distort farming systems and world trade with price supports and import barriers.

Sweden, Switzerland, and Norway are all moving to small-farmer payments. The Swedes are buying out the commercial farmers' franchise rights, and the Swiss and Norwegians hardly have any commercial farmers.

Australia and New Zealand have abolished all of their farm subsidies. They couldn't afford them. (No nation which really needs its farm export earnings can afford to subsidize its farms.) They also are hoping to lead other nations into farm trade liberalization through their example, and thus stimulate their food exports.

Even the fabulously wealthy Saudis have decided that a 3 million ton annual surplus of desert wheat is more than it bargained for. The Saudis are now telling their farmers they must switch to lower-priced barley, which the nation still needs. That won't save the Saudis' fossil water, but it does demonstrate a glaring truth of the late-20th century:

No nation in the world has been able to keep price support promises to its farmers when those farmers had access to the full range of modern high-yield technology.

It may sound inconsistent for a self-professed champion of high-yield farming to complain that farm subsidies have raised yields too high—but that is exactly what I'm doing.

The biggest sin of the farm subsidy programs is that they ignore comparative advantage. The richest countries overstimulate their agricultures the most, even if they have the least comparative advantage. The outstanding examples are Saudi Arabia and Libya, which have both spent billions of dollars to develop unsustainable farming operations based on short-term mining of fossil water.

The second biggest sin of the subsidies, as we have seen, has been to bring wetlands and droughty soils needlessly into food production.

Third is that, the farm subsidies have overfertilized surface waters, disturbing marine ecologies.

Fourth, the subsidies have overcharged poor consumers all over the world for the food they need, and subtracted huge sums of money from First World economic growth and job creation. What is the cost of unemployment for 30 percent of the males in Spain under 25 years of age, and 27 percent of them in Italy? The EC's Common Agricultural policy was heavily taxing employers all over the Community, and two-thirds of it was spent on farm subsidies that did *not* provide new farming jobs or even maintain all of the old ones. Farm subsidies have had much the same effect in the U.S. and other countries as they industrialized and became affluent. The overall cost today may well exceed $500 billion per year.

Fifth, subsidies have had negative consequences on human nutrition. India has been overcharging for high protein foods rather than permit imports. Countries like Japan and Sweden have refused to allow imports of fruits and vegetables critical to the health of its affluent citizens.

If the world is lucky, clever or wise, it may soon be able to get the benefits of high-yield productivity without having to accept the side-effects of subsidies. It will have reached the radical—and highly productive—middle ground.

Notes

[1] A.V. Krebs, *The Corporate Reapers*, Essential Books, Washington, D.C., 1991, p. 44.

[2] Reprinted in A.V. Krebs, *The Corporate Reapers*, op. cit., p. 447-448.

[3] Tweeten and Forster, "Looking Forward to Choices for the 21st Century," *Choices*, Fourth Quarter, 1993, American Agricultural Economic Association, Ames, Iowa.

[4] David Dodwell, "West's Farmers Reap $354 Billion in Subsidies," (citing new OECD study), *Financial Times*, June 3, 1993.

[5] U.S. Agricultural Attaché Reports from the Hague, Netherlands, 1985-93.

[6] Able, Daft, and Early, *Large-Scale Land Idling Has Retarded Growth of U.S. Agriculture*, Study for the National Grain and Feed Foundation, May 1994, p. III-4

[7] Able, Daft, and Early, op. cit., p. III-5.

[8] Kramer and Shabman, "Incentives for Agricultural Development of U.S. Wetlands: A Case Study of the Bottomland Hardwoods of the Lower Mississippi River Valley," *Agriculture and the Environment*, Resources for the Future, Washington, D.C., 1986, pp. 175-199.

[9] Zulauf and Tweeten, "Reordering the Mission of Agricultural Research at Land-Grant Universities," *Choices*, American Agricultural Economics Association, Second Quarter, 1993, p. 32.

[10] *Aid to Agriculture: Reversing the Decline*, Food Policy Statement No. 17, International Food Policy Research Institute, Washington, D.C., December 1993.

[11] *Science*, Vol. 260, June 25, 1993, p. 1868.

21

The Environmental Need for Free Farm Trade

MYTHMAKERS SAY:

". . . [A] people unable to protect itself from starvation could not be protected from any other danger. The inescapable conclusion is that a government that makes itself the servant of international free trade is not protecting its land and people, it is protecting the supranational corporations that thrive at the expense of land and people."

> Wendell Berry, Kentucky poet and philosopher, "Free Trade and the Environment," *The Amicus Journal*, Fall 1993

"The Business-as-Usual system . . . is clearly leading us rapidly to disaster. One apparent route of escape is . . . a 'soft path' system making use of . . . empathetic technologies. At the end of this path is a food supply made up of whole fresh foods produced by environmentally benign methods *somewhere in the vicinity of where they are to be eaten.*" [emphasis added]

> Dr. Joan D. Gussow, *Chicken Little, Tomato Sauce & Agriculture*, The Bootstrap Press, New York, 1991, p. 34

"New international trade rules are threatening to shift food safety decisions away from Federal and state elected officials and regulators to international trade bureaucrats operating in secret in Geneva. . . . This would make it difficult . . . for citizens to have control over the safety of the foods they eat. . . ."

> Public Citizen and the Environmental Working Group, Trading *Away U.S. Food Safety*, April 1994[1]

REALITY SAYS:

"Trade and environment are actually complementary . . . and could be much more so. . . . The one commodity-producing sector specifically exempted from the principles of the GATT . . . is agriculture. And, throughout this 40-year period, agriculture's environmental and economic problems have steadily worsened as the direct result . . . ."

> Robert Repetto, *Trade and Environment Policies: Achieving Complementarities and Avoiding Conflicts,*" World Resources Institute, July 1993

"Farmers in Australia and North America are not the only ones affected adversely by the protectionist policies of Western Europe and East Asia. . . . Farmers in other countries are estimated to lose $46 billion per year, while consumers in Western Europe and East Asia are worse off by more than $100 billion per year."

> Kym Anderson and Rodney Tyers, *Agricultural Policies of Industrial Countries and their Effects on Traditional Food Exporters*, University of Adelaide (Australia), Working Paper 86-4, 1986

The eco-activists' confusion over what they really want and how to achieve it in agricultural trade mirrors their more basic confusion in trying to save wildlife with low-yield farming.

If the environmental movement understood agricultural production systems, they would be on the side of high-yield farming *and on the side of free trade in farm products*.

The real mission of farm trade is to help us supply the world's food needs with as little environmental and economic cost as possible.

In practice, this means farming the safest and highest-yielding acres, wherever they may be.

The Shenandoah and Corn

Let's review the comparison between the steep, rocky land in my Shenandoah Valley and the flat rich plains of the Corn Belt:

- Corn yields in the Shenandoah are only about half the yields in central Iowa and Indiana. More land planted means less land left for other uses.

- Any farmer trying to till land in the Shenandoah is going to hit lots of rocks, and even some shale ridges. He will have to travel more slowly, stop more often—and will still break more expensive parts on his machinery.
- To prevent heavy soil erosion losses, my Shenandoah farmer needs to plant on the contour. That means a lot of surveying, plus some tricky work with the tillage equipment and the planter. His labor costs are higher.
- The Shenandoah farmer should also alternate strips of clover or other "filter" crops to stop any soil that erodes from the corn rows from moving very far. The green strips lower the overall average output of the field. Again, that means less output per acre of land.
- No matter what the Shenandoah farmer does, he's going to take up more land per bushel of production—and generate more soil erosion per bushel—than the flat, rich soils of Indiana. Those are both major environmental negatives.

All in all, both the cash outlays and the environmental costs of corn production can be twice as high in the Shenandoah as in the Corn Belt. That's why the Shenandoah grows virtually no corn for grain. (It does grow some corn silage for its dairy cows on the more level pieces of ground.)

The Valley's marginal land has been returned to grass and trees. Soil erosion has been substantially reduced, food costs have also been reduced, and the nation has more wildlife habitat.

If We Let the Tropics Grow Our Sugar

Comparative advantage is one of the basic truths of economics:

- If country A has iron ore and lots of coal, it can readily be a steel producer.
- If country B has lots of low-cost labor, it may well become a garment producer, because both capital costs and wages tend to be low in that industry.
- If A needs clothing and B needs steel, they can trade and

both be better off. Plus, B doesn't have to invest resources in costly steel plants that will operate at an economic loss.

One of tropical farming's big comparative advantages is sugar. Tropical land can produce sucrose through sugar cane nearly twice as efficiently as temperate-zone farmers. Beet sugar in the U.S. and Europe yields only about 60 percent as much sucrose per acre, even though the beets sop up more fertilizer and need more pesticides. Equally important, we haven't found much else that can be grown efficiently on the sugar cane land. We could grow a whole roster of grains and oilseeds on the high-quality temperate land that sugar beets need.

Because of national farm self-sufficiency policies, however, temperate-zone sugar beets provide nearly one-third of the world's sugar.

What would happen if we let the tropics grow our sugar?

- The world would be able to farm less-fragile land, suffer less soil erosion, and use fewer farm chemicals.
- Western Europe could shift nearly 9 million acres of its best farmland to better uses, probably feed crops, with lower chemical usage.
- Tropical sugar-growing countries would have somewhat more foreign exchange with which to import wheat and other food needs they can't grow efficiently.

In case after case, free trade in nonfarm products has increased economic growth and human well-being enormously. Free trade has proven to be the world's most successful strategy—by far—for making the Third World rich enough to be environmentally sensitive and responsible.

Foreign aid, by comparison, has been a miserable and corrupting failure.

Free trade in farm products is even more important to the environment than nonfarm free trade. This is so for at least three reasons:

- No other human activity is as important to wise land use as farming
- Comparative advantages in farming are even bigger and

more permanent than in manufacturing
- The world is just now entering its last and biggest surge in human food demand.

Three-fourths of the world's increased food demand by 2050 will be centered in its most densely populated region—Asia. If Asia tries to meet that food demand on a self-sufficient basis, it will have to destroy virtually all of its remaining environmental resources. Meanwhile, prime farmland—already cleared—would lie idle in countries like the United States and Argentina.

Both sides would be part of a needless crime against the environment.

Food Self-Sufficiency: Recipe for Hunger?

In 1994, Japan needed to import more than 1 million tons of food-quality rice, due to extremely poor weather following a near-failure of its 1993 rice crop. There weren't enough high-quality rice stocks in the world to supply this demand. So, the Japanese have had to make do with industrial-quality rice that rice consumers in other countries don't want.

How did a country with the purchasing power of Japan land in such a predicament? Because of its own policies of rice self-sufficiency.

For 40 years, Japan has adamantly opposed rice imports. Japan has offered its rice growers prices as much as ten times higher than world market prices to insure its self-sufficiency. It has spent billions of dollars stockpiling Japanese rice. But even all this expenditure wasn't enough. When the Japanese ran into two bad rice harvests in a row, they needed imports. And because they've been so rabid against imports, nobody else had been producing or stockpiling rice for a possible Japanese sale.

Thailand could have done it. Instead, they planted more corn, because the Japanese themselves said there would be no market.

America could have produced more rice—but instead we severely limited U.S. rice acreage, to avoid stockpiling more costly surplus rice in government storage bins.

Thus Japanese politicians had the "interesting" task of explaining to the Japanese consumers how their policy of self-sufficiency is "protecting" the country.

In 1987, I was in Finland, during the wettest summer in its history. For 40 years the Finns had trumpeted the importance of growing their own grain. I watched combines trying to harvest wheat with water standing in the fields, rain still coming down, and the combines throwing rooster-tails of water from their wheels. But it was September at the Arctic Circle, and the last chance to save the Finnish wheat crop. Naturally, most of the wet grain sprouted in storage.

The Finnish government quietly went out and bought two-thirds of a year's wheat supply in the world market, for half the price it paid its own farmers, from a variety of willing exporters—and promptly went back to declaiming the virtues of its high-cost food self-sufficiency.

It would have served the Finns right if there had been an international grain monopoly that charged them double the fair price. After all, they're charging their voters about $4,000 per family per year to subsidize Finnish farmers.[2] Instead, and fortunately for the Finns, there was a highly competitive world grain market trying to sell wheat to any and all comers at attractive prices.

All Countries Experience Crop Failures

Any country can have a crop failure, even big, extensive agricultural countries like the U.S. and China. When that happens, the country's food security depends on the ability to import from another country that had good weather and has a surplus for export.

No one country's farm output is anywhere near as stable as worldwide production measured as a whole. In almost any year, at least one country will have a crop failure and another will have a bumper crop.

Under a free-trade regimen, we wouldn't need to keep extra grain sitting expensively and unused every year in every country's storage bins. Trade evens out the *inevitable unpredictability* of the weather.

What About Wars?

The most common rationale for the self-sufficiency approach has to do with historical experiences of wartime. Europe and Japan, for example, say they were hungry at the end of World War II, and they must produce their own food because they have such a deep-down fear of being hungry again.

But would Germany and Japan have been any *less* hungry in 1945 if their agricultures had been twice as big in 1937? No. The farms would still have been devastated by the fighting in World War II.

Nor was there widespread famine in Germany or Japan at the end of the war. As quickly as the fighting ceased in a region, the Allies brought in food for the populace. The German and Japanese peoples were saved from famine in 1945-46—by imports!

What About Embargoes?

But (the argument continues) what if other countries in the world embargo our country? What if they won't ship grain to us?

History itself rejects the argument. Remember the Jimmy Carter embargo of the USSR? The Soviets simply turned to Argentina and immediately replaced all the embargoed American grain contracts—without so much as a price increase. (The Argentines were hoping to build future business with the USSR.)

The Nixon embargo of soybeans backfired even more explosively. Americans were afraid of a protein meal shortage that would raise meat prices. But the Japanese were even more fearful—that the U.S. embargo would create shortages of their traditional soy foods. There's no comparison in the emotional intensity of a food shortage versus a feed shortage.

Japan immediately launched a research and development partnership with the Brazilian soybean industry, which has helped Brazil raise its soybean output from around 2 million tons in 1972 to more than 20 million tons per year today.

The whole civilized world embargoed Iraq before Desert Storm. However, Iraq's consumers suffered no major food problem—until after the U.S. started bombing its roads and bridges. The Iraqis were very adept at smuggling food into their country. After the attacks on their transport system, however, they could no longer distribute it. The embargo, alone, had little effect.

MYTHMAKER:

"Their proposed revisions in the General Agreement on Tariffs and Trade are an attempt to place the agriculture of the world under the rule of the same economic forces that have already virtually ruined agriculture in the United States."

Wendell Berry, "Free Trade and the Environment,"
Amicus Journal, Fall 1993, p. 31

Who Stockpiles Food?

Actually, if a country is truly concerned about food security, there is a better way to achieve it than expanding the local farms. The answer is to stockpile food. Put grain in a silo. That way it's not going to be wrecked by a rainy summer, or a drought, and probably not even by a war.[3]

How many countries stockpile food for security purposes?

One—India. India does it because it suffers a monsoon failure about one year in five. In 1987, it was able to replace practically all of the losses from the worst monsoon in a century—from its own storage stocks.

U.S. and EC grain stockpiles, by contrast, are for politics, not food security. The stocks are vastly larger than any food security need.

Japan, the most import-dependent feed buyer among the world's countries, keeps one month's supply of feed imports on hand. It keeps another month's supply on vessels headed toward the islands. That's their cost-effective food security policy.

Why do so many other countries "protect" their agricultures for "food security" when that lowers real food security? Because of farmer politics.

The Fallacy of Protest-Based Farm Policy

Farmers in every country hate to see food imports. The last year I was at the State Department, we saw violent demonstrations against apple imports in both Sweden and Taiwan, both "highly civilized" countries. And apples aren't even a food-security staple!

The trade barriers that keep American farm products out of growth markets in other countries have nothing to do with food security. So long as farmers constitute a major proportion of a country's population, and the international farm trade rules are lax enough to let politicians buy farm votes with hidden "food taxes" on consumers, farm trade will be suppressed.

During the latter stages of the GATT Uruguay Round trade negotiations, French farmers protested the idea of freer farm trade by blocking major highways with burning tires. They also stomped McDonald's hamburgers (full of French beef) and smashed Coke machines (full of French sugar) in their anger at America's insistence on liberalizing farm trade rules.

In a further irony, the French government says its farmers' incomes in 1996 will be down 14 percent from 1991—primarily because of the subsidy cutbacks mandated by the EC's own budget deficit. Virtually all of the decline in farm income will be suffered by France's commercial farmers, because the government is making special payments to the "politically correct" small farmers. The French commercial farmers now have the worst of both worlds: Their subsidies are being cut back, and they do not have the trade access to help meet Asia's rising food needs.

Think about a world without GATT. All of its trade negotiations might be carried on by similar protests. Detroit auto workers might have randomly smashed foreign cars with sledge hammers—and the clean-burning Honda engines might not have made their pro-environmental impact on America's air quality. Nor would we have gotten the competitive pressure which brought us disc brakes and automatic braking systems from Europe.

The Environmental Problems of Farm Self-Sufficiency

- Food self-sufficiency in Indonesia means cutting down tropical forest to grow soybeans—when the U.S. and Argentina already have more than 50 million acres of prime soybean land lying cleared and uncropped.
- Food self-sufficiency in Saudi Arabia means using petroleum-powered pumps to raise fossil water from as deep as 3,000 feet to grow gritty wheat on the desert. Yet Argentina is producing

only half the wheat it could cost-effectively grow on the rich, level rain-fed Pampas.

• Japanese farmers' protests against rice imports have kept virtually all of that country's land in rice paddies, with no room for housing, parks, or recreation. (Tokyo's superhighways have been built *over its rivers* because the land area was so densely populated and legally entangled.)

• Food self-sufficiency in China will mean putting enormous amounts of chemical fertilizers on China's limited supply of farmland. As recently as 1980, China was using about 14 million tons of chemical fertilizer. Today, the total is more than 90 million tons, and the government's forecast for 2000 is 150 million tons. Farm self-sufficiency for the years after 2030 would likely mean more than 300 million tons of fertilizer—on the same farmland base![4]

• Food self-sufficiency in India will mean building lots of dams, irrigating lots of additional land, and putting on huge amounts of fertilizer (as in China). It may also mean pushing crops and pasture out onto the already-scarce wildlife habitat of species like the Bengal tiger and the barking deer.

• Milk self-sufficiency for India already means compensating for the shrinking pastures available by relying still more heavily on crop residues as virtually their sole source of feed. These crop residues should actually be going back onto the cropland to preserve its fertility and tilth. To the extent that farmers cannot compensate for the "stolen" residues with green manures and fertilizers, India risks mining some of its soil fertility. In this era when dairy products can readily be imported (as dry milk, as concentrated milk, and/or as butter and cheese) India should at least examine the trade alternative.

• Brazil's wheat crop has dropped sharply since the government ran out of money to pay wheat subsidies. The crop is down from a peak of about 6 million tons per year in the 1980s to a little over 2 million tons at present. Now Brazil is importing the rest of the wheat it needs from next-door Argentina, where the yields are twice as high and the per-unit costs are low.

Vegetable Oil Self-Sufficiency in India

India is making dramatic economic progress. Its economy has been growing three times as fast as its population since 1980. There are already reportedly 150 million middle-class consumers among the country's 900 million people.

Now, in the 1990s, India is beginning to relax the red tape bonds of socialism, starting to welcome foreign capital and thinking seriously about exports and imports. Dairy consumption is rising 2 million tons per year, previewing a huge increase in food demand as economic growth spreads across the countryside.

Unfortunately, India is also dramatically demonstrating how modern farm technology can amplify the worst aspects of farm trade barriers. In 1987, India produced less than 14 million tons of oilseeds and was the world's largest importer of vegetable oil (1.8 million tons). Then the government decided to ban vegetable oil imports. Seven years later, the price of cooking oil for the Indian housewife has been as much as three times the world market price. And India's farmers have responded:

- Oilseed production for 1993 was estimated at 25 million tons, up 11 million tons and 75 percent in six years.
- Soybean production has soared from less than 1 million tons to more than 4 million tons predicted for 1994.
- Sunflowerseed production has leapt from 600,000 tons to 1.5 million tons.
- Oilseed meal production has soared from 5.8 million tons to more than 11 million tons. Since India doesn't yet have a modern feed industry, 3 million tons per year of oilmeals are being exported to compete with U.S. soymeal exports.

Hybrid sunflowerseed has been one of the big factors. India's sunflowerseed yields averaged only 0.4 tons per hectare in 1987. Eight years later, hybrids have helped boost the average by 50 percent—with experimental plots getting 3 tons under irrigation and 1.5 tons on rainfed land! The farmers are growing them on India's top-quality irrigated land, which should probably be in more valuable crops like cotton. (Cotton would produce more off-farm textile jobs and help meet India's growing cotton clothing needs.)

Continued on next page

MYTHMAKER:

"The real aim of American policy is to use food as a weapon in post-Cold War geopolitical strategy. They want to control the markets on grain and oilseed exports both through their own produce and that of Third World countries, whose even cheaper exports they control in various ways; for example, the huge soybean plantations in South America, which are owned or controlled by U.S. companies."
                    French farmer, quoted in *Whole Earth Review*, Winter 1993[5]

Reality Comment: American farmers feel as big a threat from South America's oilseed expansion as French farmers. If there is a "foreign devil" to blame, it is Japan. But the impetus came not from an attempted monopoly but from the anti-trade Nixon soybean embargo of the early 1970s.

The Imperative of Good Public Nutrition

Throughout this book I have repeatedly stressed the importance of good diet in preventing disease. I must stress it again in this chapter on trade.

Farm trade has been one of the important factors in improving American and European nutrition in the past two decades. It will be equally important for nutrition in Japan and other Asian countries in the two decades ahead.

USDA data indicate that farm trade has helped to raise America's

India is also building a major dam system on the Narmada River in western India, to irrigate the light soils of its peanut basin in Gujarat State. This could produce still another expensive increase in India's oilseed production.

The country is investing money in oilseeds which should almost certainly go into its manufacturing base. Machine tools and textile mills would yield a much higher return—and pose far less threat to India's wildlife than crop expansion.

Lower food costs to consumers, made possible through food imports, are *not* a waste of India's foreign exchange. They should simply be a spur to seizing further export opportunities for the things India produces best.

consumption of fruits by 25 percent and vegetables by 11 percent since 1970. These gains have reversed a long-term decline in U.S. per capita produce consumption.[6] Years ago, we didn't have many fresh fruits and vegetables in our stores and restaurants in the off-season. Instead, winter meant wilted cabbage and withering apples. Trade with Latin America has been a major factor in the wide variety, low cost, and attractive array of produce being offered to the American public today: lettuce and melons from Mexico; peaches and apples from Chile; tiny cocktail vegetables from Honduras; and flash-frozen asparagus from Guatemala, to name a few.

All have helped to stimulate American fruit and vegetable consumption. Such imports have helped keep the salad bars and fruit bowls stocked attractively and cost-effectively, even during the winter.

MYTHMAKER SAYS:

"Great advantages will be reaped (from GATT) by agribusiness transnationals which will take over vast tracts of Third World land to grow cash crops, while peasants will suffer and forests be destroyed. Of course, they will use ample amounts of toxic pesticides and artificial fertilizers to grow this food."

Helen Caldicott, Australian antiwar and environmental activist,
If You Love This Planet, 1992[7]

Reality Comment: Ask the small farmers of the highlands in Honduras and Guatemala who are supplying the produce taken to their airport for flight to the U.S. or to the new flash-freezing plant nearby. Ask the small farmers in Kenya and Zimbabwe supplying the same sorts of demand from Europe. Ask the farmers of Chile who have rescued the entire economy of their country from stagnation with winter produce. Mrs. Caldicott should probably not stand for election in any of those districts.

The Challenge of Population Density

The biggest reality of world food production is that farming resources aren't spread equitably for the world of the 21st century.

By 2050, for example, Asia will have nine times as many people per acre of farmland as North America. Moreover, Asia is already using its farmland potential more fully than North America. Asia's

Figure 21.1

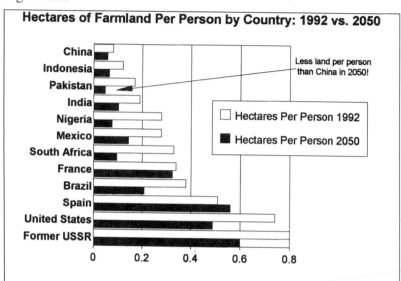

development of its wet rice culture was one of the early triumphs of human knowledge. But it has left Asia with such a dense population that the 21st century food challenge can only be met by huge investments of capital and chemicals—or by trade.

A policy of nation-by-nation food self-sufficiency would foolishly leave more than 100 million acres of the world's best cropland idle in places like the U.S. and Argentina—while it encouraged Asian farmers to plow down every scrap of land they could reach. One proposed dam (Three Gorges) on the Yangtse River in China would force relocation of at least 1 million people!

The slogan of the environmental movement is "Think globally, act locally." Yet eco-activists opposing farm trade are obviously thinking locally, without much regard for the world as a whole.

Anyone who advocates farm self-sufficiency for environmental reasons is either ignorant of the world's farm resource distribution—or selfishly worrying about his own neighborhood while he endangers huge tracts of wildlife and acre-feet of fossil water in other countries.

That is the antithesis of real environmentalism.

Keeping Our Food Safe—With Trade

Public Citizen and the Environmental Working Group recently published a report entitled *Trading Away U.S. Food Safety*. The 86-page document did its best to frighten people and their legislators into rejecting freer trade in farm products:

> The Uruguay Round of GATT Promotes Downward Harmonization of Food Safety Standards. . . . Domestic standards that do not conform to international ones must pass a battery of Uruguay Round tests in order *not* to be considered an unfair trade barrier. Specifically, food safety standards that do not conform to Codex (Alimentarius) standards:
>
> - Must be based on scientific principles;
> - Must not be maintained without sufficient scientific evidence;
> - Must be based on a risk assessment;
> - Must not achieve a higher level of public health protection than the Codex standard unless the regulating country . . . has a scientific justification for concluding that the Codex standard will not achieve its level of protection;
> - Must use the least trade-restrictive means of achieving the country's goals.

But why would an environmental group—or *any* group—oppose such a sensible set of principles?

The requirement for scientific data is basic. There's no way to assess public risk *at all* without scientific evidence. Without it we are forced to rely on public emotion alone, too often fanned to white heat by misinformation. *No* safety standard would be "safe" enough. Even the environmental movement, the reader will recall, has based its opposition to pesticides on the scientific data from the high-dose rat tests.

The Uruguay Round disciplines even give member countries the leeway to have higher standards than the GATT has agreed to, so long as they make a scientific showing that the GATT standards wouldn't achieve the country's level of protection.

Then the "environmental" paper tips its hand. It continues:

The Uruguay Round science and risk assessment criteria could have a severe impact on domestic food safety standards that are based on the precautionary principle, which supports the prevention of certain public health risks, or those that are based on consumer preferences in the face of such uncertain risks.

In other words, the GATT would make it harder for eco-activists to pass legislation through scare campaigns! GATT might actually force them to develop a scientific data base to support their contentions. The past campaigns against DDT and Alar, the current campaigns against atrazine and chlorine—all would have flunked the GATT "science" test.

Because of the GATT, environmental zealots might even have to go head-to-head on high-dose rat tests with European countries that don't use them. And they might lose in such an international scientific "court."

Of course, if the environmental movement comes to understand the importance of high yields and trade in saving wildlife, they will not want to ban useful pesticides or block farm trade. They will not want to fan public fears over foods that are actually safe. And if foods or food production systems are truly dangerous, it will be a simple matter to bring forward the scientific evidence.

Nor will First World farmers want to hang onto subsidies and trade protection once they understand the combination of environmental challenge and economic opportunity that awaits them.

Once the importance of high yields and trade is clear, the only likely opponents of free farm trade will be the farmers in the newly industrializing countries, who do not yet understand the importance of preserving wildlife habitat and wild genes. Both the First World and their own political leaders will need to help them understand—for the world can reasonably take no other path.

Notes

[1]Public Citizen and the Environmental Working Group, *Trading Away U.S. Food Safety*, Washington, D.C., April 1993, p. 1. Public Citizen was founded by Ralph Nader. The Environmental Working Group is

relatively new and describes itself as an "environmental research " organization.

[2]David Dodwell, "West's Farmers Reap $354 bn in Subsidies," reporting on an annual OECD study, *Financial Times*, June 3, 1993.

[3]I used to be involved at the State Department in occasional "nuclear war" games. I could always astonish the other players by noting that most of the grain stored in the Commodity Credit Corporation's surplus silos would be usable after a nuclear exchange—just by peeling off the radioactive "hot layer" on the outside.

[4]Bruce Stone, International Food Policy Research Institute, "Chinese Fertilizer Development 1990: Status and Prospects," presented at the 13th Phosphate-Sulphur Symposium, Boca Raton, Florida, January 22, 1991.

[5]"Sustainability vs. Agribusiness-as-Usual in France," *Whole Earth Review*, No. 81, Winter 1993, pp. 42-47.

[6]Judith Jones Putnam, *Food Consumption, Prices and Expenditures*, 1967-88, Statistical Bulletin No. 501, Washington, D.C. U.S. Department of Agriculture, Washington, D.C., May 1990. See also Stephen Hiemstra, *Food Consumption, Prices and Expenditures*, Agricultural Economic reports No. 138, USDA, July 1968 and USDA/ERS, *Vegetables and Specialties*, TVS-249, Washington D.C., November 1989.

[7]Helen Caldicott, *If You Love this Planet: A Plan to Heal the Earth*, op. cit.

22

New Incentives for
Bad Regulation

MYTHMAKERS SAY:

"The most important thing is to reduce the overall use of pesticides. By doing that, we will automatically reduce risks and we won't have to spend all this time worrying about lots of complicated things."

> EPA Administrator Carol Browner, interviewed in *E, The Environmental Magazine*, December 1993[1]

"On the whole, agrichemicals *do* pose worrisome, chronic and *avoidable* risks to the health of farmers and the public. Farming without the use of any synthetic pesticides or fertilizers is one solution along a continuum of alternative solutions. It is being practiced successfully by a growing number of commercial farmers, who produce a wide variety of crops."

> Kenneth Cook, Center for Resource Economics, in Testimony before the House Committee on Agriculture, July 13, 1989

"In an interview, the [Natural Resources Defense Council's] chief lobbyist, attorney Janet Hathaway, described for me NRDC's ultimate goal. If pesticide residues can be detected on food even in 'minute amounts,' she explained to me, and if a massive dose of that pesticide 'causes tumors in any laboratory animals, then it should be illegal.' [NRDC staffer Lawrie] Mott told me that the NRDC would ban all such chemicals 'no matter how great their benefits are.'"

> Robert J. Bidinotto, *Readers' Digest* staff writer, 1993[2]

REALITY SAYS:

". . . Modern synthetic pesticides replaced more hazardous substances, such as lead arsenate, one of the major pesticides before the

modern era. Lead and arsenic are both natural, highly toxic, and carcinogenic. . . . Each new generation of pesticides is more environmentally
and toxicologically benign."
> Drs. Bruce Ames and Lois Gold, "Environmental Pollution and
> Cancer: Some Misconceptions," *Rational Readings on
> Environmental Concerns*[3]

". . . [C]hemical makers and the farmers who use [chemicals] are
troubled by a fly in the ointment: a [Clinton Administration] proposal to
allow citizen suits under the Federal Insecticide, Fungicide and Rodenticide Act. . . . They fear that the addition of this provision would lay
them naked as untreated tomatoes to a plague of frivolous lawsuits by
pesky trial lawyers and flighty environmentalists."
> Jim McTague, "Makers of Farm Chemicals Gird to Fight New
> Proposal for Citizen Lawsuits," *Barron's*, March 7, 1994, p. 51

"Chemically Sensitive Woman Files Lawsuit Over Condominium
Pesticides"
"A woman who says she is sensitive to lawn chemicals sued a
homeowners organization in her condominium complex Tuesday charging its use of pesticides violated her fair housing rights. . . .
"The lawsuit, which seeks damages of at least $300,000, names Coun-
try Creek, four of its past and present officers and a grounds management company. . . .
"The Trial Lawyers for Public Justice, a Washington-based public-in-
terest law firm that filed the lawsuit on Ms. Lebens' behalf, said it hopes the
case will establish chemical sensitivity as a legal disability. . . .
"In March 1994, HUD determined that there was reason to believe
that Ms. Lebens was discriminated against. But the Justice Department,
which would have had to pursue the case, declined to get involved."
> From a news story in the Staunton, Virginia, *Daily News Leader*,
> July 20, 1994, p. A5

There is now a serious danger that the chemophobes in America
may get their wish for a radical cut in farm chemical use.

I fervently hope it does not come to pass—until and unless we
have developed better ways to raise crop yields without chemicals.
Moving to cut chemical use for its own sake would mean less wildlife, more soil erosion, and more cancer for people.

The Critical Moment for Farm Chemicals

The 1990s will be a critical period for farm chemicals:

- All pesticides registered before 1984 are supposed to be re-registered by 1997. The process may force de-registration of many of the "minor" pesticides that control pests and diseases on fruits and vegetables. Their sales volume is too small to warrant the big testing costs for re-registration.
- The Federal Insecticide, Fungicide and Rodenticide Act (FIFRA), under which cost/benefit standards and requirements for the registration of pesticides are established, must be reauthorized.
- The Ninth Circuit Court of Appeals decision enforces the zero tolerance Delaney standard of the Federal Food, Drug and Cosmetic Act for processed foods. That decision must be rationalized by Congress against the reduced supply and availability of fruits and vegetables which would result from strict application of Delaney.
- The Clean Water Act and The Endangered Species Act, both of which can affect the use of pesticides generally or on specific lands, must be reauthorized.
- The first fruits of the biotechnical revolution in farming will be applying for regulatory approval and trying to make their way into the marketplace. Eco-activists are attempting both to stymie the regulatory process and to poison the public reception for them.

I have no fear about public acceptance of biotech in the long run; it is already generating so many live-saving and life-enriching opportunities for the genetically handicapped that its public acceptance as a blessing is assured. These benefits, of course, have not prevented some of the less scrupulous activists from attacking such food applications as bovine growth hormone and non-rotting tomatoes. That's why the short run is uncertain.

Today, farmers in 20 other countries—mostly in western Europe—are already losing the *right* to use fertilizer and pesticides. Governments are mandating cutbacks in pesticide volume with little thought to their real dangers or to the impact of the reductions on wildlife, erosion, and human health. The chemicals are being lost due to unfounded fears of their dangers, and to a backlash against their overuse under high farm price supports.

Here in America, the Congress in 1988 imposed deadlines on the EPA (backed up by fees on chemical companies) for reregistering the "old" pesticides which were registered before the current testing system was fully in place.

These chemicals have been used for decades, and have been considered safe, by scientists. ("Nature" groups are fond of saying, "Pesticide X has never been fully tested for its long-term environmental effects." Usually, that means all we have is 40 years of positive experience to go on.)

But the markets for many of these "untested but safe-by-experience" chemicals tend to be small. Running the full set of rat and environmental tests on these chemicals would cost millions of dollars per compound. In fact, chemical companies have already voluntarily dropped the registration of 28 active ingredients and 5,000 pesticide products in the past five years rather than go through the full re-registration process.

In 1993, the Clinton Administration added to the problem. It proposed sweeping new pesticide regulations deliberately aimed at a sharp cut in U.S. pesticide use.

First, the Clinton proposals would eliminate the so-called "economic justification" for keeping some pesticides on the market. (Until now, EPA could keep on the market a compound that hasn't gone through the full set of tests, if banning it would significantly raise food prices.) *The result of this Clinton proposal would be to shrink the supply of fruits and vegetables, and raise their costs.*

Second, the Clinton food safety proposals would give the EPA authority to suspend "suspicious" chemicals even if they had not been proven a threat.

On the surface, this seems a reasonable degree of authority for a government regulatory agency. But remembering the public furors raised over chemicals in the past—from DDT to aminotriazole in cranberries and continuing up to Alar—it seems all too likely that the EPA would quickly succumb to future public scare campaigns.

Giving EPA "suspicion" authority might actually eliminate the current requirement for scientific proof. Whenever the eco-activists decide to turn up the heat on a particular chemical, EPA might simply suspend it to get the public off its back. Few of the compounds suspended "on suspicion" would ever make it back to the market.

The New Regulatory Climate

The new regulatory climate may fairly be characterized by the plight of potato growers in the Northeastern U.S. in 1994. They were beset by intense infestations of the Colorado potato beetle, one of the most destructive potato pests. The EPA had just taken away a compound called Trigard (cyromazine) because it had decided to eliminate temporary exemptions for compounds in the "suspected carcinogenic" category. The EPA made this ruling in spite of the fact that the use of Trigard leaves no residue on the potatoes. The compound does form a metabolite in the soil, but this washes off with the dirt when the potatoes are made ready for use. (Ironically, Trigard is still registered for use on celery.)

Nor would EPA give a temporary exception for the use of a new product named Admire (imidacloprid). This new product is not sprayed, but rather is applied in the furrows *between* the rows of potato plants—so both wildlife and applicators are safer. It would cut the number of applications from 10 to 3, and the active chemical volume by 40 percent. Admire also has a different mode of action, so it would help to break the potato beetle's population buildup and force it to develop a new type of resistance.[4]

Apple growers, in the meantime, have lost an insecticide—phosphamidon—which controls aphids without destroying the natural predators of mites. That had allowed apple growers to nearly eliminate their use of miticides. But with phosphamidon off the market, farmers have had to use other aphid-killers—which do kill the beneficial mite predators. Thus, apple growers are back to using two chemicals instead of one, and relying less heavily on the natural predators to kill mites.[5]

The EPA, of course, has little incentive to help the potato and apple growers produce crops. The agency gets criticized by the public for allowing too much pesticide use. It rarely gets criticized for the high price of potatoes—because the public rarely sees the connection. Nor does the public think much about the cancer connection between high produce prices and lower fruit and vegetable consumption.

DANGEROUS REALITY:

". . . [Banning] of fungicides could lead to food scarcities. An increase in the contamination of foods by fungal products that include carcinogens and nerve, liver, and kidney poisons would also follow. . . . An immediate cause for concern is . . . a Consent Decree dated 20 September, 1994, in which the Environmental Protection

WEED-FREE WITH HERBICIDES—Such fields produce higher yields because they don't have to share the moisture and plant nutrients with competing weeds. Nor do the herbicides pose a threat to people or wildlife.

Agency is a participant . . . many of the most effective fungicides would ultimately be banned . . . because they can be shown to induce cancer in one strain and one sex of a rodent when huge, nearly lethal doses are administered. An example is the important, widely used fungicide, captan. Captan is relatively nontoxic. It is rarely detected on produce or in ground water. It is readily decomposed. . . . [T]he benefits of fungicides in the production and distribution of health-enhancing fruits and vegetables should not be jeopardized by the folly of the Delaney clause and actions of a regulation-proliferating agency."

Philip H. Abelson, *Science* editorial, "Adequate Supplies of Fruits and Vegetables," Vol. 266, November 25, 1994, p. 1303

The facts about current pesticide use include these:

- The only category of pesticides in which U.S. use has been rising has been herbicides. Herbicide use rose because of its broadening use in no-till and conservation tillage farming systems—designed expressly to combat soil erosion!
- Since 1982, even herbicide usage has dropped significantly due to new safer and lower-volume compounds.
- The only way for a Clinton initiative to show big reductions in pesticide *poundage* used would be to reduce the use of herbicides—the soil-savers.
- The only major *category* of pesticides which would be forced off the market by the Clinton proposals would be the small-volume pesticides used to grow fruits and vegetables.
- In all other categories of pesticides, usage has declined significantly without government interference—due to cost factors and the reduced levels of active ingredients needed with the modern low-volume pesticides. (See Fig. 2.1)

What is the rationale for such heavy-handed efforts to slash farm chemical use?

The only rationale offered seems to be the one embodied in EPA Administrator Browner's opening quote. It seems to the an emotional commitment to the assumptions made by Rachel Carson:

"Pesticides are dangerous to people because they kill pests."
"Pesticides are dangerous because they are manmade."

What's new in today's regulatory mix? After all, neither pesticides nor Rachel Carson's fears are new.

What's new seems to be *first and foremost* that the current generation of regulators has grown up with unquestioning repetition of the antipesticide message in their books, within their families, on their TV programs, and in their dorm-room discussions. They have fully digested the concept that pesticides are inherently bad. The policy debaters rarely even stop to offer a public reason for being so anxious to reduce pesticide volumes and coverage. Nor does the public seem to feel the need for one.

We have moved farther and farther from the destructive pest experiences of the past. I recently met an older federal regulator who grew up hoeing cotton on a small family farm. Thus he understood the real danger of weeds taking over the crop. Moreover, his father had contracted malaria in the cotton fields, so he understood the real evils of human disease which pesticides have helped to eliminate from our culture. But this man is nearing retirement.

His younger cohorts grew up in a world where pests were an annoyance, not a real threat.

America has lost that understanding.

Some of our young mothers today don't even bother to get their children immunized against diseases like typhoid and diphtheria, because they have no real understanding of the devastating power of those diseases. Yet, it is only the vaccines that protect us from the return of epidemics.

Similarly, we run a serious risk of throwing away our weapons against the pests, *because we haven't been through the devastation they can inflict recently enough*. We're more likely to react to the bad smell of a sulphur spray on grapes, or to the emotional idea that a manmade chemical has been inserted into Nature's supposedly careful balance.

Target: Atrazine!

The eco-activist drums have now started rolling for another "vicious" pesticide called atrazine. It's a big target—and a highly valuable one, both to farmers and to eco-activists.

Atrazine is a weed control herbicide used annually on 50 million acres of U.S. corn production. There is no cost-effective replacement for atrazine; it can be sprayed *once*, at a pound or so per acre, and give full-season weed control.

Wisconsin, which banned atrazine for 1992, found that its corn farmers subsequently had to spend an extra $11 per acre on weed control. Extended nationwide, *a ban on atrazine would apparently cost American farmers more than $1 billion extra per year*—or force lower corn yields and eventually larger plantings to meet the world's corn demand.

Atrazine is a valuable target for the activists for several reasons:

- It is the pesticide that turns up most commonly in our drinking water. It often shows up seasonally at measurable levels in reservoirs in the spring and early summer (depending on rainfall patterns).
- Because atrazine has been associated with mammary tumors in one strain of laboratory rat, the activists can also raise the dreaded spectre of "breast cancer."
- Recently, we have been finding three metabolites (breakdown products) of atrazine in water. These breakdown products, which are also formed in laboratory rats and as such have been studied in animal cancer tests, have the same health safety profile as atrazine itself. Hence, when activists say that there are more "triazines" (atrazine is just one) in our water than we thought, they are technically correct.
- EPA has warned many cities and community water systems that they are facing multi-million-dollar investments for atrazine testing and remediation, because of seasonal peaks that exceed the current safety levels.
- All that's lacking for a first-rate scare story is some threat to New York and Los Angeles. (Nobody grows much corn in their watersheds, so there's no atrazine in the drinking water of those media meccas.)

How risky *is* atrazine?

- It has been broadly used for 30 years and has not been linked with any demonstrated human cancer risk.
- It is not a reproductive toxin, a teratogen, or a mutagen.
- It does not bioconcentrate, or "build up" in the food chain.
- Studies of workers in the plants where it is made show no elevated risks, even over periods of 30 years. That's true even though its production dates back to times when industrial plants were far less careful than they are today.
- A definitive study on atrazine and farmers was done recently to examine the potential for increases in non-Hodgkin's lymphoma. The study found "little or no increase in the risks . . . attributable to the agricultural use of atrazine."[6]

Atrazine does have one "safety" problem.

The potential for atrazine to produce cancer has been evaluated in at least seven lifetime studies in rats and four studies in mice. No potential to induce cancer was seen in the studies using the U.S. Government's choice of rats or in three different strains of mice. It does seem to hasten the onset of mammary tumors in the females of one variety of laboratory rat. However, scientists say this is probably not applicable to humans for several reasons:

- These rats are especially susceptible to mammary tumors; 40 to 70 percent of the females get such tumors with a normal diet and in the absence of any chemical exposure.
- A woman would have to drink 22,000 gallons of water per day at the current water-safety level of 3 parts per billion just to reach the *no effect threshold* in rats.
- Atrazine has been widely used in both farming and forestry for 30 years. If atrazine caused breast cancer, women in farming and forestry should have more breast cancer than the national average. Yet women involved in farming and forestry have *less* breast cancer—only 84 percent as much as the average American woman.[7]
- The tumors in this strain of rat apparently result from prolonged periods of estrogen secretion; these occur more often in the older female rats. (Atrazine seems to acceler-

ate this process.) By contrast, human females have *less* estrogen as they get older. Thus it is unlikely that atrazine affects human breast cancer rates.

The biggest reason of all for confidence in atrazine's safety?

The EPA has recently reevaluated statistical "false positives" in the atrazine rat reproduction tests and raised the "no-effect" level by *tenfold*. In effect, that says atrazine is *far safer than originally rated*.

The maker of atrazine agrees with the environmentalists that the metabolites of atrazine should be lumped with the atrazine itself. The net effect of the latest findings, however, is that atrazine's reference dose which is used to assess safety is seven times higher than originally determined (seven times safer than originally assumed). That includes both the increase in residues (atrazine *plus* the metabolites) and the reevaluated rat reproduction test results.

The manufacturer has accordingly asked the EPA to raise the Maximum Contaminant Level (MCL) from the current 3 ppb to 20 ppb. This would make the MCL consistent with the EPA's own new Reference Dose—and with the scientific evidence on atrazine's health effects.

If the EPA calculates the MCL using the new reference dose, it will eliminate virtually all of the multi-million-dollar testing and remediation requirements under the Safe Drinking Water Act. No expensive carbon filters would be needed by city and community water systems.

Well water, even with the metabolites counted, would be rated about three times as safe as before. Surface water, where the metabolites seldom appear, would be about *seven times as safe* as currently rated. (It is the surface water which is involved with most of the seasonal peaks in American drinking-water exposures.)

To put atrazine into proper perspective, let's look at what the new atrazine safety rating means to the average urban female whose water comes from a riverine reservoir. Since most of the urban "threat" from atrazine was in surface waters (small rivers), she would now have to drink 154,000 gallons of water per day to reach the no effect level. Even then, she'd have to take atrazine doses directly during the 9 months of the year when there are virtually no traces of atrazine in the urban water supplies. (Presumably she could buy atrazine directly from some agricultural supply house.)

An atrazine ban in the U.S. would do far more than raise U.S. corn production costs.

It would probably produce a ripple effect in other countries, as was the case with DDT. (The U.S. after all is looked to as a leader in environmental science.) In the long run, it would likely mean lower corn yields throughout large parts of the world.

Absent a shift to vegetarian diets (none is apparent yet) this lowering of yields would mean more world acres required for corn production—and less wildlife habitat.

The most likely consequences of an atrazine ban, then, would be less wildlife, more cancer and more soil erosion—all because Washington, D.C. is now populated with the first generation that grew up reading the well-meaning and eloquent Rachel Carson.[8]

Reality Can Also Strike the Environmental Movement

The environmental movement has been highly critical of the Food and Drug Administration for not being tougher in banning pesticides. As we have seen, activists have often demanded use limits or bans on pesticides when there was no evidence to indicate the need for such actions.

Recently, however, the FDA has riled the environmental movement itself with a regulatory thrust. FDA ruled that any health and nutritional claims made for *"natural" foods and nutrition supplements* have to be documented. The environmentalists have predictably been outraged by the very idea.

Buzzworm's Earth Journal fulminated:

The government maintains a strong bias against vitamins, minerals, amino acids, herbs and other dietary supplements, conducting at times a War on Drugs-style battle on substances that do not threaten the public and may be the key to the nation's health care problems. . . . If out of 100 million consumers, 20 individuals were diagnosed with nerve damage from taking a vitamin, is this a sufficient number of cases to warrant labeling vitamins as "dangerous" . . . ?

[Author's note: In the case of pesticides, eco-activists have certainly thought so.]

Supplement advocates argue such an approach isn't needed for products that are essentially safe, are often already backed by significant scientific support, and have, in the case of many herbs, centuries of history as effective medical tools.[9]

[Author's note: Again, what about their objections to the pesticides that were grandfathered into approval because of decades of safe experience?]

In sum, it is amazing how much the environmentalists sound like farmers when it's *their* products that are tied to the regulatory stake.

Notes

[1]Will Nixon, "Twenty Minutes with Carol Browner," *E, The Environmental Magazine*, December 1993, pp. 14-17.

[2]Robert Bidinotto, "The Green Machine," lecture before the Institute for Objectivist Studies, New York City, March 21, 1993.

[3]Ames and Gold, "Environmental Pollution and Cancer: Some Misconceptions," *Rational Readings on Environmental Concerns*, op. cit., pp. 165-166.

[4]Ben Kudwa, executive director, Michigan Potato Commission, December 15, 1993, personal communication.

[5]Dr. Leonard Gianessi, "The Quixotic Quest for Chemical-Free Farming," *Issues in Science and Technology*, Fall 1993, p. 32.

[6]S. Hoar Zahm et al., *Scandinavian Journal of Worker and Environmental Health*, Vol. 19, 1993, pp. 108-114.

[7]C. Rubin et al., *American Journal of Public Health*, 1993: 83: 1311-1315.

[8]Albert Gore, *Earth in the Balance,* op. cit., p. 3.

[9]Michael O'Keefe, "Food Fights and Drug Wars," *Buzzworm's Earth Journal*, January/February 1994, pp. 35-36.

23

Who Are These People?

MYTHMAKERS SAY:

"Just now one of the significant historical roles of the primal people of the world is . . . to call the entire civilized world back to a more authentic mode of being."
Thomas Berry, *The Dream of the Earth*, Sierra Club Books, 1988

"On December 28, 1954, the American Association for the Advancement of Science held a symposium on 'Population Problems,' at which Dr. Alan Gregg, vice-president of the Rockefeller Foundation (1951-56) came up with a startling idea: the thought that the human species is to the planet Earth what a cancer is to an individual human being."
Van Rensselaer Potter, *Global Bioethics: Building on the Leopold Legacy*, Michigan State University Press, 1988

"But the assumption of continued affluence at today's level is unfounded. If our numbers continue to rise, our standard of living will fall so sharply that by the year 2000, any surviving Americans might consider today's average Asian to be well off."
Wayne H. Davis, "Overpopulated America," *The New Republic*, January 10, 1970. Far from being "dated" and unrepresentative of current environmentalism, this 1970 essay continues to be cited as a classic at meetings such as the 1994 Cairo Population Conference. It was recently reprinted in *Learning to Listen to the Land*, a collection of important environmental essays published by Island Press in 1992

REALITY SAYS:

"Until very recently, ordinary people spent most of their time out-doors—farming, hunting, gathering nuts and berries, pillaging the countryside in armed bands. The more contact people actually have with nature, the less likely they are to 'appreciate' it in a big, mushy ecumenical way. And the more likely they are to get chiggers. . . . For most of history, mankind has managed to keep a reasonable balance between thinking nature's adorable and thinking it wants to kill us."

P. J. O'Rourke, *All the Trouble in the World: The Lighter Side of Overpopulation, Famine, Ecological Disaster, Ethnic Hatred, Plague and Poverty*, Atlantic Monthly Press, New York, 1994, pp. 122-124

"We cannot produce harmony simply by setting up sacred wilderness temples, while downgrading, excluding and eventually learning to despise human beings. . . . Humanity has spent most of its history trying to 'tame' wilderness . . . because people found it hostile and constricting. . . . Only after we have provided ourselves with the basic necessities is it fun to go back and see what untamed nature is really like."

William Tucker, *Progress and Privilege: America in the Age of Environmentalism*[1]

We've never before seen the huge, powerful, narrowly fixated environmental movement known today. Most of us are startled by it and the ways in which it seems to be changing our lives.

So let's examine this new phenomenon.

First, we must realize that the environmental movement has welded together several major groups of people. Most of these people are wholly sincere in their belief that they are doing good. However, they all come to the environmental movement with values and beliefs that make them willing to risk major changes in our social and economic systems without having much solid evidence that those changes will produce a better society—or even a more environmentally responsible one.

Environmental Purists

The environmental movement is led primarily by a group of purists. These are people who value "nature" over humanity.

The intensity of the eco-activists has been captured by Philip Shabecoff, until recently the chief environmental reporter for the *New York Times*, in his book, *A Fierce Green Fire*:

Our negligent use of the Promethean forces of science and technology has brought us to the verge of disaster.[2]

The beginnings of the ecology movement can be traced to the success of the Industrial Revolution—and the reactions against it—during the early part of the 20th Century. People welcomed the new productivity, but many hated the ugly urbanization, the pollution, and the exploitation of human and natural resources. Many affluent idealists then looked back fondly on the pastoral past, even though for most rural people that had also been a harsh world of unremitting toil and poverty.

One of the early pivotal figures in the creation of environmentalism was Gifford Pinchot, the first chief of the U.S. Forest Service under President Teddy Roosevelt. Another was John Muir, a lover

TRADITIONAL FARMING—It may have allowed husband and wife to work together, but you would have a hard time convincing them that it represents the farming ideal for the future.

of raw nature who founded the Sierra Club.

Both men believed fervently in public ownership of natural resources. Such collectivism, they believed, was the only way to prevent the exploitation and ultimate destruction of the wild lands.
Pinchot, in fact, was instrumental in expanding American public
ownership to one-third of the land area of the United States.

The next step in deepening the ecology movement is credited to
Aldo Leopold, the cofounder of the Wilderness Club, who wrote his
widely quoted *Sand County Almanac* in 1949.

Leopold's concept was a "pyramid of life" which required preserving the diversity of all species. He wanted to "enlarge the bound-
aries of the community to include soils, waters, plants and animals,"
thus justifying "changes in the role of Homo Sapiens from conqueror
of the land-community to plain member and citizen of it."[3]

It is no accident that several of the founders of the environmental movement are among the few people who *have* lived alone in the
wilderness but without having to wrest their livings directly from
natural resources:

- Muir lived in the California mountains for some years as a
  trail guide. (He met a number of important philanthropists
  and political figures that way.)
- Brad and Vena Angier, Bostonians who fled to the Canadian
  forest, became famous writing on survival skills and wilderness living. Yet they were ready to quit and return to Boston—rather than, say, take jobs in the nearby logging town—
  when they sold their first wildlife story.
- Aldo Leopold was a park ranger in New Mexico's Gila National Forest.

Each of these people lived *in* the wilderness without having to
live *from* it. The pioneers of the deep ecology movement nevertheless acquired a proprietary feeling about natural resources. No matter that the very idea of a "friendly wilderness" is totally unrealistic
unless the ecologists are backed by the products and safety factors
of modern civilization, such as down sleeping bags, freeze-dried
foods, and butane stoves.

Their solution was creative, and for the most part successful:

They got the government to reserve much of the wilderness for the things they liked—hiking, backpacking, photographing birds, and the few other activities that can be done in the wilderness without leaving a "human imprint."

Then came the next step for the purists. By the middle of the antiestablishment 1960s, UCLA historian Lynn White, Jr., was calling for a "new religion" based on "the spiritual autonomy of all parts of nature," and "the equality of all creatures, including man."[4]

White thus rejected the Judeo-Christian concept of man having dominion over the other creatures of the world.

Today, the basic tenet of the environmental movement is that "all living things are created equal" and are valuable in and of themselves, regardless of their relationship to man.

Some environmental purists go even further. William McKibben, in *The End of Nature*, quotes a biologist for the National Park Service, David Graber:

> Human happiness and certainly human fecundity, are not as important as a wild and healthy planet. . . . We have become a plague upon ourselves and upon the Earth. . . . Until such time as Homo Sapiens should decide to rejoin nature, some of us can only hope for the right virus to come along.[5]

This is not man and nature, it is nature *instead* of man.

Such radical groups as Greenpeace and Earth First! are led by angry deep ecologists who are inclined to strike out violently against the perceived threats to 'their' wilderness. These angry and violent purists, though few in number, have nonetheless managed to set the stage for the rest of the movement.

THEY ADMIT IT:

"The fact is we wish to preserve because we wish to preserve. If that's not a valid concept, then we haven't got one. To make believe we hold a different view is pure hypocrisy."
Environmental consultant Ian Parker, interviewed in the
New York Times Magazine in 1982[6]

"I founded Friends of the Earth to make the Sierra Club look reasonable. Then I founded the Earth Island Institute to make Friends of the Earth look reasonable. Earth First! now makes us look reasonable."
David Brower, author of *Confessions of an Eco-Warrior*[7]

The Greens

The Greens, in contrast to the purists, are the ecology movement's more worldly politicians and pragmatists. They profess at least a nominal concern for human values and modern culture, but their goal seems to be a highly regulated, socialist society that will impose and enforce a simpler, more austere lifestyle on the rest of us.

There are quite a few Greens, and they have proven very adept at politics.

Working together, the "deep" ecologists, or purists, and the broader group of Greens have achieved some major gains for society. They were the groups that set aside the national parks years ago. These parks now represent an enormously valuable set of national assets for recreation, timber, grazing, fishing—and even that cherished wilderness contemplation.

They also led the cleanup of rivers and industrial effluents which has given the Western world major improvements in its environmental quality since 1970.

However, the deep ecologists and the Greens may now have gotten *too* effective at preservation:

- They are virtually withdrawing the national forests from the timber business, are halfway to eliminating grazing on public lands—and are casting covetous eyes on the rest of the nation's land uses. This could represent major environmental problems in time, such as fire damage from overaged tree stands and the destruction of communities and industries..
- They have not only banned DDT, but are now attempting to ban chlorine from our lives, even though without it we risk sudden death from cholera (water treatment) and going without paper and other modern necessities. The eco-activists have not proven any threat from chlorine but then they didn't prove a threat from DDT either.

The general public may not realize that preservation and anti-technology policies have gone too far until they are already locked in place as the law of the land. By then, such policies will be enormously difficult to change.

My personal vivid fear is that the eco-activists' unwarranted fear of pesticides will lead to banning of key farm chemicals, followed by famine and the very wildlife losses that the ecology movement claims to be preventing.

THEY BELIEVE:

"We projected our own vicious qualities onto such animals as the wolf, the rat, the snake, the worm and the insects."
Thomas Berry, *The Dream of the Earth*, Sierra Club Books, 1988[8]

"A civilization is comparable to a living organism. Its longevity is a function of its metabolism. The higher the metabolism (affluence) the shorter the life. . . . We have now run our course."
Wayne H. Davis, "Overpopulated America,"
The New Republic, 1970

Fans of Big Government

There are also millions of people in the world who honestly trust government more than private enterprise, and/or think we're too rich for our own good. Most of these people are now also collected under the Green banner—because they have virtually nowhere else to go.

After all, most other adversarial political movements have lost out to democratic capitalism. The Soviet Union has collapsed. The Communist myth that human dictatorship and central planning are good for us has been completely discredited. Socialism, especially as demonstrated in Western Europe, looks moribund. Utopian communities are out of fashion. Nevertheless, many of the people in the environmental movement still urgently believe in the efficacy of non-democratic collectivist "solutions."

Jane Fonda, who used to recommend Communist big government, now recommends environmental big government instead. What hasn't changed is her belief in big government (and, of course, the

importance of Jane Fonda in a highly visible role as a key advisor to
that government).

Power Seekers

Many members of the environmental movement have not chosen to pursue power through the traditional methods, but that doesn't
mean they don't want power. They pursue it for what they feel are
valid reasons, following in the footsteps of other special interest groups
throughout American history.

Jeremy Rifkin, for example, spent his student years learning to
lead antiwar protests that attracted TV cameras. He liked the work
and the attention. Later in life, he turned his talent for protests into a
lucrative career, writing fear books, making speeches, and even setting up a 900 number so anxious housewives can pay for his advice
on what foods to buy and where to buy them. Fortune 500 food
companies tremble at his works.

Many 1960s-style law students didn't want to go into corporate
law—and found they could carve out lucrative niches with environmental lawsuits that not only got them fees but praise from their
peers.

Whole troops of environmentalists are generating millions of
dollars per year from memberships, grants, book sales, and speaking
fees—and getting the psychological rewards of "saving the world" in
the bargain.

Bureaucrats, especially, get power from the environmental movement. The EPA, state regulatory agencies, local trash recycling agencies, water authorities, and Soil Conservation Service employees get
higher salaries, bigger empires, and added job security if they can
make themselves seem more important to an environmentally sensitive public.

THE REALITY:

"John Stossel, ABC reporter extraordinaire and host of the cliché-
busting special, 'Are We Scaring Ourselves to Death?' confirmed the
bias that allowed such hysteria to go from activist group to news story
unchallenged. . . . 'We approached it from the bias that on the one hand is

business, which is greedy and has an ulterior motive, and will distort the data, and on the other hand is the noble environmental group, which has no motive other than to help the public. I'm embarrassed to say that it took me years to realize that their data were often soft, if not absurd, and that they had their own venal motives . . . to get on TV, to get famous, to get more grant money.'"

Brent Bozell III, "When the Media Looks at Risk," Washington
Times, October 17, 1994, p. A17

Vice President Al Gore is another example of how well-meaning activists can obtain power through environmentalism. His bestselling book, *Earth in the Balance*, helped to strengthen his national political ambitions. The case of Gore is particularly illuminating, in fact, as the box nearby shows.

The Rich and the Near-Rich

William Tucker's *Progress and Privilege: America in the Age of Environmentalism* is one of the most perceptive and powerful books on environmentalism. Tucker says:

> Every survey that has ever been taken (including the Sierra Club's extensive polling of its own membership) has shown that support for environmentalism has been concentrated in the upper-middle-class, professional segment of Society. Academics, attorneys, doctors, dentists, journalists and upper-income suburbanites have been, without question, the backbone of the movement. One extensive polling showed that support for environmental causes picks up strongly when income levels reach about $30,000. . . . The "plain old rich people" have brought the ideas and attitudes. . . . The idea of looking on material progress and economic security as an irrelevant and vulgar nuisance cannot be picked up overnight. . . . It is usually the sons and daughters of people who have achieved complete material security who make the most strident environmentalists.

The following is a *Washington Times* editorial, March 2, 1994, reprinted with permission.

Mr. Gore In the Balance

In the summer of 1992, the *New Republic* published an article reproving then-Senator Albert Gore for inviting journalists to ignore scientific findings that undermined his warnings of impending environmental doom. Encouraging that kind of "self-censorship," wrote Gregg Easterbrook, is dangerous ground for liberals who are supposed to be champions of skeptical debate. . . .

Apparently, Mr. Gore's fears have worsened. Now vice president, he is . . . personally attempting to put scientists skeptical of the sort of apocalyptic outlook one finds in Mr. Gore's *Earth in the Balance* on a media blacklist. . . .

Mr. Gore urged ["Nightline"] to examine the connections between scientific skeptics and assorted politically incorrect business, religious and other groups. . . . "Nightline" examined the material and found that "in a manner of speaking" there were links between the scientists and the groups. For example, Fred Singer, oft-published in peer-reviewed scientific journals . . . "is on the executive advisory board of . . . *The World and I*, which is funded by the Unification Church International, . . . however . . . Mr. Singer has other noteworthy credentials as a former Environmental Protection Agency official, University of Virginia professor of environmental sciences and Department of Transportation scientist.

Patrick Michaels, an associate professor of Environmental Sciences at University of Virginia . . . receives funding from a consortium of coal companies to publish his *World Climate Review*. But every major environmental group in the country receives industry funding of one sort of another.

Does it taint the findings of climate change skeptics? Apparently not. Three years ago on "Nightline" Mr. Singer predicted, correctly as it turns out, that the oil fires in Kuwait would have only limited environmental effects. Mr. Gore's fellow apocalyptic, Carl Sagan, wrongly predicted disaster.

Computer models apparently led Mr. Sagan astray, and Mr. Koppel pointed out computer models are the basis for Mr. Gore's predictions on so-called global warming. With that in mind, Mr.

Continued on next page

Those Who Fear Chemicals

Another group of environmental leaders are the people with an intense dread of manmade chemicals. All of us, of course, must cope today with far more technology, a much more rapid pace of technological change, and more highly specialized socioeconomic systems than any people in the previous history of the world.

It's tough to be constantly adapting to change. Still, some people retreat from modern living's intimidating challenges by focusing instead on the "solvable" challenge of making their lives "toxin-free."

They often carry the concept to amazing lengths.

Some are afraid of aluminum cookware. They fear that the traces of aluminum that can be picked up from the food cooked in such pans can cause severe reactions in the nervous system—or even be the source of Alzheimer's disease. (It was never very likely that such tiny amounts of aluminum were causing problems, and it now appears that the whole scare may have been due to dust-contaminated samples.)

Others are afraid of pressure-treated lumber. One writer noted

---

Koppel allowed scientists to debate the relative merits of climate models and proposed government remedies. And there was plenty of debate. If the program showed anything, it's that there clearly is no scientific consensus on the matter.

Showing that debate was itself a rebuke to Mr. Gore, who wants to stifle one side of it. But Mr. Koppel . . . concluded, "There is some irony in the fact that Vice President Gore, one of the most scientifically literate men to sit in the White House in this century . . . is resorting to political means to achieve what should ultimately be resolved on a purely scientific basis. . . . The measure of good science is neither the politics of the scientists nor the people with whom the scientist associates. It is the immersion of hypotheses into the acid of truth. That's the hard way to do it, but it's the only way that works."

To date, Mr. Gore has taken the easy way out. He's tried guilt by association. He's tried blacklisting scientific critics—using tax-paid staff, by the way. He's tried journalistic self-censorship. Such tactics prove nothing about the Earth's environment. They only put his integrity in the balance.

that "tests had proved" that carrots grown under a deck made from
pressure-treated lumber had a higher level of arsenic. The arsenic
level was not high in any absolute sense of representing a health
hazard—but that fact didn't stop pressure-treated lumber from going on the danger list.

They hate and fear plastics of virtually all kinds.

Again, there are not many chemophobes. But they are vocal and
persistent.

Here are a few quotes from just one issue of one magazine—
Green Alternatives for Health and the Environment (Vol. 3, No. 4,
October/November 1993):

"Admittedly, the many factors involved in causing such complex diseases as Alzheimer's and osteoporosis are not known. However, aluminum has no known use in the human body. . . . While no definitive conclusions have been reached (about aluminum cookware) there are enough
results to warrant caution about ingesting too much aluminum."
                    Kathy Gibbons, "Aluminum in My What?" p. 14

"Our Certified Kitchen Designer staff is well versed in alternative
products. . . . [S]teel cabinets are inert, meaning virtually no outgassing
of toxic chemicals. . . . [We can provide] optional non-tox doors and
sides with special non-tox stain finishes to create the 'wood look' over
the steel cabinets. We can supply whatever wood species would be chemically tolerant to the user."
                    kitchen-design advertisement, p. 35.

"Rachel Perry believes that while natural makeup is good for the
surface layer of the skin, its ingredients do not actually penetrate into
the bloodstream. . . . On the other side . . . Logona stated that one's skin
is a membrane that absorbs materials and that whatever you want to avoid
eating you should also avoid applying to your skin."
                    "Natural Cosmetics," pp. 38-41

"The chemicals in bedding most often cited as potential sources of
concern are pesticides, herbicides, fire retardants, the various substances
in synthetic fibers and the formaldehyde sometimes used to wrinkle-
proof sheets. Even minute amounts of any of these chemicals could cause
immediate health problems in a chemically sensitive individual. . . .
Michael Dimock of Jantz Design, another natural bedding manufacturer,

says 'There is no hard data, but people's (health) problems clear up' when they switch to organic bedding."

"Bedding," pp. 44-45

Organic Farmers

The organic farmers are obviously part of the environmental movement, but a small part of it because there are very few of them. Moreover, organic farming doesn't leave much time for organizing the general public.

The major significance of organic farmers is to serve as visible examples.

I attended the 1993 organic farming association's conference in Amherst, Mass. It was charming. Kids ran sack races. People tasted organic wine. Gardeners were taught how to attract more butterflies. Members sold one another handmade brooms and llamas (which produce a "really fine fiber for hand-woven garments"). There was a wood-chopping contest.

A local grower taught us how to prune raspberry bushes so that they would live twice as long (but produce only half as many berries per year).

There was only one problem. Nobody said anything about productivity. There was none of the usual "farmer talk" about yields per acre or milk per cow. Nobody mentioned the need to raise the world's farm output by threefold to supply an adequate diet to a redoubled world population in 2050.

I spoke to the conference on biotechnology's potential to produce more food from fewer acres. I pointed out that shifting to organic farming at its current low yields would mean plowing down wildlife habitat equal to the land area of North America. I noted that the world had less than 20 percent of the organic nitrogen needed to *support* global organic farming.

In response, one hot-eyed organic grower likened biotechnology and farm chemicals to nuclear radiation.

Another wanted a "philosophical" decision on biotechnology. I admitted I am no philosopher; I admire biotech purely for its practical ability to save people and wild creatures from famine-related destruction.

The organic community felt *no* urgency about the world food problem. They mainly wanted enough cash from the produce of their little farms to maintain their hand-crafted communities.

I came away wondering, *who are the press agents for organic farming?* Who's touting them as the world food solution? Certainly not these sandaled folks!

The organic farmers believe in what they're doing, but few of them have demonstrated any media skills or effective lobbying capacity. The people pushing organic farming are apparently the eco-activists, most of them wearing business clothes and roaming the governmental and media capitals of the country.

Population-Phobes

There seem to be millions of people who are afraid of more people. In fact, there may be more "environmentalists" in this category than any other. Because of their numbers and secretly radical beliefs they are politically quite dangerous.

They don't *want* high-yield farming to feed more people. Naturally, they have no open intent to cause the deaths of billions of humans. However, they are extremely uncomfortable with the idea of living in a more crowded world.

They want to solve the population equation *only* by suppressing births, even though this is not realistic. Hence Senator Bumpers' proposal to gut the funding for the Green Revolution agricultural research effort, even though it has been the salvation of humanity and wildlife over the last 30 years and is even more urgently needed for the next 30. Instead, the politicians and the environmentalists are quite comfortable putting that money into "population management" programs that simply cannot stop the population growth quickly.

It's almost as if they're saying, "Let them use the condoms or starve. We'll stop the population growth one way or the other."

In reality, we don't have the "luxury" of starving the people and keeping the wildlife. If we don't feed the larger population by raising crop yields, they will feed themselves by plowing down every inch of ground possible.

But many people instinctively react like Senator Bumpers, in his

Appropriations Committee hearing. He didn't *want* to hear that more people could be fed.

There seem to be millions of others like him:

- Why else would authors such as Lester Brown, Paul Ehrlich, and the Paddock brothers (*Famine 1975!*) be able to the recycle their same failed famine predictions over and over to renewed success in the bookstores?
- Why else would the *Amicus Journal* of the Natural Resources Defense Fund name Brown its "humanitarian of the year" for loudly being antihuman?
- Why else would the National Education Association and the teachers of America make green publications some of the most widely used "outside source materials" in U.S. education?

MYTHS SUPERIMPOSED ON HISTORY:

"Our species once did live in stable harmony with the natural environment. . . . That was not because men were incapable of changing their environment but for some more enveloping and deeper reasons still. The change began between five and ten thousand years ago and become more destructive and less accountable with the progress of civilization. The economic and material needs of growing villages and towns are, I believe, not causes but results of this change. . . . [I]t wrenched the ancient social machinery that had limited human births . . . a kind of failure in some fundamental dimension of human existence . . . a kind of madness."

Paul Shepard, *Nature and Madness*, Sierra Club Books, 1982[9]

Reality Comment: Shepard, perhaps without realizing it, is actually describing the impact of society's shift from hunting to agriculture. That shift began about 10,000 years ago and spread gradually around the world. It did not occur on account of raising birth rates, as Shepard implies. It was rather the direct result of lower *death* rates—as higher food output from farming staved off more famine and supported additional people. Shepard's willingness to misread birth rate causes and effects emphasizes how deeply antagonistic the environmental movement truly has been to high-yield farming.

HISTORICAL REALITY:

"In 1845, the twenty-eight-year-old Thoreau . . . built himself a little cabin near Walden Pond in Concord, Mass. The land was owned by Emerson and was about as far out of town as the average modern driving range. . . . Thoreau frequently went to dinners and parties in Concord, and according to his list of household expenses in *Walden*, he sent his laundry out to be done. Thoreau lived in his shack for two years, devoting his time to being full of sanctimonious beatnik. . . . And he is the source of the loathsome self-righteousness that turns every kid who's ever thought 'a tree is better looking than a parking lot' into Saint Paul of the Recycling Bin."

> P. J. O'Rourke, *All the Trouble in the World: The Lighter Side of Overpopulation, Famine, Ecological Disaster, Ethnic Hatred, Plague and Poverty*, Atlantic Monthly Press, New York, 1994, pp. 129-30

"Urbanization (in ancient times) meant that a number of new problems had to be solved. . . . Urbanization was accompanied by rapid progress in the technology of large-scale construction, transport and agriculture. . . . The inhabitants of large, sparsely populated continents were doomed to be illiterate subsistence producers. Their rich natural resources were of little use to them."

> E. Boserup, *Population and Technological Change*, University of Chicago Press, 1981

Even though past population growth has stimulated powerful improvements in human technology and public administration, there is no question that things would be simpler and easier for everybody if it stopped at 6 billion.

Unfortunately, that is wishful thinking. Neither Lester Brown nor Senator Bumpers nor you nor I are making life's intimate decisions for mothers and fathers in the Third World.

Sheer crowding doesn't seem to be frightening Calcutta or Hong Kong. Neither does it seem to frighten the affluent but densely residential Dutch. Even the residents of Manhattan Island, who enthusiastically support Planned Parenthood and the Worldwatch Institute, stack themselves into a population density that makes an anthill seem spacious.

WHO WILL COMPILE THE SUBTRACTION LIST?

"It is imperative that we reduce U.S. population to no more than 150 million and stabilize it there. . . . But the path we are on now is propelling us headlong toward a catastrophic size of 400 million and more."

Mailing from Negative Population Growth, Inc., Teaneck, N.J.,
Spring 1994

Reality Comment: If NPG plans to "reduce" the U.S. population by over 100 million, they will outrank Hitler and Stalin as history's foremost mass murderers.

The Worriers

There are *lots* of hand-wringers. Nature and evolution have seen to that.

Careful people tend to live longer than daredevils. They are more likely to reproduce. They try to teach their children caution. They surround themselves with fences, zoning ordinances, and vaccinations.

In the days of the wilderness, it was wise to keep looking over your shoulder—and to both sides. Lethal dangers were waiting just a paw-swipe away.

Today, however, both evolution and technology have left us with far fewer dangers. About all we have left of statistical importance are mistakes like doing drugs, smoking cigarettes, and not wearing seat-belts.

Most of the people reading this book can count on living into their eighties.

If we eat lots of fruits and vegetables and get regular exercise, we can even count on *enjoying* those "golden years."

That leaves a lot of anxiety with no valid place to go.

No saber-toothed tiger. No typhoid or cholera in the chlorinated water. No undulant fever or campylobacter in the pasteurized milk. No fear of personal famine; the supermarket is a few blocks away and probably open at least 15 hours per day.

Inevitably, at least some of the anxiety that saved our forefathers from sabre-toothed tigers winds up targeted inappropriately at such irrational worries as these:

- All of the good jobs in America will disappear.
- Our children, the best-educated and best-equipped generation in the world's most successful economy, will never live
  as well as their parents (many of whom remember the threat
  of polio and the death of playmates from ailments now easily cured by antibiotics).
- Electronic emissions from computer terminals are ruining our
  health.

There are *lots* of hand-wringers. Their attention span, however,
tends to be short.

The Guilt-Ridden

Many people in the world believe that there's only a limited supply of wealth. Thus, if one person or country has more, they must
have gotten it at the expense of another person or country.

More and more people fear that they got their affluence by ex-
ploiting more than their share of natural resources. They don't understand that most of the credit goes to their being members of a
successful society with constructive institutions, productive values,
and lots of knowledge.

There is no rational basis for the "limited-wealth" belief. If the
world ever was constrained by "natural resources," that time passed
at least 200 years ago. Today, knowledge is creating new wealth out
of very unlikely resources—such as sand which we turn into silicone
chips and glass fiber telecommunications cables. Hard work, investment, and commerce are making billions of people affluent all at
once.

Two hundred years ago, people understood where wealth came
from, because it came directly. The farmer who had the best land
and worked the hardest usually got the best crop. The shoemaker
who made the best shoes got the business, and so on.

Today, millions of people do such specialized things that those
things may not make total sense even to those who do them successfully (such as floor traders on commodity exchanges). Thus, there's
lots of uncertainty about wealth and poverty and the reasons for
them.

That may be why the environmental movement has had huge success in tapping guilt feelings about wealth, in America and the other affluent countries. When a supposedly selfless, confident-sounding "expert" says that people should feel guilty for living too well and "endangering the spotted owls," lots of them do.

AS AN EXAMPLE:

"Rising expectations for the poor is a cruel joke foisted upon them by the Establishment. As our new economy of use-it-once-and-throw-it-away produces more and more products for the affluent, the share of our resources available for the poor declines. Blessed be the starving blacks of Mississippi with their outdoor privies, for they are ecologically sound, and they shall inherit a nation."

Wayne H. Davis, "Overpopulated America," *The New Republic,*
January 1970

True Believers Lacking Something to Believe In

The declining depth of America's religious beliefs has also played an important role in the rise of environmentalism. In fact, environmentalism can be viewed as a return to the pagan nature-worship of pre-Biblical times.

There are many reasons put forward for the declining importance of religion in America and the Western World, all representing arguments that are beyond the scope of this book. However, if we look at the prescriptions of most religions, we see that they are aimed at telling us how to live our lives productively and harmoniously— and to build our societies rather than tearing them apart. Such messages, which represent thousands of years of learning about human behavior, have now been pitched out in the secular revolution.

Ironically, the very "freedom" delivered by the secular revolt has left many people looking for some larger ideal to justify their lives. "Nature" has become the religious substitute for many of them. That is unfortunate, mainly because nature-worship is unlikely to be truly satisfying or to deliver a successful society that protects its children and resources. It has already been abandoned time and again in history for visions that offered a more elevated understanding of human beings and their place in the world.

MYTHMAKERS ON HIGH:

"In his compelling work, *Broken Trust, Broken Land*, University of Washington natural resource sociologist Robert G. Lee reminds readers of a point made by many scholars—that environmentalism is a religion. But Lee goes farther, suggesting it to be a reincarnation of Calvinism, the faith of early Puritans. A central tenet of Calvinism . . . is that while 'the elect' are 'predestined to eternal salvation,' everyone else is 'predestined for eternal damnation.' This . . . makes it easier for true believers to inflict pain and ignore suffering. They feel justified punishing, and withholding sympathy from, those deemed to break God's law."

Alston Chase, environmental columnist, "The Election of 1994 Was A Religious War," Creators Syndicate, Inc., November 1994

The Environmental Strategies

How, in the face of its many intellectual and moral weaknesses, has the environmental movement achieved so much?

The evidence suggests three answers:

- The movement makes heavy use of fear as a strategy, constantly declaring new crises even though each may be based on shaky science. Environmental zealots attempt to create a constant crisis mentality, with new threats linked to the "dangers" of modern technology. If a "crisis" resonates with the public, they pursue it. If science effectively refutes a danger, they simply shift to a new one.
- The environmental movement has successfully exploited the media and the typical reporter's breathless hunger for scary front-page headlines. Often, this media impact has translated into political power even without the environmentalists having to win elections. Polling results have been more than enough to swing politicians and bureaucrats into line.
- The movement is made up of people who enjoy networking and organizing. Many of them have lots of spare time and energy. When I attended a big national environmental meeting in Louisville, Kentucky, in 1993, the entire meeting seemed to be affluent housewives, retired professionals, and salaried activists.

ON-LINE MYTHMAKING:

"Ecoline, a toll-free, global information system developed by the University of Vermont's Environmental Studies Program and the Together Foundation, connects callers to live operators who can provide the names, addresses and phone numbers of more than 60,000 organizations world-wide working on sustainable development, environmental projects and 'environmentally friendly products.'"

"Good News," *Earth Island Journal*, Winter 1993/94[10]

Beyond Political Correctness

To date, the only justification farmers have offered for high-yield farming is to save people from famine.

In truth, however, and as we have seen, high-yield farming saves *both* wildlife and people.

At the Hudson Institute's 1994 agricultural conference in Indianapolis, one of our panelists was Dr. Adam Finkel of Resources for the Future. Dr. Finkel was defending the use of the high-dose rat tests to find the least little scrap of potential "cancer risk" in pesticide residues—but he volunteered that if the use of low-risk pesticides would save wildlife, we should use them. Finkel is a graduate of the Harvard School of Public Health—and a former staffer for Vice President Al Gore!

When I was on a call-in radio show in Los Angeles last fall, a young lady called up and disagreed with me about the need for bio-technology.

"We have plenty of food," she said.

I told her I wasn't very worried about famine, but I was worried that low-yield farming would plow down wildlife in other parts of the world.

"Oh," she said. And hung up.

She would have debated me on biotech food safety all day, but she was not about to argue against preserving wildlife habitat in front of environmentally sensitive Los Angeles.

Among well-meaning people like these, high-yield farming remains politically incorrect. Yet, by any rational assessment, high-yield farming and the environmental movement must complement each other. Neither can reach its goals without the other.

I have written this book because I am convinced that we cannot afford to stand quietly and let public policy be based on false famine predictions and lies about pesticides harming people and wildlife. We must loudly proclaim farming's ability to feed people safely and sustainably—leaving room for wildlife and nature.

Notes

[1] William Tucker, *Progress and Privilege: America in the Age of Environmentalism*, Anchor Press/Doubleday, Garden City, New York, 1982, pp. 151-152.

[2] Philip Shabecoff, *A Fierce Green Fire: The American Environmental Movement*, New York, Hill and Wang, 1993, p. xiii.

[3] Shabecoff, op. cit., pp. 88-90.

[4] Lynn White, "The Historical Roots of Our Ecologic Crisis," *Science*, March 10, 1967.

[5] McKibben, *The End of Nature*, Random House, New York, 1989.

[6] Clifford D. May, "Preservation for Profit," *New York Times Magazine*, September 12, 1982, p. 146.

[7] David Brower, quoted by Virginia Postrel in "The Green Road to Serfdom," *Reason*, April 1990, pp. 23-4.

[8] Thomas Berry from *The Dream of the Earth*, excerpted in *Learning to Listen to the Land*, Island Press, Washington, D.C., 1992, p. 257.

[9] Paul Shepard, excerpt from *Nature and Madness*, Sierra Club Books, San Francisco, 1982, reprinted in *Learning to Listen to the Land*, op. cit., pp. 136-149.

[10] *Earth Island Journal*, Vol. 9, No. 1, published by Earth Island Institute, San Francisco, p. 5.

Epilogue

Think with me about a future time on the planet Earth. It might be about 2050.

Think about 8 to 9 billion humans who have the wealth and technology to coexist cooperatively, constructively, and enjoyably with their environment. Population growth has now stopped. Birth rates all over the world have now come down to match the low death rates produced by modern medicine. Population growth has leveled out, even with the remarkable death-delaying progress in biotechnology and gene therapy.

Contemplate the following events that brought this about:

- long-term birth control technologies;
- reform of outdated welfare systems, which used to encourage births among the poor of the First World;
- the rapid spread of affluence to all of the Third World except remote parts of sub-Saharan Africa and the high valleys of the Andes, thanks in large part to the open trade and financial flows mandated by the General Agreement on Tariffs and Trade; and
- a broad and fundamental change in the way societies view women and women view themselves, giving full credit for childbearing and child-rearing—but also giving full credit for their entire economic and social potential.

Virtually all of the world's expanded human population now has access to rewarding careers. There is less economic pressure to "work," but new knowledge and information systems have made "work" one of the most interesting human activities. None of these careers depend on cutting tropical rain forests or old-growth fir trees in America's Northwest. Some do involve helping to protect and manage those areas as wilderness/wildlife habitats. Few jobs are on the old "assembly lines," because these have been automated. Most of the new jobs utilize information technologies and provide eagerly sought and well-rewarded services to the billions of other people and creatures on the planet.

Humans now treat their sewage so thoroughly that it no longer overfertilizes surface waters. Landfills are no longer hermetically sealed to preserve their trash, but managed for rapid degradation back into "compost." Nonpolluting energy systems no longer depend heavily on burning fossil fuels. Though the new energy systems have been enormously expensive, they have been phased in slowly enough to avoid stopping economic growth; otherwise there would have been severe suffering and even violent opposition in the Third World.

This large number of people lives on less than 4 percent of the earth's land area—from choice. People will always be basically gregarious. In addition, new transport and housing technologies and the end of the "welfare ghettoes" have made cities more pleasant than ever.

These people produce ample food—in wondrous variety—from less land than they used in 1994. They still have to contend with pests, but they are able to do it more successfully than ever, thanks to the higher productivity, stress tolerance, and pest resistance which have been genetically engineered into most crop plants and domestic livestock and poultry. Any pesticide sprays are used in grams per acre, biodegrade quickly, and have extremely narrow toxicity aimed directly at pest species only. Domestic crop species have been engineered so they are unharmed by the safest pesticides, ensuring that we can use the safest compounds the most broadly.

This world in the future produces ample supplies of renewable lumber, paper and other forest products from a small amount of land—equal to only 5 percent of the closed forests that existed in the world in 1994. High-yielding hybrid trees grow faster, straighter, and disease-free on tree plantations. The plantations are themselves fine wildlife habitat for much of their growth cycle. Their real purpose, however, it is to totally eliminate human pressures on the other 95 percent of the wild forests. Thus the wild forests do not even have to be logged, let alone clear-cut.

Is this picture too good to be true? Probably not.

I am not an expert in non-fossil energies, nor on automation. I will not attempt to explain how the big improvements can be made in those areas. (People who *are* experts in those fields assure me that the potential is there.) In agriculture and forestry, I know that this "impossible future" is attainable.

It is attainable because of humanity's expanding knowledge.

It is attainable because better knowledge continues to give us higher yields per acre—safely.

Index

About the Author

Dennis T. Avery is a Senior Fellow at Hudson Institute and is director of Hudson's Center for Global Food Issues. He is a recognized expert on international agriculture, specializing in the study of how technology and national farm policies interact to affect farm output.

Mr. Avery grew up on a Michigan dairy farm and studied agricultural economics at Michigan State University and the University of Wisconsin. He holds awards for outstanding performance from three different government agencies and was awarded the National Intelligence Medal of Achievement in 1983.

Mr. Avery served for nearly a decade (1980-88) as senior agricultural analyst for the U.S. Department of State, where he was responsible for assessing the foreign-policy implications of food and farming developments worldwide.

Mr. Avery is author of *Biodiversity: Saving Species with Biotechnology,* a Hudson Institute Executive Briefing that challenges the conventional wisdom on loss of species, arguing that destruction of habitat, not industrialization, is the primary threat, and that biotechnology and economic growth are the keys to the solution. He has also authored *Global Food Progress 1991,* an overview of the state of the world's ability to produce food and a critique of myths about impending global starvation. He is editor of Hudson's *Global Food Quarterly* newsletter.

Mr. Avery's articles have appeared in *The Wall Street Journal, Baltimore Sun, Washington Times, Detroit News, Christian Science Monitor,* and other publications. He is frequently quoted in publications such as the *New York Times, USA Today, Time, Newsweek, U.S. News and World Report, Insight,* and *Successful Farming.*

About Hudson Institute

Hudson Institute is a private, not-for-profit research organization founded in 1961 by the late Herman Kahn. Hudson analyzes and makes recommendations about public policy for business and government executives, as well as for the public at large. The institute does not advocate an express ideology or political position. However, more than thirty years of work on the most important issues of the day has forged a viewpoint that embodies skepticism about the conventional wisdom, optimism about solving problems, a commitment to free institutions and individual responsibility, an appreciation of the crucial role of technology in achieving progress, and an abiding respect for the importance of values, culture, and religion in human affairs.

Since 1984, Hudson has been headquartered in Indianapolis, Indiana. It also maintains offices in Washington, D.C.; Madison, Wisconsin; and Brussels, Belgium.